Peter Norton's Assembly Language Book

for the IBM PC

Other Brady Books by Peter Norton

Inside the IBM PC, Revised and Enlarged
MS-DOS and PC-DOS User's Guide
PC-DOS: The Guide to High Performance Computing

Peter Norton's Assembly Language Book for the IBM PC

Peter Norton

and

John Socha

A Brady Book
Published by Prentice Hall Press
New York, New York 10023

Portions of this work were previously published in a work entitled:
Assembly Language Safari On The IBM PC.

A Brady Book
Published by Prentice Hall Press
A Division of Simon & Schuster, Inc.
Gulf+Western Building
One Gulf+Western Plaza
New York, New York 10023

PRENTICE HALL PRESS is a trademark of Simon & Schuster, Inc.

Manufactured in the United States of America

3 4 5 6 7 8 9 10

Library of Congress Cataloging-in-Publication Data

Norton, Peter, 1943–
    Peter Norton's Assembly Language book for
the IBM PC.

    "A Brady book."
    Includes index.
    1. IBM Personal Computer—Programming.
2. Assembler language (Computer program language)
I. Socha, John, 1958–   . II. Title.
III. Title: Assembly language book for the IBM PC.
QA76.8.I2594N66 1986   005.265   86-25363

ISBN 0-13-661901-0

Contents

Trademarks

IBM, IBM PC, XT, and AT are registered trademarks of International Business Machines Corporation.

COMPAQ is a registered trademark of Compaq Computer Corporation.

MS-DOS and Microsoft are registered trademarks of Microsoft Corporation.

SideKick and SuperKey are trademarks of Borland International.

ProKey is a trademark of Rosesoft.

Lotus and 1-2-3 are trademarks of Lotus Development Corporation.

Intel is a registered trademark of Intel Corporation.

Limits of Liability and Disclaimer of Warranty

The authors and publisher of this book have used their best efforts in preparing this book and the programs contained in it. These efforts include the development, research, and testing of the theories and programs to determine their effectiveness. The authors and publisher make no warranty of any kind, expressed or implied, with regard to these programs or the documentation contained in this book. The authors and publisher shall not be liable in any event for incidental or consequential damages in connection with, or arising out of, the furnishing, performance, or use of these programs.

Introduction

By the time you finish reading this book, you'll know how to write full-scale, assembly language programs: text editors, utilities, and so on. Along the way, you'll learn many techniques that professional programmers use to make their work simpler. These techniques, which include modular design and step-wise refinement, will double or triple your programming speed, as well as help you write more readable and reliable programs.

The technique of step-wise refinement, in particular, takes a lot of the work out of writing complex programs. If you've ever had that sinking, where-do-I-start feeling, you'll find that step-wise refinement gives you a simple and natural way to write programs. And it's also fun!

This book isn't all theory, though. We'll build a program, too. The program is called Dskpatch (for Disk Patch), and you'll find it useful for several reasons. First of all, you'll see step-wise refinement and modular design at work in a real program, so you'll have an opportunity to see why these techniques are so useful. Also, as you'll see shortly, Dskpatch is, in its own right, a general-purpose, full-screen editor for disk sectors—one that you can continue to use both in whole and in part long after you've finished with this book.

Why Assembly Language?

We'll assume that you've picked up this book because you are interested in learning assembly language. But you may not be exactly certain why you'd want to learn it.

One reason, perhaps the least obvious, is that assembly language programs are at the heart of any IBM PC or compatible computer. In relation to all other programming languages, assembly language is the lowest common denominator. It takes you closer to the machine than higher-level languages do, so learning assembly language also means learning to understand the 8088 microprocessor inside your computer. We'll teach you the instructions of the 8088 microprocessor, as do the authors of other introductory books, but we'll go much farther and also cover *advanced* material that you'll find invaluable when you start to write your own programs.

Once you understand the 8088 microprocessor inside your IBM PC, many elements you'll see in other programs and in high-level languages will have greater meaning for you. For example, you may have noticed that the largest integer you can have in BASIC is 32767. Where did this number come from? It's an odd number for an upper limit. But as you'll see later, the number 32767 is directly related to the way your IBM PC stores numbers.

Then, too, you may be interested in speed or size. As a rule, assembly language programs are much faster than those written in any other language.

Typical assembly language programs are two to three times as fast as equivalent C or Pascal programs, and they generally outpace interpreted BASIC programs by 15 times or more. Assembly language programs are also smaller. The Dskpatch program we'll build in this book will be full-grown at about one kilobyte. Compared with programs in general, that's small. A similar program written in C or Pascal would be about ten times the size. For these reasons, among others, the Lotus Development Corporation wrote 1-2-3 entirely in assembly language.

Assembly language programs also provide you with full access to the features in your computer. A number of programs, such as SideKick, ProKey, and SuperKey, stay in memory after you run them. Such programs change the way your machine works, and they use system features available only to assembly language programs.

Dskpatch

In our work with assembly language, we'll look directly at disk sectors, displaying characters and numbers stored there by DOS in hexadecimal notation. Dskpatch is a full-screen editor for disks, and it will allow us to change these characters and numbers in a disk sector. Using Dskpatch you could, for example, look at the sector where DOS stores the directory for a disk and you could change file names or other information. Doing so is a good way to learn how DOS stores information on a disk.

You'll get more out of Dskpatch than just one program, though. Dskpatch contains about 50 subroutines. Many of these are general-purpose subroutines you'll find useful when you write your own programs. Thus, not only is this book an introduction to the 8088 and assembly language programming, it's also a source of useful subroutines.

In addition, any full-screen editor needs to use features specific to the IBM PC family of computers. Through the examples in this book, you'll also learn how to write useful programs for IBM PCs, ATs, or compatible computers, such as the COMPAQ.

Equipment Requirements

What equipment will you need to run the examples in this book? You'll need an IBM PC or compatible with at least 128K of memory and one disk drive. You'll also need version 2.00 or later of PC-DOS (or MS-DOS). And, starting in Part II, you'll need either the IBM or the Microsoft Macro Assembler.

Organization of This Book

This book is divided into three parts, each with a different emphasis. Whether you know anything about microprocessors or not, and whether you already know assembly language or not, you'll find sections that are of interest to you.

Part I focuses on the 8088 microprocessor. Here, you'll learn the mysteries of bits, bytes, and machine language. Each of the seven chapters contains a wealth of real examples that use a program called Debug, which comes on your DOS disk. Debug will allow us to look *inside* the famous 8088 microprocessor nestled deep in your IBM PC as it runs DOS. Part I assumes only that you have a rudimentary knowledge of BASIC and know how to work with your computer.

Part II, Chapters 8 to 16, moves on to assembly language and how to write programs in the assembler. The approach is gentle, and rather than cover all the details of the assembler itself, we'll concentrate on a set of assembler commands we need to write useful programs.

We'll use the assembler to rewrite some of the programs from Part I, and then move on to begin creating Dskpatch. We'll build this program slowly, so you'll learn how to use step-wise refinement in building large programs. We'll also cover techniques like modular design that help in writing clear programs. As mentioned, these techniques will simplify programming by removing some of the complexities normally associated with writing assembly language programs.

In Part III, which includes Chapters 17 to 29, we'll concentrate on using more advanced features found in IBM PCs. These features include moving the cursor and clearing the screen.

In Part III we'll also discuss techniques for debugging larger assembly language programs. Assembly language programs grow very quickly and can easily be two or more pages long without doing very much (Dskpatch will be longer). Even though we'll use these debugging techniques on programs larger than a few pages, you'll find them useful with small programs, too.

Now, without further ado, let's jump into the 8088 and take a look at the way it stores numbers.

PART I

Machine Language

1

DEBUG AND ARITHMETIC

Let's begin our foray into assembly language by learning how computers count. That may sound simple enough. After all, we count to 11 by starting at one and counting up: 1, 2, 3, 4, 5, 6, 7, 8, 9, 10, 11.

But a computer doesn't count that way. Instead, it counts to five like this: 1, 10, 11, 100, 101. The numbers 10, 11, 100, and so on are binary numbers, based a number system with only two digits, one and zero, instead of the ten associated with our more familiar decimal numbers. Thus, the binary number 10 is equivalent to the decimal number we know as two.

We're interested in binary numbers because they are the form in which numbers are used by the 8088 microprocessor inside your IBM PC. But while computers thrive on binary numbers, those strings of ones and zeros can be long and cumbersome to write out. The solution? Hexadecimal numbers—a far more compact way to write binary numbers. In this chapter, you'll learn both ways to write numbers: hexadecimal and binary. And as you learn how computers count, you'll also learn about how they store numbers—in bits, bytes, and words.

If you already know about binary and hexadecimal numbers, bits, bytes, and words, you can skip to the chapter summary.

Hexadecimal Numbers

Since hexadecimal numbers are easier to handle than binary numbers—at least in terms of length—we'll begin with hexadecimal (hex for short), and use DEBUG.COM, a program you'll find on your PC-DOS supplemental disk. We'll be using Debug here and in later chapters to enter and run machine-language programs one instruction at a time. Like BASIC, Debug provides a nice, interactive environment. But unlike BASIC, it doesn't know decimal numbers. To Debug, the number 10 is a hexadecimal number—not ten. And since Debug only speaks in hexadecimal, you'll need to learn something about hex numbers. But first, let's take a short side trip and find out a little about Debug itself.

Debug

Why does this program carry the name Debug? *Bugs*, in the computer world, are mistakes in a program. A working program has no bugs, while a non-working or "limping" program has at least one bug. By using Debug to run a program one instruction at a time, and watching how the program works, we can find mistakes and correct them. This is known as *debugging*, hence the name Debug.

According to computer folklore, the term debugging stems from the early days of computing—in particular, a day on which the Mark I computer at Harvard failed. After a long search, the technicians found the source of their troubles: a small moth caught between the contacts of a relay. The technicians removed the moth and wrote a note in the log book about "debugging" the Mark I.

Find Debug on your DOS supplemental disk and we'll get started. You should also have a work disk handy, and you'll want to copy DEBUG.COM to it. We'll make heavy use of Debug in Part I of this book.

> **Note:** From here on, in interactive sessions like this one, the text you type will be against a gray background to distinguish it from your computer's responses. Type the text, press the Enter key, and you should see a response similar to the ones we show in these sessions. You won't always see exactly the same responses, because your computer probably has a different amount of memory from the computer on which we wrote this book. (We'll begin to encounter such differences in the next chapter.) In addition, notice that we use uppercase letters in all examples. This is only to avoid any confusion between the lowercase letter l (el) and the number 1 (one). If you prefer, you can type all examples in lowercase letters.

Now, with those few conventions noted, start Debug by typing its name after the DOS prompt (which is A> in this example):

```
A>DEBUG
-
```

The hyphen you see in response to your command is Debug's prompt symbol, just as A> is a DOS prompt. It means Debug is waiting for a command.

To leave Debug and return to DOS, just type Q (for *Quit*) at the hyphen prompt and press Enter. Try quitting now, if you like, and then return to Debug:

```
-Q
A>DEBUG
-
```

Now we can get down to learning about hex numbers.

Hexarithmetic

We'll use a Debug command called H. H is short for *Hexarithmetic*, and, as its name suggests, it adds and subtracts two hex numbers. Let's see how H works by starting with 2 + 3. We know that 2 + 3 = 5 for decimal numbers. Is this true for hex numbers? Make sure you're still in Debug and, at the hyphen prompt, type the following screened text:

```
-H 3 2
0005   0001
```

Debug prints both the sum (0005) and the difference (0001) of 3 and 2. The Hexarithmetic command always calculates the sum and difference of two numbers, as it did here. And so far, the results are the same for hex and decimal numbers: 5 is the sum of 3 + 2 in decimal, and 1 is the difference (3 − 2). But sometimes, you can encounter a few surprises.

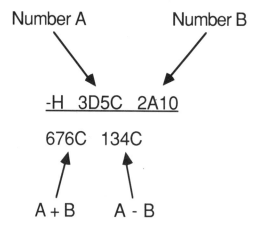

Figure 1-1. The Hexarithmetic Command.

For example, what if we typed *H 2 3*, to add and subtract two and three, instead of three and two? If we try it:

```
-H 2 3
0005  FFFF
```

we get FFFF instead of −1, for 2 − 3. Strange as it may look, however, FFFF is a number. In fact, it is hex for −1.

We'll come back to this rather unusual −1 shortly. But first, let's explore the realm of slightly larger numbers to see how an F can appear in a number.

To see what the Hexarithmetic command does with larger numbers, let's try nine plus one, which would give us the decimal number 10:

```
-H 9 1
000A  0008
```

Nine plus one equals A? That's right: A is the hex number for ten. Now, what if we try for an even larger number, such as 15:

```
-H 9 6
000F  0003
```

If you try other numbers between ten and fifteen, you'll find 16 digits altogether—0 through F (0 through 9 and A through F). The name hexadecimal comes from hexa- (6), plus deca- (10) which, when combined, represent 16. The digits 0 through 9 are the same in both hexadecimal and decimal; the hexadecimal digits A through F are equal to the decimals 10 through 15.

Why does Debug speak in hexadecimal? Soon you'll see that we can write 256 different numbers with two hex digits. As you may already suspect, 256 also bears some relationship to the unit known as a byte, and the byte plays a major role in computers and in this book. You'll find out more about bytes near the end of this chapter, but for now we'll continue to concentrate on learning hex, the only number system known to Debug, and hex math.

Converting Hexadecimal to Decimal

Thus far we've looked at single-digit hex numbers. Now, let's see how to represent larger hex numbers, and how to convert these numbers to decimal numbers.

Just as with decimal numbers, we build multiple-digit hex numbers by add-

Decimal	Hex digit
0	0
1	1
2	2
3	3
4	4
5	5
6	6
7	7
8	8
9	9
10	A
11	B
12	C
13	D
14	E
15	F

Figure 1-2.   Hexadecimal Digits.

ing more digits on the left. Suppose, for example, we add the number 1 to the largest single-digit decimal number, 9. The result is a two-digit number, 10 (ten). What happens when we add 1 to the largest single-digit hex number, F? We get ten again.

But wait, ten in hex is really 16, not ten. This could become rather confusing. We need some way to tell these two tens apart, so from now on we'll place the letter h after any hex number. Thus, we'll know that 10h is hexadecimal 16 and 10 is decimal ten.

Now we come to the question of how to convert numbers between hex and decimal. We know that 10h is 16, but how do we convert a larger hex number, such as D3h, to a decimal number without counting up to D3h from 10h? Or, how do we convert the decimal number 173 to hex?

We can't rely on Debug for help, because Debug can't speak in decimal. In Chapter 10, we'll write a program to convert a hex number into decimal notation so that our programs can talk to us in decimal. But right now, we'll have to do these conversions by hand, so let's begin by returning to the familiar world of decimal numbers.

What does the number 276 mean? In grade school, we learned that 276 means we have two hundreds, seven tens, and six ones. Or, more graphically:

```
2   * 100 =  200
7   *  10 =   70
6 * 1 =    6
276          =  276
```

Well, that certainly helps us visualize the meanings of those digits. Can we use the same graphic method with a hex number? Of course.

Consider the number D3h we mentioned earlier. D is the hexadecimal digit 13, and there are 16 hex digits, versus 10 for decimal, so D3h is thirteen sixteens and three ones. Or, presented graphically:

```
D → 13 * 16 =  208
3 → 3 * 1 =    3
D3h          =  211
```

For the decimal number 276, we multiplied the digits by 100, 10, and 1; for the hex number D3, we multiplied the digits by 16 and 1. If we had four decimal digits we'd multiply by 1000, 100, 10, and 1. Which four numbers would we use with four hex digits?

For decimal, the numbers 1000, 100, 10, and 1 are all powers of 10:

```
10³ = 1000
10² =  100
10¹ =   10
10⁰ =    1
```

We can use exactly the same method for hex digits, but with powers of 16, instead of 10, so our four numbers are:

```
16³ = 4096
16² =  256
16¹ =   16
16⁰ =    1
```

Let's convert 3AC8h to decimal using the four numbers we just calculated:

```
7     -->  7  *  16  =  112
C     --> 12  *   1  =   12
7Ch            =         124


3     -->  3  * 256  =  768
F     --> 15  *  16  =  240
9     -->  9  *   1  =    9
3F9h           =       1,017


A     --> 10  * 4,096  =  40,960
F     --> 15  *   256  =   3,840
1     -->  1  *    16  =      16
C     --> 12  *     1  =      12
AF1Ch            =         44,828


3     -->  3  * 65,536  =  196,608
B     --> 11  *  4,096  =   45,056
8     -->  8  *    256  =    2,048
D     --> 13  *     16  =      208
2     -->  2  *      1  =        2
3B8D2h            =         243,922
```

Figure 1-3.   **More Hexadecimal to Decimal Conversions.**

```
3   →  3 * 4096  = 12288
A   → 10 *  256  =  2560
C   → 12 *   16  =   192
8   →  8 *    1  =     8
3AC8h           = 15048
```

Now let's discover what happens when we add hex numbers that have more than one digit. For this, we'll use Debug and the numbers 3A7h and 1EDh:

```
-H 3A7 1ED
0594 01BA
```

So we see that 3A7h + 1EDh = 594h. You can check the results by converting these numbers to decimal and doing the addition (and subtraction, if you wish) in decimal form; if you're more adventurous, do the calculations directly in hex.

```
    1                 1                    1
   3A7               F451                  C
 + 92A             + CB03                + D
   CD1              1BF54                 19


  1111             1  1
  BCD8             BCD8
 + FAE9           + 0509
  1B7C1            C1E1
```

Figure 1-4. **More Examples of Hexadecimal Addition.**

Five-Digit Hex Numbers

So far, hex math is quite straightforward. What happens when we try adding even larger hex numbers? Let's try a five-digit hex number:

```
-H 5C3F0 4BC6
         ^ Error
-
```

That's an unexpected response. Why does Debug say we have an error here? The reason has to do with a unit of storage called the *word*. Debug's Hex-arithmetic command works only with words, and words happen to be long enough to hold four hex digits, no more.

We'll find out more about words in a few pages, but for now, remember that you can work only with four hex digits. Thus, if you try to add two four-digit hex numbers, such as C000h and D000h (which should give you 19000h), you get 9000h, instead:

```
-H C000 D000
9000  F000
-
```

Debug keeps only the four rightmost digits of the answer.

Converting Decimal to Hex

So far we've only looked at the conversion from hex to decimal. Now we'll learn how to convert decimal numbers to hex. As we mentioned earlier, in Chapter 10 we'll create a program to write the 8088's numbers as decimal numbers; in Chapter 23, we'll write another program to read decimal numbers into the 8088. But, as with decimal-to-hex conversions, let's begin by learning how to do the conversions by hand. Again, we'll start by recalling a bit of grade-school math.

When we first learned division, we would divide 9 by 2 to get 4 with a remainder of 1. We'll use the remainder to convert decimal numbers to hex.

Let's see what happens when we repeatedly divide a decimal number, in this case 493, by 10:

```
493 / 10  =   49 remainder 3 ─────────────┐
   │                                       │
   ▼                                       │
  49 / 10  =    4 remainder 9 ─────────┐   │
   │                                   │   │
   ▼                                   │   │
   4 / 10  =    0 remainder 4 ─────┐   │   │
                                   ▼   ▼   ▼
                                   4   9   3
```

The digits of 493 appear as the remainder in reverse order—that is, starting with the rightmost digit (3). We saw in the last section that all we needed for our hex-to-decimal conversion was to replace powers of 10 with powers of 16.

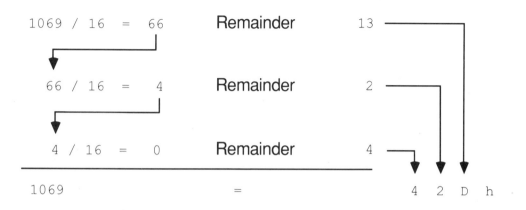

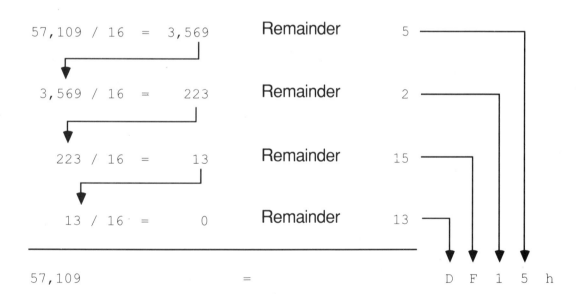

Figure 1-5. **More Examples of Hexadecimal Conversions.**

For our decimal-to-hex conversion, can we divide by 16 instead of 10? Indeed, that's our conversion method.

For example, let's find the hex number for 493. Dividing by 16, as shown here:

```
493 / 16  =  30 remainder 13 (Dh) ─────────┐
  │                                         │
  ▼                                         │
  30 / 16  =  1 remainder 14 (Eh) ────────┐ │
  │                                       │ │
  ▼                                       │ │
  1 / 16  =  0 remainder  1 (1h) ───────┐ │ │
493                  =                  ▼ ▼ ▼
                                        1 E D h
```

We find that 1EDh is the hex equivalent of decimal 493. In other words, keep dividing by 16, and form the final hex number from the remainders. That's all there is to it.

Negative Numbers

If you recall, though, we still have an unanswered puzzle in the number FFFFh. We said that FFFFh is actually -1. Yet, if we convert FFFFh to decimal, we get 65535. How can that be? Does it behave as a negative number?

Well, if we add FFFFh (alias -1) to 5, the result should be 4, because $5 - 1 = 4$. Is that what happens? Using Debug's H command to add 5 and FFFFh, we find:

```
-H 5 FFFF
0004  0006
-
```

Debug *seems* to treat FFFFh as -1. But FFFFh won't always behave as -1 in programs we'll write. To see why not, let's do this addition by hand.

When we add two decimal numbers, we often find ourselves carrying a one to the next column, like this:

```
1 1
  9 5
+ 5 8
1 5 3
```

The addition of two hex numbers isn't much different. Adding 3 to F gives us 2, with a carry into the next column:

```
   1
     F
 +   3
   1 2 h
```

Now, watch what happens when we add 5 to FFFFh:

```
 1 1 1 1
   0 0 0 5 h
 + F F F F h
 1 0 0 0 4 h
```

Since Fh + 1h = 10h, the successive carries neatly move a 1 into the far left position. And, if we ignore this 1, we have the correct answer for 5 − 1: namely, 4. Strange as it seems, FFFFh behaves as −1 when we ignore this *overflow*. It's called an overflow because the number is now five digits long, but Debug keeps only the first (rightmost) four digits.

Is this overflow an error, or is the answer correct? Well, yes and yes. We can choose either answer. Don't the answers contradict each other? Not really, because we can view these numbers in either of two ways.

Let's suppose we take FFFFh as equal to 65536. This is a positive number, and it happens to be the largest number we can write with four hex digits. We say that FFFFh is an *unsigned* number. It is unsigned because we've just defined all four digit numbers as positive. Adding 5 to FFFFh gives us 10004h; no other answer is correct. In the case of unsigned numbers, then, an overflow is an error.

On the other hand, we can also treat FFFFh as a negative number, as Debug did when we used the H command to add FFFFh to 5. FFFFh behaves as −1 as long as we ignore the *overflow*. In fact, the numbers 8000h through FFFFh all behave nicely as negative numbers. For *signed* numbers, as here, the overflow isn't an error.

The 8088 microprocessor can view numbers either as unsigned or signed; the choice is yours. There are slightly different instructions for each, and we'll explore these differences in later chapters as we begin to use numbers on the 8088. Right now, before you can learn to actually write the negative of, say, 3C8h, we need to unmask the bit and see how it fits into the scheme of bytes, words, and hex.

Bits, Bytes, Words, and Binary Notation

It's time for us to dig deeper into the intricacies of your IBM PC—time to learn about the arithmetic of the 8088: binary numbers. The 8088 microprocessor, with all its power, is rather dumb. It knows only the two digits 0 and 1, so any number it uses must be formed from a long string of zeros and ones. This is the *binary* (base 2) number system.

When Debug prints a number in hex, it uses a small program to convert it's internal numbers from binary to hexadecimal. In Chapter 5, we'll build such a program to write binary numbers in hex notation, but first we need to learn more about binary numbers themselves.

Let's take the binary number 1011b (the b stands for binary). This number is equal to the decimal 11, or Bh in hex. To see why, multiply the digits of 1011b by the number's base, 2:

Powers of 2:

$$2^3 = 8$$
$$2^2 = 4$$
$$2^1 = 2$$
$$2^0 = 1$$

So that:

```
1 * 8  =  8
0 * 4  =  0
1 * 2  =  2
1 * 1  =  1
1011b  =  11    or    Bh
```

Likewise, 1111b is Fh, or 15. And 1111b is the largest unsigned four-digit binary number we can write, while 0000b is the smallest. Thus, with four binary digits we can write 16 different numbers. There are exactly 16 hex digits, so we can write one hex digit for every four binary digits.

A two-digit hex number, such as 4Ch, can be written as 0100 1100b. It's composed of eight digits, which we separate into groups of four for easy reading. Each one of these binary digits is known as a *bit*, so a number like 0100 1100b, or 4Ch, is eight bits long.

Very often, we find it convenient to number each of the bits in a long string, with bit 0 farthest to the right. The 1 in 10b then is bit number 1, and the leftmost bit in 1011b is bit number 3. Numbering bits in this way makes it easier for us to talk about any particular one, as we'll want to later on.

A group of eight binary digits is known as a *byte*, while a group of 16 binary

Binary	Decimal	Hexadecimal
0000	0	0
0001	1	1
0010	2	2
0011	3	3
0100	4	4
0101	5	5
0110	6	6
0111	7	7
1000	8	8
1001	9	9
1010	10	A
1011	11	B
1100	12	C
1101	13	D
1110	14	E
1111	15	F

Figure 1-6.   Binary, Hex, and Decimal for 0 Through F.

digits, or two bytes, is a *word*. We'll use these terms frequently throughout this book, because bits, bytes, and words are all fundamental to the 8088.

We can see now why hexadecimal notation is convenient; two hex digits fit exactly into one byte (four bits per hex digit), and four digits fit exactly into one word. We can't say the same for decimal numbers. If we try to use two decimal digits for one byte, we can't write numbers larger than 99, so we lose the values from 100 to 255—more than half the range of numbers a byte can hold. And if we use three decimal digits, we must ignore more than half the three-digit decimal numbers, because the numbers 256 through 999 can't be contained in one byte.

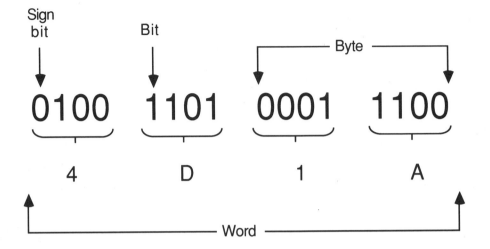

Figure 1-7. A Word is Made Out of Bits and Bytes.

Two's Complement—An Odd Sort of Negative Number

Now we're ready to learn more about negative numbers. We said before that the numbers 8000h through FFFFh all behave as negative numbers when we ignore the overflow. There is an easy way to spot negative numbers when we write them in binary:

```
Positive numbers:
        0000h                 0000 0000 0000 0000b
          .                          .
          .                          .
          .                          .
        7FFFh                 0111 1111 1111 1111b

Negative numbers:
        8000h                 1000 0000 0000 0000b
          .                          .
          .                          .
          .                          .
        FFFFh                 1111 1111 1111 1111b
```

In the binary forms for all the positive numbers, the first bit (bit 15) is always 0. For all negative numbers, this first bit is always 1. This difference is, in fact, the way that the 8088 microprocessor knows when a number is negative: It looks at bit 15, the *sign bit*. If we use instructions for unsigned numbers in our programs, the 8088 will ignore the sign bit, and we will be free to use signed numbers at our convenience.

These negative numbers are known as the *Two's Complement* of positive numbers. Why complement? Because the conversion from a positive number, such as 3C8h, to its two's-complement form is a two-step process, with the first being the conversion of the number to its *complement*.

We won't need to negate numbers often, but we'll do the conversion here just so you can see how the 8088 microprocessor negates numbers. The conversion will seem a bit strange. You won't see why it works, but you will see that it does work.

To find the two's-complement form (negative of) any number, first write the number in binary, ignoring the sign. For example, 4Ch becomes 0000 0000 0100 1100b.

To negate this number, first reverse all the zeros and ones. This process of reversing is called *complementing*, and taking the complement of 4Ch, we find that:

```
          0 0 0 0    0 0 0 0    0 1 0 0    1 1 0 0
becomes:
          1 1 1 1    1 1 1 1    1 0 1 1    0 0 1 1
```

In the second step of the conversion, we add 1:

```
                                    1 1
      1 1 1 1    1 1 1 1    1 0 1 1    0 0 1 1
    +                                        1
    _____
      1 1 1 1    1 1 1 1    1 0 1 1    0 1 0 0
                                   -4Ch = FFB4h
```

The answer, FFB4h, is the result we get if we use Debug's H command to subtract 4Ch from 0h.

If you wish, you can add FFB4h to 4Ch by hand, to verify that the answer is 10000h. And from our earlier discussion, you know that you should ignore this leftmost 1 to get 0 (4C + (−4C) = 0) when you do two's-complement addition.

Summary

This chapter has been a fairly steep climb into the world of hexadecimal and binary numbers, and it may have required a fair amount of mental exercise. Soon, in Chapter 3, we'll slow down to a gentler pace—once you've learned enough to converse with Debug in hex. Now, let's take a breath of fresh air and look back on where we've been and what we've found.

We started out by meeting Debug. In chapters to come, we'll become intimate friends with Debug but, since it doesn't understand our familiar decimal numbers, we've begun the friendship by learning a new numbering system, hexadecimal notation.

In learning about hex numbers, you also learned how to convert decimal numbers to hex, and hex numbers to decimal. We'll write a program to do these translations later, but for now it's been necessary to learn the language itself.

Once we'd covered the basics of hexadecimal notation, we were able to wander off for a look at bits, bytes, words, and binary numbers—important characters you'll encounter frequently as we continue to explore the world of the 8088 and assembly language programming.

Finally, we moved on to learn about negative numbers in hex—the two's-complement numbers. They led us to signed and unsigned numbers, where we also witnessed overflows of two different types: one in which an overflow leaves the correct answer (addition of two signed numbers), and one in which the overflow leads to the wrong answer (addition of two unsigned numbers).

All this learning will pay off in later chapters, because we'll use our knowledge of hex numbers to speak with Debug, and Debug will act as an interpreter between us and the 8088 microprocessor waiting inside your IBM PC.

In the next chapter, we'll use the knowledge we've gained so far to learn about the 8088. We'll rely on Debug again, and use hex numbers, rather than binary, to talk to the 8088. We'll learn about the microprocessor's registers—the places where it stores numbers—and, in Chapter 3, we'll be ready to write a real program that will print a character on the screen. We'll also learn more about how the 8088 does its math; by the time we reach Chapter 10, we'll be able to write a program to convert binary numbers to decimal.

8808 ARITHMETIC

2

Knowing something of Debug's hex arithmetic and the 8088's binary arithmetic, we can begin to learn how the 8088 does its math. It uses internal commands called *instructions*.

Registers as Variables

Debug, our guide and interpreter, knows much about the 8088 microprocessor inside the IBM PC. We'll use it to delve into the inner workings of the 8088, and begin by asking Debug to display what it can about small pieces of memory called *registers*, in which we can store numbers. Registers are like variables in BASIC, but they are not exactly the same. Unlike the BASIC language, the 8088 microprocessor contains a fixed number of registers, and these registers are not part of your IBM PC's memory.

We'll ask Debug to display the 8088's registers with the R, for *Register*, command:

```
-R
AX=0000  BX=0000  CX=0000  DX=0000  SP=FFEE  BP=0000  SI=0000  DI=0000
DS=3756  ES=3756  SS=3756  CS=3756  IP=0100   NV UP DI PL NZ NA PO NC
3756:0100 E485          IN       AL,85
-
```

(You'll probably see different numbers in the second and third lines of your display; those numbers reflect the amount of memory in a computer. You'll continue to see such differences, and later we'll learn more about them.)

For now, Debug has certainly given us a lot of information. Let's concentrate on the first four registers, AX, BX, CX, and DX, all of which Debug tells us are equal to 0000, both here and on your display. These registers are the *general-purpose* registers. The other registers, SP, BP, SI, DI, DS, ES, SS, CS, and IP, are special-purpose registers we'll deal with in later chapters.

The four-digit number following each register name is in hex notation. In Chapter 1, we learned that one word is described exactly by four hex digits. Here, you can see that each of the 13 registers in the 8088 is one word, or 16 bits, long. This is why computers based on the 8088 microprocessor are known as 16-bit machines.

We mentioned that the registers are like BASIC variables. That means we should be able to change them, and we can. Debug's R command does more than display registers. Followed by the name of the register, the command tells Debug that we wish to view the register, and then change it. For example, we can change the AX register like this:

```
-R AX
AX 0000
:3A7
-
```

Let's look at the registers again to see if the AX register now contains 3A7h:

```
-R
AX=03A7  BX=0000  CX=0000  DX=0000  SP=FFEE  BP=0000  SI=0000  DI=0000
DS=3757  ES=3756  SS=3756  CS=3756  IP=0100   NV UP DI PL NZ NA PO NC
3756:0100 E485         IN     AL,85
-
```

It does. Furthermore, we can put any hex number into any register with the R command by specifying the register's name and entering the new number after the colon, as we just did. From here on, we'll be using this command whenever we need to place numbers into the 8088's registers.

You may recall seeing the number 3A7h in Chapter 1, where we used Debug's Hexarithmetic command to add 3A7h and 1EDh. Back then, Debug did the work for us. This time, we'll use Debug merely as an interpreter so we can work directly with the 8088. We'll give the 8088 instructions to add numbers from two registers: We'll place a number in the BX register and then instruct the 8088 to add the number in BX to the number in AX and put the answer back into AX. First, we need a number in the BX register. This time, let's add 3A7h and 92Ah. Use the R command to store 92Ah into BX.

Memory and the 8088

The AX and BX registers should, respectively, contain 3A7h and 92Ah, as we can verify with the R command:

```
AX=03A7  BX=092A  CX=0000  DX=0000  SP=FFEE  BP=0000  SI=0000  DI=0000
DS=3756  ES=3756  SS=3756  CS=3756  IP=0100   NV UP DI PL NZ NA PO NC
3756:0100 E485         IN     AL,85
```

Now that we have our two numbers in the AX and BX registers, how do we tell the 8088 to add BX to AX? We put some numbers into the computer's memory.

Your IBM PC probably has at least 128K of memory—far more than we'll need to use here. We'll place two bytes of *machine code* into a corner of this vast amount of memory. In this case, the machine code will be two binary numbers that tell the 8088 to add the BX register to AX. Then, so we can watch what happens, we'll *execute* this instruction with the help of Debug.

Now, where in memory should we place our two-byte instruction, and how will we tell the 8088 where to find it? As it turns out, the 8088 chops memory into 64K pieces known as *segments*. Most of the time, we'll be looking at memory within one of these segments without really knowing where the segment starts. We can do this because of the way the 8088 labels memory.

All bytes in memory are labeled with numbers, starting with 0h and working up. But remember the four-digit limitation on hex numbers? That means the highest number the 8088 can use is the hex equivalent of 65535, which means the maximum number of labels it can use is 64K. Even so, we know from experience that the 8088 can call on more than 64K of memory. How does it do this? By being a little bit tricky: It uses two numbers, one for each 64K segment, and one for each byte, or *offset*, within the segment. Each segment begins at a multiple of 16 bytes, so by overlapping segments and offsets, the 8088 effectively can label more than 64K of memory. In fact, this is precisely how the 8088 uses up to one million bytes of memory.

All the addresses (labels) we'll be using are offsets from the start of a segment. We'll write addresses as a segment number, followed by the offset within the segment. For example, 3756:0100 will mean we are at an offset of 100h within segment 3756h.

Later, in Chapter 11, we'll learn more about segments and see more about why we have such a high segment number. But for now, we'll simply trust Debug to look after the segments for us, so that we can work within one segment without having to pay attention to segment numbers. And for the time being, we'll refer to addresses only by their offsets. Each of these addresses refers to one byte in the segment, and the addresses are sequential, so 101h is the byte following 100h in memory.

Written out, our two-byte instruction to add BX to AX looks like this: ADD AX,BX. We'll place this instruction at locations 100h and 101h, in whatever segment Debug starts to use. In referring to our ADD instruction, we'll say that it's at location 100h, since this is the location of the first byte of the instruction.

Debug's command for examining and changing memory is called E, for *Enter*. Use this command to enter the two bytes of the ADD instruction, as follows:

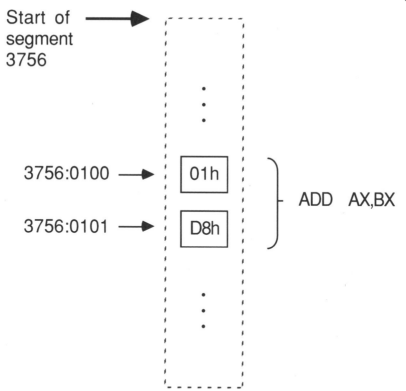

Figure 2-1. Our Instruction Begins 100h Bytes From the Start of the Segment.

```
-E 100
3756:0100  E4.01
-E 101
3756:0101  85.D8
-
```

The numbers 01h and D8h are the 8088's machine language for our ADD instruction at memory locations 3756:0100 and 3756:0101. The segment number you see will probably be different, but that difference won't affect our program. Likewise, Debug probably displayed a different two-digit number for each of your E commands. These numbers (E4h and 85h in our example) are the old numbers in memory at offset addresses 100h and 101h of the segment

Debug chose—that is, the numbers are data from previous programs left in memory when you started Debug. (If you just started your computer, the numbers should be 00.)

Addition, 8088 Style

Now your register display should look something like this:

```
AX=03A7  BX=092A  CX=0000  DX=0000  SP=FFEE  BP=0000  SI=0000  DI=0000
DS=3756  ES=3756  SS=3756  CS=3756  IP=0100   NV UP DI PL NZ NA PO NC
3756:0100 01D8         ADD     AX,BX
```

Our ADD instruction is neatly placed in memory, just where we want it to be. We know this from reading the third line of the display. The first two numbers, 3756:0100, give us the address (100h) for the first number of our ADD instruction. Next to this, we see the two bytes for ADD: 01D8. The byte equal to 01h is at address 100h, while D8h is at 101h. Finally, since we entered our instruction in *machine language*—numbers that have no meaning to us, but which the 8088 will interpret as an add instruction—the message ADD AX,BX confirms that we entered the instruction correctly.

Even though we've placed our ADD instruction in memory, we're not quite ready to run it through the 8088 (*execute* it). First, we need to tell the 8088 where to find the instruction.

The 8088 finds segment and offset addresses in two special registers, CS and IP, which you can see listed in the preceding register display. The segment number is stored in the CS, or *Code Segment*, register, which we'll discuss shortly. If you look at the register display, you can see that Debug has already set the CS register for us (CS=3756, in our example). The full starting address of our instruction, however, is 3756:0100.

The second part of this address (the offset within segment 3756) is stored in the IP (*Instruction Pointer*) register. The 8088 uses the offset in the IP register to actually find our first instruction. We can tell it where to look by setting the IP register to the address of our first instruction—IP=0100.

But the IP register is already set to 100h. We've been clever: Debug sets IP to 100h whenever you first start it. Knowing this, we've deliberately chosen 100h as the address of our first instruction and have thus eliminated the need to set the IP register in a separate step. It's a good point to keep in mind.

Now, with our instructions in place and the registers set correctly, we'll tell Debug to execute our one instruction. We'll use Debug's T (for *Trace*) command, which executes one instruction at a time and then displays the registers. After each trace, the IP should point to the next instruction. In this case, it will point to 102h. We haven't put an instruction at 102h, so in the last line of the register display we'll just see an instruction left from some other program.

Let's ask Debug to trace one instruction with the T command:

```
-T
AX=0CD1  BX=092A  CX=0000  DX=0000  SP=FFEE  BP=0000  SI=0000  DI=0000
DS=3756  ES=3756  SS=3756  CS=3756  IP=0102   NV UP DI PL NZ AC PE NC
3756:0102 AC           LODSB
-
```

That's it. The AX register now contains CD1h, which is the sum of 3A7h and 92Ah. And the IP register points to address 102h, so the last line of the register display shows some instruction at memory location 102h, rather than 100h.

We mentioned earlier that the instruction pointer, together with the CS register, always points to the next instruction for the 8088. If we typed T again, we'd execute the next instruction, but don't do it just yet—your 8088 might head for limbo.

Instead, what if we want to execute our ADD instruction again, adding 92Ah to CD1h and storing the new answer in AX? For that we need to tell the 8088 where to find its next instruction, and want this to be our ADD instruction at 0100h. Can we just change the IP register to 0100h? Let's try it. Use the R command to set IP to 100, and look at the register display:

```
AX=0CD1  BX=092A  CX=0000  DX=0000  SP=FFEE  BP=0000  SI=0000  DI=0000
DS=3756  ES=3756  SS=3756  CS=3756  IP=0100   NV UP DI PL NZ AC PE NC
3756:0100              ADD      AX,BX
```

That's done it. Try the T command again and see if the AX register contains 15FBh. It does.

As you can see here, you should always check the IP register and the instruction at the bottom of an R display before using the T command. That way, you'll be sure the 8088 executes the instruction you want it to.

Now, set the IP register to 100h once again, make certain the registers contain AX = 15FB, BX = 092A, and let's try subtraction.

AX: 03A7   BX: 092A

IP:100 ⟹ ADD AX,BX
LODSB

Figure 2-2.   Before Executing the ADD Instruction.

AX: 0CD1   BX: 092A

ADD AX,BX
IP:102 ⟹ LODSB

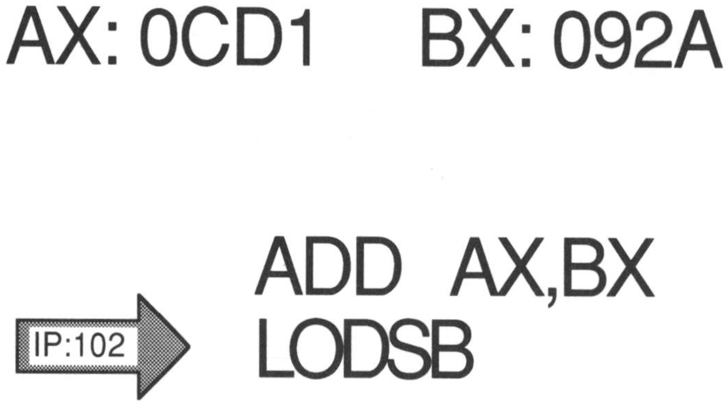

Figure 2-3.   After Executing the ADD Instruction.

Subtraction, 8088 Style

We're going to write an instruction to subtract BX from AX so that, after two subtractions, we'll have 3A7h in AX: the point from which we started before our two additions. You'll also see how we can save a little effort in entering two bytes into memory.

When we entered the two bytes for our ADD instruction, we typed the E command twice: once with 0100h for the first address, and once with 0101h for the second address. The procedure worked, but as it turns out we can actually enter the second byte without another E command if we separate it from the first byte with a space. When you've finished entering bytes, pressing the

Enter key will exit from the Enter command. Try this method for our subtract instruction:

```
-E 100
3756:0100  01.29   D8.D8
```

The register display (remember to reset the IP register to 100h) should now show the instruction *SUB AX,BX*, which subtracts the BX register from the AX register and leaves the result in AX. The order of AX and BX may seem backward, but the instruction is like the BASIC statement AX = AX − BX except that the 8088, unlike BASIC, always puts the answer into the first variable (register).

Execute this instruction with the T command. AX should contain CD1. Change IP to point back to this instruction, and execute it again (remember to check the instruction at the bottom of the R display first). AX should now be 03A7.

Negative Numbers in the 8088

In the last chapter, we learned how the 8088 uses the two's-complement form for negative numbers. Now, let's work directly with the SUB instruction to calculate negative numbers. Let's put the 8088 to a little test, to see if we get FFFFh for −1. We'll subtract one from zero and, if we're right, the subtraction should place FFFFh (−1) into AX. Set AX equal to zero and BX to one, then trace through the instruction at address 0100h. Just what we expected: AX = FFFFh.

While you have this subtraction instruction handy, you may wish to try some different numbers to gain a better feel for two's-complement arithmetic. For example, see what result you get for −2.

Bytes in the 8088

All of our arithmetic thus far has been performed on words, hence the four hex digits. Does the 8088 microprocessor know how to perform math with bytes? Yes, it does.

Since one word is formed from two bytes, each general-purpose register can be divided into two bytes, known as the *high byte* (the first two hex digits) and the *low byte* (the second two hex digits). Each of these registers can be called by its letter (A through D), followed by X for a word, H for the high byte, or L for the low byte. For example, DL and DH are byte registers, and DX is a word register. (This terminology can become somewhat confusing, however, because words stored in memory have their low byte first, and the high byte second.)

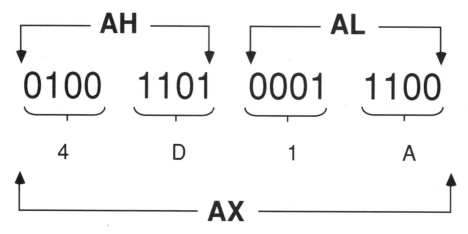

Figure 2-4.   The AX Register Split into Two Byte Registers (AH and AL).

Let's test byte-sized math with an ADD instruction. Enter the two bytes 00h and C4h, starting at location 0100h. At the bottom of the register display, you'll see the instruction *ADD AH, AL*, which will add the two bytes of the AX register and place the result in the high byte, AH.

Next, load the AX register with 0102h. This places 01h in the AH register and 02h in the AL register. Set the IP register to 100h, execute the T command, and you'll find that AX now contains 0302. The result of 01h + 02h is 03h, and that value is in the AH register.

But suppose you hadn't meant to add 01h and 02h. Suppose you really meant to add 01h and 03h. If the AX register already contained 0102, could you change the AL register to 03h? No. You would have to change the AX register to 0103h. Why? Because Debug only allows us to change *entire* word registers. There isn't a way to change just the low or high part of a register with Debug. But, as you saw in the last chapter, this isn't a problem. With hex numbers, we can split a word into two bytes by breaking the four-digit hex number in half. Thus, the word 0103h becomes the two bytes 01h and 03h.

To try this ADD instruction, load the AX register with 0103h. Your ADD

AH,AL instruction is still at memory location 0100h, so reset the IP register to 100h and, with 01h and 03h now in the AH and AL registers, trace through this instruction. This time, AX contains 0403h: 04h, the sum of 01h + 03h is now in the AH register.

Multiplication and Division, 8088 Style

We've seen the 8088 add and subtract two numbers. Now we'll see that it can also multiply and divide—clever processor. The multiply instruction is called MUL, and the machine code to multiply AX and BX is F7h E3h. We'll enter this into memory, but first a word about the MUL instruction.

Where does the MUL instruction store its answer? In the AX register? Not quite; we have to be careful here. As you'll soon see, multiplying two 16-bit numbers can give a 32-bit answer, so the MUL instruction stores its result in two registers, DX and AX. The higher 16 bits are placed in the DX register; the lower, into AX. We can also write this register combination as DX:AX.

Let's get back to Debug and the 8088. Enter the multiply instruction, F7h E3h, at location 0100h, just as you did for the addition and subtraction instructions, and set AX = 7C4Bh and BX = 100h. You'll see the instruction in the register display as *MUL BX*, without any reference to the AX register. To multiply words, as here, the 8088 *always* multiplies the register you name in the instruction by the AX register, and stores the answer in the DX:AX pair of registers.

Before we actually execute this MUL instruction, let's do the multiplication by hand. How do we calculate 100h * 7C4Bh? The three digits 100 have the same effect in hex as in decimal, so to multiply by 100h simply add two zeros to the right of a hex number. Thus, 100h * 7C4Bh = 7C4B00h. This result is too long to fit into one word, so we'll split it into the two words 007Ch and 4B00h.

Use Debug to trace through the instruction. You'll see that DX contains the word 007Ch, and AX contains the word 4B00h. In other words, the 8088 returned the result of the *word-multiply* instruction in the DX:AX pair of registers. Since multiplying two words together can never be longer than two words, but will often be longer than one word (as we just saw), the word-multiply instruction always returns the result in the DX:AX pair of registers.

And what about division? When we divide numbers, the 8088 keeps both the result and the remainder of the division. Let's see how the 8088's division

DX

AX

BX

MUL BX
LODSB

Figure 2-5.   Before Executing the MUL Instruction.

DX

AX

BX

MUL BX
LODSB

Figure 2-6.   After Executing the MUL Instruction.

DX

AX

BX

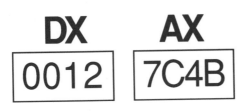

DIV BX
LODSB

Figure 2-7.   Before Executing the DIV Instruction.

DX

AX

BX

DIV BX

LODSB

Figure 2-8.   After Executing the DIV instruction.

works. First, place the instruction F7h F3h at 0100h (and 101h). Like the MUL instruction, DIV uses DX:AX without being told, so all we see is *DIV BX*. Now, load the registers so that DX = 007Ch and AX = 4B12h; BX should still contain 0100h.

Again, we'll first calculate the results by hand: 7C4B12h / 100h = 7C4Bh, with 12h left over. When we execute our division instruction at 0100h, we find that AX = 7C4Bh, the result of our division, and DX = 0012h, which is the remainder. (We'll put this remainder to very good use in Chapter 10, when we write a program to convert decimal numbers to hex by using the remainders, just as we did in Chapter 1.)

Summary

It's almost time for us to write a real program—one to print a character on the screen. We've put in our time learning the basics. Let's take a look at the ground we've covered, and then we'll be all set to push on.

We began this chapter by learning about registers and noticing their similarity to variables in BASIC. Unlike BASIC, however, we saw that the 8088 has a small, fixed number of registers. We concentrated on the four general-purpose registers, with a quick look at the CS and IP registers, which the 8088 uses to locate segment and offset addresses.

After learning how to change and read registers, we moved on to build some single-instruction programs by entering the machine codes to add, subtract, multiply, and divide two numbers with the AX and BX registers. In future chapters we'll use much of what we learned here, but you won't need to remember the machine codes for each instruction.

We also learned how to tell Debug to execute, or trace through, a single instruction. We'll come to rely heavily on Debug to trace through our programs. Of course, as our programs grow in size, this tracing will become both more useful and more tedious. Later on we'll build on our experience and learn how to execute more than one instruction with a single Debug command.

Let's turn back to real programs and learn how to make a program that speaks.

3

PRINTING CHARACTERS

Now we know enough to do something solid, so roll up your sleeves and flex your fingers. We're going to begin by instructing DOS to send a character to the screen, then we'll move on to even more interesting work. We'll build a small program with more than one instruction, and from there, learn another way to put data into registers—this time, from within a program. Now, let's see if we can get DOS to speak.

INT—The Powerful Interrupt

To our four math instructions, ADD, SUB, MUL, and DIV, we'll add a new instruction called INT (for *Interrupt*). INT is something like BASIC's GOSUB statement. We'll use the INT instruction to ask DOS to print a character, A, on the screen for us.

Before we learn how INT works, let's run through an example. Start Debug and place 200h into AX and 41h into DX. The INT instruction for DOS functions is INT 21h—in machine code, CDh 21h. This is a two-byte instruction like the DIV instruction in the last chapter. Put INT 21h in memory, starting at location 100h, and use the R command to confirm that the instruction reads INT 21 (remember to set IP to 100h if it isn't already there).

Now we're ready to execute this instruction, but we can't use the trace command here as we did in the last chapter. The trace command executes one instruction at a time, but the INT instruction calls upon a large program in DOS to do the actual work, much as BASIC programs can call a subroutine with the GOSUB statement.

We don't want to execute each of the instructions in the entire DOS "subroutine" by tracing through it one instruction at a time. Instead, we want to *run* our one-line program, but stop before executing the instruction at location 102h. We can do this with Debug's G (for *Go*) command, followed by the address at which we want to stop:

```
-G 102
A
AX=0241  BX=0000  CX=0000  DX=0041  SP=FFEE  BP=0000  SI=0000  DI=0000
DS=3970  ES=3970  SS=3970  CS=3970  IP=0102   NV UP DI PL NZ NA PO NC
3970:0102 8BE5          MOV     SP,BP
```

DOS printed the character A, and then returned control to our small program.

(Remember, the instruction at 102h is just data left behind by another program, so you'll probably see something different.)

Our small program here is, in a sense, two instructions long, the second instruction being whatever is at location 102h. That is, it is something like this:

```
INT     21
MOV     SP,BP           (Or whatever is on your computer)
```

We'll soon replace this random second instruction with one of our own. For now, since it isn't anything we want to execute, we told Debug to run our program, stop execution when it reached this second instruction, and display the registers when it was done.

And how did DOS know to print the A? The 02h in the AH register told DOS to print a character. Another number in AH would tell DOS to execute a different function. (We'll see others later, but if you're curious right now, you can find a list of functions in your *DOS Technical Manual*.)

As for the character itself, DOS uses the number in the DL register as the ASCII code for the character to print when we ask it to send a character to the screen. We stored 41h, the ASCII code for an uppercase A.

In Appendix E, you'll find a chart of ASCII character codes for all the characters your IBM PC can display. For your convenience, the numbers are in both decimal and hex notation. But since Debug reads hex only, here is a good chance for you to practice converting decimal numbers to hex. Pick a character from the table and convert it to hex on your own. Then, verify your conversion by typing your hex value into the DL register and running the INT instruction again (remember to reset IP to 100h).

You may have wondered what would have happened if you had tried the trace command on the INT instruction. We'll pretend we had not executed the G 102 command and, instead, trace a short distance through, to see what happens. If you try this yourself, don't go too far: You may find your IBM PC doing something strange. After you've traced through a few steps, exit Debug with the Q command. This will clean up any mess you've left behind.

```
-R
AX=0200  BX=0000  CX=0000  DX=0041  SP=FFEE  BP=0000  SI=0000  DI=0000
DS=3970  ES=3970  SS=3970  CS=3970  IP=0100   NV UP DI PL NZ NA PO NC
3970:0100 CD21          INT    21
-T
```

```
AX=0200  BX=0000  CX=0000  DX=0041  SP=FFE8  BP=0000  SI=0000  DI=0000
DS=3970  ES=3970  SS=3970  CS=3372  IP=0180   NV UP DI PL NZ NA PO NC
3372:0180 80FC4B           CMP      AH,4B
-T


AX=0200  BX=0000  CX=0000  DX=0041  SP=FFE8  BP=0000  SI=0000  DI=0000
DS=3970  ES=3970  SS=3970  CS=3372  IP=0183   NV UP DI NG NZ AC PE CY
3372:0183 7405             JZ       018A
-T


AX=0200  BX=0000  CX=0000  DX=0041  SP=FFE8  BP=0000  SI=0000  DI=0000
DS=3970  ES=3970  SS=3970  CS=3372  IP=0185   NV UP DI NG NZ AC PE CY
3372:0185 2E               CS:
3372:0186 FF2EAB0B         JMP      FAR [0BAB]              CS:0BAB=0BFF
-Q
```

Notice that the first number of the address changed here, from 3970 to 3372. These last three instructions were part of DOS, and the program for DOS is in another segment. In fact, there are many, many more instructions that DOS executes before it prints a single character; even such an apparently simple task is not as easy as it sounds. Now you can see why we used the G command to run our program to location 102h. Otherwise, we'd have seen a torrent of instructions from DOS. (If you're using a different version of DOS than we used, the instructions you see when you try this may be different.)

A Graceful Exit—INT 20h

Remember that our INT instruction was 21h? If we changed the 21h to a 20h, we'd have INT 20h instead. INT 20h is another interrupt instruction, and it tells DOS we want to exit our program, so that DOS can take full control again. In our case, INT 20h will send control back to Debug, since we're executing our programs from Debug, rather than from DOS.

Enter the instruction CDh 20h, starting at location 100h, then try the following (remember to check the INT 20h instruction with the R command):

```
-G 102

Program terminated normally
-R
AX=0000  BX=0000  CX=0000  DX=0000  SP=FFEE  BP=0000  SI=0000  DI=0000
DS=3970  ES=3970  SS=3970  CS=3970  IP=0100   NV UP DI PL NZ NA PO NC
3970:0100 CD20             INT      20
-G
```

```
Program terminated normally
-R
AX=0000  BX=0000  CX=0000  DX=0000  SP=FFEE  BP=0000  SI=0000  DI=0000
DS=3970  ES=3970  SS=3970  CS=3970  IP=0100   NV UP DI PL NZ NA PO NC
3970:0100 CD20        INT    20
```

The command G, with no number after it, executes the entire program (which is just one instruction now, because INT 20 is an *exit* instruction), and then returns to the start. IP has been reset to 100h, where we started. The registers in this example are 0 only because we started Debug afresh.

We can use this INT 20h instruction at the end of a program to return control gracefully to DOS (or Debug), so let's put this instruction together with INT 21h and build a two-line program.

A Two-Line Program—Putting the Pieces Together

Starting at location 100h, enter the two instructions INT 21h, INT 20h (CDh 21h CDh 20h) one after the other. (From now on, we'll always start programs at location 100h).

When we had only one instruction we could "list" that instruction with the R command, but now we have two instructions. To see them, we have the U (*Unassemble*) command, which acts like BASIC's List command:

```
-U 100
3970:0100 CD21        INT    21
3970:0102 CD20        INT    20
3970:0104 D98D460250B8 ESC    09,[DI+0246][DI+B850]
3970:010A 8D00        LEA    AX,[BX+SI]
3970:010C 50          PUSH   AX
3970:010D E82A23      CALL   243A
3970:0110 8BE5        MOV    SP,BP
3970:0112 83C41A      ADD    SP,+1A
3970:0115 5D          POP    BP
3970:0116 C3          RET
3970:0117 55          PUSH   BP
3970:0118 83EC02      SUB    SP,+02
3970:011B 8BEC        MOV    BP,SP
3970:011D 823E0E0000  CMP    BYTE PTR [000E],00
```

The first two instructions we recognize as the two instructions we just entered. The other instructions are remnants left in memory. As our program grows, we'll fill this display with more of our own code.

Now, fill the AH register with 02h and the DL register with the number for any character (just as you did earlier when you changed the AX and DX registers), then simply type the G command to see your character. For example, if you place 41h into DL, you'll see:

```
-G
A
Program terminated normally
-
```

Try this a few times before we move on to other ways to set these registers.

Entering Programs

From here on, most of our programs will be more than one instruction long, and to present these programs we'll use an unassemble display. Our last program would thus appear like this:

```
3970:0100 CD21        INT    21
3970:0102 CD20        INT    20
```

So far, we've entered the instructions for our programs directly as numbers, such as CDh, 21h. But that's a lot of work, and, as it turns out, there is a much easier way to enter instructions.

In addition to the unassemble command, Debug includes an A (*Assemble*) command, which allows us to enter the mnemonic, or human-readable, instructions directly. So rather than entering those cryptic numbers for our short program, we can use the assemble command to enter the following:

```
-A 100
3970:0100 INT 21
3970:0102 INT 20
3970:0104
-
```

When you've finished assembling instructions, all you have to do is press the Enter key, and the Debug prompt reappears.

Here, the A command told Debug that we wished to enter instructions in mnemonic form, and the 100 in our command told Debug to start entering instructions at location 100h. Since Debug's assemble command makes entering programs much simpler, we'll use it from now on to enter instructions.

MOVing Data into Registers

Although we've relied on Debug quite a bit so far, we won't always run programs with it. Normally, a program would set the AH and DL registers itself before an INT 21h instruction. To do this, we'll learn about another instruction, MOV. Once we know enough about this instruction, we'll be able to take our small program to print a character and make a real program—one that we can execute directly from DOS.

Soon, we'll use the MOV instruction to load numbers into registers AH and DL. But let's start learning about MOV by moving numbers between registers. Place 1234h into AX (12h into the AH register, and 34h in AL) and ABCDh into DX (ABh in DH, and CDh in DL). Now, enter the following instruction with the A command:

```
396F:0100 88D4        MOV    AH,DL
```

This instruction *moves* the number in DL into AH by putting a copy of it into AH; AL is not affected. If you trace through this one line, you'll find that AX = CD34h and DX = ABCDh. Only AH has changed. It now holds a copy of the number in DL.

Like the BASIC statement LET AH = DL, a MOV instruction copies a number from the second register to the first, and for this reason we write AH before DL. Although there are some restrictions, which we'll find out about later, we can use other forms of the MOV instruction to copy numbers between other pairs of registers. For example, reset IP and try this:

```
396F:0100 89C3        MOV    BX,AX
```

You've just moved words, rather than bytes, between registers. The MOV instruction always works between words and words, or bytes and bytes; never between words and bytes. It makes sense, for how would you move a word into a byte?

We originally set out to move a number into the AH and DL registers. Let's do so now with another form of the MOV instruction:

```
396F:0100 B402        MOV    AH,02
```

This instruction moves 02h into the AH register without affecting the AL register. The second byte of the instruction, 02h, is the number we wish to move. Try moving a different number into AH: Change the second byte to another, such as C1h, with the E 101 command.

Now, let's put all the pieces of this chapter together and build a longer program. This one will print an asterisk, *, all by itself, with no need for us to set the registers (AH and DL). The program uses MOV instructions to set the AH and DL registers before the INT 21h call to DOS:

```
396F:0100 B402        MOV     AH,02
396F:0102 B22A        MOV     DL,2A
396F:0104 CD21        INT     21
396F:0106 CD20        INT     20
```

Enter the program and check it with the U command (U 100). Make sure IP points to location 100h, then try the G command to run the entire program. You should see the * character appear on your screen:

```
-G
*
Program terminated normally
-
```

Now that we have a complete, self-contained program, let's write it to disk as a .COM program, so we will be able to execute it directly from DOS. We can run a .COM program from DOS simply by typing its name. Since our program doesn't yet have a name, we need to give it one.

The Debug command N (for *Name*) gives a name to a file before we write it to disk. Type:

```
-N WRITESTR.COM
```

to give the name WRITESTR.COM to our program. This command doesn't write our file to the disk, though—it simply names the file.

Next, we must give Debug a byte count, telling it the number of bytes in our program so it will know how much memory we want to write to our file. If you refer to the unassemble listing of our program, you can see that each instruction is two bytes long (this won't always be true). We have four instructions, so our program is 4 * 2 = 8 bytes long. (We could also put Debug's H command to work, and use hexarithmetic to determine the number of bytes in our program. Typing *H 108 100*, where 108 is the address of the instruction after INT 20, will produce 8.)

Once we have our byte count, we need somewhere to put it. Debug uses the pair of registers BX:CX for the length of our file, so putting 8h into CX tells Debug that our program is eight bytes long. Finally, since our file is only eight bytes long, we also need to set BX to zero.

Once we've set the name and length of our program, we can then write it to disk with Debug's W (for *Write*) command:

```
-W
Writing 0008 bytes
-
```

We now have a program on our disk called WRITESTR.COM, so let's exit Debug, with a Q, and look for it. Use the DOS Dir command to list the file:

```
A>DIR WRITESTR.COM

  Volume in drive A has no label
  Directory of  A:\

WRITESTR COM       8   6-30-83  10:05a
        1 File(s)     18432 bytes free

A>
```

The directory listing tells us that WRITESTR.COM is on the disk and that it's eight bytes long, just as it should be. To run the program, simply type *Writestr* at the DOS prompt. You'll see a * appear on the display. Nothing to it.

Writing a String of Characters

As a final example for this chapter, we'll use INT 21h, with a different function number in the AH register, to write a whole string of characters. We'll have to store our string of characters in memory and we'll have to tell DOS where to find the string, so in the process, we'll also learn more about addresses and memory.

We've already seen that function number 02h for INT 21H prints one character on the screen. Another function, number 09h, prints an entire string, and stops printing characters when it finds a $ symbol in the string. Let's put a string into memory. We'll start at location 200h, so the string won't become tangled with the code for our program. Enter the following numbers, using the instruction E 200:

```
48      65      6C      6C
6F      2C      20      44
4F      53      20      68
65      72      65      2E
24
```

The last number, 24h, is the ASCII code for a $ sign, and it tells DOS that this is the end of our string of characters. You'll see what this string says in a minute, when you run the program we'll enter now:

```
396F:0100 B409        MOV    AH,09
396F:0102 BA0002      MOV    DX,0200
396F:0105 CD21        INT    21
396F:0107 CD20        INT    20
```

200h is the address of the string we entered, and loading 200h into the DX register tells DOS where to find the string of characters. Check your program with the U command, then run it with a G command:

```
-G
Hello, DOS here.
Program terminated normally
```

Now that we've stored some characters in memory, it's time to meet another Debug command, D (for *Dump*). The dump command dumps memory to the screen somewhat like U lists instructions. Just as when you use the U command, simply place an address after D to tell Debug where to start the dump. For example, type the command D 200 to see a dump of the string you just entered:

```
-D 200
396F:0200  48 65 6C 6C 6F 2C 20 44-4F 53 20 68 65 72 65 2E   Hello, DOS here.
396F:0210  24 5D C3 55 83 EC 30 8B-EC C7 06 10 00 00 00 E8   $]CU.10.1G.....h
   .
   .
   .
```

After each pair of address numbers (such as 396F:0200 in our example), we see 16 hex bytes, followed by the 16 ASCII characters for these bytes. Thus, on the first line you see most of the ASCII codes and characters you typed in. The ending $ sign you typed is the first character on the second line; the remainder of that line is a miscellaneous assortment of characters.

Wherever you see a period (.) in the ASCII window, it represents either a period or a special character, such as the Greek letter pi. Debug's D command displays only 96 of the 256 characters in the IBM PC character set, so a period is used for the remaining 160 characters.

We'll use the D command in the future to check numbers we enter for data, whether those data are characters or ordinary numbers. (For more information, refer to the Debug section in your DOS manual.)

Our string-writing program is complete, so we can write it to the disk. The procedure is the same one we used to write WRITESTR.COM to disk, except this time we have to set our program length to a value long enough to include the string at 200h. Our program begins at line 100h, and we can see from the memory dump just performed that the first character ( ]) following the $ sign that ends our string is at location 211h. Again, we can use the H command to find the difference between these two numbers. Find 211h − 100h and store this value into the CX register, again setting BX to zero. Use the N command to give the program a name (add the .COM extension to run the program directly from DOS), then use the W command to write the program and data to a disk file.

That's it for writing characters to the screen—aside from one final note: You may have noticed that DOS never sends the $ character. Quite so, because DOS uses the $ sign to mark the end of a string of characters. That means we can't use DOS to print a string with a $ in it, but in a later chapter, we'll see how to print a string with a $ sign or any other special character.

Summary

Our preparations in the first two chapters brought us to the point where we could work on a real program. In this chapter, we used our knowledge of hex numbers, Debug, 8088 instructions, and memory to build short programs to print a character and a string of characters on the screen. In the process we also learned some new things.

First we learned about INT instructions—not in much detail, but enough for us to write two short programs. In later chapters, we'll gain more knowledge about interrupt instructions as we increase our understanding of the 8088 microprocessor tucked under the cover of your IBM PC.

Debug has, once again, been a useful and faithful guide. We've been relying heavily on Debug to display the contents of registers and memory, and in this chapter we used its abilities even more. Debug ran our short programs with the G command.

We also learned about the INT 20 exit instruction, and the MOV instruction for moving numbers into and between registers. The exit instruction (INT 20) allowed us to build a complete program that we could write to the disk and run directly from DOS without the help of Debug. And the MOV instruction gave us the ability to set registers before an INT 21 (print) instruction, so we could write a self-contained program to print one character.

Finally, we rounded out the chapter with the INT 21h function to print an entire string of characters. We'll use all these instructions heavily throughout the rest of this book, but as you saw from using the Debug assemble and unassemble commands, you won't need to remember the machine codes for these instructions.

Now we know enough to move on to printing binary numbers. In the next chapter we'll build a short program to take one byte and print it on the screen as a string of binary digits (zeros and ones).

4

PRINTING BINARY NUMBERS

In this chapter we'll build a program to write binary numbers to the screen as strings of zeros and ones. We have most of the knowledge we need, and our work here will help solidify ideas we've already covered. We'll also add a few instructions to those we know, including another version of ADD and some instructions to help us repeat parts of our program. Let's begin by learning something completely new.

Rotations and the Carry Flag

In Chapter 2, when we first encountered hex arithmetic, we found that adding 1 to FFFFh should give 10000h, but doesn't. Only the four hex digits to the right fit into one word; the 1 doesn't fit. We also found that this 1 is an overflow and that it is not lost. Where does it go? It is put into something called a *flag*—in this case, the *Carry Flag*, or *CF*. Flags contain one-bit numbers, so they can hold either a zero or a one. If we need to carry a one into the fifth hex digit, it goes into the carry flag.

Let's go back to our ADD instruction of Chapter 3 (ADD AX,BX). Put FFFFh into AX and 1 into BX, then trace through the ADD instruction. At the end of the second line of Debug's R display, you'll see eight pairs of letters. The last of these, which can read either NC or CY, is the carry flag. Right now, because your add instruction resulted in an overflow of 1, you'll see that the carry status reads CY (*Carry*). The carry bit is now 1 or, as we'll say, it's *set*.

Just to confirm that we've stored a seventeenth bit here (it would be the ninth bit for a byte addition), add one to the zero in AX by resetting IP to 100h and tracing through the add instruction again. The carry flag is affected by each add instruction, and this time there shouldn't be any overflow, so the carry should be reset. And, indeed, the carry does become zero, as indicated by the NC, which stands for *No Carry*, in the R display.

(We'll learn about the other status flags later, but if you're curious, you can find information about them right now under Debug's R command in your DOS manual.)

Let's review the task of printing a binary number, to see how the carry information could be useful. We print only one character at a time, and want to pick off the bits of our number, one by one, from left to right. For example, the first character we would want to print in the number 1000 0000b would be the one. If we could move this entire byte left one place, dropping the one into the carry flag and adding a 0 to the right side, then repeat the process for each succeeding digit, the carry flag would pick off our binary digits. And we can do just this with a new instruction called RCL (*Rotate Carry Left*).

To see how it works, enter the short program:

```
3985:0100 D0D3        RCL    BL,1
```

This instruction *rotates* the byte in BL to the left by one bit (hence the ,1), and it does so through the carry flag. The instruction is called rotate, because RCL moves the leftmost bit into the carry flag, while moving the bit currently in the carry flag into the rightmost bit position (0). In the process, all the other bits are moved, or rotated, to the left. After enough rotations (17 for a word, nine for a byte) the bits are moved back into their original positions, and you get back the original number.

Place B7h in the BX register, then trace through this rotate instruction several times. Converting your results to binary, you'll see the following:

```
Carry          BL register
  0         1 0 1 1   0 1 1 1     B7h      We start here
  1         0 1 1 0   1 1 1 0     6Eh
  0         1 1 0 1   1 1 0 1     DDh
  1         1 0 1 1   1 0 1 0     BAh
                         .
                         .
                         .
  0         1 0 1 1   0 1 1 1     B7h      After 9 rotations
```

In the first rotation, bit 7 of BL moves into the carry flag, the bit in the carry flag moves into bit 0 of BL, and all the other bits move left one position. Succeeding moves continue rotating the bits to the left until, after nine rotations, the original number is back in the BL register.

We're getting closer to building our program to write binary numbers to the screen, but we still need a few other pieces. Let's see how we can convert the bit in the carry flag into the character 0 or 1.

Adding With the Carry Flag

The normal ADD instruction, for example, ADD AX,BX, simply adds two numbers. Another instruction, ADC (*Add with Carry*) adds three numbers: the two, as before, *plus* one bit from the carry flag. If you look in your ASCII table, you'll discover that 30h is the character 0 and 31h is the character 1. So, adding the carry flag to 30h gives the character 0 when the carry is clear, and 1 when the carry is set. Thus, if DL = 0 and the carry flag is set (1), executing:

```
ADC  DL,30
```

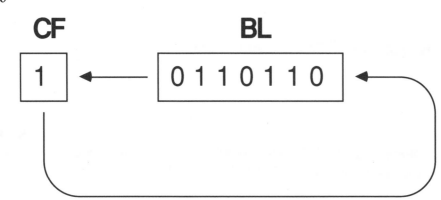

Figure 4-1.   The RCL BL,1 Instruction.

adds DL (0) to 30h ('0') and to 1h (the carry) to give 31h ('1'). And, with one instruction we've converted the carry to a character we can print.

At this point, rather than run through an example of ADC, let's wait for our complete program. Once we've built our program, we'll execute its instructions one at a time, in a procedure called *single-stepping*, and through this, we'll see both how the ADC instruction works and how it fits nicely into our program. But first we need one more instruction, which we'll use to repeat our RCL, ADC, and INT 21h (print) instructions eight times: once for each bit in a byte.

Looping

As mentioned, the RCL instruction isn't limited to rotating bytes; it can also rotate entire words. We'll use this ability to demonstrate the *LOOP* instruction. LOOP is something like a FOR-NEXT loop in BASIC, but it's not as general. As with BASIC's FOR-NEXT loop, however, we need to tell LOOP how many times to run through a loop. We do this by placing our repeat count in register CX. Each time through the loop, the 8088 subtracts one from CX, and, when CX becomes zero, LOOP ends the loop.

Why the CX register? The C in CX stands for *Count*. We can use this register as a general-purpose register, but, as you'll see in the next chapter, the CX register is used with other instructions when we wish to repeat operations.

Here's a simple program that rotates the BX register left eight times, moving BL into BH (but not the reverse, since we rotate through the carry flag):

```
396F:0100 BBC5A3        MOV    BX,A3C5
396F:0103 B90800        MOV    CX,0008
396F:0106 D1D3          RCL    BX,1
396F:0108 E2FC          LOOP   0106
396F:010A CD20          INT    20
```

Our loop starts at 106h (RCL BX,1) and ends with the LOOP instruction. The number following LOOP (106h) is the address of the RCL instruction. When we run the program, LOOP subtracts one from CX, then jumps to address 106h if CX is not zero. The instruction RCL BX,1 (rotate carry left, one place) is executed eight times here, because CX is set to eight before the loop.

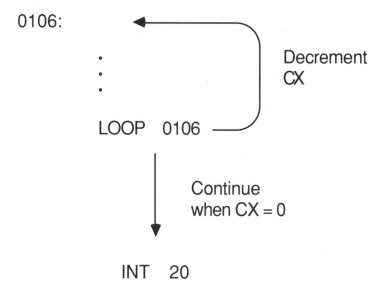

Figure 4-2. The LOOP Instruction.

You may have noticed that, unlike the FOR-NEXT loop in BASIC, the LOOP instruction is at the end of our loop (where we'd put the NEXT statement in BASIC). And the start of the loop, the RCL instruction at 106h, has no special instruction like FOR has in BASIC. If you know a language like Pascal, you can see that the LOOP instruction is somewhat akin to the RE-PEAT-UNTIL pair of instructions, where the REPEAT instruction just labels the start of the block of instructions to loop through.

There are different ways you could execute our small program. If you simply type G, you won't see any change in the register display, because Debug saves all the registers before it starts carrying out a G command. Then, if it encounters an INT 20 instruction (as it will in our program), it restores all the registers. Try G. You'll see that IP has been reset to 100h (where you started), and that the other registers don't look any different, either.

If you have the patience, you can trace through this program instead. Taking it one step at a time, you can watch the registers change at each step:

```
-R
AX=0000  BX=0000  CX=0000  DX=0000  SP=FFEE  BP=0000  SI=0000  DI=0000
DS=0CDE  ES=0CDE  SS=0CDE  CS=0CDE  IP=0100   NV UP DI PL NZ NA PO NC
0CDE:0100 BBC5A3        MOV     BX,A3C5
-T

AX=0000  BX=A3C5  CX=0000  DX=0000  SP=FFEE  BP=0000  SI=0000  DI=0000
DS=0CDE  ES=0CDE  SS=0CDE  CS=0CDE  IP=0103   NV UP DI PL NZ NA PO NC
0CDE:0103 B90800        MOV     CX,0008
-T

AX=0000  BX=A3C5  CX=0008  DX=0000  SP=FFEE  BP=0000  SI=0000  DI=0000
DS=0CDE  ES=0CDE  SS=0CDE  CS=0CDE  IP=0106   NV UP DI PL NZ NA PO NC
0CDE:0106 D1D3          RCL     BX,1
-T

AX=0000  BX=478A  CX=0008  DX=0000  SP=FFEE  BP=0000  SI=0000  DI=0000
DS=0CDE  ES=0CDE  SS=0CDE  CS=0CDE  IP=0108   OV UP DI PL NZ NA PO CY
0CDE:0108 E2FC          LOOP    0106
-T
AX=0000  BX=478A  CX=0007  DX=0000  SP=FFEE  BP=0000  SI=0000  DI=0000
DS=0CDE  ES=0CDE  SS=0CDE  CS=0CDE  IP=0106   OV UP DI PL NZ NA PO CY
0CDE:0106 D1D3          RCL     BX,1
                            .
                            .
                            .

-T

AX=0000  BX=C551  CX=0001  DX=0000  SP=FFEE  BP=0000  SI=0000  DI=0000
DS=0CDE  ES=0CDE  SS=0CDE  CS=0CDE  IP=0108   NV UP DI PL NZ NA PO CY
0CDE:0108 E2FC          LOOP    0106
-T

AX=0000  BX=C551  CX=0000  DX=0000  SP=FFEE  BP=0000  SI=0000  DI=0000
DS=0CDE  ES=0CDE  SS=0CDE  CS=0CDE  IP=010A   NV UP DI PL NZ NA PO CY
0CDE:010A CD20          INT     20
```

Alternatively, you can type G 10A to execute the program up to, but not including, the INT 20 instruction at 10Ah; then the registers will show the result of the program.

If you try this, you'll see CX = 0 and either BX = C551 or BX = C5D1, depending on the value of the carry flag before you ran the program. The C5 our program's MOV instruction put into BL at the start is now in the BH register, but BL doesn't contain A3, because we rotated BX *through* the carry. Later, we'll see other ways of rotating without going through the carry. Let's get back to our goal of printing a number in binary notation.

Writing a Binary Number

We've seen how to strip off binary digits one at a time, and convert them to ASCII characters. If we add an INT 21h instruction to print our digits, our program will be done. Here's the program; the first instruction sets AH to 02 for the INT 21h function call (recall, 02 tells DOS to print the character in the DL register):

```
3985:0100 B402       MOV    AH,02
3985:0102 B90800      MOV    CX,0008
3985:0105 B200       MOV    DL,00
3985:0107 D0D3       RCL    BL,1
3985:0109 80D230      ADC    DL,30
3985:010C CD21       INT    21
3985:010E E2F5       LOOP   0105
3985:0110 CD20       INT    20
```

We've seen how all the pieces work, and put them together now. Use rotate BL (with the instruction RCL BL,1) to pick off the bits of a number, pick a number you want printed in binary, load it into the BL register, then run this program with a G command. After the INT 20h instruction, the G command restores the registers to the values they had before, so BL still contains the number you see printed in binary.

The ADC DL,30 instruction in our program converts the carry flag to a zero or a one character. The instruction MOV DL,0 sets DL to zero first, then the ADC instruction adds 30h to DL, and then finally adds the carry. Since 30h is the ASCII code for a 0, the result of ADC DL,30 is the code for 0 when the carry is clear (NC) or 1 if the carry is set (CY).

If you want to see what happens when you run this program, trace through it. Keep in mind that you'll need to be a bit careful in single-stepping through it with the T command. It contains an INT 21h instruction and, as you saw when we first encountered INT 21h, DOS does a great deal of work for that one instruction. That's why you can't use T on the INT 21.

You can, however, trace through all the other instructions in this program except the final INT 20, which won't concern you until the very end. During your tracing, each time you loop through and reach the INT 21h instruction, type G 10E. Your G command, followed by an address, will tell Debug to continue running the program, but to stop when IP becomes the address (10E) you entered. That is, Debug will execute the INT 21h instruction without your tracing through it, but stops before executing the LOOP instruction at 10E, so you can return to tracing through the program. (The number you type after G is known as a *breakpoint* in the DOS manual; breakpoints are very useful when you're trying to understand the inner workings of programs.)

Finally, terminate the program when you reach the INT 20h instruction by typing the G command by itself.

The Proceed Command

Whether or not you tried out the instructions to trace through our program, you've seen that an instruction like G 10E allows us to trace *over* an INT instruction that starts at, say, 10Ch. But that means each time we want to trace over an INT instruction, we need to find the address of the instruction immediately following the INT instruction.

As it turns out, there is a Debug command that makes tracing through INT instructions much simpler. The P (for *Proceed*) command does all the work for us. To see, trace through the program, but this time, when you reach the INT 21h instruction, type P, rather than G 10E, as described before.

We'll make heavy use of the P command in the rest of this book, because it's a very nice way to trace over commands like INT, which call on large programs, such as the routines inside DOS. Before going on, though, we should mention one thing about the P command—it wasn't documented in the DOS manuals for versions of DOS before 3.00. This lack of documentation may have been an oversight or, more likely, because Microsoft didn't have time to test the P command completely before delivering version 2.00 of DOS. Whatever the reason, if you have a version of DOS before 3.00, you should be aware that the P command *may not* work all the time—although we've never had any problems using it.

That's about all we'll do for printing binary numbers as strings of zeros and ones, but here's a simple exercise for you to practice on: See if you can modify this program to print a *b* at the end of our binary number (**Hint**: The ASCII code for b is 62h).

Summary

In this chapter, we had a chance to catch our breath a bit after our hard work on new concepts in Chapters 1 through 3. So where have we been, and what have we seen?

We had our first encounter with flags, and had a look at the carry flag, which was of special interest here, because it made our job of printing a binary number quite simple. It did so as soon as we learned about the rotate instruction RCL, which rotates a byte or word to the left, one bit at a time.

Once we learned about the carry flag and rotating bytes and words, we tucked a new version of the add instruction, ADC, under our belts and were almost ready to build our program to print a number in binary notation.

This is where the LOOP instruction entered the scene. By loading the CX register with a loop count, we could keep the 8088 executing a loop of instructions a number of times. We set CX to 8, to execute a loop eight times.

That's all we needed to write our program. We'll use these tools again in the following chapters. In the next chapter we'll print a binary number in hexadecimal notation, just as Debug does, so by the time we finish Chapter 5, we'll have a better idea of how Debug translates numbers from binary to hex. Then, we'll move on to the other end of Debug: reading the numbers typed in hex and converting them to the 8088's binary notation.

5

PRINTING IN HEX

Our program in Chapter 4 was fairly straightforward. We were lucky, because the carry flag made it easy to print a binary number as a string of 0 and 1 characters. Now we'll move on to printing numbers in hex notation. Here, our work will be a bit less direct, and we'll begin to repeat ourselves in our programs, writing the same sequence of instructions more than once. But that type of repetition won't last forever: In Chapter 7, we'll learn about procedures, or subroutines, that eliminate the need to write more than one copy of a group of instructions. First, let's learn some more useful instructions and see how to print numbers in hex.

Compare and Status Bits

In the last chapter, we learned something about status flags and examined the carry flag, which is represented as either CY or NC in Debug's R display. The other flags, which are equally useful, keep track of the *status* for the last arithmetic operation. There are eight flags altogether, and we'll learn about them as they are needed.

Recall that CY means the carry flag is 1, or set, whereas NC means the carry flag is 0. In all flags 1 means *true* and 0 means *false*. For example, if you did a SUB instruction with a result of 0, the flag known as the Zero Flag would be set to 1—true—and you would see it in the R display as ZR (*Zero*). Otherwise, the zero flag would be reset to 0—NZ (*Not Zero*).

Let's look at an example that tests the zero flag. We'll use the SUB instruction to subtract two numbers. If the two numbers are equal, the result will be zero, and the zero flag will appear as ZR on your display. Enter the following subtract instruction:

```
396F:0100 29D8        SUB     AX,BX
```

Now, trace through the instruction with a few different numbers, watching for ZR or NZ to appear in the zero flag. If you place the same number (F5h in the following example) into both the AX and BX registers, you'll see the zero flag set after one subtract instruction, and cleared after another:

```
-R
AX=00F5  BX=00F5  CX=0000  DX=0000  SP=FFEE  BP=0000  SI=0000  DI=0000
DS=0CDE  ES=0CDE  SS=0CDE  CS=0CDE  IP=0100    NV UP DI PL NZ NA PO NC
0CDE:0100 29D8          SUB     AX,BX
-T

AX=0000  BX=00F5  CX=0000  DX=0000  SP=FFEE  BP=0000  SI=0000  DI=0000
DS=0CDE  ES=0CDE  SS=0CDE  CS=0CDE  IP=0102    NV UP DI PL ZR NA PE NC
0CDE:0102 3F            AAS
-R IP
IP 0102
:100
-R
AX=0000  BX=00F5  CX=0000  DX=0000  SP=FFEE  BP=0000  SI=0000  DI=0000
DS=0CDE  ES=0CDE  SS=0CDE  CS=0CDE  IP=0100    NV UP DI PL ZR NA PE NC
0CDE:0100 29D8          SUB     AX,BX
-T

AX=FF0B  BX=00F5  CX=0000  DX=0000  SP=FFEE  BP=0000  SI=0000  DI=0000
DS=0CDE  ES=0CDE  SS=0CDE  CS=0CDE  IP=0102    NV UP DI NG NZ AC PO CY
0CDE:0102 3F            AAS
```

If we subtract one from zero, the result is FFFFh, which, as we saw in Chapter 1, is -1 in two's-complement form. Can we tell from the R display whether a number is positive or negative? Yes, another flag, called the *Sign Flag*, changes between NG (*Negative*) and PL (*Plus*), and is set to 1 when a number is a negative two's-complement number.

And another new flag we'll be interested in is the Overflow Flag, which changes between OV (*Overflow*) when the flag is 1 and NV (*No Overflow*) when the flag is 0. The overflow flag is set if the sign bit changes when it shouldn't. For example, if we add two positive numbers, such as 7000h and 6000h, we get a negative number, D000h, or -12288. This is an error because the result overflows the word. The result should be positive, but isn't, so the 8088 sets the overflow flag. (Remember, if we were dealing with unsigned numbers, this wouldn't be an error, in which case we would ignore the overflow flag.)

Try several different numbers to see if you can set and reset each of these flags, trying them out until you're comfortable with them. For the overflow, subtract a large negative number from a large positive number— for example, 7000h $-$ 8000h, since 8000h is a negative number equal to -32768 in two's-complement form.

Now we're ready to look at a set of instructions called the *conditional jump* instructions. They allow us to check status flags more conveniently than we've been able to so far. The instruction JZ (*Jump if Zero*) jumps to a new address if the last arithmetic result was zero. Thus, if we follow a SUB instruction with, say, JZ 15A, a result of zero for the subtraction would cause the 8088 to jump to, and start executing, statements at address 15Ah, rather than at the next instruction.

The JZ instruction tests the zero flag, and, if it's set (ZR), does a jump just like a jump with the BASIC statement IF A = 0 THEN 100. The opposite of JZ is JNZ (*Jump if Not Zero*). Let's look at a simple example that uses JNZ and subtracts one from a number until the result is zero:

```
396F:0100 2C01        SUB    AL,01
396F:0102 75FC        JNZ    0100
396F:0104 CD20        INT    20
```

Put a number like three in AL, so you'll go through the loop a few times, then trace through this program, one instruction at a time, to see how conditional branches work. We put the INT 20h instruction at the end so typing G by accident won't drop off the end of our program: It's a good defensive practice.

You may have noticed that using SUB to compare two numbers, as we just did, has the potentially undesirable side effect of changing the first number. Another instruction, CMP (*Compare*) allows us to do the subtraction without storing the result anywhere and without changing the first number. The result is used only to set the flags, so we can use one of the many conditional jump instructions after a compare. To see what happens, set both AX and BX to the same number, F5h, and trace through this instruction:

```
-A 100
0CDE:0100 CMP AX,BX
0CDE:0102
-T

AX=00F5  BX=00F5  CX=0000  DX=0000  SP=FFEE  BP=0000  SI=0000  DI=0000
DS=0CDE  ES=0CDE  SS=0CDE  CS=0CDE  IP=0102    NV UP DI PL ZR NA PE NC
0CDE:0102 3F                AAS
```

The zero flag is now set (ZR), but F5h remains in both registers.

Let's use CMP to print a single hex digit. We'll create a set of instructions that use flags to alter the flow of our program, as LOOP did in the last chapter, in a manner similar to BASIC's IF-THEN statement. This new set of instructions will use the flags to test for such conditions as less than, greater than, and so on. We won't have to worry about which flags are set when the first number is less than the second; the instructions know which flags to look at.

Printing a Single Hex Digit

Let's start by putting a small number (between 0 and Fh) into the BL register. Since any number between 0 and Fh is equivalent to one hex digit, we can convert our choice to a single ASCII character and then print it. Let's look at the steps we need to take to do the conversion.

The ASCII characters 0 through 9 have the values 30h through 39h; the characters A through F, however, have the values 41h through 46h. Herein lies a problem: These two groups of ASCII characters are separated by seven characters. As a result, the conversion to ASCII will be different for the two groups of numbers (0 through 9 and Ah through Fh), so we must handle each group differently. A BASIC program to do this two-part conversion looks like this:

```
100 IF  BL < &H0A
        THEN BL = BL + &H30
        ELSE BL = BL + &H37
```

(Notice that we wrote 0Ah for the number A, rather than AH, so we wouldn't confuse the number Ah with the register AH. We'll often place a zero before hex numbers in situations like this, that could be confusing. In fact, since it never hurts to place a zero before a hex number, it's a good idea to place a zero before *all* hex numbers.)

Our BASIC conversion program is fairly simple. Unfortunately, the 8088's machine language doesn't include an ELSE statement; it's far more primitive than BASIC is, so we'll need to be somewhat clever. Here's another BASIC program, this time one that mimics the method we'll use for our machine-language program:

```
100 BL = BL + &H30
110 IF  BL >= &H3A
        THEN  BL = BL + &H7
```

You can convince yourself that this program works by trying it with some choice examples. The numbers 0, 9, Ah, and Fh are particularly good because

Character	ASCII Code (Hex)
/	2F
0	30
1	31
2	32
3	33
4	34
5	35
6	36
7	37
8	38
9	39
:	3A
;	3B
<	3C
=	3D
>	3E
?	3F
@	40
A	41
B	42
C	43
D	44
E	45
F	46
G	47

Figure 5-1. Partial ASCII Table Showing the Characters Used by Hex Digits.

these four numbers cover all the *boundary* conditions—areas where we often run into problems.

Here, 0 and Fh are, respectively, the smallest and largest single-digit hex numbers, so by using 0 and Fh, we check the bottom and top of our range. The numbers 9 and 0Ah, although next to each other, require two different conversion schemes in our program. By using 9 and 0Ah, we confirm that we've chosen the correct place to switch between these two conversion schemes.

The machine-language version of this program contains a few more steps, but it's essentially the same as the BASIC version. It uses the CMP instruction, as well as a conditional jump instruction called JL (*Jump if Less Than*). Here's the program to take a single-digit hex number in the BL register and print it in hex:

```
3985:0100 B402      MOV   AH,02
3985:0102 88DA      MOV   DL,BL
3985:0104 80C230    ADD   DL,30
3985:0107 80FA3A    CMP   DL,3A
3985:010A 7C03      JL    010F
3985:010C 80C207    ADD   DL,07
3985:010F CD21      INT   21
3985:0111 CD20      INT   20
```

The CMP instruction, as we saw before, subtracts two numbers (DL − 3Ah) to set the flags, but it doesn't change DL. So if DL is less than 3Ah, the JL 10F instruction skips to the INT 21h instruction at 10Fh. Place a single-digit hex number in BL and trace through this example to get a better feeling for CMP and our algorithm to convert hex to ASCII. Remember to use either the G command with a breakpoint or the P command when you run the INT instructions.

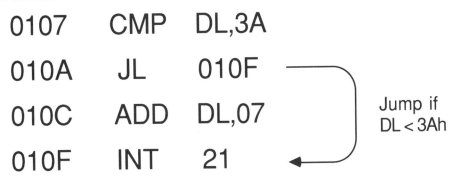

Figure 5-2. The JL Instruction.

Another Rotate Instruction

Our program works for any single-digit hex number, but if we wish to print a two-digit hex number, we need a few more steps. We need to isolate each digit (four bits, which are often called a *nibble*) of this two-digit hex number. In this section, we'll see that we can easily isolate the first, or higher, four bits, and in the next section, we'll encounter a concept known as a *logical operation*, which we'll use to isolate the lower four bits—the second of our two hex digits.

To begin, recall that the RCL instruction rotates a byte or a word to the left, through the carry flag. In the last chapter we used the instruction RCL BL,1, in which the one told the 8088 to rotate BL by one bit. We can rotate by more than one bit if we want, but we can't simply write the instruction RCL BL,2. (**Note**: Although RCL BL,2 isn't a legal 8088 instruction, it works just fine with the 80286 processor found in IBM ATs. But since the older IBM PCs are more common than ATs, it's best to write your programs for the lowest common denominator — the older 8088.) For rotations by more than one bit, we must place a rotate count in the CL register.

The CL register is used here in much the same way as the CX register is used by the LOOP instruction to determine the number of times to repeat a loop. Use CL for the number of times to rotate a byte or word, rather than the CX register, because it makes no sense to rotate more than 16 times; thus the eight-bit CL register is more than large enough to hold our maximum shift count.

How does all this tie in with printing a two-digit hex number? Our plan now is to rotate the byte in DL four bits to the right. To do so, we'll use a slightly different rotate instruction called SHR (*Shift Right*). Using SHR, we will be able to move the upper four bits of our number to the rightmost nibble (four bits).

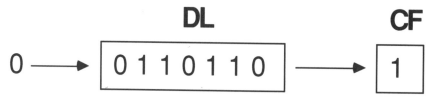

Figure 5-3. The SHR DL,1 Instruction.

We also want the upper four bits of DL set to zero, so that the entire register becomes equal to the byte we are shifting into the right nibble. If we were to enter SHR DL,1, our instruction would move the byte in DL one bit to the right, and at the *same* time, it would move bit 0 into the carry flag, while *shifting* a zero into bit 7 (the highest, or leftmost, bit in DL). If we do that three more times, we'll have just what we want: The upper four bits will end up shifted down into the lower four bits, while the upper four bits will all have had zeroes shifted into them. We can do all that shifting in one instruction, using the CL register as the *shift count*. By setting CL to four before the instruction SHR DL,CL, we will ensure that DL becomes equal to the upper hex digit.

Let's see how this works. Place 4 into CL and 5Dh into DL, then enter and trace through the following SHR instruction:

```
3985:0100 D2EA        SHR     DL,CL
```

DL should now be 05h, which is the first digit in the number 5Dh, and we can now print this digit with a program like the one we used earlier. Thus, putting together the pieces we have so far, we can build the following program to take a number in the BL register and print the first hex digit:

```
3985:0100 B402        MOV     AH,02
3985:0102 88DA        MOV     DL,BL
3985:0104 B104        MOV     CL,04
3985:0106 D2EA        SHR     DL,CL
3985:0108 80C230      ADD     DL,30
3985:010B 80FA3A      CMP     DL,3A
3985:010E 7C03        JL      0113
3985:0110 80C207      ADD     DL,07
3985:0113 CD21        INT     21
3985:0115 CD20        INT     20
```

Logic and AND

Now that we can print the first of the two digits in a hex number, let's see how we can isolate and print the second digit. Here, we'll learn how to clear the upper four bits of our original (not shifted) number to zero, leaving DL equal to the lower four bits. It's simple: Set the upper four bits to zero with an instruction called AND. The AND instruction is one of the *logical* instructions—those that have their roots in formal logic. Let's see how AND works.

In formal logic, we can say, "A is true, if B and C are both true." But if either B or C is false, then A must also be false. If we take this statement, substitute one for true and zero for false, then look at the various combinations of A, B, and C, we can create what is known as a *truth* table. Here's the truth table for ANDing two bits together:

```
AND │ F  T              AND │ 0  1
 F  │ F  F       =       0  │ 0  0
 T  │ F  T               1  │ 0  1
```

Down the left and across the top are the values for the two bits. The results for the AND are in the table, so you see that 0 AND 1 gives 0.

The AND instruction works on bytes and words by ANDing together the bits of each byte or word that are in the same position. For example, the statement AND BL,CL successively ANDs bits 0 of BL and CL, bits 1, bits 2, and so on, and places the result in BL. Let's make this clearer with an example in binary:

```
      1 0 1 1   0 1 0 1
AND   0 1 1 1   0 1 1 0
      0 0 1 1   0 1 0 0
```

Furthermore, by ANDing 0Fh to any number, we can set the upper four bits to zero:

```
      0 1 1 1   1 0 1 1
AND   0 0 0 0   1 1 1 1
      0 0 0 0   1 0 1 1
```

Let's put this logic into a short program that takes the number in BL, isolates the lower hex digit by ANDing 0Fh to the upper four bits, and then prints the result as a character. We saw most of the details of this program when we printed the upper hex digit; the only new detail is the AND instruction.

```
3985:0100 B402        MOV   AH,02
3985:0102 88DA        MOV   DL,BL
3985:0104 80E20F      AND   DL,0F
3985:0107 80C230      ADD   DL,30
3985:010A 80FA3A      CMP   DL,3A
3985:010D 7C03        JL    0112
3985:010F 80C207      ADD   DL,07
3985:0112 CD21        INT   21
3985:0114 CD20        INT   20
```

Try this with some two-digit hex numbers in BL before we move on to put the pieces together to print both digits. You should see the rightmost hex digit of your number in BL on the screen.

Putting It All Together

There really isn't much to change when we put all the pieces together. We need only change the address of the second JL instruction we used to print the second hex digit. Here is the complete program:

```
3985:0100 B402        MOV   AH,02
3985:0102 88DA        MOV   DL,BL
3985:0104 B104        MOV   CL,04
3985:0106 D2EA        SHR   DL,CL
3985:0108 80C230      ADD   DL,30
3985:010B 80FA3A      CMP   DL,3A
3985:010E 7C03        JL    0113
3985:0110 80C207      ADD   DL,07
3985:0113 CD21        INT   21
3985:0115 88DA        MOV   DL,BL
3985:0117 80E20F      AND   DL,0F
3985:011A 80C230      ADD   DL,30
3985:011D 80FA3A      CMP   DL,3A
3985:0120 7C03        JL    0125
3985:0122 80C207      ADD   DL,07
3985:0125 CD21        INT   21
3985:0127 CD20        INT   20
```

Once you've entered this program, you'll have to type *U 100*, followed by *U*, to see the entire unassembled listing. Note that we've repeated one set of five instructions: the instructions at 108h through 113h, and 11Ah through 125h. In Chapter 7 we'll see how to write this sequence of instructions just once by using an instruction similar to BASIC's GOSUB statement.

Summary

In this chapter, we learned more about how Debug translates numbers from the 8088's binary format to a hex format we can read. What did we add to our growing store of knowledge?

First, we learned about some of the two-letter flags we see on the right side of the register (R) display. These status bits give us a great deal of information about our last arithmetic operation. By looking at the zero flag, for example, we could tell whether the result of the last operation was zero. We also found we could compare two numbers with a CMP instruction.

Next, we learned how to print a single-digit hex number. And, armed with this information, we went on to learn about the SHR instruction, which enabled us to move the upper digit of a two-digit hex number into the lower four bits of BL. That done, we could print the digit, just as we've done before.

Finally, we found that the AND instruction allowed us to isolate the lower hex digit from the upper. And, putting all these pieces together, we wrote a program to print a two-digit hex number.

We could have continued on to print a four-digit hex number, but at this point, we'd find ourselves repeating instructions. Before we try to print a four-digit hex number, we'll learn about procedures in Chapter 7. Then, we'll know enough to write a procedure to do the job. By then we'll also be ready to learn about the assembler—a program that will do much of our work for us. But now, let's move on to reading hex numbers.

6

READING CHARACTERS

Now that we know how to print a byte in hex notation, we're going to reverse the process by reading two characters—hex digits—from the keyboard and converting them into a single byte.

Reading One Character

The DOS INT 21h function call we've been using has an input function, number 1, that reads a character from the keyboard. When we learned about function calls in Chapter 4, we saw that the function number must be placed in the AH register before an INT 21h call. Let's try function 1 for INT 21h. Enter INT 21h at location 0100h:

```
396F:0100 CD21          INT    21
```

Then, place 01h into AH and type either *G 102* or *P* to run this one instruction. Nothing happens? It doesn't seem to—all you'll see is the blinking cursor. But actually, DOS has paused and is waiting until you press a key (don't do so yet). Once you press a key, DOS will place the ASCII code for that character into the AL register. We'll use this instruction later, to read the characters of a hex number, but right now, let's see what happens when we press a key like F1.

Try pressing the F1 key. DOS will return a 0 in AL, and you'll also see a semicolon (;) appear just after Debug's hyphen prompt.

This is what happened. F1 is one of a set of special keys with *extended codes*, which DOS treats differently from the keys representing normal ASCII characters. (You'll find a table listing these extended codes in Appendix E, as well as at the end of your BASIC manual.) For each of these special keys, DOS sends *two* characters, one right after the other. The first character returned is always zero, indicating that the next character is the *scan code* for a special key.

To read both characters, we'd need to execute INT 21h twice. But in our example, we read only the first character, the zero, and left the scan code in DOS. When Debug finished with the G 102 (or P) command, it began to read characters, and the first character it read was the scan code left behind from the F1 key: namely, 59, which is the ASCII code for a semicolon.

Later, when we develop our Dskpatch program, we'll begin to use these extended codes to bring the cursor and function keys to life. Until then, we'll just work with the normal ASCII characters.

Reading a Single-Digit Hex Number

Let's reverse the conversion used in Chapter 5, when we transformed a single-digit hex number to the ASCII code for one of the characters in 0 through 9 or A through F. To convert one character, such as C or D, from a hex character to a byte, we must subtract either 30h (for 0 through 9) or 37h (for A through F). Here is a simple program that will read one ASCII character and convert it to a byte:

```
3985:0100 B401        MOV     AH,01
3985:0102 CD21        INT     21
3985:0104 2C30        SUB     AL,30
3985:0106 3C09        CMP     AL,09
3985:0108 7E02        JLE     010C
3985:010A 2C07        SUB     AL,07
3985:010C CD20        INT     20
```

Most of these instructions should be familiar now, but there is one new one, JLE (*Jump if Less than or Equal to*). In our program, this instruction jumps if AL is less than or equal to 9h.

To see the conversion from hex character to ASCII, you need to see the AL register just before the INT 20h is executed. Since Debug restores the registers when it executes the INT 20h, you'll need to set a breakpoint, as you did in Chapter 4. Here, type *G 10C*, and you'll see that AL will contain the hex number converted from a character.

Try typing some characters, such as *k* or a lowercase *d*, that are not hex digits, to see what happens. You'll notice that this program works correctly only when the input is one of the digits 0 through 9 or the uppercase letters A through F. We'll correct this minor failing in the next chapter, when we learn about subroutines, or procedures. Until then, we'll be temporarily sloppy and ignore error conditions: We'll have to type correct characters for our program to work properly.

Reading a Two-Digit Hex Number

Reading two hex digits isn't much more complicated than reading one, but it does require many more instructions. We'll begin by reading the first digit, then we'll place its hex value in the DL register and multiply it by 16. To perform this multiplication, we'll shift the DL register left four bits, placing a hex zero (four zero bits) to the right of the digit we just read. The instruction SHL DL,CL, with CL set to four does the trick by inserting zeros at the right. In fact, the SHL (*Shift Left*) instruction is known as an *arithmetic shift*, because it has the same affect as an arithmetic multiplication by two, four, eight, and so on, depending on the number (such as one, two, or three) in CL.

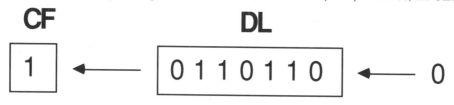

Figure 6-1.   The SHL DL,1 Instruction.

Finally, with the first digit shifted over, we'll add the second hex digit to the number in DL (the first digit * 16). You can see and work through all these details in this program:

```
3985:0100 B401        MOV     AH,01
3985:0102 CD21        INT     21
3985:0104 88C2        MOV     DL,AL
3985:0106 80EA30      SUB     DL,30
3985:0109 80FA09      CMP     DL,09
3985:010C 7E03        JLE     0111
3985:010E 80EA07      SUB     DL,07
3985:0111 B104        MOV     CL,04
3985:0113 D2E2        SHL     DL,CL
3985:0115 CD21        INT     21
3985:0117 2C30        SUB     AL,30
3985:0119 3C09        CMP     AL,09
3985:011B 7E02        JLE     011F
3985:011D 2C07        SUB     AL,07
3985:011F 00C2        ADD     DL,AL
3985:0121 CD20        INT     20
```

Now that we've got a working program, it's a good idea to check the boundary conditions to confirm that it's working properly. For these boundary conditions, use the numbers 00, 09, 0A, 0F, 90, A0, F0, and some other number, such as 3C. Use a breakpoint to run the program without executing the INT 20h instruction. (Make sure you use uppercase letters for your hex input.)

Summary

We've finally had a chance to practice what we learned in previous chapters without being flooded with new information. Using a new INT 21 function (number 1) to read characters, we developed a program to read a two-digit hex number. Along the way, we emphasized the need to test programs with all the boundary conditions.

Now we're ready to wrap up Part I by learning about procedures in the 8088.

PROCEDURES—COUSINS
TO SUBROUTINES

In the next chapter, we'll meet MASM, the macro assembler, and begin to use *assembly*, or *assembler*, language. But before we leave Debug, we'll look at one last set of examples, and learn about subroutines and a special place to store numbers called the stack.

Procedures

A procedure is a list of instructions that we can execute from many different places in a program, rather than having to repeat the same list of instructions at each place they're needed. In BASIC such lists are called *subroutines*, but we'll call them *procedures* for reasons that will become clear later.

We move to and from procedures just as we do in BASIC. We call a procedure with one instruction, *CALL*, which is just like BASIC's GOSUB. And we return from the procedure with a *RET* instruction, which is just like BASIC's RETURN.

Here's a simple BASIC program we'll soon rewrite in machine language. This program calls a subroutine ten times, each time printing one character, starting with A and ending with J:

```
10 A = &H41              'ASCII for 'A'
20 FOR I = 1 TO 10
30 GOSUB 1000
40 NEXT I
50 END
1000 PRINT CHR$(A);
1100 A = A + 1
1200 RETURN
```

The subroutine, following a common practice in BASIC programs, begins at line 1000 to leave room for us to add more instructions to the main program without affecting our subroutine. We'll do the same with our machine-language procedure by putting it at 200h, far away from our main program at 100h. We'll also replace GOSUB 1000 with the instruction CALL 200h, which *calls* the procedure at memory location 200h. The CALL sets IP to 200h, and the 8088 starts executing the instructions at 200h.

The FOR-NEXT loop of the BASIC program, as we saw in Chapter 4, can be written as a LOOP instruction. The other pieces of the main program should be familiar.

```
3985:0100 B241        MOV    DL,41
3985:0102 B90A00       MOV    CX,000A
3985:0105 E8F800       CALL   0200
3985:0108 E2FB         LOOP   0105
3985:010A CD20         INT    20
```

The first instruction places 41h (ASCII for A) into the DL register, because the INT 21h instruction prints the character given by the ASCII code in DL. The INT 21h instruction itself is located some distance away, in the procedure at location 200h. Here's the procedure you should enter at 200h:

```
3985:0200 B402         MOV    AH,02
3985:0202 CD21         INT    21
3985:0204 FEC2         INC    DL
3985:0206 C3           RET
```

There are two new and two old instructions here. Recall that the 02h in AH tells DOS to print the character in DL when we execute the INT 21h instruction. INC DL, the first of our two new instructions, *increments* the DL register. That is, it adds one to DL. The other new instruction, RET, *returns* to the first (LOOP) instruction following the CALL in our main program.

Type G to see the output of this program, then single-step through it to see how it works (remember to use either a breakpoint or the P command to run the INT 21 instruction).

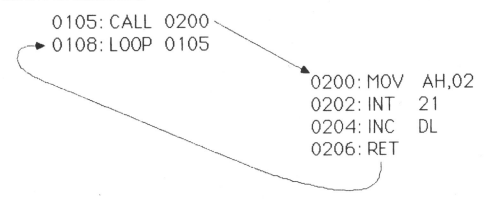

Figure 7-1. The CALL and RET Instructions.

The Stack and Return Addresses

The CALL instruction in our program needs to save the *return address* somewhere so the 8088 will know where to resume executing instructions when it sees the RET instruction. For the storage place itself, we have a portion of memory known as the stack. And for tracking what's on the *stack*, there are two registers that we can see on the R display: the SP (*Stack Pointer*) register, which points to the top of the stack, and the SS (*Stack Segment*), which holds the segment number.

In operation, a stack for the 8088 is just like a stack of trays in a cafeteria, where placing a tray on the top covers the trays underneath. The last tray on the stack is the first to come off, so another name for a stack is LIFO, for *Last In, First Out*. This order, LIFO, is precisely what we need for retrieving return addresses after we make *nested* CALLs like this one:

```
396F:0100 E8FD00        CALL    0200
                                  .
                                  .
                                  .
396F:0200 E8FD00        CALL    0300
396F:0203 C3            RET
                                  .
                                  .
                                  .
396F:0300 E8FD00        CALL    0400
396F:0303 C3            RET
                                  .
                                  .
                                  .
396F:0400 C3            RET
```

Here, the instruction at 100h calls one at 200h, which calls one at 300h, which calls one at 400h, where we finally see a return (RET) instruction. This RET returns to the instruction following the *previous* CALL instruction, at 300h, so the 8088 resumes executing instructions at 303h. But there it encounters a RET instruction at 303h, which pulls the next oldest address (203h) off the stack. So the 8088 resumes executing instructions at 203h, and so on. Each RET *pops* the topmost return address off the stack, so each RET follows the same path backward as the CALLs did forward.

Try entering a program like the preceding one. Use multiple calls, and trace through the program to see how the calls and returns work. Although the process may not seem very interesting right now, there are other uses for this stack, and a good understanding of how it works will come in handy. (In a later chapter, we'll go looking for the stack in memory.)

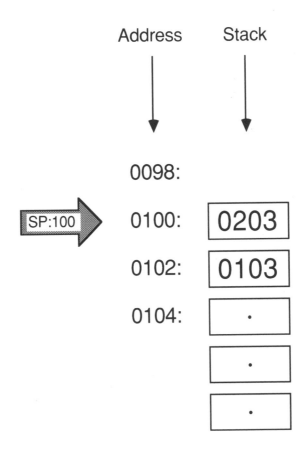

Figure 7-2. The Stack Just Before Executing the CALL 400 Instruction.

PUSHing and POPping

The stack is a useful place to store words of data for a while, provided we're careful to restore the stack before a RET instruction. We've seen that a CALL instruction *pushes* the return address (one word) onto the top of the stack, while a RET instruction *pops* this word off the top of the stack, loads it into the IP register, and exposes the word that was lying underneath it. We can do much the same thing with the instructions PUSH and POP, which allow us to push and pop words. When might we want to do this?

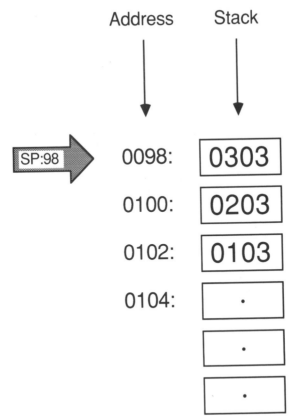

Figure 7-3. The Stack Just After Executing the CALL 400 Instruction.

It's often convenient to save the values of registers at the beginning of a procedure and restore them at the end, just before the RET instruction. Then we're free to use these registers in any way we like within the procedure, as long as we restore their values at the end.

Programs are built from many levels of procedures, with each level calling the procedures at the next level down. By saving registers at the beginning of a procedure and restoring them at the end, we remove unwanted interactions between procedures at different levels, and this makes our job of programming much easier. You'll see more about saving and restoring registers in Chapter 13, when we talk about modular design. But right now, here's an example (don't enter it) to use to save and restore CX and DX:

```
396F:0200 51          PUSH    CX
396F:0201 52          PUSH    DX
396F:0202 B90800      MOV     CX,0008
396F:0205 E8F800      CALL    0300
396F:0208 FEC2        INC     DL
396F:020A E2F9        LOOP    0205
396F:020C 5A          POP     DX
396F:020D 59          POP     CX
396F:020E C3          RET
```

Notice that the POPs are in reverse order from the PUSHes, because a POP removes the word placed most recently on the stack, and the old value of DX is on top of the old CX.

Saving and restoring CX and DX allows us to change these registers in the procedure that begins at 200h, but without changing the values used by any procedure that calls this one. And once we've saved CX and DX, we can use these registers to hold *local* variables—variables we can use within this procedure without affecting the values used by the calling program.

We'll use such local variables to simplify our programming tasks. As long as we're careful to restore the original values, we won't have to worry about our procedures changing any of the registers used by the calling program. This will become clearer in the next example, which is a procedure to read a hex number. Unlike the program in Chapter 6, our program now will allow only valid characters such as A, but not K.

Reading Hex Numbers with More Ease

We want to create a procedure that keeps reading characters until it receives one it can convert to a hex number between 0 and Fh. We don't want to display any invalid characters, so we'll sift our input by using a new INT 21h function, number 8, that reads a character but doesn't let it pass on to the screen. That way we can *echo* (display) characters only if they are valid.

Place 8h into the AH register and run through this instruction, typing an A just after you type G 102:

```
3985:0100 CD21        INT     21
```

The ASCII code for A (41h) is now in the AL register, but the A didn't appear on the screen.

Using this function, our program can read characters without echoing them until it reads a valid hex digit (0 through 9 or A through F), which it will then echo. Here is the procedure to do this and to convert the hex character to a hex number:

```
3985:0200 52       PUSH  DX
3985:0201 B408      MOV   AH,08
3985:0203 CD21      INT   21
3985:0205 3C30      CMP   AL,30
3985:0207 72FA      JB    0203
3985:0209 3C46      CMP   AL,46
3985:020B 77F6      JA    0203
3985:020D 3C39      CMP   AL,39
3985:020F 770A      JA    021B
3985:0211 B402      MOV   AH,02
3985:0213 88C2      MOV   DL,AL
3985:0215 CD21      INT   21
3985:0217 2C30      SUB   AL,30
3985:0219 5A        POP   DX
3985:021A C3        RET
3985:021B 3C41      CMP   AL,41
3985:021D 72E4      JB    0203
3985:021F B402      MOV   AH,02
3985:0221 88C2      MOV   DL,AL
3985:0223 CD21      INT   21
3985:0225 2C37      SUB   AL,37
3985:0227 5A        POP   DX
3985:0228 C3        RET
```

The procedure reads a character in AL (with the INT 21h at 203h) and checks to see if it's valid with the CMPs and conditional jumps. If the character just read is not a valid character, the conditional jump instructions send the 8088 back to location 203, where the INT 21h reads another character. (JA is *Jump if Above*, and JB is *Jump if Below*; both treat the two numbers as unsigned numbers, whereas the JL instruction we used earlier treated both as signed numbers.)

By line 211h, we know that we have a valid digit between 0 and 9, so we subtract the code for the character 0 and return the result in the AL register, remembering to pop the DX register, which we saved at the beginning of the procedure. The process for hex digits A through F is much the same. Notice that we have two RET instructions in this procedure; we could have had more, or we could have had just one.

Here is a very simple program to test the procedure:

```
3985:0100 E8FD00    CALL  0200
3985:0103 CD20      INT   20
```

As you've done before, use either the G command, with a breakpoint, or use the P command. You want to execute the CALL 200h instruction without executing the INT 20h instruction, so you can see the registers just before the program terminates and the registers are restored.

You'll see the cursor at the left side of the screen, waiting patiently for a character. Type *k*, which isn't a valid character. Nothing should happen. Now, type any of the uppercase hex characters. You should see the character's hex value in AL and the character itself echoed on the screen. Test this procedure with the boundary conditions: '\' (the character before zero), 0, 9, ':' (the character just after 9), and so on.

Now that we have this procedure, the program to read a two-digit hex number, with error handling, is fairly straightforward:

```
3985:0100 E8FD00    CALL    0200
3985:0103 88C2      MOV     DL,AL
3985:0105 B104      MOV     CL,04
3985:0107 D2E2      SHL     DL,CL
3985:0109 E8F400    CALL    0200
3985:010C 00C2      ADD     DL,AL
3985:010E B402      MOV     AH,02
3985:0110 CD21      INT     21
3985:0112 CD20      INT     20
```

You can run this program from DOS, since it reads in a two-digit hex number and then displays the ASCII character that corresponds to the number you typed in.

Aside from the procedure, our main program is much simpler than the version we wrote in the last chapter, and we haven't duplicated the instructions to read characters. We did add error handling, though, and even if it did complicate our procedure, it also ensures that the program now accepts only valid input.

Here we can also see the reason for saving the DX register in the procedure. The main program stores the hex number in DL, so we don't want our procedure at 200h to change DL. On the other hand, the procedure at 200h must use DL itself to echo characters. So, by using the instruction PUSH DX at the beginning of the procedure, and POP DX at the end, we save ourselves from problems.

From now on, to avoid complicated interactions between procedures, we'll be very strict about saving any registers used by a procedure.

Summary

Our programming is becoming more sophisticated. We've learned about procedures that allow us to reuse the same set of instructions without rewriting them each time. We've also discovered the stack and seen that a CALL stores a return address on the top of the stack, while a RET instruction returns to the address on the top of the stack.

We saw how to use the stack for more than just saving return addresses. We used the stack to store the values of registers (with a PUSH instruction) so we could use them in a procedure. By restoring the registers (with a POP instruction) at the end of each procedure, we avoided unwanted interactions between procedures. By always saving and restoring registers in procedures that we write, we can CALL other procedures without worrying about which registers are used within the other procedure.

And finally, armed with this knowledge, we moved on to build a better program to read hex numbers—this time, with error checking. The program we built here is similar to one we'll use in later chapters, when we begin to develop the Dskpatch program.

Now we're ready to move on to Part II, where we'll learn how to use the assembler. In the next chapter, we'll see how to use the assembler to convert a program to machine language. We'll also see that there won't be any reason to leave room between procedures, as we did in this chapter, when we put our procedure way up at location 200h.

PART II

Assembly Language

8

WELCOME TO THE ASSEMBLER

W ell, at long last we're ready to meet the assembler, a DOS program that will make our programming much simpler. From now on, we'll write mnemonic, human-readable instructions directly, using the assembler to turn our programs into machine code.

Of necessity, this chapter and the next will be somewhat heavy with details on the assembler, but learning these details will be well worth the effort. Once we know how to use the assembler, we'll get back on course in learning how to write assembly language programs. Meanwhile, let's jump right in.

A Program Without Debug

Up to this point, we've just typed *DEBUG*, and then typed in our program instructions. Now we're about to leave Debug behind, and to write programs without it, and we'll have to use either an editor or a word processor to create text, or human-readable, files containing our assembly language instructions.

We begin by creating a *source file*—the name for the text version of an assembly language program. We'll create a source file now, for the program we built and named Writestr back in Chapter 3. To refresh your memory, here is our Debug version:

```
396F:0100 B402        MOV     AH,02
396F:0102 B26l        MOV     DL,2A
396F:0104 CD21        INT     21
396F:0106 CD20        INT     20
```

Use your editor to enter the following lines of code into a file named WRITESTR.ASM (the extension .ASM means this is an assembler source file). Here, as with Debug, lowercase works just as well as uppercase, but we'll continue to use uppercase letters to avoid confusion between the number 1 (one) and the lowercase letter l (el):

```
CODE_SEG        SEGMENT
        MOV     AH,2h
        MOV     DL,2Ah
        INT     21h
        INT     20h
CODE_SEG        ENDS
        END
```

This is the same program we created in Chapter 3, but it contains a few necessary changes and additions. Ignoring for now the three new lines in our source file, notice that there is an *h* after each hex number. This *h* tells the assembler that the numbers are in hexadecimal. Unlike Debug, which assumes all numbers are in hexadecimal, the assembler assumes that all numbers are decimal. We tell it otherwise by placing an h after any hexadecimal number.

> NOTE: Here's a warning before we move on: The assembler can become confused by numbers, such as ACh, that look like a name or an instruction. To avoid this, always type a zero before a hex number that begins with a letter. For example, type 0Ch—*not* ACh.

Watch what happens when we assemble a program with ACh, rather than 0ACh. Here's the program:

```
CODE_SEG        SEGMENT
        MOV     DL,ACh
        INT     20h
CODE_SEG        ENDS
        END
```

Here's the output:

```
A>MASM TEST;
Microsoft (R) Macro Assembler  Version 4.00
Copyright (C) Microsoft Corp 1981, 1983, 1984, 1985.  All rights reserved.

TEST.ASM(2) : error 9: Symbol not defined AC

  51070 Bytes symbol space free

      0 Warning Errors
      1 Severe  Errors

A>
```

Definitely not encouraging. But changing the ACh to 0ACh will satisfy the assembler.

Also notice the spacing of the commands in our assembler program. We used tabs to align everything neatly and make the source text more readable. Compare the program you entered with this version:

```
CODE_SEG SEGMENT
MOV AH,2h
MOV DL,2Ah
INT 21h
INT 20h
CODE_SEG ENDS
END
```

A bit of a mess; the assembler doesn't care, but we do.

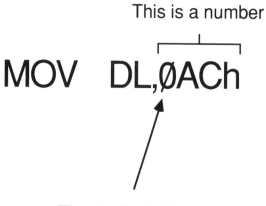

Figure 8-1.   Put a zero before hexadecimal numbers starting with a letter, otherwise the assembler will treat the number as a name.

Now let's return to the three new lines in our source file. The three new lines are all *pseudo-ops*, or pseudo-operations. They're called pseudo-ops because, rather than generate instructions, they just supply information to the assembler. The END pseudo-op marks the end of the source file, so the assembler knows that it's done when it sees an END. Later on, we'll see that END is useful in other ways, too. But right now, let's put aside any further discussion of it or the other two pseudo-ops and see how to use the assembler.

Creating Source Files

Even though you've entered the lines of WRITESTR.ASM, there's one more consideration before we move on to actually assemble our program. The assembler can use source files that contain standard ASCII characters only. If you are using a word processor, bear in mind that not all word processors write disk files using only the standard ASCII characters. WordStar is one such culprit; Microsoft Word is another. For both these word processors, use the non-document, or unformatted, mode when you save your files.

Before you try assembling WRITESTR.ASM, make sure it's still ASCII. From DOS, type:

```
A>TYPE WRITESTR.ASM
```

You should see the same text you entered, as you entered it. If you see strange characters in your program, you may have to use a different editor or word processor to enter programs. You'll also need a blank line after the END statement in your file.

Now, let's begin to assemble Writestr (be sure to type the semicolon).

```
A>MASM WRITESTR;
The IBM Personal Computer Assembler
Version 1.00 (C) Copyright IBM Corp 1981

Warning Severe
Errors  Errors
0       0

A>
```

We're not done yet. At this point, the assembler has produced a file called WRITESTR.OBJ, which you'll now find on your disk. This is an intermediate file, called an *object file*. It contains our machine language program, along with a lot of bookkeeping information used by another DOS program called the *Linker*.

Linking

Right now, we want the linker to take our .OBJ file and create an .EXE version of it. Copy LINK.EXE from your DOS disk to the disk containing your source file and the assembler. Then, link WRITESTR.OBJ by typing:

```
A>LINK WRITESTR;

IBM Personal Computer Linker
Version 1.10 (C)Copyright IBM Corp 1982

Warning: No STACK segment

There was 1 error detected.

A>
```

One error? Not really; the linker counts its warning as an error, but in this case it's really just what we want. (In some versions of MS-DOS, the Linker doesn't report this warning as an error.) Even though the linker warns us that there is no stack segment, we don't need one right now. After we learn how to add more of the trappings, we'll see why we might want a stack segment.

Now we have our .EXE file, but this still isn't the last step. We have one more step—to create a .COM version, which is just what we created with Debug. Again, you'll see later why we need all these steps. For now, let's create a .COM version of Writestr.

For our final step, we need the program EXE2BIN.EXE from the DOS supplemental disk. Exe2bin, as its name implies, converts an .EXE file to a .COM, or binary (bin) file. There's a difference between .EXE and .COM files, but we won't see it until much later, so for now let's just create the .COM file. Type:

```
A>EXE2BIN WRITESTR WRITESTR.COM

A>
```

The response didn't tell us very much. To see whether Exe2bin worked, let's list all the Writestr files we've created so far:

```
A>DIR WRITESTR.*

 Volume in drive A has no label
 Directory of  A:\

WRITESTR ASM      78   7-25-83   5:00p
WRITESTR OBJ      46   7-25-83   7:02p
WRITESTR EXE     640   7-25-83   7:04p
WRITESTR COM       8   7-25-83   7:06p
        7 File(s)    23552 bytes free

A>
```

This is quite a number of files, including WRITESTR.COM. Type *writestr* to run the .COM version and verify that your program functions properly (recall that it should print an asterisk on your screen). The exact sizes DOS reports for the first three files may vary a bit.

The results may seem a little anticlimactic, since we are seemingly back where we were in Chapter 3, but we aren't: We've gained a great deal. It will all become much clearer when we deal with calls again. Notice that we never once had to worry about where our program was put in memory, as we did about IP in Debug. The addresses were all taken care of for us.

Very soon you'll come to appreciate this feature of the assembler: It will make programming much easier. For example, recall that in the last chapter we wasted space by having our main program at 100h and the procedure we called at 200h. We'll see that using the assembler allows us to place the procedure immediately after the main program without any gap. But first, let's see how our program looks to Debug.

Back in Debug

Let's read our .COM file into Debug and unassemble it to see how Debug reconstructs our program from the machine code of WRITESTR.COM:

```
A>DEBUG WRITESTR.COM
-U
397F:0100 B402          MOV     AH,02
397F:0102 B22A          MOV     DL,2A
397F:0104 CD21          INT     21
397F:0106 CD20          INT     20
```

Exactly what we had in Chapter 3. This is all Debug sees in WRITESTR.COM. The END and our additional instructions about segments—CODE_SEG SEGMENT and CODE_SEG ENDS—didn't make it through at all. What happened to them?

These instructions don't appear in the final machine language version of the program because they are pseudo-ops, and pseudo-ops are for bookkeeping only. The assembler takes care of a lot of bookkeeping at the cost of some extra lines. We'll make good use of pseudo-ops to simplify our job, and we'll see how they affect our program, when we take a closer look at segments in Chapter 11.

Comments

Since we are no longer operating directly with Debug, we're free to add more to our program that the assembler sees but won't pass on to the 8088. Perhaps the most important such additions we can make are comments, which are invaluable in making a program clear. In assembly language programs, we place comments after a semicolon, which works like a single quotation mark (') in BASIC. The assembler ignores anything on the line after a semicolon, so we can add anything we want. If we add comments to our brief program:

```
CODE_SEG      SEGMENT
        MOV   AH,2h          ;Select DOS function 2, character output
        MOV   DL,2Ah         ;Load the ASCII code for '*' to be printed
        INT   21h            ;Print it with INT 21h
        INT   20h            ;And exit to DOS
CODE_SEG      ENDS
        END
```

we see quite an improvement—we can understand this program without having to think back and remember what each line means.

Labels

To round off this chapter, let's look at another bookkeeping feature of the assembler that makes programming smoother: labels.

Until now, when we wanted to jump from one part of a program to another with one of the jump commands, we had to know the specific address we were jumping to. In everyday programming, inserting new instructions forces us to change the addresses in jump instructions. The assembler takes care of this problem with *labels*—names we give to the addresses of any instructions or memory locations. A label takes the place of an address. As soon as the assembler sees a label, it replaces the label with the correct address before sending it on to the 8088.

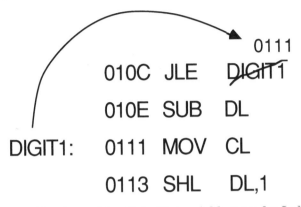

Figure 8-2. **The Assembler Substitutes Addresses for Labels.**

Labels can be up to 31 characters long and can contain letters, numbers, and any of the following symbols: a question mark (?), a period (.), an *at* symbol (@), an underline (_), or a dollar sign ($). They can't start with a digit (0 through 9), and a period can be used only as the first character.

As a practical example, let's take a look at our program from Chapter 6 that reads a two-digit hex number. It contains two jumps, JLE 0111 and JLE 011F. Here's the old version:

```
3985:0100 B401          MOV     AH,01
3985:0102 CD21          INT     21
3985:0104 88C2          MOV     DL,AL
3985:0106 80EA30        SUB     DL,30
3985:0109 80FA09        CMP     DL,09
3985:010C 7E03          JLE     0111
3985:010E 80EA07        SUB     DL,07
3985:0111 B104          MOV     CL,04
3985:0113 D2E2          SHL     DL,CL
3985:0115 CD21          INT     21
3985:0117 2C30          SUB     AL,30
3985:0119 3C09          CMP     AL,09
3985:011B 7E02          JLE     011F
3985:011D 2C07          SUB     AL,07
3985:011F 00C2          ADD     DL,AL
3985:0121 CD20          INT     20
```

It's certainly not obvious what this program does, and if it's not fresh in your mind, you may have to work a little to understand the program again. Let's add labels and comments to clarify its function:

```
CODE_SEG        SEGMENT
        ASSUME  CS:CODE_SEG     ;(To be explained in chapter 11)
        MOV     AH,1h           ;Select DOS function 1, character input
        INT     21h             ;Read a character, and return ASCII code in AL
        MOV     DL,AL           ;Move ASCII code into DL
        SUB     DL,30h          ;Subtract 30h to convert digit to 0 - 9
        CMP     DL,9h           ;Was it a digit between 0 and 9?
        JLE     DIGIT1          ;Yes, we have the first digit (four bits)
        SUB     DL,7h           ;No, subtract 7h to convert letter A - F
DIGIT1:
        MOV     CL,4h           ;Prepare to multiply by 16
        SHL     DL,CL           ;Multiply by shifting, becomes upper four bits
        INT     21h             ;Get next character
        SUB     AL,30h          ;Repeat conversion
        CMP     AL,9h           ;Is it a digit 0 - 9?
        JLE     DIGIT2          ;Yes, so we have the second digit
        SUB     AL,7h           ;No, subtract 7h
DIGIT2:
        ADD     DL,AL           ;ADD second digit
        INT     20h             ;And exit
CODE_SEG        ENDS
        END
```

The labels here, DIGIT1 and DIGIT2, are of a type known as *NEAR* labels, because a colon (:) appears after the labels when they're defined. The term *NEAR* has to do with segments, which we'll talk about in Chapter 11, along with the SEGMENT, ENDS, and ASSUME pseudo-ops. Here, if you assembled the preceding program and then unassembled it with Debug, you'd see DIGIT1 replaced by 0111h and DIGIT2 replaced by 011Fh.

Summary

This has been quite a chapter. It's as if we've stepped into a new world, and, in a sense, we have. The assembler's much simpler to work with than Debug was, so we can now begin to write real programs, because the assembler does much of the bookkeeping for us.

What have we learned here? We began by learning how to create a source file and then go through the steps of assembling, linking, and converting it from an .OBJ file to an .EXE, and then a .COM file, using a simple program from Chapter 3. The assembly language program we created contained a few pseudo-ops, which we've never seen before, but they'll become familiar, once we've become more comfortable using the assembler. In fact, we'll place SEG-MENT, ENDS, and END pseudo-ops in all our programs from now on, since we need them, even though we won't really see the reason why until Chapter 11.

Next, we learned about comments. You may have wondered how we could survive without comments. We won't from now on. Comments add so much to the readability of programs that we won't skimp on them.

Finally came labels, to make our programs even more readable. We'll use all these ideas and methods throughout the rest of this book. Let's move on to the next chapter and see how the assembler makes procedures easier to use.

9

PROCEDURES AND THE ASSEMBLER

Now that we've met the assembler, let's become a little more comfortable with writing assembly language programs. In this chapter, we'll return to the subject of procedures. You'll see how we can write procedures much more easily with the help of our hard-working assembler. Then, we'll move on to build some useful procedures, which we'll use when we begin to develop our Dskpatch program a few chapters from now.

We'll begin with two procedures to print a byte in hexadecimal. Along the way, we'll meet several more pseudo-ops. But, like SEGMENT, END, and ENDS in the last chapter, we'll leave them pretty much undefined until Chapter 11, where we'll learn more about segments.

The Assembler's Procedures

When we first learned about procedures, we left a large gap between the main program and its procedures, so that we'd have room for changes without having to worry about our main program overlapping a procedure. But now we have the assembler, and since it does all the work of assigning addresses to instructions, we no longer need to leave a gap between procedures. With the assembler, each time we make a change, we can just assemble the program again.

In Chapter 7, we built a small program with one CALL. The program did nothing more than print the letters A through J, and it looked like this:

```
3985:0100 B241        MOV     DL,41
3985:0102 B90A00      MOV     CX,000A
3985:0105 E8F800      CALL    0200
3985:0108 E2FB        LOOP    0105
3985:010A CD20        INT     20

3985:0200 B402        MOV     AH,02
3985:0202 CD21        INT     21
3985:0204 FEC2        INC     DL
3985:0206 C3          RET
```

Let's turn this into a program for the assembler. It will be hard to read without labels and comments, so we'll add those embellishments to make our program far more readable:

Listing 9-1. The Program PRINTAJ.ASM

```
CODE_SEG        SEGMENT
        ASSUME  CS:CODE_SEG
        ORG     100h                    ;Make this a .COM file (to be explained)

PRINT_A_J       PROC    NEAR
        MOV     DL,'A'                  ;Start with the character A
        MOV     CX,10                   ;Print 10 characters, starting with A
PRINT_LOOP:
        CALL    WRITE_CHAR              ;Print character, and move to next one
        LOOP    PRINT_LOOP              ;Continue for 10 characters
        INT     20h                     ;Return to DOS
PRINT_A_J       ENDP

WRITE_CHAR      PROC    NEAR
        MOV     AH,2                    ;Set function code for character output
        INT     21h                     ;Print the character already in DL
        INC     DL                      ;Move to the next char in the alphabet
        RET                             ;Return from this procedure
WRITE_CHAR      ENDP

CODE_SEG        ENDS
        END     PRINT_A_J
```

There are four new pseudo-ops here: ASSUME, ORG, PROC, and ENDP. ASSUME is related to segments, and ORG is related to the way DOS loads programs; we'll find out more about them in Chapter 11.

PROC and ENDP are pseudo-ops for defining procedures. As you can see, both the main program and the procedure at 200h are surrounded by matching pairs of the pseudo-ops PROC and ENDP, which, themselves, are enclosed in the pseudo-ops SEGMENT and ENDS (End Segment).

PROC defines the beginning of a procedure; ENDP defines the end. The label in front of each is the name we give to the procedure they define. Thus, in the main procedure, PRINT_A_J, we can replace our CALL 200 instruction with the more readable CALL WRITE_CHAR. Just insert the name of the procedure, and the assembler assigns the addresses.

The NEAR and FAR pseudo-ops (more on FAR later) provide information to the assembler about our use of segments. The assembler uses this information whenever it assembles a CALL instruction since there are two types of CALL and RET instructions: near and far. A far CALL, which we won't use here, calls a procedure that is contained in another segment. A near CALL, on the other hand, calls a procedure contained in the same segment.

In this book, we'll be dealing with programs that fit in a single 64K segment, so all of our procedures will be NEAR procedures. NEAR informs the assembler the procedure is in the same segment as any procedure that calls it. When the assembler sees CALL WRITE_CHAR, it will know from the NEAR, in WRITE_CHAR PROC NEAR, that WRITE_CHAR is in the same segment as PRINT_A_J.

The assembler needs this segment information because there are two version of the CALL and RET instructions—one for when we don't change segments, and one for when we do. Here it is obvious that our two procedures are in the same segment, because we placed both procedures between one pair of segment-defining pseudo-ops: SEGMENT and ENDS. Later on, as we break our program into pieces that we put in several different source files, the uses of NEAR and FAR will become more important.

Finally, since we have two procedures, we need to tell the assembler which to use as the main procedure—where the 8088 should start executing our program. The END pseudo-op takes care of this detail. By writing END PRINT_A_J, we've told the assembler that PRINT_A_J is the main procedure. Later in our work, we'll see that the main procedure can be anywhere. Right now, however, we are dealing with .COM files, and we'll need to place the main procedure first in our source file.

You're ready to go, so if you haven't done so yet, enter the program into a file called PRINTAJ.ASM and generate the .COM version, using the same steps you did in the last chapter:

```
MASM PRINTAJ;
LINK PRINTAJ;
EXE2BIN PRINTAJ PRINTAJ.COM
```

Then give Printaj a try. (Make sure you've run Exe2bin *before* you run Printaj. Otherwise, you'll end up running the .EXE version of Printaj, which undoubtedly won't produce the results you expect.)

When you're satisfied, use Debug to unassemble our program and see how the assembler fits the two procedures together. Recall that we can read a particular file into Debug by typing its name as part of the command line. For example, we can type *DEBUG PRINTAJ.COM*, and when we do, we see:

```
3985:0100 B241        MOV     DL,41
3985:0102 B90A00      MOV     CX,000A
3985:0105 E80400      CALL    010C
3985:0108 E2FB        LOOP    0105
3985:010A CD20        INT     20
3985:010C B402        MOV     AH,02
3985:010E CD21        INT     21
3985:0110 FEC2        INC     DL
3985:0112 C3          RET
```

Our program is nice and snug, with no gap between the two procedures.

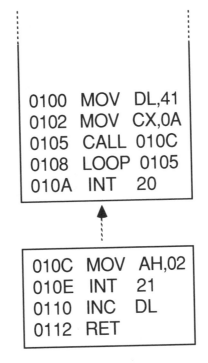

```
0100  MOV   DL,41
0102  MOV   CX,0A
0105  CALL  010C
0108  LOOP  0105
010A  INT   20
```

```
010C  MOV   AH,02
010E  INT   21
0110  INC   DL
0112  RET
```

Figure 9-1. MASM Assembles Separate Procedures Without a Gap.

The Hex-Output Procedures

We've seen hex-output procedures twice before: Once in Chapter 5, where we learned how to print a number in hex, and again in Chapter 7, where we saw how to simplify the program, using a procedure to print one hex digit. Now we're going to add yet another procedure to print one character. Why? Well, let's just call it foresight.

By using a central procedure to write a character to the screen, we can change the way this procedure writes characters without affecting the rest of the program. We will change it several times.

Enter the following program into the file VIDEO_IO.ASM:

Listing 9-2. The New File VIDEO_IO.ASM

```
CODE_SEG        SEGMENT
        ASSUME  CS:CODE_SEG
        ORG     100h

TEST_WRITE_HEX  PROC    NEAR
        MOV     DL,3Fh                  ;Test with 3Fh
        CALL    WRITE_HEX
        INT     20h                     ;Return to DOS
TEST_WRITE_HEX  ENDP

        PUBLIC  WRITE_HEX
;----------------------------------------------------------------------;
; This procedure converts the byte in the DL register to hex and writes ;
; the two hex digits at the current cursor position.                    ;
;                                                                       ;
;       DL      Byte to be converted to hex.                           ;
;                                                                       ;
; Uses:         WRITE_HEX_DIGIT                                         ;
;----------------------------------------------------------------------;
WRITE_HEX       PROC    NEAR            ;Entry point
        PUSH    CX                      ;Save registers used in this procedure
        PUSH    DX
        MOV     DH,DL                   ;Make a copy of byte
        MOV     CX,4                    ;Get the upper nibble in DL
        SHR     DL,CL
        CALL    WRITE_HEX_DIGIT         ;Display first hex digit
        MOV     DL,DH                   ;Get lower nibble into DL
        AND     DL,0Fh                  ;Remove the upper nibble
        CALL    WRITE_HEX_DIGIT         ;Display second hex digit
        POP     DX
        POP     CX
        RET
WRITE_HEX       ENDP

        PUBLIC  WRITE_HEX_DIGIT
;----------------------------------------------------------------------;
; This procedure converts the lower 4 bits of DL to a hex digit and     ;
; writes it to the screen.                                              ;
;                                                                       ;
;       DL      Lower 4 bits contain number to be printed in hex.       ;
;                                                                       ;
; Uses:         WRITE_CHAR                                              ;
;----------------------------------------------------------------------;
WRITE_HEX_DIGIT         PROC    NEAR
        PUSH    DX                      ;Save registers used
        CMP     DL,10                   ;Is this nibble <10?
        JAE     HEX_LETTER              ;No, convert to a letter
        ADD     DL,"0"                  ;Yes, convert to a digit
        JMP     Short WRITE_DIGIT       ;Now write this character
HEX_LETTER:
```

Listing 9-2. *continued*

```
        ADD     DL,"A"-10               ;Convert to hex letter
WRITE_DIGIT:
        CALL    WRITE_CHAR              ;Display the letter on the screen
        POP     DX                      ;Restore old value of AX
        RET
WRITE_HEX_DIGIT ENDP

        PUBLIC  WRITE_CHAR
;-------------------------------------------------------------------;
; This procedure prints a character on the screen using the DOS     ;
; function call.                                                    ;
;                                                                   ;
;       DL      Byte to print on screen.                           ;
;-------------------------------------------------------------------;
WRITE_CHAR      PROC    NEAR
        PUSH    AX
        MOV     AH,2                    ;Call for character output
        INT     21h                     ;Output character in DL register
        POP     AX                      ;Restore old value in AX
        RET                             ;And return
WRITE_CHAR      ENDP

CODE_SEG        ENDS

        END     TEST_WRITE_HEX
```

The DOS function to print characters treats some characters specially. For example, using the DOS function to output 07 results in a beep, without printing the character for 07, which is a small diamond. We'll see a new version of WRITE_CHAR in Part III, where we'll learn about the ROM BIOS routines inside your IBM PC. For now, though, we'll just use the DOS function to print characters.

The new pseudo-op PUBLIC is here for future use: We'll use it in Chapter 13, when we learn about modular design. PUBLIC simply tells the assembler to generate some more information for the linker. The linker allows us to bring separate pieces of our program, assembled from different source files, together into one program. And PUBLIC informs the assembler that the procedure named after the PUBLIC pseudo-op should be made public, or available to procedures in other files.

Right now, Video_io contains the three procedures to write a byte as a hex number, and a short main program to test these procedures. We'll be adding many procedures to the file as we develop Dskpatch, and by the end of this book, VIDEO_IO.ASM will be filled with many general-purpose procedures.

The procedure TEST_WRITE_HEX that we've included does just what it says: It's here to test WRITE_HEX, which, in turn, uses WRITE_HEX_ DIGIT and WRITE_CHAR. As soon as we've verified that these three procedures are all correct, we'll remove TEST_WRITE_HEX from VIDEO_ IO.ASM.

Create the .COM version of Video_io, and use Debug to thoroughly test WRITE_HEX. Change the 3Fh at memory location 101h to each of the boundary conditions we tried in Chapter 5, then use G to run TEST_WRITE_HEX.

We'll use many simple test programs to test new procedures we've written. In this way, we can build a program piece by piece, rather than try to build and debug it all at once. This incremental method is much faster and easier, since we can confine bugs to just the new code.

The Beginnings of Modular Design

Notice that, ahead of each procedure in Video_io, we've included a block of comments briefly describing the function of each procedure. More importantly, these comments tell which registers the procedure uses to pass information back and forth, as well as what other procedures it uses. As one feature of our modular approach, the comment block allows us to use any procedure by looking at the description. There's no need to relearn how the procedure does its work. This also makes it fairly easy to rewrite one procedure without having to rewrite any of the procedures that call it.

We've also used PUSH and POP instructions to save and restore any registers we use within each procedure. We'll do this for every procedure we write, except for our test procedures. This approach, too, is part of the modular style we'll be using.

Recall that we save and restore any register used so that we never have to worry about complex interactions between procedures trying to fight over the small number of registers in the 8088. Each procedure is free to use as many registers as it likes, *provided* it restores them before the RET instruction. It's a small price to pay for the added simplicity. In addition, without saving and restoring registers, the task of rewriting procedures would be mind-rending. You'd be sure to lose much hair in the process.

We also try to use many small procedures, instead of one large one. This, too, makes our programming task simpler, although we'll sometimes be forced to write longer procedures when the design becomes particularly convoluted.

These ideas and methods will all be borne out more fully in the chapters to come. In the next chapter, for example, we'll add another procedure to Video_ io: a procedure to take a word in the DX register and print the number in decimal on the screen.

A Program Skeleton

As we've seen in this and the preceding chapter, the assembler imposes a certain amount of overhead on any programs that we write. In other words, we need to write a few pseudo-ops that tell the assembler the basics. For future reference, here is the absolute minimum you'll need for programs you write:

```
CODE_SEG        SEGMENT
        ASSUME  CS:CODE_SEG
        ORG     100h

Some_procedure  PROC    NEAR
        .
        .
        .
        INT     20h
Some_procedure  ENDP

CODE_SEG        ENDS
        END     Some_procedure
```

We'll add some new pseudo-ops to this program skeleton in later chapters, but you can use it, as shown here, as the starting point for new programs you write. Or, even better, you can use some of the programs and procedures from this book as your starting point.

Summary

We're really making progress now. In this chapter, we learned how to write procedures in assembly language. From now on we'll use procedures all the time, and by using small procedures, we'll make our programs more manageable.

We saw that a procedure begins with a PROC definition and ends with an ENDP pseudo-op. We rewrote PRINT_A_J to test our new knowledge of procedures, then went on to rewrite our program to write a hex number—this time with an extra procedure. Now that procedures are so easy to work with, there's little reason not to break our programs into more procedures. In fact, we've seen that there are many reasons for using many small procedures.

At the end of this chapter we talked briefly about modular design, a philosophy that will save us a great deal of time and effort. Our modular programs will be easier to write, easier to read, and easier for someone else to modify than programs created with the well-worn technique of spaghetti logic: programs written with very long procedures and many interactions.

We're now ready to build another useful procedure. Then, in Chapter 11, we'll learn about segments. And from there, we'll move on to developing larger programs, where we'll really start to use the techniques of modular design.

10

PRINTING IN DECIMAL

We've been promising that we'd write a procedure to take a word and print it in decimal notation. WRITE_DECIMAL uses some new tricks—ways to save a byte here, a few microseconds there. Perhaps such tricks will hardly seem to be worth the effort. But if you memorize them, you'll find that you can use them to shorten and speed up programs. Through our tricks, we'll also learn about two new types of logical operations to add to the AND instruction we covered in Chapter 5. First, let's review the process for converting a word to decimal digits.

Recalling the Conversion

Division is the key to converting a word to decimal digits. Recall that the DIV instruction calculates both the integer answer and its remainder. So, calculating 12345/10 yields 1234 as the integer answer, and 5 as the remainder. In this example, 5 is simply the rightmost digit. And if we divide by 10 again,

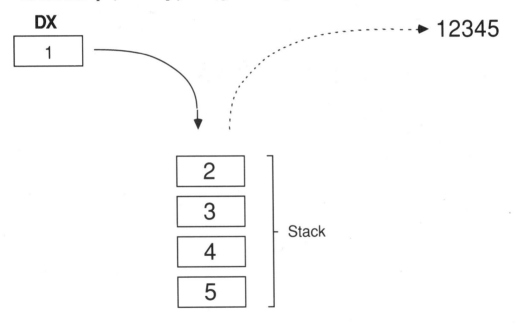

Figure 10-1. PUSHing the Digits onto the Stack Reverses Their Order.

we'll get the next digit to the left. Repeated division by 10 *strips off* the digits from right to left, each time putting them in the remainder.

Of course, the digits come out in reverse order, but in assembly language programming, we have a fix for that. Remember the stack? It's just like a stack of lunch trays: The first one to come off the top is the last tray that was set down. If we substitute digits for trays, and place the digits one on top of the other as they come out of the remainder, we'll have it. We can pull out the digits in correct order.

The top digit is the first digit in our number, and the other digits are underneath it. So, if we push the remainders as we calculate them, and print them as we pop them off the stack, the digits will be in the correct order.

The following program is the complete procedure to print a number in decimal notation. As we mentioned, there are a few tricks hiding in this procedure. We'll get to them soon enough, but let's try WRITE_DECIMAL to see if it works before we worry about how it works.

Place WRITE_DECIMAL into VIDEO_IO.ASM, along with the procedures for writing a byte in hex. Make sure you place WRITE_DECIMAL *after* TEST_WRITE_HEX, which we'll be replacing with TEST_WRITE_DECI-MAL. To save some work, WRITE_DECIMAL uses WRITE_HEX_DIGIT to convert one nibble (four bits) into a digit.

Listing 10-1. Add to VIDEO_IO.ASM

```
        PUBLIC  WRITE_DECIMAL
;---------------------------------------------------------------------;
; This procedure writes a 16-bit, unsigned number in decimal notation. ;
;                                                                      ;
;       DX      N : 16-bit, unsigned number.                          ;
;                                                                      ;
; Uses:         WRITE_HEX_DIGIT                                        ;
;---------------------------------------------------------------------;
WRITE_DECIMAL   PROC    NEAR
        PUSH    AX                      ;Save registers used here
        PUSH    CX
        PUSH    DX
        PUSH    SI
        MOV     AX,DX
        MOV     SI,10                   ;Will divide by 10 using SI
        XOR     CX,CX                   ;Count of digits placed on stack
NON_ZERO:
        XOR     DX,DX                   ;Set upper word of N to 0
        DIV     SI                      ;Calculate N/10 and (N mod 10)
        PUSH    DX                      ;Push one digit onto the stack
        INC     CX                      ;One more digit added
        OR      AX,AX                   ;N = 0 yet?
```

Listing 10-1. *continued*

```
        JNE     NON_ZERO                ;Nope, continue
WRITE_DIGIT_LOOP:
        POP     DX                      ;Get the digits in reverse order
        CALL    WRITE_HEX_DIGIT
        LOOP    WRITE_DIGIT_LOOP
END_DECIMAL:
        POP     SI
        POP     DX
        POP     CX
        POP     AX
        RET
WRITE_DECIMAL   ENDP
```

Notice that we've included a new register, the SI (*Source Index*), register. Later we'll see why it's been given that name, and we'll meet its brother, the DI, or *Destination Index*, register. Both registers have special uses, but they can also be used as if they were general-purpose registers. Since WRITE_ DECIMAL needs four general-purpose registers, we used SI, even though we could have used BX, simply to show that SI (and DI) can serve as general-purpose registers if need be.

Before we try out our new procedure, we need to make two other changes to VIDEO_IO.ASM. First, we must remove the procedure TEST_WRITE_HEX, and insert this test procedure in its place:

Listing 10-2. Replace TEST_WRITE_HEX in VIDEO_IO.ASM with This
           Procedure

```
TEST_WRITE_DECIMAL      PROC    NEAR
        MOV     DX,12345
        CALL    WRITE_DECIMAL
        INT     20h                     ;Return to DOS
TEST_WRITE_DECIMAL      ENDP
```

This procedure tests WRITE_DECIMAL with the number 12345 (which the assembler converts to the word 3039h).

Second, we need to change the END statement at the end of VIDEO_ IO.ASM to read END TEST_WRITE_DECIMAL, because TEST_WRITE_ DECIMAL is now our main procedure.

Make these changes and give VIDEO_IO a whirl. Convert it to its .COM version and see if it works. If it doesn't, check your source file for errors. If you're adventurous, try to find your bug with Debug. After all, that's what Debug is for.

Some Tricks

Hiding in WRITE_DECIMAL are two tricks of the trade garnered from the people who wrote the ROM BIOS procedures we'll meet in Chapter 17. The first is an efficient instruction to set a register to zero. It's not much more efficient than MOV AX,0, and perhaps it's not worth the effort, but it's the sort of trick you'll find people using, so here it is. The instruction:

```
XOR     AX,AX
```

sets the AX register to zero. How? To understand that, we need to learn about the logical operation called an Exclusive OR, hence the name XOR.

The exclusive OR is similar to an OR (which we'll see next), but the result of XORing two trues:

$$
\begin{array}{c|cc}
\text{XOR} & 0 & 1 \\
\hline
0 & 0 & 1 \\
1 & 1 & 0
\end{array}
$$

is true if *only* one bit is true, not if both are true. Thus, if we exclusive OR a number to itself, we get zero:

$$
\begin{array}{r}
1\ 0\ 1\ 1 \quad 0\ 1\ 0\ 1 \\
\text{XOR} \quad 1\ 0\ 1\ 1 \quad 0\ 1\ 0\ 1 \\
\hline
0\ 0\ 0\ 0 \quad 0\ 0\ 0\ 0
\end{array}
$$

That's the trick. We won't find other uses for the XOR instruction in this book, but we thought you'd find it interesting.

As a short aside, you'll also find many people using another quick trick to set a register to zero. Rather than using the XOR instruction, we could have used:

```
SUB     AX,AX
```

to set the AX register to zero.

Now for the other trick. It's just about as devious as our XOR scheme to clear a register, and it uses a cousin to the exclusive OR—the OR function.

We want to check the AX register to see if it's zero. To do this, we could use the instruction CMP AX,0. But no, we'd rather use a trick: It's more fun, and a little more efficient, too. So, we write OR AX,AX and follow this instruction with a JNE (Jump if Not Equal) conditional jump. (We could also have used JNZ—Jump if Not Zero.)

The OR instruction, like any of the math instructions, sets the flags, including the zero flag. Like AND, OR is a logical concept. But here, a result is true if one *OR* the other bit is true:

```
OR │ 0  1
───┼──────
 0 │ 0  1
 1 │ 1  1
```

If we take a number and OR it to itself, we get the original number back again:

```
      1 0 1 1   0 1 0 1
OR    1 0 1 1   0 1 0 1
      ─────────────────
      1 0 1 1   0 1 0 1
```

The OR instruction is also useful for setting just one bit in a byte. For example, we can set bit 3 in the number we just used:

```
      1 0 1 1   0 1 0 1
OR    0 0 0 0   1 0 0 0
      ─────────────────
      1 0 1 1   1 1 0 1
```

We'll have more tricks to play before we're through in this book, but these two are the only ones that are entirely for fun.

The Inner Workings

To see how WRITE_DECIMAL performs its task, study the listing; we won't cover more details here. We do need to point out a few more things.

First, the CX register is used to count how many digits we've pushed onto the stack, so that we know how many to remove. The CX register is a particularly convenient choice, because we can build a loop with the LOOP instruction and use the CX register to store the repeat count. Our choice makes the digit-output loop (WRITE_DIGIT_LOOP) almost trivial, because the LOOP instruction uses the CX register directly. We'll use CX very often when we have to store a count.

Next, be careful to check the boundary conditions here. The boundary condition at 0 isn't a problem, as you can check. The other boundary condition is 65535, or FFFFh, which you can check easily with Debug. Just load VIDEO_ IO.COM into Debug by typing *DEBUG VIDEO_IO.COM* and change the 12345 (3039h) at 101h to 65535 (FFFFh). (WRITE_DECIMAL works with unsigned numbers. See if you can write a version to write signed numbers).

You may have noticed a sticky point here, having to do with the 8088, not our program. Debug works mostly with bytes (at least the E command does) but we want to change a word. We must be careful, since the 8088 stores the bytes in a different order. Here is an unassemble for the MOV instruction:

```
3985:0100 BA3930     MOV     DX,3039
```

You can tell from the *BA3930* part of this display that the byte at 101h is 39h, and the one at 102h is 30h (BA is the MOV instruction). The two bytes are the two bytes of 3039h, but seemingly in reverse order. Confusing? Actually, the order is logical, after a short explanation.

A *word* consists of two parts, the lower byte and the upper byte. The lower byte is the least significant byte (39h in 3039h), while the upper byte is the other part (30h). It makes sense, then, to place the lower byte at the lower address in memory. (Some computers actually reverse these two bytes, and this can be a bit confusing if you're using several different computers.)

Try different numbers for the word starting at 101h, and you'll see how this storage works. Use TEST_WRITE_DECIMAL to see if you got it right, or unassemble the first instruction.

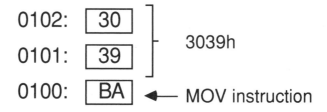

Figure 10-2.   The 8088 Stores Numbers With the Lower Byte First in Memory.

Summary

We added a few new instructions to our repertoire here, as well as a few tricks for fun. We also learned about two other registers, SI and DI, that we can use as general-purpose registers. They also have other uses, which we'll see in later chapters.

We learned about the XOR and OR logical instructions, which allow us to work between individual bits in two bytes or words. And in our WRITE_DEC-IMAL procedure, we used the XOR AX,AX instruction as a tricky way to set the AX register to zero. We used OR AX,AX as a devious way to write the equivalent of CMP AX,0 to test the AX register and see if it is zero.

Finally, we learned about how the 8088 stores a word in memory by checking the boundary conditions of our new procedure, WRITE_DECIMAL.

Here, at the end of this chapter, we now have another general-purpose procedure, WRITE_DECIMAL, that we'll be able to use in the future for our own programs.

Take a breather now. We've got a few *different* chapters scheduled next. Chapter 11 covers segments in detail. Segments are perhaps the most complicated part of the 8088 microprocessor, so the chapter may prove to be rather heavy going. Even so, though, we need to cover the topic for following chapters.

After that, we'll make a slight course correction and get back on track by learning about what we want to do with our program Dskpatch. We'll do a bit of probing on disks, and learn about sectors, tracks, and other such things.

From there, we can plot a simple course for preliminary versions of Dskpatch. En route, you'll get a chance to see how to develop large programs. Programmers don't write an entire program, then debug it. They write sections and try each section before they move on—programming is much less work that way. We've used this approach to a limited extent by writing and testing WRITE_HEX and WRITE_DECIMAL, for which the test programs were very simple. The test programs from here on will be more complex, but more interesting, too.

11

SEGMENTS

In the preceding chapters, we've encountered several pseudo-ops that deal with segments. Now the time has come to look at segments themselves, and at how the 8088 manages to address a full megabyte (1,048,576 bytes) of memory. From this, we'll begin to understand why segments need their own pseudo-ops in the assembler, and in later chapters we'll begin to use different segments (thus far, we've used only one). Then, in Chapter 13, when we learn about modular design, we'll see how to group segments together into a .COM file.

Let's start at the 8088 level by learning how it constructs the 20-bit addresses needed for a full megabyte of memory.

Sectioning the 8088's Memory

Segments are about the only part of the 8088 we haven't covered yet, and they are, perhaps, the most confusing part of this microprocessor to most people. In fact, segments are what we call a *kludge* in this business: computerese for a makeshift fix to a problem.

The problem, in this case, is being able to address more than 64K of memory—the limit with one word, since 65535 is the largest number a single word can hold. Intel, designers of the 8088, used segments and segment registers to "fix" this problem, and in the process made the 8088 more confusing.

So far, we haven't concerned ourselves with this problem. We've been using the IP register to hold the address of the next instruction for the 8088 to execute ever since we met Debug in Chapter 2. Back then, you may recall that we said the address is actually formed from both the CS register and the IP register. But we never really said how. Now, let's find out.

Although the complete address is formed from two registers, the 8088 doesn't form a two-word number for the address. If you were to take CS:IP as a 32-bit number (two 16-bit numbers side by side), the 8088 would be able to address about four billion bytes—far more than the one million bytes it can actually address. The 8088's method is slightly more complicated: The CS register provides the *starting* address for the code segment, where a segment is 64K of memory. Here's how it works.

As you can see in Figure 11-1, the 8088 divides memory into many overlapping segments, with a new segment starting every 16 bytes. The first segment (segment 0) starts at memory location 0; the second (segment 1) starts at 10h (16); the third starts at 20h (32), and so on.

The actual address is just CS * 16 + IP. For example, if the CS register contains 3FA8 and IP contains D017, the absolute address is:

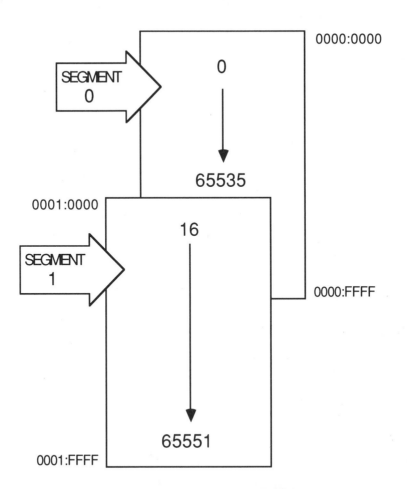

Figure 11-1. Overlapping Segments Start Every 16 Bytes, and Are 65536 Bytes Long.

```
CS * 16 :  0 0 1 1   1 1 1 1   1 0 1 0   1 0 0 0   0 0 0 0
   IP   :            1 1 0 1   0 0 0 0   0 0 0 1   0 1 1 1
           0 1 0 0   1 1 0 0   1 0 1 0   1 0 0 1   0 1 1 1
```

We multiplied by 16 just by shifting CS left four bits, and injecting zeros at the right.

Now, this may seem like a strange way to address more than 64K of memory, and it is—but it works. Soon, we'll begin to see how well it really works.

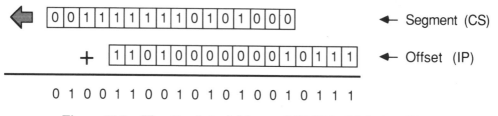

Figure 11-2. The Absolute Address of CS:IP is CS * 16 + IP.

The 8088 actually has four segment registers: CS (Code Segment), DS (Data Segment), SS (Stack Segment), and ES (Extra Segment). The CS register we've been looking at is used by the 8088 for the segment where the next instruction is stored. In much the same way, DS is the segment where the 8088 looks for data, and SS is where the 8088 places the stack.

Before we go on, let's look at a short program, quite different from any we've seen before, that uses two different segments. Enter this program into the file TEST_SEG.ASM:

Listing 11-1. The Program TEST_SEG.ASM

```
CODE_SEG        SEGMENT
        ASSUME  CS:CODE_SEG
TEST_SEGMENT    PROC    NEAR
        MOV     AH,4Ch                  ;Ask for the exit-to-dos function
        INT     21h                     ;Return to DOS
TEST_SEGMENT    ENDP
CODE_SEG        ENDS

STACK_SEGMENT   SEGMENT STACK
        DB      10 DUP ("Stack    ")    ;Three spaces after Stack
STACK_SEGMENT   ENDS

        END     TEST_SEGMENT
```

Then assemble and link Test_seg, but don't generate a .COM file for it. The result will be TEST_SEG.EXE, which is slightly different from a .COM file.

> **Note**: We have to use a different method for exiting from .EXE files. For .COM files, INT 20h works perfectly well, but it doesn't work at all for .EXE files because the organization of segments is very different, as we'll see in this chapter; more on this difference later.

When we used Debug on a .COM file, Debug sets all the segment registers to the same number, with the program starting at an *offset* of 100h from the start of this segment. The first 256 bytes (100h) are used to store various pieces of information which we really aren't that interested in, but we'll take a peek at part of this area in a little bit.

Now, try loading TEST_SEG.EXE into Debug, to see what happens with segments in an .EXE file:

```
A>DEBUG TEST_SEG.EXE
-R
AX=0000  BX=0000  CX=0080  DX=0000  SP=0050  BP=0000  SI=0000  DI=0000
DS=3985  ES=3985  SS=3996  CS=3995  IP=0000   NV UP DI PL NZ NA PO NC
3995:0000 CD20          INT    20
```

The values of the SS and CS registers are different from those for DS and ES.

In our program, we defined two segments. The STACK_SEGMENT is where we place the stack (hence, the word *STACK* after the word SEGMENT). We defined the stack to be 80 bytes long: The instruction DB 10 DUP ("Stack   ") tells the assembler to convert the string in quotation marks to bytes, and to repeat the string ten times in memory. DB (*Define Byte*) tells the assembler we are defining bytes of memory. Here, we're initializing the stack with ten repetitions of the ASCII code for *Stack* and three spaces. The code for this is 53 74 61 63 6B 20 20 20, so if we look at the stack segment, we should see these numbers repeated ten times. Ask Debug to dump this area of memory with the following command, which tells Debug to dump memory starting at offset 0 within the Stack Segment (SS:0):

```
-D SS:0
3996:0000  53 74 61 63 6B 20 20 20-53 74 61 63 6B 20 20 20   Stack   Stack
3996:0010  53 74 61 63 6B 20 20 20-53 74 61 63 6B 20 20 20   Stack   Stack
3996:0020  53 74 61 63 6B 20 20 20-53 74 61 63 6B 20 20 20   Stack   Stack
3996:0030  53 74 61 63 6B 20 20 20-53 74 61 63 6B 20 20 20   Stack   Stack
3996:0040  53 74 61 63 6B 20 20 20-53 74 61 63 6B 20 00 00   Stack   Stack ..
3996:0050  00 00 00 00 00 00 00 00-00 00 00 00 00 00 00 00   ................
            .
            .
            .
        ↑    ↑
        SS   SP
```

The address for the top of the stack is given by SS:SP. SP is the Stack Pointer, like IP and CS for code, and is an offset within the current Stack Segment.

Actually, "top-of-stack" is a misnomer, because the stack grows from high

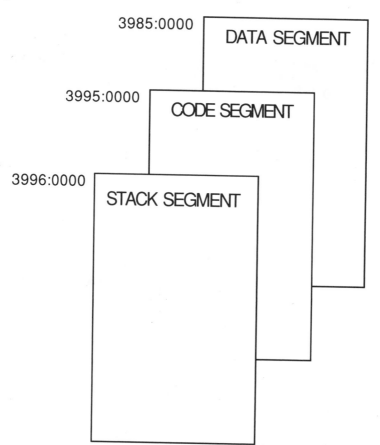

Figure 11-3. Memory Layout for TEST_SEG.EXE.

memory toward low memory. Thus, the top of the stack is really at the bottom of the stack in memory, and new entries to the stack are placed progressively lower in memory. Here, SP is 50h, which is 80 decimal, because we defined a stack area 80 bytes long. We haven't placed anything on the stack as yet, so top-of-stack is still at the top of the memory we set aside for the stack: 50h.

Now that you know how to find the stack, you may wish to watch how it changes for the programs in previous chapters. Here, though, let's continue with the example already in Debug.

Notice that the Stack Segment (SS) is segment number 3996 (this will probably be different for you), while our Code Segment (CS) is at segment 3995—

one less than SS, or just 16 bytes lower in memory. That means if we do an unassemble starting at CS:0, we'll see our program (the INT 20h instruction) followed by 14 bytes equal to zero (the INT 20h takes two bytes), and then we'll see the bytes from the stack segment. We'll also see the data for *Stack*, followed by three spaces, unassembled:

```
-U CS:0
3995:0000 CD20        INT     20
3995:0002 0000        ADD     [BX+SI],AL
3995:0004 0000        ADD     [BX+SI],AL
3995:0006 0000        ADD     [BX+SI],AL
3995:0008 0000        ADD     [BX+SI],AL
3995:000A 0000        ADD     [BX+SI],AL
3995:000C 0000        ADD     [BX+SI],AL
3995:000E 0000        ADD     [BX+SI],AL
3995:0010 53          PUSH    BX
3995:0011 7461        JZ      0074
3995:0013 63          DB      63
3995:0014 6B          DB      6B
3995:0015 2020        AND     [BX+SI],AH
3995:0017 205374      AND     [BP+DI+74],DL
3995:001A 61          DB      61
3995:001B 63          DB      63
3995:001C 6B          DB      6B
3995:001D 2020        AND     [BX+SI],AH
3995:001F 205374      AND     [BP+DI+74],DL
-
```

Just as we expected, the number 53h—the ASCII code for S, the first letter in our stack area—is at offset 10h (16) within our Code Segment.

In looking at the register display, you may have noticed that the ES and DS registers contain 3985h, 10h less than the beginning of the program at segment 3995h. Multiplying by 16 to get the number of bytes, we can see that there are 100h (or 256) bytes before our program starts. This is the same area placed at the beginning of a .COM file.

Among other things, this 256 byte *scratch area* at the start of programs contains the characters we type after the name of our program. For example:

```
A>DEBUG TEST_SEG.EXE And now for some characters we'll see in the memory dump
-D DS:80
3985:0080 39 20 41 6E 64 20 6E 6F-77 20 66 6F 72 20 73 6F   9 And now for so
3985:0090 6D 65 20 63 68 61 72 61-63 74 65 72 73 20 77 65   me characters we
3985:00A0 27 6C 6C 20 73 65 65 20-69 6E 20 74 68 65 20 6D   'll see in the m
3985:00B0 65 6D 6F 72 79 20 64 75-6D 70 0D 20 6D 65 6D 6F   emory dump. memo
3985:00C0 72 79 20 64 75 6D 70 0D-00 00 00 00 00 00 00 00   ry dump.........
                 .
                 .
                 .
```

The first byte tells us we typed 39h (or 57) characters, including the first space after TEST_SEG.EXE. We won't use this information in this book, but it helps show why you might want such a large scratch area.

Note: The "scratch area" is actually called a PSP (Program Segment Prefix) and contains information for use by DOS. In other words, you should not assume that you can make use of this area.

The scratch area also contains information that DOS uses when we exit from a program, with either the INT 20h or the INT 21h, function 4Ch, instructions. But for reasons that are not at all clear, the INT 20h instruction expects the CS register to point to the start of this scratch area, which it does for a .COM program, but *not* for a .EXE program. This is an historical question. And, in fact, the exit function (INT 21h, function 4Ch) was added to DOS with the introduction of version 2.00.

The code for .COM files must always start at an offset of 100h in the code segment to leave room for this 256-byte scratch area at the start. This is unlike the .EXE file, which had its code start at IP = 0000, because the code segment started 100h bytes after the beginning of the area in memory.

Recall that, in our .COM files in Chapter 10, we had to explicitly place an ORG 100h pseudo-op at the beginning of our programs to set aside 100h bytes. The ORG 100h pseudo-op sets the *origin* of our code to 100h. That's all it does, but we'll continue to use the ORG 100h in our files, because we'll be using .COM programs in the rest of the book.

We presented an .EXE file here just so you could learn about segments. Later on, you'll learn more about them, but we'll use .COM files from now on, because they are smaller and load into memory more quickly. You'll see the reasons for this when we reach the last chapter, but now let's move on. Let's learn about the pseudo-ops for segments.

Segment Pseudo-Ops

We have several pseudo-ops to cover here: SEGMENT, ENDS, ASSUME, and the NEAR and FAR from the PROC pseudo-op. We also need to take a closer look at the CALL and RET instructions. When we've covered all this ground, we'll learn more about the INT instruction and see how it is similar to

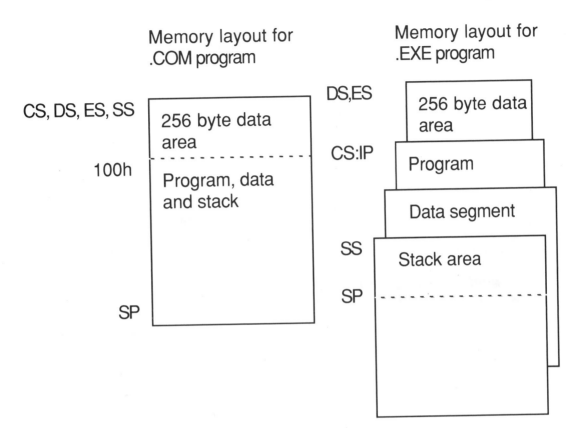

Figure 11-4. .COM vs .EXE Programs.

a CALL instruction. But let's take these all in order, beginning with SEG-MENT and ENDS.

The SEGMENT and ENDS pseudo-ops are much like the PROC and ENDP pseudo-ops we encountered in Chapter 9. We define a segment by surrounding part of the source file with a SEGMENT/ENDS pair, just as we defined a procedure with a PROC/ENDP pair. The name before the SEGMENT pseudo-op is a label.

We'll use this label in Chapter 13, when we divide our source file into many different source files and two segments; a data segment and a code segment. With two segments, we can easily separate the variables in memory from our program. There will be more on memory variables, too, in Chapter 13, and we'll also add more pieces to the SEGMENT pseudo-op. There are myriad details, though, and we won't spend much time on them. You can find the information in your assembler manual if you need it.

The ASSUME Pseudo-Op

The ASSUME pseudo-op is slightly trickier than SEGMENT. It provides the assembler with information about segments and how we want to use the segment registers. To understand ASSUME, we need to understand how the assembler keeps track of labels and variable names.

Every time you create a label, such as a procedure (like WRITE_CHAR PROC NEAR) or a memory variable, the assembler remembers several pieces of information along with the name: the type (procedure, byte, word, and so on), the address of the name, and the segment in which it is defined. This last piece of information is where ASSUME becomes involved.

The assembler doesn't automatically assume that all the procedures of a program are in the same segment. In many cases, such as for large programs like Lotus 1-2-3, they aren't. Such programs actually use a number of different code segments. So in the interest of generality, we need to provide information to the assembler in the form of ASSUME statements, which tell the assembler which segments the segment registers are pointing to.

For example, let's look at the ASSUME statement we used in previous chapters:

```
ASSUME  CS:CODE_SEG
```

This ASSUME statement tells the assembler that the CS register is pointing to the code segment we named CODE_SEG. Without this information, the assembler will throw up its hands whenever we try to use a label (as in CALL WRITE_CHAR), saying that it doesn't know which segment we're currently in with the message *No or unreachable CS*.

Since the CS register is always pointing to the code that we're executing, it may seem a bit odd that the assembler complains when we have no ASSUME statement. As a matter of fact, we wouldn't need the ASSUME pseudo-op, if it weren't for something called *segment overrides*.

The 8088 normally reads data (as in MOV AL,SOME_VARIABLE) from the data segment (DS). But it can also read information from any other segment, such as the code segment (CS), by using a segment override. And this is why the assembler needs the ASSUME pseudo-op: so that it knows which segment register to use when you read or write memory.

Don't worry if you didn't quite understand this explanation of the ASSUME pseudo-op. We'll be making minimal use of it until we reach Chapter 29. There, we'll learn more about both the ASSUME pseudo-op and segment overrides, when we look at multiple-segment programs.

The rest of the information in this chapter is purely for your interest, since we won't be making use of it in this book. You can skip the next two sections and read them later if you find the going tough or you're anxious to get back to programming.

Near and Far CALLs

Let's step back for a minute and take a closer look at the CALL instructions we used in previous chapters. Specifically, let's look at the short program in Chapter 7, where we first learned about the CALL instruction. Back then, we wrote a very short program that looked like this (without the procedure at 200h):

```
3985:0100 B241      MOV    DL,41
3985:0102 B90A00    MOV    CX,000A
3985:0105 E8F800    CALL   0200
3985:0108 E2FB      LOOP   0105
3985:010A CD20      INT    20
```

You can see by looking at the machine code on the left that the CALL instruction occupies only three bytes (E8F800). The first byte (E8h) is the CALL instruction, and the second two bytes form an offset. The 8088 calculates the address of the routine we're calling by adding this offset of 00F8h (remember that the 8088 stores the lower byte of a word in memory *before* the high byte, so we have to reverse the bytes) to the address of the next instruction (108h in our program). In this case, then, we have F8h + 108h = 200h. Just what we expected.

The fact that this instruction uses a single word for the offset means that CALLs are limited to a single segment, which is 64K bytes long. So how is it that we can write a program like Lotus 1-2-3 that is larger than 64K? We do it by using FAR, rather than NEAR, calls.

NEAR CALLs, as we've seen, are limited to a single segment. In other words, they change the IP register without affecting the CS register. And for this reason they're sometimes known as *intrasegment* CALLs.

But we can also have FAR CALLs that change both the CS and IP registers.

Such CALLs are often known as *intersegment* CALLs because they call procedures in other segments.

Going along with these two versions of the CALL instruction are two versions of the RET instruction.

The NEAR CALL, as we saw in Chapter 7, pushes a single word onto the stack for its return address. And the corresponding RET instruction pops this word off the stack and into the IP register.

In the case of FAR CALLs and RETs, a word is not sufficient, because we're dealing with another segment. In other words, we need to save a two-word return address on the stack: one word for the instruction pointer (IP) and the other for the code segment (CS). The FAR RET, then, pops two words off the stack—one for the CS register, and the other for IP.

Now we come to a sticky issue. How does the assembler know which of these two CALLs and RETs to use? When should it use the FAR CALL, and when should it use the NEAR CALL? This is where the NEAR and FAR pseudo-ops take command.

By way of example, look at the following program:

```
PROC_ONE        PROC    FAR
        .
        .
        .
        RET
PROC_ONE        ENDP

PROC_TWO        PROC    NEAR
        CALL    PROC_ONE
        .
        .
        .
        RET
PROC_TWO        ENDP
```

When the assembler sees the CALL PROC_ONE instruction, it hunts in its table for the definition of PROC_ONE, which, in this case, is PROC_ONE PROC FAR. This definition tells whether the procedure is a near or far procedure.

In the case of a NEAR procedure, the assembler generates a NEAR CALL. And conversely, it generates a FAR CALL if the procedure you're calling was defined as a FAR procedure. In other words, the assembler uses the definition of the procedure that you're *calling* to determine the type of CALL instruction that's needed.

For the RET instruction, on the other hand, the assembler looks at the defi-

PROC_TWO PROC NEAR
CALL PROC_ONE

.
.
.

RET
PROC_TWO ENDP

PROC_ONE PROC FAR

.
.

RET
PROC_ONE ENDP

Figure 11-5. The Assembler Produces a FAR CALL.

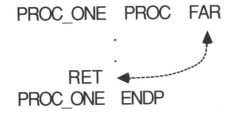

PROC_ONE PROC FAR

.
.

RET
PROC_ONE ENDP

Figure 11-6. The Assembler Produces a FAR RET.

nition of the procedure that contains the RET instruction. In our program, the RET instruction for PROC_ONE will be a FAR RET, because PROC_ONE is declared to be a FAR procedure. Likewise, the RET in PROC_TWO is a NEAR RET.

More on the INT Instruction

The INT instruction is much like a CALL instruction, but with a minor difference. The name INT comes from the word *interrupt*. An interrupt is an external signal that causes the 8088 to execute a procedure and then return to what it was doing before it received the interrupt. An INT instruction doesn't interrupt the 8088, but it's treated as if it did.

When the 8088 receives an interrupt, it needs to store more information on the stack than just the two words for the return address. It has to store the values of the status flags—the carry flag, the zero flag, and so on. These values are stored in one word known as the Flag Register, and the 8088 pushes this information onto the stack before the return address. Here's why we need to save the status flags.

Your IBM PC regularly responds to a number of different interrupts. The 8088 inside your IBM PC receives an interrupt from the clock 18.2 times every second, for example. Each of these interrupts causes the 8088 to stop what it's doing and execute a procedure to count the clock pulses.

Now, envision such an interrupt occurring between these two program instructions:

```
CMP     AH,2
JNE     NOT_2
```

Let's assume AH = 2, so the zero flag will be set after the CMP instruction, which means that the JNE instruction will not branch to NOT_2.

Now, imagine that the clock interrupts the 8088 between these two instructions. That means the 8088 runs off to carry out the interrupt procedure before it checks the zero flag (with the JNE instruction). If the 8088 didn't save and restore the flag registers, the JNE instruction would use flags set by the interrupt procedure, *not* from our CMP instruction. To prevent such disasters, the 8088 *always* saves and restores the flag register for interrupts. An interrupt saves the flags, and an IRET (*Interrupt Return*) instruction restores the flags at the end of the interrupt procedure.

The same is true for an INT instruction. Thus, after executing the instruction:

```
INT     21
```

the 8088's stack will look like this:

```
Top of stack →      Old IP (return address part I)
                    Old CS (return address part II)
                    Old Flag Register
```

(The stack grows into lower memory, so the top-of-stack is below the Old Flag Register).

When we place an INT instruction in a program, however, the interrupt is no surprise. Why, then, do we want to save the flags? Isn't saving the flags useful only when we have an external interrupt that comes at an unpredictable time? As it turns out, the answer is no. There is a very good reason for saving and restoring the flags for INT instructions. In fact, without this feature, Debug wouldn't be possible.

Debug uses a special flag in the flag register called the Trap Flag. This flag puts the 8088 into a special mode known as *single-step* mode, which Debug uses to trace through programs one instruction at a time. When the trap flag is set, the 8088 issues an INT 1 after it executes any instruction.

The INT 1 also clears the trap flag, so the 8088 won't be in single-step mode while we're inside Debug's INT 1 procedure. But since INT 1 saved the flags to the stack, issuing an IRET to return to the program we're debugging restores the trap flag. Then, we'll receive another INT 1 interrupt after the next instruction in our program. This is just one example of when it's useful to save the flag registers. But, as we'll see next, this restore-flag feature isn't always appropriate.

Some interrupt procedures bypass the restoration of the flag registers. For example, the INT 21h procedure in DOS sometimes changes the flag registers by short-circuiting the normal return process. Many of the INT 21h procedures that read or write disk information return with the carry flag set if there was an error of some sort (such as no disk in the drive).

Interrupt Vectors

Where do these interrupt instructions get the addresses for procedures? Each interrupt instruction has an interrupt number, such as the 21h in INT 21h. The 8088 finds addresses for interrupt procedures in a table of *interrupt vectors*, which is located at the very bottom of memory. For example, the two-word address for the INT 21h procedure is at 0000:0084. We get this address by multiplying the interrupt number by 4 (4 * 21h = 84h), since we need four bytes, two words, for each vector, or procedure address.

These vectors are exceedingly useful for adding features to DOS, because they enable us to intercept calls to interrupt procedures by changing the addresses in the vector table. We won't do that in this book, though. Such tricks are too advanced for us just now.

All these ideas and methods should become clearer as we see more examples. Most of this book from here on will be filled with examples, so there will be plenty to study. If you've been feeling a bit overwhelmed by new information, rest easy. We'll take a short breather in the next chapter, and get ourselves reoriented and back on course.

Summary

As we said, this chapter contained a lot of information. We won't use it all, but we did need to learn more about segments. Chapter 13 will bring us to modular design, and we'll use some aspects of segments to make our job easier.

We began this chapter by learning how the 8088 divides memory into segments. To understand segments in more detail, we built an .EXE program with two different segments. We won't use .EXE programs in this book, but an .EXE program demonstrated the idea of segments nicely here.

We also found that the 100h (256 byte) scratch area at the start of our programs contains a copy of what we typed on the command line. Again, we won't use this knowledge in this book, but it helps us see why DOS sets aside such a large chunk of memory for the purpose.

And, we finally got around to learning about the SEGMENT, ENDS, ASSUME, NEAR, and FAR pseudo-ops. These are all pseudo-ops that help us work with segments. In this book, we'll barely use the power of these pseudo-ops, because our .COM programs will use only one segment. But for programmers who write *huge* programs in assembly language, these pseudo-ops are invaluable. If you're interested, you'll find the details in your macro assembler manual.

At the very end of this chapter we learned more about the roots of our helpful INT instruction. Now, we're just about ready to slow down and learn how to *write* larger and more useful assembly language programs.

12

COURSE CORRECTIONS

We've been poking our noses into a lot of new and interesting places, and you may, at times, have wondered whether we've been wandering about somewhat aimlessly. We haven't been, of course. We're now familiar enough with our new surroundings to fix our sights and plot a course for the rest of this book. And that's what we'll do in this chapter: We'll take a close look at a design for our Dskpatch program. Then we'll spend the rest of this book developing Dskpatch, much as you will later develop programs of your own.

We won't present the finished version of Dskpatch all at once; that isn't the way we wrote it. Instead, we'll present short test programs to check each stage of our program as we write it. To do this, we need to know where we want to go. Hence, our course correction here.

Since Dskpatch will deal with information on disks, that's where we'll begin.

Diskettes, Sectors, and Dskpatch

The information on your floppy disks is divided into *sectors*, with each sector holding 512 bytes of information. A double-sided disk formatted with DOS 2.0 or above has a total of 720 sectors, or 720 * 512 = 368,640 bytes. If we could look directly at these sectors, we could examine the directory directly, or we could look at the files on the disk. We can't—not by ourselves—but Dskpatch will. Let's use Debug to learn more about sectors and get an idea of how we'll display a sector with Dskpatch.

Debug has a command, L (*Load*), to read sectors from disk into memory, where we can look at the data. As an example, let's look at the directory that starts at sector 5 on a double-sided disk. Load sector 5 from the disk in drive A (that's drive 0 to Debug) by using the L command like this:

```
-L 100 0 5 1
```

As you can see in Figure 12-1, this command loads sectors into memory, starting with sector 5 and continuing through one sector at an offset of 100 within the data segment. To display sector 5, we can use a Dump command:

```
-D 100
396F:0100  49 42 4D 42 49 4F 20 20-43 4F 4D 27 00 00 00 00   IBMBIO  COM'....
396F:0110  00 00 00 00 00 00 00 60-68 06 02 00 00 12 00 00   .......`h.......
396F:0120  49 42 4D 44 4F 53 20 20-43 4F 4D 27 00 00 00 00   IBMDOS  COM'....
```

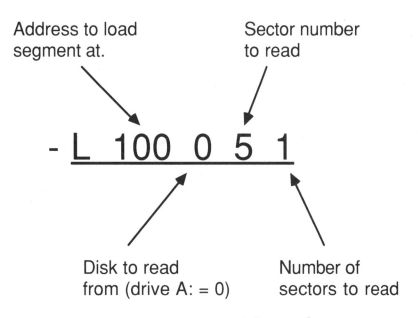

Figure 12-1.   DEBUG's Load Command.

```
396F:0130  00 00 00 00 00 00 00 60-68 06 07 00 00 43 00 00   .......`h....C..
396F:0140  43 4F 4D 4D 41 4E 44 20-43 4F 4D 20 00 00 00 00   COMMAND COM ....
396F:0150  00 00 00 00 00 00 00 60-68 06 18 00 00 45 00 00   .......`h....E..
396F:0160  41 53 53 45 4D 42 4C 45-52 20 20 08 00 00 00 00   ASSEMBLER  .....
396F:0170  00 00 00 00 00 00 33 9C-B0 06 00 00 00 00 00 00   ......3.0.......
-D
396F:0180  46 57 20 20 20 20 20 20-43 4F 4D 20 00 00 00 00   FW      COM ....
396F:0190  00 00 00 00 00 00 00 00-6F 05 2A 00 80 AF 00 00   ........o.*../..
396F:01A0  46 57 20 20 20 20 20 20-4F 56 4C 20 00 00 00 00   FW      OVL ....
396F:01B0  00 00 00 00 00 00 00 00-72 05 56 00 81 02 00 00   ........r.V.....
396F:01C0  46 57 20 20 20 20 20 20-53 57 50 20 00 00 00 00   FW      SWP ....
396F:01D0  00 00 00 00 00 00 9B 8A-FF 06 57 00 00 C8 00 00   ..........W..H..
396F:01E0  43 4F 4E 46 49 47 20 20-44 41 54 20 00 00 00 00   CONFIG  DAT ....
396F:01F0  00 00 00 00 00 00 1D 82-A1 06 89 00 00 28 00 00   ........!....(..
```

We'll use a format much like this for Dskpatch, but with many improvements. Dskpatch will be the equivalent of a full-screen editor for disk sectors. We'll be able to display sectors on the screen and move the cursor about the sector display, changing numbers or characters as we want. We'll also be able to write this altered sector back to the disk, and this is why we call it Disk Patch—or rather Dskpatch, since we can't have more than eight characters in the name.

Dskpatch is the motivation for the procedures we write. It is by no means an end in itself. In using Dskpatch as an example for this book, we'll also manage to present many procedures that you'll find useful when you attempt to write your own programs. That means you'll find many general-purpose procedures for display output, display manipulation, keyboard input, and more.

Let's take a closer look at some improvements we'll make to Debug's sector dump. The display from Debug only shows the "printable" characters—96 out of the 256 different characters that an IBM PC can display. Why is that? Because MS-DOS, PC-DOS's cousin, runs on many different computers. Some of these computers display only 96 characters, so Microsoft (the author of Debug) chose to write one version of Debug that would work on all machines.

Dskpatch is for IBM Personal Computers and near cousins, so we can display all 256 different characters; to do so will require a bit of work. Using the DOS function 2 for character output, we can display almost all characters, but DOS gives special meaning to some, such as 7, which rings the bell. There are characters for special codes like 7, and in Part III we'll see how to display them.

We'll also make heavy use of the function keys so that, for example, we can display the next sector just by pressing the F2 key. And we'll be able to change any byte by moving the cursor to that byte and typing in a new number. It will be just like using a word processor, where we can change characters very easily. More of these details will appear as we slowly build Dskpatch. (Figure 12-2 shows what its normal display will look like—a vast improvement over the display from Debug.)

The Game Plan

In Chapter 13, we'll learn how to break our program into many different source files. Then, we'll begin serious work on Dskpatch in Chapter 14. At the end, we'll have nine source files for Dskpatch that have to be linked together. And even if you don't enter and run all these programs now, they'll be here when you're ready for them, or when you want to borrow some of the general-purpose procedures. In any case, you'll get a better idea of how to write long programs as you read through the following chapters.

We've already created several useful procedures, such as WRITE_HEX to write a byte as a two-digit hex number and WRITE_DECIMAL to write a number in decimal. Now, we'll write some programs to display a block of memory in much the same way Debug's D command does. We'll start by displaying 16 bytes of memory, one line of Debug's display, and then work

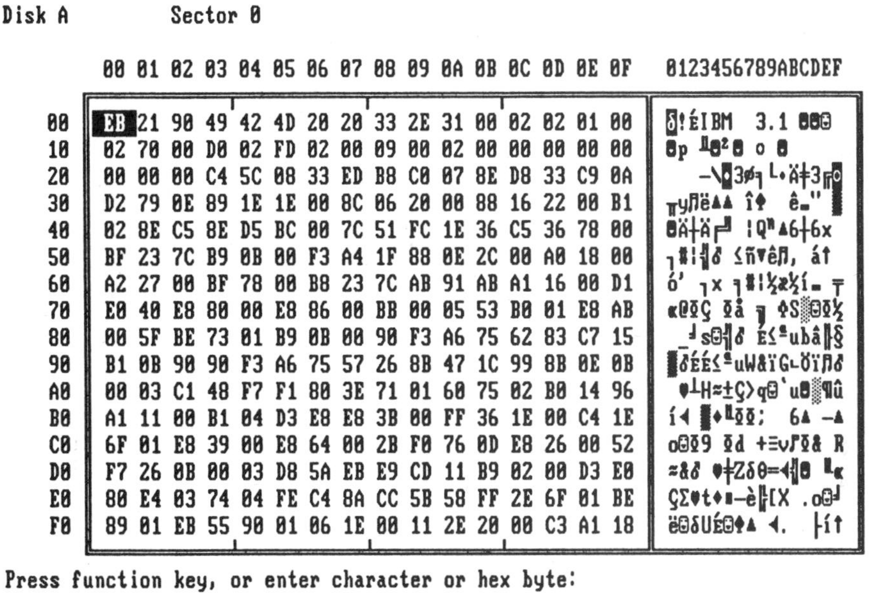

Disk A   Sector 0

```
     00 01 02 03 04 05 06 07 08 09 0A 0B 0C 0D 0E 0F   0123456789ABCDEF

00   EB 21 90 49 42 4D 20 20 33 2E 31 00 02 02 01 00   δ!éIBM  3.1 ☺☺☺
10   02 70 00 D0 02 FD 02 00 09 00 02 00 00 00 00 00   ☻p ▐☻²☺ o ☻
20   00 00 00 C4 5C 00 33 ED B8 C0 07 8E D8 33 C9 0A   –\� 3♪┐ L·Ä‡3╓♂
30   D2 79 0E 89 1E 1E 00 8C 06 20 00 88 16 22 00 B1   ┬y♫ë▲▲ î♦  ê."▌
40   02 8E C5 8E D5 BC 00 7C 51 FC 1E 36 C5 36 78 00   ☻Ä┼Ä╒┘ |Q▪▲6┼6x
50   BF 23 7C B9 0B 00 F3 A4 1F 88 8E 2C 00 A0 18 00   ┐#|┤♂ ≤ñvê╖, á↑
60   A2 27 00 BF 78 00 B8 23 7C AB 91 AB A1 16 00 D1   ó' ┐x ┐#|½æ½í▬ ┬
70   E0 40 E8 80 00 E8 86 00 BB 00 05 53 B0 01 E8 AB   α@Θ╜ ☼å ╗ ♣S░☺Θ½
80   00 5F BE 73 01 B9 0B 00 90 F3 A6 75 62 83 C7 15   _┐s♦ ┤♂ É≤¦ubâ╟§
90   B1 0B 90 90 F3 A6 75 57 26 8B 47 1C 99 8B 0E 0B   ▌♂ÉÉ≤¦uW&ïG∟Öï♫♂
A0   00 03 C1 48 F7 F1 80 3E 71 01 60 75 02 B0 14 96   ♥┴H≈±ç>q♦'u░¶û
B0   A1 11 00 B1 04 D3 E8 E8 3B 00 FF 36 1E 00 C4 1E   í◄ ▌♦╙ΘΘ; 6▲ ─▲
C0   6F 01 E8 39 00 E8 64 00 2B F0 76 0D E8 26 00 52   o☺Θ9 Θd +≡▌¶Θ& R
D0   F7 26 0B 00 03 D8 5A EB E9 CD 11 B9 02 00 D3 E0   ≈&♂ ♥▐Zδθ═◄┤☻ ╙α
E0   80 E4 03 74 04 FE C4 8A CC 5B 58 FF 2E 6F 01 BE   çΣ▪♦■─è╠[X .o☺▒
F0   89 01 EB 55 90 01 06 1E 00 11 2E 20 00 C3 A1 18   ë☺δUÉ☺♠▲ ◄. ├í↑
```

Press function key, or enter character or hex byte:

Figure 12-2.   **Example of Dskpatch's Display.**

toward displaying 16 lines of 16 bytes each (half a sector). A full sector won't fit on the display at one time with the format we've chosen, so Dskpatch includes procedures for scrolling through a sector using the ROM BIOS—not DOS—interrupts. That will come much later, though, after we've built a full-screen display of half a sector.

Once we can dump 256 bytes from memory, we'll build another procedure to read a sector from the disk into our area of memory. We'll dump half a sector on the screen, and we'll be able to use Debug to alter our program, so we can dump different sectors. At that point, we'll have a functional, but not very attractive display, so making it pretty comes next.

With a bit more work and some more procedures, we'll rebuild the half-sector display to be much more pleasing aesthetically. It still won't be a full-screen display, so it will just scroll past like Debug's dump did. But the full-screen display will come next, and through it, we'll learn about the ROM BIOS routines that allow us to control the display, move the cursor . . . that sort of thing. Then, we'll be ready to learn how to use more ROM BIOS routines to print all 256 different characters.

Next will come the keyboard input and command procedures that will let us start interacting with Dskpatch. About that time we'll also need another course correction.

Summary

We've seen enough of the future here. You should have a better idea of where we're headed, so let's move on to the next chapter, where we'll lay the groundwork for modular design and learn how to split a program into many different source files. Then, in Chapter 14, we'll write some test procedures to display sections of memory.

13

MODULAR DESIGN

Without modular design, Dskpatch wouldn't have been much fun to write. Using a modular design greatly eases the task of writing any but the smallest program. We'll use this chapter to set some ground rules for modular design, and we'll follow those rules throughout the rest of this book. Let's begin by learning how to separate a large program into many different source files.

Separate Assembling

In Chapter 10, we added the procedure WRITE_DECIMAL to VIDEO_ IO.ASM, and we also added a short test procedure called TEST_WRITE_ DECIMAL. Let's take this test procedure out of VIDEO_IO.ASM and put it in a file of its own, called TEST.ASM. Then, we'll assemble these two files separately and link them together into one program. Here is the TEST.ASM file:

Listing 13-1. The File TEST.ASM

```
CODE_SEG        SEGMENT PUBLIC
        ASSUME  CS:CODE_SEG
        ORG     100h

        EXTRN   WRITE_DECIMAL:NEAR

TEST_WRITE_DECIMAL      PROC    NEAR
        MOV     DX,12345
        CALL    WRITE_DECIMAL
        INT     20h                     ;Return to DOS
TEST_WRITE_DECIMAL      ENDP

CODE_SEG        ENDS

        END     TEST_WRITE_DECIMAL
```

We've seen most of this source file before, but some of it is new, so let's begin at the top and work our way down. First, the word *PUBLIC* now appears after SEGMENT. This tells the assembler we want this segment (CODE_SEG) combined into one segment along with all other segments that have the same name—the code segment, in this case. The assembler just passes this information on to the linker, which, as its name implies, *links* different files. The linker does the work of stitching the different pieces of each segment together.

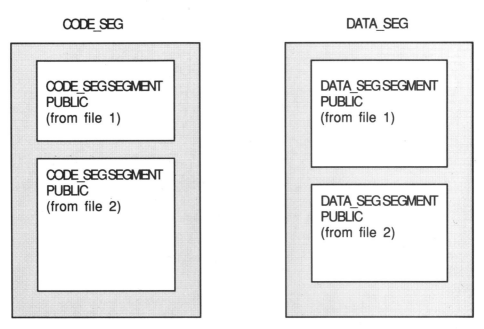

CODE_SEG

DATA_SEG

Figure 13-1.   LINK Stitches Together Segments From Different Files.

Our file now contains the EXTRN pseudo-op. The statement EXTRN-WRITE_DECIMAL:NEAR tells the assembler two things: that WRITE_DECIMAL is in another, *external*, file, and that it's defined as a NEAR procedure in that file, so it should be in the same segment. The assembler thus generates a NEAR CALL for this procedure; it would generate a FAR CALL if we had placed a FAR after WRITE_DECIMAL.

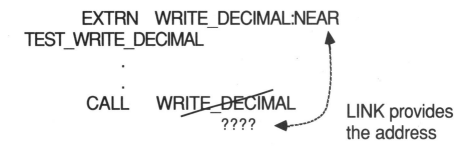

Figure 13-2.   LINK Assigns the Addresses for External Names.

These are about the only changes we need for separate source files until we begin to store data in memory. At that point, we'll introduce another segment for data. Now, let's modify VIDEO_IO.ASM, and then assemble and link these two files.

Remove the procedure TEST_WRITE_DECIMAL from VIDEO_IO.ASM. We've placed this in TEST.ASM, so we don't need it in Video_io. Then, remove the ORG 100h statement from Video_io. We moved this, too, to TEST.ASM, which now has the first procedure in our program. As we saw in Chapter 11, the ORG 100h statement is needed to save 256 bytes for the scratch area at the beginning of our program—that is, before TEST_WRITE_ DECIMAL in the source file TEST.ASM.

Next, we have to put the word *PUBLIC* after SEGMENT, like this:

```
CODE_SEG      SEGMENT PUBLIC
```

so the linker will know that it should combine this segment with the same segment in TEST.ASM.

Finally, change END TEST_WRITE_DECIMAL at the end of VIDEO_ IO.ASM to just END. Once again, we moved the main procedure to TEST.ASM. The procedures in VIDEO_IO.ASM are now *external* procedures, nothing more. That is, they have no function by themselves; they must be linked to procedures that call them from other files. We don't need a name after the END pseudo-op in VIDEO_IO.ASM, because our main program is now in TEST.ASM.

When you've finished making these changes, your VIDEO_IO.ASM source file should look something like this:

```
CODE_SEG      SEGMENT PUBLIC
       ASSUME CS:CODE_SEG

       PUBLIC  WRITE_HEX_DIGIT
          .
          .
          .
WRITE_HEX_DIGIT      ENDP

       PUBLIC  WRITE_HEX
          .
          .
          .
WRITE_HEX      ENDP
```

```
        PUBLIC   WRITE_CHAR
            .
            .
            .
WRITE_CHAR      ENDP

        PUBLIC   WRITE_DECIMAL
            .
            .
            .
WRITE_DECIMAL   ENDP

CODE_SEG        ENDS

        END
```

with an ASSUME at the the start.

Assemble these two files just as you assembled Video_io before. TEST.ASM knows all it needs to know about VIDEO_IO.ASM through the EXTRN statement. The rest will come when we link the two files.

You should now have the files TEST.OBJ and VIDEO_IO.OBJ. Use the following command to link these two files into one program named TEST.EXE:

```
A>LINK TEST VIDEO_IO;
```

LINK stitches the procedures of these two files together to create one file containing the entire program. It uses the first file name we entered as the name for the resulting .EXE file, so we now have TEST.EXE.

Finally, create a .COM file, just as you did before, by typing *EXE2BIN TEST TEST.COM*. That's it, we created one program from two source files. The final .COM program is identical to the version we created from the single file VIDEO_IO.ASM, when it contained the main procedure TEST_WRITE_DECIMAL.

We'll make heavy use of separate source files from here on, and their value will become clearer as the procedures stack up. In the next chapter, we'll write a test program to dump sections of memory in hex. We'll usually write a simple test version of a procedure before we write the complete version. Doing so will allow us to see how to write a good final version, as well as saving much effort and mental turmoil in the process.

There are several other useful ways to save effort. We call them the *Three Laws of Modular Design*.

The Three Laws of Modular Design

These laws are summarized in Table 13-1. They aren't really *laws*, they're suggestions. But we'll use them throughout this book. Define your own laws if you like, but either way, stick to the same ones all the time. Your job will be much easier if you're consistent.

Table 13-1. The Three Laws of Modular Design

1. Save and restore <u>all</u> registers, *unless* the procedure returns a value in that register.

2. Be consistent about which registers you use to pass information. For example:
   * DL, DX—Send byte and word values.
   * AL, AX—Return byte and word values.
   * BX:AX—Return double-word values.
   * DS:DX—Send and return addresses.
   * CX—Repeat counts and other counts.
   * CF—Set when there is an error; an error code should be returned in one of the registers, such as AL or AX.

3. Define <u>all</u> external interactions in the comment header:
   * Information needed on entry.
   * Information returned (registers changed).
   * Procedures called.
   * Variables used (read, written, and so on).

There's an obvious parallel between modular design in programming and modular design in engineering. An electrical engineer, for example, can build a very complicated piece of equipment from boxes that perform different functions, without knowing how each box works. But if each box uses different voltages and different connections, the lack of consistency creates a major headache for the poor engineer, who must somehow provide a different voltage for each box and create special connections between boxes. Not much fun, but fortunately for the engineer, there are standards providing for only a small number of standard voltages. So, perhaps only four different voltages need to be provided, instead of a different voltage for each box.

Modular design and standard interfaces are just as important in assembly-language programs, and that's why we'll lay down the laws (so to speak), and use those laws from here on. As you'll see by the end of this book, these rules will make our task much simpler. Let's take a look at these laws in detail.

Save and restore *all* **registers,** *unless* **the procedure returns a value in that register.**   There aren't that many registers in the 8088. By saving registers at the start of a procedure, we free them for use within that procedure. But we must be careful to restore them at the end of the procedure. You'll see us doing this in all our procedures, with PUSH instructions appearing first in each procedure, and POPs at the end.

The only exception is for procedures that must return some information to the calling procedure. For example, a procedure that reads a character from the keyboard must somehow return the character. We won't save any registers that we use to return information.

Short procedures also help the register-shortage problem. At times, we'll write a procedure that's used only once. Not only does this help with the shortage of registers, it also makes the program easier to write and, often, easier to read. We'll see more of this as we write procedures for Dskpatch.

Be consistent about which registers you use to pass information. Our job becomes simpler if we set standards for exchanging information between procedures. We'll use one register for sending information, and one for receiving information. We'll also need to send addresses for long pieces of data, and for this we'll use the pair of registers DS:DX, so that our data can be anywhere in memory. You'll learn more about this when we introduce a new segment for data and begin to make use of the DS register.

We reserve the CX register for repeat counts. We'll soon write a procedure to write one character several times, so that we can write ten spaces by calling this procedure (WRITE_CHAR_N_TIMES) with CX set to 10. We'll use the CX register whenever we have a repeat count or when we want to return some count, such as the number of characters read from the keyboard (we'll do this when we write a procedure named READ_STRING).

Finally, we'll set the Carry Flag (CF) whenever there is an error, and we'll clear it whenever there isn't an error. Not all procedures use the carry flags. For example, WRITE_CHAR always works, so there's no reason to return an error report. But a procedure that writes to the disk can encounter many errors (no disk, write-protection, and so on). In this case, we'll use a register to return an error code. There's no standard here, because DOS uses different registers for different functions. Its fault, not ours.

Define all external interactions in the comment header.   There's no need to learn how a procedure works if all we want to do is use it, and this is why we place a detailed comment header before each procedure. This header

contains all the information we need to know. It tells us what to place in each
register before calling the procedure, and it tells what information the procedure returns. Most procedures use registers for their variables, but some of
the procedures we'll soon see use variables in memory. The comment header
should say which of these memory variables are read and which are changed.
And lastly, each header should list other procedures called. Here is an example of a full-blown header with much of this information:

```
;----------------------------------------------------------------------;
; This is an example of a full-blown header.  This part would normally  ;
; be a brief description of what this procedure does.  For example,     ;
; this procedure will write the message "Sector   " on the first line.  ;
;                                                                       ;
;        DS:DX    Address of the message "Sector   "                    ;
;                                                                       ;
; Calls:          GOTO_XY, WRITE_STRING  (procedures called)            ;
; Reads:          STATUS_LINE_NO         (memory variables read only)   ;
; Writes:         DUMMY                  (memory variables altered)     ;
;----------------------------------------------------------------------;
```

Whenever we want to use any procedure we've written, we can just glance
at this comment header to learn how to use it. There will be no need to delve
into the inner workings of the procedure to find out what it does.

These laws make assembly language programming easier, and we'll be certain to abide by them, but not necessarily on the first try—we often won't. The
first version of a procedure or program is a test case. Frequently, we don't
know exactly how to write the program we have in mind, so on these "rough
drafts," we'll write the program without concern for the laws of modular design. We'll just plow through and get something that works. Then we can
backtrack and do a good job by rewriting each procedure to conform to these
laws.

Programming is a process that goes by leaps and bounds. Throughout this
book we'll show much of the stuttering that went into writing Dskpatch, but
we certainly can't show it all. There isn't room enough to contain all the versions we wrote before we settled on the final version. Our first tries often bore
very little resemblance to the final versions you'll see, so when you write programs, don't worry about getting everything right the first time. Be prepared
to rewrite each procedure as you learn more about what you really want.

In the next chapter, we'll build a simple test program to print a block of
memory. It won't be the final version; we'll go through others before we're
satisfied, and even then, there will be other changes we'd like to make. The
moral is: A program is never done . . . but we must stop somewhere.

Summary

This has been a chapter for you to remember and use in the future. We began by learning how to separate a program into a number of different source files that we can assemble independently, then stitch together with the linker. We used the PUBLIC and EXTRN pseudo-ops to inform the linker that there are connections between different source files. PUBLIC says that other source files can CALL the procedures named after PUBLICs, while EXTRN tells the assembler that the procedure we want to use is in another file.

We also used PUBLIC after the SEGMENT definition so that the linker will stitch together segments of the same name that are in different source files.

Then we moved on to the Three Laws of Modular Design. These rules are meant to make your programming job simpler, so use them when you write your own programs, just as you'll see us use them in this book. You'll find it easier to write, debug, and read programs if they conform to these Three Laws.

14

DUMPING MEMORY

From here on, we'll concentrate on building Dskpatch in much the same way we originally wrote it. Some of the instructions in procedures to come may be unfamiliar; we'll explain each briefly as we come across them, but for detailed information, you'll need a book that covers all of the instructions in detail.

Rather than cover all the 8088 instructions, we'll concentrate on new concepts, such as the different modes of addressing memory, which we'll cover in this chapter. In Part III, we'll move even farther away from the details of instructions and begin to see information specific to the IBM Personal Computer and its near cousins.

Now, let's learn about *addressing modes* by writing a short test program to dump 16 bytes of memory in hex notation. To begin, we need to learn how to use memory as variables.

Addressing Modes

We've seen two addressing modes; they're known as the *register* and *immediate* addressing modes. The first one we learned about was the register mode, which uses registers as variables. For example, the instruction:

```
MOV     AX,BX
```

uses the two registers AX and BX as variables.

Then, we moved on to the immediate addressing mode, in which we moved a number directly into a register, as in the example:

```
MOV     AX,2
```

This moves the byte or word of memory *immediately* following the instruction into a register. In this sense, the MOV instruction in our example is one byte long, with two more bytes for the data (0002):

```
396F:0100 B80200        MOV     AX,0002
```

The instruction is B8h, and the two bytes of data (02h and 00h) follow this (remember that the 8088 stores the low byte, 02h, first in memory).

Now, we'll learn how to use memory as a variable. The immediate mode allows us to read the piece of fixed memory immediately following that one instruction, but it doesn't allow us to change memory. For this, we'll need other addressing modes.

Let's begin with an example. The following program reads 16 bytes of memory, one byte at a time, and displays each byte in hex notation, with a single space between each of the 16 hex numbers. Enter the program into the file DISP_SEC.ASM and assemble it. Later, we'll want to change VIDEO_ IO.ASM slightly, but first, let's take care of DISP_SEC.ASM:

Listing 14-1. The New File DISP_SEC.ASM

```
CGROUP  GROUP   CODE_SEG, DATA_SEG     ;Group two segments together
        ASSUME  CS:CGROUP, DS:CGROUP


CODE_SEG        SEGMENT      PUBLIC
        ORG     100h

        EXTRN   WRITE_HEX:NEAR
        EXTRN   WRITE_CHAR:NEAR
;------------------------------------------------------------------;
; This is a simple test program to dump 16 bytes of memory as hex  ;
; numbers, all on one line.                                        ;
;------------------------------------------------------------------;
DISP_LINE       PROC    NEAR
        XOR     BX,BX                  ;Set BX to 0
        MOV     CX,16                  ;Dump 16 bytes
HEX_LOOP:
        MOV     DL,SECTOR[BX]          ;Get 1 byte
        CALL    WRITE_HEX              ;Dump this byte in hex
        MOV     DL,' '                 ;Write a space between numbers
        CALL    WRITE_CHAR
        INC     BX
        LOOP    HEX_LOOP
        INT     20h                    ;Return to DOS
DISP_LINE       ENDP

CODE_SEG        ENDS


DATA_SEG        SEGMENT PUBLIC
        PUBLIC  SECTOR
SECTOR  DB      10h, 11h, 12h, 13h, 14h, 15h, 16h, 17h  ;Test pattern
        DB      18h, 19h, 1Ah, 1Bh, 1Ch, 1Dh, 1Eh, 1Fh
DATA_SEG        ENDS


        END     DISP_LINE
```

Notice that we've put the data segment (DATA_SEG) *after* the code segment (CODE_SEG). We've put it at the end of the file so the linker will load the data in memory at the end of our program.

We've also added a few new tricks to this program, and for this reason we need to make some small changes to VIDEO_IO.ASM. First, remove the ASSUME statement in Video_io and place the following two lines at the beginning of VIDEO_IO.ASM:

```
CGROUP  GROUP   CODE_SEG                ;Group two segments together
        ASSUME  CS:CGROUP
```

We'll place these two lines at the beginning of each file from now on, with one slight variation. We'll write:

```
CGROUP  GROUP   CODE_SEG, DATA_SEG      ;Group two segments together
        ASSUME  CS:CGROUP, DS:CGROUP
```

(with DATA_SEG) whenever we have both a code segment and a data segment in the file.

The ASSUME here replaces the old ASSUME, and we'll see later what these two statements actually do. But now, let's try our new program to see how it works. Assemble both Disp_sec and Video_io.

We're ready to link DISP_SEC.OBJ and VIDEO_IO.OBJ and run the result through Exe2bin, so first use LINK to create an .EXE file named DISP_SEC.EXE. The first file name in the LINK command must be the name of the file that contains the main procedure (Disp_sec in this case), and a semicolon must appear at the end of the list of files, so type:

```
A>LINK DISP_SEC VIDEO_IO;
```

Linking will always be the same, with more names before the semicolon when we have more files, but the main procedure must always be in the first file listed.

Now, convert the .EXE file to a .COM file by typing:

```
A>EXE2BIN DISP_SEC DISP_SEC.COM
```

In general, the two preceding steps for the files *file1, file2,* and so on, look like this:

```
LINK file1 file2 file3 ...;
EXE2BIN file1 file1.COM
```

Now, run the .COM file. Make sure you've run Exe2bin *before* you run Disp_sec. Otherwise, you'll end up running the .EXE version of Disp_sec, and who knows what will happen. At worst, you'll have to turn your computer off, wait about a minute, and then turn it on again to reset it.

If you don't see:

```
10 11 12 13 14 15 16 17 18 19 1A 1B 1C 1D 1E 1F
```

when you run the program, go back and check carefully for a mistake.

Now, let's see how Disp_sec works. The instruction:

```
MOV    DL,SECTOR[BX]              ;Get 1 byte
```

uses a new addressing mode known as *Indirect Memory Addressing*—addressing memory through the *Base* register with *offset*, or more simply, *Base Relative*. Let's see what this really means.

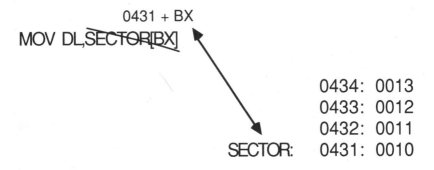

Figure 14-1. Translation of SECTOR[BX].

Looking at Disp_sec, you'll see that the label SECTOR is in a segment named DATA_SEG. This is a new segment used for memory variables. Any time we want to store and read data in memory, we'll set aside some space in this segment. We'll get back to memory variables in just a minute, but first let's learn a little more about segments.

The ASSUME DS:CGROUP tells the assembler where to find memory variables. You might have guessed we'd want ASSUME DS:DATA_SEG. Not quite, because we want to build a .COM file, we must build only one segment. Yet, it's convenient to work with two: one for the code, and one for the data. This is where the GROUP pseudo-op enters the scene. GROUP groups different segments into what is effectively one segment, with the name we give before the GROUP pseudo-op. So the statement:

```
CGROUP  GROUP   CODE_SEG, DATA_SEG
```

merges the two segments CODE_SEG and DATA_SEG into a single 64K segment with the name CGROUP. The inner workings of groups are a bit more complicated than this, but we don't need to know any more details. If you want the details, you'll find them in your macro assembler manual. Be warned, however: They are a bit difficult to read.

It's time to get back to our base-relative addressing mode. The two lines:

```
SECTOR  DB      10h, 11h, 12h, 13h, 14h, 15h, 16h, 17h  ;Test pattern
        DB      18h, 19h, 1Ah, 1Bh, 1Ch, 1Dh, 1Eh, 1Fh
```

set aside 16 bytes of memory in the data segment starting at SECTOR, which the assembler converts to an address. DB, you may recall, stands for *Define Byte*; the numbers after each DB are initial values. So, when we first start DISP_SEC.COM, the memory starting at SECTOR will contain 10h, 11h, 12h, and so on. If we wrote:

```
MOV     DL,SECTOR
```

the instruction would move the first byte (10h) into the DL register. This is known as *direct* memory addressing. But we didn't write that. Instead, we placed [BX] after SECTOR. This may look suspiciously like an index into an array, like the BASIC statement:

```
K = L(10)
```

which moves the 10th element of L into K.

In fact, our MOV instruction is much the same. The BX register contains an *offset* in memory from SECTOR. So if BX is 0, the MOV DL,SECTOR[BX] moves the first byte (10h here) into DL. If BX is 0Ah, this MOV instruction moves the eleventh byte (1Ah—remember, we started at 0) into DL.

CS,DS ⟶

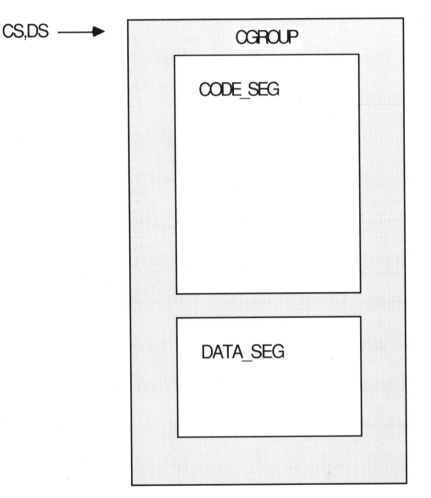

Figure 14-2.   **Groups Treat Multiple Sectors as a Single Segment.**

On the other hand, the instruction MOV DX,SECTOR[BX] would move the sixth word into DX, since an offset of 10 bytes is the same as 5 words, and the first word is at offset zero. (For enthusiasts: This last MOV instruction is not legal, because SECTOR is a byte label, whereas DX is a word register. We would have to write MOV DX,Word Ptr SECTOR[BX] to tell the assembler that we really want to use SECTOR as a word label in this instruction.)

There are many other addressing modes; some we'll encounter later, but most we won't. All the addressing modes are summarized in Table 14-1.

Table 14-1. Addressing Modes

Addressing Mode	Format of Address	Segment Register Used
Register	register (such as AX)	None
Immediate	data (such as 12345)	None
Memory Addressing Modes		
Register Indirect	[BX]	DS
	[BP]	SS
	[DI]	DS
	[SI]	DS
Base Relative*	label[BX]	DS
	label[BP]	SS
Direct Indexed*	label[DI]	DS
	label[SI]	DS
Base Indexed*	label[BX + SI]	DS
	label[BX + DI]	DS
	label [BP + SI]	SS
	label[BP + DI]	SS
String Commands: (MOVSW, LODSB, *and so on*)		Read from DS:SI Write to ES:DI

* Label[...] can be replaced by [disp + ...], where disp is a displacement. Thus, we could write [10 + BX] and the address would be 10 + BX.

Adding Characters to the Dump

We're almost through the procedure for a dump display similar to Debug's. So far we've dumped the hex numbers for one line; in the next step we'll add the character display following the hex display. It's not very involved, so without further delay, here's the new version of DISP_LINE (in DISP_SEC.ASM), with a second loop added to display the characters:

Listing 14-2. Changes to DISP_LINE in DISP_SEC.ASM

```
DISP_LINE       PROC     NEAR
        XOR     BX,BX                   ;Set BX to 0
        MOV     CX,16                   ;Dump 16 bytes
HEX_LOOP:
        MOV     DL,SECTOR[BX]           ;Get 1 byte
        CALL    WRITE_HEX               ;Dump this byte in hex
        MOV     DL,' '                  ;Write a space between numbers
        CALL    WRITE_CHAR
        INC     BX
        LOOP    HEX_LOOP

        MOV     DL,' '                  ;Add another space before characters
        CALL    WRITE_CHAR
        MOV     CX,16
        XOR     BX,BX                   ;Set BX back to 0
ASCII_LOOP:
        MOV     DL,SECTOR[BX]
        CALL    WRITE_CHAR
        INC     BX
        LOOP    ASCII_LOOP

        INT     20h                     ;Return to DOS
DISP_LINE       ENDP
```

Assemble this, link it to Video_io, run it through Exe2bin, and try it. Just the display we wanted. (See Figure 14-3.)

```
A>disp_sec
10 11 12 13 14 15 16 17 18 19 1A 1B 1C 1D 1E 1F  ▶◀‼!¶§▬↨↑↓→∟↔▲▼
A>
```

Figure 14-3.   DISP_LINE's Output.

Try changing the data to include a 0Dh or a 0Ah. You'll see a rather strange display. Here's why: 0Ah and 0Dh are the characters for the line-feed and carriage-return characters. DOS interprets these as commands to move the cursor, but we'd like to see them as just ordinary characters for this part of the display. To do this, we'll have to change WRITE_CHAR to print all characters, without applying any special meaning. We'll do that in Part III, but for now, let's rewrite WRITE_CHAR slightly so that it prints a period in place of the low characters (between 0 and 1Fh).

```
A>disp_sec
18 11 12 13 14 15 16 17 18 19 1A 1B 1C 1D 1E 1F ................
A>
```

Figure 14-4. Modified Version of DISP_LINE.

Replace the WRITE_CHAR in VIDEO_IO.ASM with this new procedure:

Listing 14-3. A New WRITE_CHAR in VIDEO_IO.ASM

```
        PUBLIC  WRITE_CHAR
;-----------------------------------------------------------------;
; This procedure prints a character on the screen using the DOS   ;
; function call. WRITE_CHAR replaces the characters 0 through 1Fh with ;
; a period.                                                       ;
;       DL      byte to print on screen.                          ;
;-----------------------------------------------------------------;
WRITE_CHAR      PROC    NEAR
        PUSH    AX
        PUSH    DX
        CMP     DL,32           ;Is character before a space?
        JAE     IS_PRINTABLE    ;No, then print as is
        MOV     DL,'.'          ;Yes, replace with a period
IS_PRINTABLE:
        MOV     AH,2            ;Call for character output
        INT     21h             ;Output character in DL register
        POP     DX              ;Restore old value in AX and DX
        POP     AX
        RET
WRITE_CHAR      ENDP
```

Try this new procedure with Disp_sec, and change the data to various characters to check the boundary conditions.

Dumping 256 Bytes of Memory

Now we've managed to dump one line, or 16 bytes, of memory. The next step is to dump 256 bytes of memory. This happens to be exactly half the number of bytes in a sector, so we're working toward building a display of half a sector. We still have many more improvements to make; this is just a test version.

We'll need two new procedures here, and a modified version of DISP_LINE. The new procedures are DISP_HALF_SECTOR, which will soon evolve into a finished procedure to display half a sector, and SEND_CRLF, which just sends the cursor to the beginning of the next line (CRLF stands for *Carriage*

Return-Line Feed, the pair of characters that move the cursor to the next line).

SEND_CRLF is very simple, so let's start with it. Place the following procedure into a file called CURSOR.ASM:

Listing 14-4. The New File CURSOR.ASM

```
CR              EQU    13              ;Carriage return
LF              EQU    10              ;Line feed

CGROUP  GROUP   CODE_SEG
        ASSUME  CS:CGROUP

CODE_SEG        SEGMENT PUBLIC

        PUBLIC  SEND_CRLF
;--------------------------------------------------------------------;
; This routine just sends a carriage return-line feed pair to the    ;
; display, using the DOS routines so that scrolling will be handled   ;
; correctly.                                                          ;
;--------------------------------------------------------------------;
SEND_CRLF       PROC    NEAR
        PUSH    AX
        PUSH    DX
        MOV     AH,2
        MOV     DL,CR
        INT     21h
        MOV     DL,LF
        INT     21h
        POP     DX
        POP     AX
        RET
SEND_CRLF       ENDP

CODE_SEG        ENDS

        END
```

This procedure sends a Carriage Return and Line Feed pair, using the DOS function 2 to send characters. The statement:

```
    CR              EQU    13              ;Carriage return
```

uses the EQU pseudo-op to define the name CR to be equal to 13. So the instruction MOV DL,CR is equivalent to MOV DL,13. As shown in Figure 14-5, the assembler substitutes 13 whenever it sees CR. Likewise, it substitutes 10 whenever it sees LF.

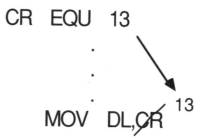

Figure 14-5.   The EQU Pseudo-Op Lets Us Use Names in Place of Numbers.

The file Disp_sec now needs much work. Here's the new version of DISP_
SEC.ASM. From here on, additions to our programs will be shown against a
gray background; text you should delete will be printed in blue:

Listing 14-5. The New Version of DISP_SEC.ASM

```
CGROUP   GROUP    CODE_SEG, DATA_SEG        ;Group two segments together
         ASSUME   CS:CGROUP, DS:CGROUP

CODE_SEG          SEGMENT PUBLIC
         ORG      100h

         PUBLIC   DISP_HALF_SECTOR
         EXTRN    SEND_CRLF:NEAR
;------------------------------------------------------------------------;
; This procedure displays half a sector (256 bytes)                      ;
;                                                                        ;
; Uses:          DISP_LINE, SEND_CRLF                                    ;
;------------------------------------------------------------------------;
DISP_HALF_SECTOR          PROC    NEAR
         XOR      DX,DX                      ;Start at beginning of SECTOR
         MOV      CX,16                      ;Display 16 lines
HALF_SECTOR:
         CALL     DISP_LINE
         CALL     SEND_CRLF
         ADD      DX,16
         LOOP     HALF_SECTOR
         INT      20h
DISP_HALF_SECTOR          ENDP

         PUBLIC   DISP_LINE
         EXTRN    WRITE_HEX:NEAR
         EXTRN    WRITE_CHAR:NEAR
```

Listing 14-5. *continued*

```
;--------------------------------------------------------------;
; This procedure displays one line of data, or 16 bytes, first in hex, ;
; then in ASCII.                                                ;
;                                                               ;
;        DS:DX    Offset into sector, in bytes.                 ;
;                                                               ;
; Uses:           WRITE_CHAR, WRITE_HEX                         ;
; Reads:          SECTOR                                        ;
;--------------------------------------------------------------;
DISP_LINE       PROC    NEAR
        XOR     BX,BX
        PUSH    BX
        PUSH    CX
        PUSH    DX
        MOV     BX,DX                   ;Offset is more useful in BX
        MOV     CX,16                   ;Dump 16 bytes
        PUSH    BX                      ;Save the offset for ASCII_LOOP
HEX_LOOP:
        MOV     DL,SECTOR[BX]           ;Get 1 byte
        CALL    WRITE_HEX               ;Dump this byte in hex
        MOV     DL,' '                  ;Write a space between numbers
        CALL    WRITE_CHAR
        INC     BX
        LOOP    HEX_LOOP

        MOV     DL,' '                  ;Add another space before characters
        CALL    WRITE_CHAR
        MOV     CX,16
        POP     BX                      ;Get back offset into SECTOR
        XOR     BX,BX
ASCII_LOOP:
        MOV     DL,SECTOR[BX]
        CALL    WRITE_CHAR
        INC     BX
        LOOP    ASCII_LOOP

        POP     DX
        POP     CX
        POP     BX
        RET
        INT     20h
DISP_LINE       ENDP

CODE_SEG        ENDS

DATA_SEG        SEGMENT PUBLIC
        PUBLIC  SECTOR
SECTOR  DB      10h, 11h, 12h, 13h, 14h, 15h, 16h, 17h  ;Test pattern
        DB      18h, 19h, 1Ah, 1Bh, 1Ch, 1Dh, 1Eh, 1Fh
```

Listing 14-5. *continued*

```
SECTOR     DB        16 DUP(10h)
           DB        16 DUP(11h)
           DB        16 DUP(12h)
           DB        16 DUP(13h)
           DB        16 DUP(14h)
           DB        16 DUP(15h)
           DB        16 DUP(16h)
           DB        16 DUP(17h)
           DB        16 DUP(18h)
           DB        16 DUP(19h)
           DB        16 DUP(1Ah)
           DB        16 DUP(1Bh)
           DB        16 DUP(1Ch)
           DB        16 DUP(1Dh)
           DB        16 DUP(1Eh)
           DB        16 DUP(1Fh)
DATA_SEG             ENDS
           END       DISP_HALF_SECTOR
```

The changes are all fairly straightforward. In DISP_LINE, we've added a PUSH BX and POP BX around the HEX_LOOP, because we want to reuse the initial offset in ASCII_LOOP. We've also added PUSH and POP instructions to save and restore all the registers we use within DISP_LINE. Actually, DISP_LINE is almost done; the only changes we have left are aesthetic,

```
A>disp_sec
10 10 10 10 10 10 10 10 10 10 10 10 10 10 10 10  ................
11 11 11 11 11 11 11 11 11 11 11 11 11 11 11 11  ................
12 12 12 12 12 12 12 12 12 12 12 12 12 12 12 12  ................
13 13 13 13 13 13 13 13 13 13 13 13 13 13 13 13  ................
14 14 14 14 14 14 14 14 14 14 14 14 14 14 14 14  ................
15 15 15 15 15 15 15 15 15 15 15 15 15 15 15 15  ................
16 16 16 16 16 16 16 16 16 16 16 16 16 16 16 16  ................
17 17 17 17 17 17 17 17 17 17 17 17 17 17 17 17  ................
18 18 18 18 18 18 18 18 18 18 18 18 18 18 18 18  ................
19 19 19 19 19 19 19 19 19 19 19 19 19 19 19 19  ................
1A 1A 1A 1A 1A 1A 1A 1A 1A 1A 1A 1A 1A 1A 1A 1A  ................
1B 1B 1B 1B 1B 1B 1B 1B 1B 1B 1B 1B 1B 1B 1B 1B  ................
1C 1C 1C 1C 1C 1C 1C 1C 1C 1C 1C 1C 1C 1C 1C 1C  ................
1D 1D 1D 1D 1D 1D 1D 1D 1D 1D 1D 1D 1D 1D 1D 1D  ................
1E 1E 1E 1E 1E 1E 1E 1E 1E 1E 1E 1E 1E 1E 1E 1E  ................
1F 1F 1F 1F 1F 1F 1F 1F 1F 1F 1F 1F 1F 1F 1F 1F  ................

A>
```

Figure 14-6. Output From Disp_sec.

to add spaces and graphics characters so we'll have an attractive display; those will come later.

When you link the files, remember that we now have three files: Disp_sec, Video_io, and Cursor. Disp_sec must be first in this list. After you run the .EXE version through Exe2bin, you'll see a display like the one in Figure 14-6.

We'll have more files before we're done, but now, let's move on to the next chapter, where we'll read a sector directly from the disk before we dump half a sector.

Summary

We know more about the different memory modes for addressing memory and registers in the 8088 microprocessor. We learned about indirect memory addressing, which we first used to read 16 bytes of memory.

We also used indirect memory addressing in several programs we wrote in this chapter, starting with our program to print 16 hex numbers on the screen. These 16 numbers came from an area in memory labeled SECTOR, which we expanded a bit later so we could display a memory dump for 256 bytes—half a sector.

And, at last, we've begun to see dumps of the screen, as they appear on your display, rather than as they are set in type. We'll use these screen dumps to more advantage in the following chapters.

DUMPING A DISK SECTOR

Now that we have a program that dumps 256 bytes of memory, we can add some procedures to read a sector from the disk and place it in memory starting at SECTOR. Then, our dump procedures will dump the first half of this disk sector.

Making Life Easier

With the three source files we had in the last chapter, life becomes somewhat complicated. Did we change all three of the files we were working on, or just two? You probably assembled all three, rather than check to see if you made any changes since the last assemble.

But assembling all of our source files when we've only changed one of them is rather slow, and will become even slower as Dskpatch grows in size. What we'd really like to do is assemble only the files that we've changed.

Fortunately, if you are using one of the more recent Macro Assembler packages from Microsoft (or you have their C compiler), there is a way you can do just that. They include a program called Make that does exactly what we want. To use it, we create a file (we'll call it Dskpatch) that tells Make how to do its work, then just type:

```
A>MAKE DSKPATCH
```

Make then assembles only the files you've changed.

The file you create (Dskpatch) tells Make which files depend on which other files. Every time you change a file, DOS updates the modify time for this file (you can see this in the DIR display). Make simply looks at both the .ASM and .OBJ versions of a file. If the .ASM version has a more recent modify time than the .OBJ version, Make knows that it needs to assemble that file again.

That's all there is to it, but there is one caveat we need to point out: Make will work correctly only if you're diligent about setting DOS' date and time each time you start your computer. Without this information, Make won't always know when you've made changes to a file.

Format of the Make File

The format for our file, Dskpatch, that we'll use with Make is fairly simple:

Listing 15-1. The Make File DSKPATCH

```
disp_sec.obj:   disp_sec.asm
        masm disp_sec;

video_io.obj:   video_io.asm
        masm video_io;

cursor.obj:     cursor.asm
        masm cursor;

disp_sec.com:   disp_sec.obj video_io.obj cursor.obj
        link disp_sec video_io cursor;
        exe2bin disp_sec disp_sec.com
```

Each entry has a file name on the left (before the colon) and one or more file names on the right. If any of the files on the right (such as DISP_SEC.ASM in the first line) are more recent than the first file (DISP_SEC.OBJ), Make will execute all the indented commands that appear on the following lines. (**Note:** You must indent the command lines with a tab, not with spaces.)

If your assembler has the Make program, enter these lines into the file Dskpatch (without an extension) and make a small change to DISP_SEC.ASM. Then type:

```
A>MAKE DSKPATCH
```

and you'll see something like the following:

```
Microsoft (R) Macro Assembler Version 4.00
Copyright (C) Microsoft Corp 1981, 1983, 1984, 1985.  All rights reserved.

  48984 Bytes symbol space free

      0 Warning Errors
      0 Severe  Errors
        link disp_sec video_io cursor;

Microsoft (R) 8086 Object Linker  Version 3.05
```

```
Copyright (C) Microsoft Corp 1983, 1984, 1985.  All rights reserved.

Warning: no stack segment
                exe2bin disp_sec disp_sec.asm

A>
```

Make has done the minimum amount of work necessary to rebuild our program.

If you don't have a recent version of the Microsoft Macro Assembler that includes Make, you'll find this program worth the price of an upgrade. And you'll get a nice replacement for Debug, too. It's called Symdeb (*Symbolic Debugger*), and we'll take a look at it later. Now, on with Dskpatch.

Patching up Disp_sec

Disp_sec, as we left it, included a version of DISP_HALF_SECTOR, which we used as a test procedure, and the main procedure. Now, we'll change DISP_HALF_SECTOR to an ordinary procedure so we can call it from a procedure we'll name Disk_io. Our test procedure will be in Disk_io, along with a test version of the procedure to read a disk sector.

First, let's modify Disp_sec to make it a file of procedures, just as we did with Video_io. Change the END DISP_HALF_SECTOR to just END, since our main procedure will now be in Disk_io. Then remove the ORG 100h statement from CODE_SEG, again because we moved this to a different file.

Since we plan to read a sector into memory starting at SECTOR, there is no need for us to supply test data. We can replace all the 16 DB statements after SECTOR with one line:

```
SECTOR  DB      8192 DUP (0)
```

which reserves 8192 bytes for storing a sector.

But recall our earlier statement that sectors are 512 bytes long. So why do we need such a large storage area? It turns out that some hard disks (300 megabyte, for example) use very large sector sizes. These large sector sizes are by no means common, but we still want to be certain that we don't read in a sector that is too large to fit into the memory we've reserved for SECTOR. So, in the interest of safety, we've reserved 8192 bytes for SECTOR. In the rest of this book, with the exception of SECTOR, which we'll cover soon, we'll assume that sectors are only 512 bytes long.

Now what we need is a new version of DISP_HALF_SECTOR. The old version is nothing more than a test procedure that we used to test DISP_LINE. In the new version, we'll want to supply an offset into the sector so that we can display 256 bytes, starting anywhere in the sector. Among other things, this means we could dump the first half, the last half, or the middle 256 bytes. Once again, we'll supply this offset in DX. Here is the new—and final—version of DISP_HALF_SECTOR in Disp_sec:

Listing 15-2. The Final Version of DISP_HALF_SECTOR
in DISP_SEC.ASM

```
                PUBLIC  DISP_HALF_SECTOR
                EXTRN   SEND_CRLF:NEAR
;------------------------------------------------------------------;
;  This procedure displays half a sector (256 bytes)              ;
;                                                                  ;
;       DS:DX    Offset into sector, in bytes -- should be multiple of 16;
;                                                                  ;
; Uses:          DISP_LINE, SEND_CRLF                              ;
;------------------------------------------------------------------;
DISP_HALF_SECTOR          PROC    NEAR
        XOR     DX,DX
        PUSH    CX
        PUSH    DX
        MOV     CX,16                       ;Display 16 lines
HALF_SECTOR:
        CALL    DISP_LINE
        CALL    SEND_CRLF
        ADD     DX,16
        LOOP    HALF_SECTOR
        POP     DX
        POP     CX
        RET
        INT     20h
DISP_HALF_SECTOR          ENDP
```

Let's move on now to our procedure to read a sector.

Reading a Sector

In this first version of READ_SECTOR we'll deliberately ignore errors, such as having no disk in the disk drive. This is not good practice, but this isn't the final version of READ_SECTOR. We won't be able to cover error handling in this book, but you will find error-handling procedures in the version of Dskpatch on the disk that is available for this book. For now, though, we just want to read a sector from the disk. Here is the test version of the file DISK_IO.ASM:

Listing 15-3. The New File DISK_IO.ASM

```
CGROUP   GROUP   CODE_SEG, DATA_SEG
         ASSUME  CS:CGROUP, DS:CGROUP


CODE_SEG         SEGMENT PUBLIC
         ORG     100h

         EXTRN   DISP_HALF_SECTOR:NEAR
;---------------------------------------------------------------;
; This procedure reads the first sector on disk A and dumps the first   ;
; half of this sector.                                          ;
;---------------------------------------------------------------;
READ_SECTOR      PROC    NEAR
         MOV     AL,0             ;Disk drive A (number 0)
         MOV     CX,1             ;Read only 1 sector
         MOV     DX,0             ;Read sector number 0
         LEA     BX,SECTOR        ;Where to store this sector
         INT     25h              ;Read the sector
         POPF                     ;Discard flags put on stack by DOS
         XOR     DX,DX            ;Set offset to 0 within SECTOR
         CALL    DISP_HALF_SECTOR ;Dump the first half
         INT     20h              ;Return to DOS
READ_SECTOR      ENDP

CODE_SEG         ENDS

DATA_SEG         SEGMENT PUBLIC
         EXTRN   SECTOR:BYTE
DATA_SEG         ENDS

         END     READ_SECTOR
```

There are three new instructions in this procedure. The first:

```
LEA     BX,SECTOR
```

moves the *address*, or offset, of SECTOR (from the start of CGROUP) into the BX register; LEA stands for *Load Effective Address*. After this LEA instruction, DS:BX contains the full address of SECTOR, and DOS uses this address for the second new instruction, the INT 25h call, as we'll see after a few more words about SECTOR. (Actually, LEA loads the offset into the BX register without setting the DS register; we have to ensure that DS is pointing to the correct segment.)

SECTOR isn't in the same source file as READ_SECTOR. It's over in DISP_
SEC.ASM. How do we tell the assembler where it is? We use the EXTRN
pseudo-op:

```
DATA_SEG        SEGMENT PUBLIC
        EXTRN   SECTOR:BYTE
DATA_SEG        ENDS
```

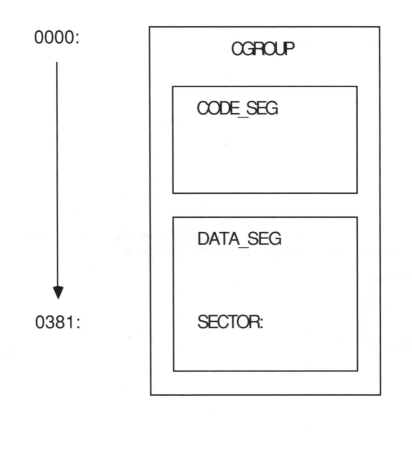

Figure 15-1.   LEA Loads the Effective Address.

This set of instructions tells the assembler that SECTOR is defined in the DATA_SEG, which is in another source file, and that SECTOR is a variable of bytes (rather than words). We'll be using such EXTRNs often in following chapters; it's the way we use the same variables in a number of source files. We just need to be careful that we define our variables in only one place.

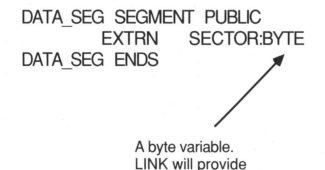

```
DATA_SEG  SEGMENT  PUBLIC
          EXTRN      SECTOR:BYTE
DATA_SEG  ENDS
```

A byte variable.
LINK will provide
the address.

Figure 15-2. The EXTRN Pseudo-Op.

Let's return to the INT 25h instruction. INT 25h is a special function call to DOS for reading sectors from a disk. When DOS receives a call from INT 25h, it uses the information in the registers as follows:

AL   Drive number (0 = A, 1 = B, and so on)
CX   Number of sectors to read at one time
DX   Number of the first sector to read (the first sector is 0)
DS:BX   Transfer address: where to write the sectors read

The number in the AL register determines the drive from which DOS will read sectors. If AL = 0, DOS reads from drive A.

DOS can read more than one sector with a single call, and it reads the number of sectors given by CX. Here, we set CX to one so DOS will read just one sector of 512 bytes.

We set DX to zero, so DOS will read the very first sector on the disk. You can change this number if you want to read a different sector; later on, we will.

DS:BX is the full address for the area in memory where we want DOS to store the sector(s) it reads. In this case, we've set DS:BX to the address of SECTOR, so that we can call DISP_HALF_SECTOR to dump the first half of the first sector read from the disk in drive A.

Finally, you'll notice a POPF instruction immediately following the INT 21h. As we mentioned before, the 8088 has a register called the status register that contains the various flags, like the zero and carry flags. POPF is a special POP instruction that pops a word into the status register. Why do we need this POPF instruction?

The INT 25h instruction pushes first the status registers, then the return address onto the stack. When DOS returns from this INT 25h, it leaves the status register on the stack. DOS does this so that it can set the carry flag on return if there was a disk error, such as trying to read from drive A: with no disk in the drive. We won't be checking for errors in this book, but we have to remove the status register from the stack—hence the POPF instruction. (**Note**: INT 25h, along with INT 24h which *writes* a disk sector, are the only DOS routines that leave the status register on the stack.)

Now you can assemble DISK_IO.ASM, and reassemble DISP_SEC.ASM. Then, link the four files Disk_io, Disp_sec, Video_io, and Cursor, with Disk_io listed first. Or, if you have Make, add these two lines to your Dskpatch file:

```
disk_io.obj:    disk_io.asm
        masm disk_io;
```

and change the last three lines to:

```
disk_io.com:    disk_io.obj disp_sec.obj video_io.obj cursor.obj
        link disk_io disp_sec video_io cursor;
        exe2bin disk_io disk_io.com
```

After you create your .COM version of Disk_io, you should see a display something like Figure 15-3.

We'll come back later to add more to Disk_io, we have enough for now. In the next chapter, we'll build a nicer sector display by adding some graphics characters to the display, and then adding a few more pieces of information.

```
A>disk_io
EB 21 90 49 42 4D 20 20 33 2E 31 00 02 02 01 00    δ!ÉIBM  3.1.....
02 70 00 D0 02 FD 02 00 09 00 02 00 00 00 00 00    .p.▌.².........
00 00 00 C4 5C 08 33 ED B8 C0 07 8E D8 33 C9 0A    ...─\.3π┐└.Ä╪3╔.
D2 79 0E 89 1E 1E 00 8C 06 20 00 88 16 22 00 B1    ╥y.ë...î. .ê.".▌
02 8E C5 8E D5 BC 00 7C 51 FC 1E 36 C5 36 78 00    .Ä╪Ä╥▐.!Q▐.6┼6x.
BF 23 7C B9 0B 00 F3 A4 1F 88 0E 2C 00 A0 18 00    ┐#!┤..≤ñ.ê.,.á..
A2 27 00 BF 78 00 B8 23 7C AB 91 AB A1 16 00 D1    ó'.┐x.┐#!½æ½í..╤
E0 40 E8 00 00 E8 86 00 BB 00 05 53 B0 01 E8 AB    α@Ç.ŝå.┐..S▐.Ç½
00 5F BE 73 01 B9 0B 00 90 F3 A6 75 62 83 C7 15    ._┘s.┤..É≤ª ubâ┐.
B1 0B 90 90 F3 A6 75 57 26 8B 47 1C 99 8B 0E 0B    ▌.ÉÉ≤ª uW&ïG.Öï..
00 03 C1 48 F7 F1 80 3E 71 01 60 75 02 B0 14 96    ..└H≈±Ç>q.`u.▐.û
A1 11 00 B1 04 D3 E8 E8 3B 00 FF 36 1E 00 C4 1E    í..▌.╙ÇÇ;. 6..─.
6F 01 E8 39 00 E8 64 00 2B F0 76 0D E8 26 00 52    o.Ç9.Çd.+≈v.Ç&.R
F7 26 0B 00 03 D8 5A EB E9 CD 11 B9 02 00 D3 E0    ≈&...╪ZδΘ=.┤..╙α
80 E4 03 74 04 FE C4 8A CC 5B 58 FF 2E 6F 01 BE    Çʃ.t.■─è╠[X .o.┘
89 01 EB 55 90 01 06 1E 00 11 2E 20 00 C3 A1 18    ë.δUÉ...... .├í.

A>
```

Figure 15-3: Screen Dump from DISK_IO.COM.

Summary

Now that we have four different source files, Dskpatch is becoming some-what more involved. In this chapter, we looked at the program Make, which helps make life simpler by assembling only the files we've changed.

We also wrote a new procedure, DISK_IO. It's in a different source file from SECTOR, so we used an EXTRN definition in DISK_IO.ASM to tell the assembler about SECTOR, and let it know that SECTOR is a byte variable.

We also learned about the LEA (Load Effective Address) instruction, which we used to load the address of SECTOR into the BX register.

DISK_IO uses a new INT number, INT 25h, to read sectors from a disk to memory. We used INT 25h to read one sector into our memory variable, SEC-TOR, so we could dump it on the screen with DISP_HALF_SECTOR.

We also learned about the POPF instruction to pop a word off the stack and into the status register. We used this instruction to remove the flags which DOS didn't remove from the stack when it returned from INT 25h.

Our half-sector display isn't very attractive yet, in the next chapter we'll use some of the graphics characters available on the IBM PC to make it more aesthetically pleasing.

ENHANCING THE SECTOR DISPLAY

We've come to the last chapter in Part II. Everything we've done so far has been applicable to MS-DOS and the 8088 (or the 8086 and other relatives of the 8088). In Part III, we'll begin to write procedures specific to the IBM Personal Computer and its close cousins.

But before we move on, we'll use this chapter to add several more procedures to Video_io. We'll also modify DISP_LINE in Disp_sec. All our modifications and additions will be to the display. Most of them will be to improve the appearance of the display, but one will add new information: It will add numbers on the left that act like the addresses in Debug's dump. Let's begin with graphics.

Adding Graphics Characters

The IBM Personal Computer has a number of line-drawing characters we can use to draw boxes around various parts of our dump display. We'll draw one box around the hex dump, and another around the ASCII dump. This change requires very little thought, just work.

Enter the following definitions near the top of the file DISP_SEC.ASM, between the ASSUME pseudo-op and the first SEGMENT pseudo-op, leaving one or two blank lines before and after these definitions:

Listing 16-1. Add to the Top of DISP_SEC.ASM

```
;--------------------------------------------------------------------;
; Graphics characters for border of sector.                         ;
;--------------------------------------------------------------------;
VERTICAL_BAR    EQU    0BAh
HORIZONTAL_BAR  EQU    0CDh
UPPER_LEFT      EQU    0C9h
UPPER_RIGHT     EQU    0BBh
LOWER_LEFT      EQU    0C8h
LOWER_RIGHT     EQU    0BCh
TOP_T_BAR       EQU    0CBh
BOTTOM_T_BAR    EQU    0CAh
TOP_TICK        EQU    0D1h
BOTTOM_TICK     EQU    0CFh
```

These are the definitions for the graphics characters. Notice that we put a zero before each hex number so the assembler will know these are numbers, rather than labels.

We could just as easily have written hex numbers instead of these definitions in our procedure, but the definitions make the procedure easier to understand. For example, compare the following two instructions:

```
MOV     DL,VERTICAL_BAR
MOV     DL,0BAh
```

Most people find the first instruction clearer.

Now, here is the new DISP_LINE procedure to separate the different parts of the display with the VERTICAL_BAR character, number 186 (0BAh). As before, additions are shown against a gray background:

Listing 16-2. Changes to DISP_LINE in DISP_SEC.ASM

```
DISP_LINE       PROC    NEAR
        PUSH    BX
        PUSH    CX
        PUSH    DX
        MOV     BX,DX                   ;Offset is more useful in BX
                                        ;Write separator
        MOV     DL,' '
        CALL    WRITE_CHAR
        MOV     DL,VERTICAL_BAR         ;Draw left side of box
        CALL    WRITE_CHAR
        MOV     DL,' '
        CALL    WRITE_CHAR
                                        ;Now write out 16 bytes
        MOV     CX,16                   ;Dump 16 bytes
        PUSH    BX                      ;Save the offset for ASCII_LOOP
HEX_LOOP:
        MOV     DL,SECTOR[BX]           ;Get 1 byte
        CALL    WRITE_HEX               ;Dump this byte in hex
        MOV     DL,' '                  ;Write a space between numbers
        CALL    WRITE_CHAR
        INC     BX
        LOOP    HEX_LOOP

        MOV     DL,VERTICAL_BAR         ;Write separator
        CALL    WRITE_CHAR
        MOV     DL,' '
        CALL    WRITE_CHAR

        MOV     CX,16
        POP     BX                      ;Get back offset into SECTOR
ASCII_LOOP:
        MOV     DL,SECTOR[BX]
        CALL    WRITE_CHAR
        INC     BX
        LOOP    ASCII_LOOP
```

Listing 16-2. *continued*

```
        MOV     DL,' '                      ;Draw right side of box
        CALL    WRITE_CHAR
        MOV     DL,VERTICAL_BAR
        CALL    WRITE_CHAR

        POP     DX
        POP     CX
        POP     BX
        RET
DISP_LINE       ENDP
```

Assemble this new version of Disp_sec and link your four files (remember to place Disk_io first in the list of files following the LINK command). You'll see nice double bars separating the display into two parts, as you can see in Figure 16-1.

Adding Addresses to the Display

Now let's try something a bit more challenging: Let's add the hex addresses down the left side of the display. These numbers will be the offset from the

```
A>disk_io
 ║ EB 21 90 49 42 4D 20 20 33 2E 31 00 02 02 01 00 ║ δ!ÉIBM  3.1.....
 ║ 02 70 00 D0 02 FD 02 00 09 00 02 00 00 00 00 00 ║ .p.▪.²..........
 ║ 00 00 00 C4 5C 08 33 ED B8 C0 07 8E D8 33 C9 0A ║ ...─\.3φ┐ └.Ä‡3╓.
 ║ D2 79 0E 89 1E 1E 00 8C 06 20 00 88 16 22 00 B1 ║ ╥y.ë...î. .ê.".█
 ║ 02 8E C5 8E D5 BC 00 7C 51 FC 1E 36 C5 36 78 00 ║ .Ä‡Äª┘.¦Qⁿ.6├6x.
 ║ BF 23 7C B9 0B 00 F3 A4 1F 88 0E 2C 00 A0 18 00 ║ ┐#¦┤..≤ñ.ê.,.á..
 ║ A2 27 00 BF 78 00 B8 23 7C AB 91 AB A1 16 00 D1 ║ ó'.┐x.┐#¦½æ½í..╤
 ║ E0 40 E8 80 00 E8 86 00 BB 00 05 53 B0 01 E8 AB ║ α@Ç.δà.╗..S▒.δ½
 ║ 00 5F BE 73 01 B9 0B 00 90 F3 A6 75 62 83 C7 15 ║ ._┐s.┤..É≤ªubâ┤.
 ║ B1 0B 90 90 F3 A6 75 57 26 8B 47 1C 99 8B 0E 0B ║ █.ÉÉ≤ªuW&ïG.Öï..
 ║ 00 03 C1 48 F7 F1 80 3E 71 01 60 75 02 B0 14 96 ║ ..┴H≈±Ç>q.`u.▒.û
 ║ A1 11 00 B1 04 D3 E8 E8 3B 00 FF 36 1E 00 C4 1E ║ í..█.└δδ;. 6..─.
 ║ 6F 01 E8 39 00 E8 64 00 2B F0 76 0D E8 26 00 52 ║ o.δ9.δd.+≡v.δ&.R
 ║ F7 26 0B 00 03 D8 5A EB E9 CD 11 B9 02 00 D3 E0 ║ ≈&...╪Zδé╤.┤..└α
 ║ 80 E4 03 74 04 FE C4 8A CC 5B 58 FF 2E 6F 01 BE ║ ÇΣ.t.■-è[X .o.┐
 ║ 89 01 EB 55 90 01 06 1E 00 11 2E 20 00 C3 A1 18 ║ ë.δUÉ...... .├í.
```

A>

Figure 16-1. Adding Vertical Bars.

beginning of the sector, so the first number will be 00, the next 10, then 20, and so on.

The process is fairly simple, since we already have the procedure WRITE_ HEX for writing a number in hex. But we do have a problem in dealing with a sector 512 bytes long: WRITE_HEX prints only two-digit hex numbers, whereas we need three hex digits for numbers greater than 255.

Here's the solution. Since our numbers will be between zero and 511 (0h to 1FFh), the first digit will either be a space, if the number (such as BCh) is below 100h, or it will be a one. So, if the number is larger than 255, we'll simply print a one, followed by the hex number for the lower byte. Otherwise, we'll print a space first. These are the additions to DISP_LINE that will print this leading three-digit hex number:

Listing 16-3. Additions to DISP_LINE in DISP_SEC.ASM

```
DISP_LINE       PROC    NEAR
        PUSH    BX
        PUSH    CX
        PUSH    DX
        MOV     BX,DX                   ;Offset is more useful in BX
        MOV     DL,' '
                                        ;Write offset in hex
        CMP     BX,100h                 ;Is the first digit a 1?
        JB      WRITE_ONE               ;No, white space already in DL
        MOV     DL,'1'                  ;Yes, then place '1' into DL for output
WRITE_ONE:
        CALL    WRITE_CHAR
        MOV     DL,BL                   ;Copy lower byte into DL for hex output
        CALL    WRITE_HEX
                                        ;Write separator
        MOV     DL,' '
        CALL    WRITE_CHAR
        MOV     DL,VERTICAL_BAR         ;Draw left side of box
                .
                .
                .
```

You can see the result in Figure 16-2.

We're getting closer to our full display. But on the screen, our display is not quite centered. We need to move it to the right by about three spaces. Let's make this one last change, then we'll have our finished version of DISP_ LINE.

We could make the change by calling WRITE_CHAR three times with a space character, but we won't. Instead, we'll add another procedure, called WRITE_CHAR_N_TIMES, to Video_io. As its name implies, this procedure

```
A>disk_io
00 ║ EB 21 90 49 42 4D 20 20 33 2E 31 00 02 02 01 00 ║ δ!ÉIBM  3.1.....
10 ║ 02 70 00 D0 02 FD 02 00 09 00 02 00 00 00 00 00 ║ .p.╨.²..........
20 ║ 00 00 00 C4 5C 08 33 ED B8 C0 07 8E D8 33 C9 0A ║ ...─\.3φ╕└.Ä╪3╔.
30 ║ D2 79 0E 89 1E 1E 00 8C 06 20 00 88 16 22 00 B1 ║ ╥y.ë...î. .ê.".▒
40 ║ 02 8E C5 8E D5 BC 00 7C 51 FC 1E 36 C5 36 78 00 ║ .Ä┼Ä╒╝.|Qⁿ.6┼6x.
50 ║ BF 23 7C B9 0B 00 F3 A4 1F 88 0E 2C 00 A0 18 00 ║ ┐#|╣..≤ñ.ê.,.á..
60 ║ A2 27 00 BF 78 00 B8 23 7C AB 91 AB A1 16 00 D1 ║ ó'.┐x.╕#|½æ½í..╤
70 ║ E0 40 E8 80 00 E8 86 00 BB 00 05 53 B0 01 E8 AB ║ α@ΦÇ.Φå.╗..S░.Φ½
80 ║ 00 5F BE 73 01 B9 0B 00 90 F3 A6 75 62 83 C7 15 ║ ._╛s.╣..É≤ªubâ╟.
90 ║ B1 0B 90 90 F3 A6 75 57 26 8B 47 1C 99 8B 0E 0B ║ ▒.ÉÉ≤ªuW&ïG.Öï..
A0 ║ 00 03 C1 48 F7 F1 80 3E 71 01 60 75 02 B0 14 96 ║ ..┴H≈±Ç>q.`u.░.û
B0 ║ A1 11 00 B1 04 D3 E8 E8 3B 00 FF 36 1E 00 C4 1E ║ í..▒.╙ΦΦ;. 6..─.
C0 ║ 6F 01 E8 39 00 E8 64 00 2B F0 76 0D E8 26 00 52 ║ o.Φ9.Φd.+≡v.Φ&.R
D0 ║ F7 26 0B 00 03 D8 5A EB E9 CD 11 B9 02 00 D3 E0 ║ ≈&...╪ZδΘ═.╣..╙α
E0 ║ 80 E4 03 74 04 FE C4 8A CC 5B 58 FF 2E 6F 01 BE ║ ÇΣ.t.■─è╠[X .o.╛
F0 ║ 89 01 EB 55 90 01 06 1E 00 11 2E 20 00 C3 A1 18 ║ ë.δUÉ...... .├í.

A>
```

Figure 16-2. Adding Numbers on the Left.

writes one character N times. That is, we place the number N into the CX register and the character code into DL, and we call WRITE_CHAR_N_TIMES to write N copies of the character whose ASCII code we placed in DL. Thus, we'll be able to write three spaces by placing 3 into CX and 20h (the ASCII code for a space) into DL.

Here's the procedure to add to VIDEO_IO.ASM:

Listing 16-4. Add this Procedure to VIDEO_IO.ASM

```
        PUBLIC  WRITE_CHAR_N_TIMES
;-----------------------------------------------------------------------;
; This procedure writes more than one copy of a character               ;
;                                                                       ;
;       DL      Character code                                          ;
;       CX      Number of times to write the character                  ;
;                                                                       ;
; Uses:         WRITE_CHAR                                              ;
;-----------------------------------------------------------------------;
WRITE_CHAR_N_TIMES      PROC    NEAR
        PUSH    CX
N_TIMES:
        CALL    WRITE_CHAR
        LOOP    N_TIMES
        POP     CX
        RET
WRITE_CHAR_N_TIMES      ENDP
```

You can see how simple this procedure is, since we already have WRITE_ CHAR. If you're wondering why we bothered to write a procedure for something so simple, it's because our program Dskpatch is much clearer when we call WRITE_CHAR_N_TIMES, rather than write a short loop to print multiple copies of a character. Besides, we'll find use for this procedure several times again.

Here are the changes to DISP_LINE to add three spaces on the left of our display. Make the changes to DISP_SEC.ASM:

```
            PUBLIC  DISP_LINE
            EXTRN   WRITE_HEX:NEAR
            EXTRN   WRITE_CHAR:NEAR
            EXTRN   WRITE_CHAR_N_TIMES:NEAR
;--------------------------------------------------------------------;
; This procedure displays one line of data, or 16 bytes, first in hex, ;
; then in ASCII.                                                      ;
;                                                                    ;
;       DS:DX   Offset into sector, in bytes                         ;
;                                                                    ;
; Uses:         WRITE_CHAR, WRITE_HEX, WRITE_CHAR_N_TIMES            ;
; Reads:        SECTOR                                               ;
;--------------------------------------------------------------------;
DISP_LINE       PROC    NEAR
            PUSH    BX
            PUSH    CX
            PUSH    DX
            MOV     BX,DX               ;Offset is more useful in BX
            MOV     DL,' '
            MOV     CX,3                ;Write 3 spaces before line
            CALL    WRITE_CHAR_N_TIMES
                                        ;Write offset in hex
            CMP     BX,100h             ;Is the first digit a 1?
            JB      WRITE_ONE           ;No, white space already in DL
            MOV     DL,'1'              ;Yes, then place '1' into DL for output
WRITE_ONE:
                    .
                    .
                    .
```

We made changes in three places. First, we had to add an EXTRN statement for WRITE_CHAR_N_TIMES, because the procedure is in Video_io, and not in this file. We also changed the comment block, to show that we use this new procedure. Our third change, the two lines that use WRITE_CHAR_N_ TIMES, is quite straightforward and needs no explanation.

Try this new version of our program to see how the display is now centered. Next we'll move on to add more features to our display—the top and bottom lines of our boxes.

Adding Horizontal Lines

Adding horizontal lines to our display is not quite as simple as it sounds, because we have a few special cases to think about. We have the ends, where the lines must go around corners, and we also have T-shaped junctions at the top and bottom of the division between the hex and ASCII windows.

We could write a long list of instructions (with WRITE_CHAR_N_TIMES) to create our horizontal lines, but we won't. We have a shorter way. We'll introduce another procedure, called WRITE_PATTERN, which will write a pattern on the screen. Then, all we'll need is a small area of memory to hold a description of each pattern. Using this new procedure, we can also easily add tick marks to subdivide the hex window, as you'll see when we finish this section.

WRITE_PATTERN uses two entirely new instructions, LODSB and CLD. We'll describe them after we see more about WRITE_PATTERN and how we describe a pattern. Right now, enter this procedure into the file VIDEO_IO.ASM:

Listing 16-5. Add This Procedure to VIDEO_IO.ASM

```
        PUBLIC  WRITE_PATTERN
;-------------------------------------------------------------------;
; This procedure writes a line to the screen, based on data in the  ;
; form                                                              ;
;                                                                  ;
;       DB      (character, number of times to write character), 0  ;
; Where (x) means that x can be repeated any number of times       ;
;       DS:DX    Address of above data statement                    ;
;                                                                  ;
; Uses:          WRITE_CHAR_N_TIMES                                 ;
;-------------------------------------------------------------------;
WRITE_PATTERN   PROC    NEAR
        PUSH    AX
        PUSH    CX
        PUSH    DX
        PUSH    SI
        PUSHF                           ;Save the direction flag
        CLD                             ;Set direction flag for increment
        MOV     SI,DX                   ;Move offset into SI register for LODSB
PATTERN_LOOP:
        LODSB                           ;Get character data into AL
        OR      AL,AL                   ;Is it the end of data (0h)?
        JZ      END_PATTERN             ;Yes, return
        MOV     DL,AL                   ;No, set up to write character N times
        LODSB                           ;Get the repeat count into AL
        MOV     CL,AL                   ;And put in CX for WRITE_CHAR_N_TIMES
        XOR     CH,CH                   ;Zero upper byte of CX
```

Listing 16-5. *continued*

```
        CALL    WRITE_CHAR_N_TIMES
        JMP     PATTERN_LOOP
END_PATTERN:
        POPF                                    ;Restore direction flag
        POP     SI
        POP     DX
        POP     CX
        POP     AX
        RET
WRITE_PATTERN   ENDP
```

Before we see how this procedure works, let's see how to write data for patterns. We'll place the data for the top-line pattern into the file Disp_sec, which is where we'll use it. To this end, we'll add another procedure, called INIT_SEC_DISP, to initialize the sector display by writing the half-sector display, then we'll modify READ_SECTOR to call our INIT_SEC_DISP procedure.

First, place the following data just after SECTOR (in DISP_SEC.ASM), inside the data segment:

Listing 16-6. Additions to DISP_SEC.ASM

```
    TOP_LINE_PATTERN        LABEL   BYTE
        DB      ' ',7
        DB      UPPER_LEFT,1
        DB      HORIZONTAL_BAR,12
        DB      TOP_TICK,1
        DB      HORIZONTAL_BAR,11
        DB      TOP_TICK,1
        DB      HORIZONTAL_BAR,11
        DB      TOP_TICK,1
        DB      HORIZONTAL_BAR,12
        DB      TOP_T_BAR,1
        DB      HORIZONTAL_BAR,18
        DB      UPPER_RIGHT,1
        DB      0
    BOTTOM_LINE_PATTERN     LABEL   BYTE
        DB      ' ',7
        DB      LOWER_LEFT,1
        DB      HORIZONTAL_BAR,12
        DB      BOTTOM_TICK,1
        DB      HORIZONTAL_BAR,11
        DB      BOTTOM_TICK,1
        DB      HORIZONTAL_BAR,11
        DB      BOTTOM_TICK,1
        DB      HORIZONTAL_BAR,12
```

Listing 16-6. *continued*

```
        DB      BOTTOM_T_BAR,1
        DB      HORIZONTAL_BAR,18
        DB      LOWER_RIGHT,1
        DB      0
```

Each DB statement contains part of the data for one line. The first byte is the character to print; the second byte tells WRITE_PATTERN how many times to repeat that character. For example, we start the top line with seven blank spaces, followed by one upper-left corner character, followed by twelve horizontal-bar characters, and so on. The last DB is a solitary hex zero, which marks the end of the pattern.

Let's continue our modifications and see the result before we discuss the inner workings of WRITE_PATTERN. Here is the test version of INIT_SEC_DISP. This procedure writes the top-line pattern, the half-sector display, and finally the bottom-line pattern. Place it in the file DISP_SEC.ASM, just before DISP_HALF_SECTOR:

Listing 16-7. Add This Procedure to DISP_SEC.ASM

```
        PUBLIC  INIT_SEC_DISP
        EXTRN   WRITE_PATTERN:NEAR, SEND_CRLF:NEAR
;---------------------------------------------------------------;
;  This procedure initializes the half-sector display.          ;
;                                                                ;
; Uses:          WRITE_PATTERN, SEND_CRLF, DISP_HALF_SECTOR      ;
; Reads:         TOP_LINE_PATTERN, BOTTOM_LINE_PATTERN           ;
;---------------------------------------------------------------;
INIT_SEC_DISP   PROC    NEAR
        PUSH    DX
        LEA     DX,TOP_LINE_PATTERN
        CALL    WRITE_PATTERN
        CALL    SEND_CRLF
        XOR     DX,DX                   ;Start at the beginning of the sector
        CALL    DISP_HALF_SECTOR
        LEA     DX,BOTTOM_LINE_PATTERN
        CALL    WRITE_PATTERN
        POP     DX
        RET
INIT_SEC_DISP   ENDP
```

We used the LEA instruction to load an address into the DX register, thus WRITE_PATTERN knows where to find the pattern data.

Finally, we need to make a small change to READ_SECTOR in the file DISK_IO.ASM, to call INIT_SECTOR_DISP, rather than WRITE_HALF_

SECTOR_DISP, so that a full box will be drawn around our half-sector display:

Listing 16-8. Changes to READ_SECTOR in DISK_IO.ASM

```
        EXTRN   INIT_SEC_DISP:NEAR
;-----------------------------------------------------------------------;
; This procedure reads the first sector on disk A and dumps the first   ;
; half of this sector.                                                  ;
;-----------------------------------------------------------------------;
READ_SECTOR     PROC    NEAR
        MOV     AL,0                    ;Disk drive A (number 0)
        MOV     CX,1                    ;Read only 1 sector
        MOV     DX,0                    ;Read sector number 0
        LEA     BX,SECTOR               ;Where to store this sector
        INT     25h                     ;Read the sector
        POPF                            ;Discard flags put on stack by DOS
        XOR     DX,DX                   ;Set offset to 0 within SECTOR
        CALL    INIT_SEC_DISP           ;Dump the first half
        INT     20h                     ;Return to DOS
READ_SECTOR     ENDP
```

That's all we need to write the top and bottom lines for our sector display. Assemble and link all these files (remember to assemble the three files we changed), run the result through Exe2bin, and give it a try. Figure 16-3 shows the output we now have.

Let's see how WRITE_PATTERN works. As mentioned, it uses two new instructions. LODSB stands for *Load String Byte*, and it is one of the *string instructions*: specially designed instructions that work with strings of characters. That's not quite what we're doing here, but the 8088 doesn't care whether we're dealing with a string of characters or just numbers, so LODSB suits our purposes just fine.

LODSB moves (loads) a single byte into the AL register from the memory location given by DS:SI, a register pair we haven't used before. All the segment registers in our .COM file are set to the beginning of our one segment, CGROUP, so DS is already set for our segment. And before the LODSB instruction, we moved the offset into the SI register with the instruction MOV SI,DX.

The LODSB instruction is somewhat like the MOV instruction, but more powerful. With one LODSB instruction, the 8088 moves one byte into the AL register and then either increments or decrements the SI register. Incrementing the SI register points to the following byte in memory; decrementing the register points to the previous byte in memory.

```
A>disk_io
```

```
00 │ EB 21 90 49 42 4D 20 20 33 2E 31 00 02 02 01 00 │ δ!ÉIBM  3.1.....
10 │ 02 70 00 D0 02 FD 02 00 09 00 02 00 00 00 00 00 │ .p.▲.²..........
20 │ 00 00 00 C4 5C 08 33 ED B8 C0 07 8E D8 33 C9 0A │ ...─\.3ε╕└.Ä╪3╔.
30 │ D2 79 0E 89 1E 1E 00 8C 06 20 00 88 16 22 00 B1 │ ┳y.ë...î. .ê.".▌
40 │ 02 8E C5 8E D5 BC 00 7C 51 FC 1E 36 C5 36 78 00 │ .Ä┼Ä╒╝.|Q⌐.6┼6x.
50 │ BF 23 7C B9 0B 00 F3 A4 1F 88 0E 2C 00 A0 18 00 │ ┐#|╣..≤ñ.ê.,.á..
60 │ A2 27 00 BF 78 00 B8 23 7C AB 91 AB A1 16 00 D1 │ ó'.┐x.╕#|½æ½í..╤
70 │ E0 40 E8 00 00 E8 86 00 BB 00 05 53 B0 01 E8 AB │ α@Φ..Φå.╗..S░.Φ½
80 │ 00 5F BE 73 01 B9 0B 00 90 F3 A6 75 62 83 C7 15 │ ._╛s.╣..É≤ªubâ╟.
90 │ B1 0B 90 90 F3 A6 75 57 26 8B 47 1C 99 8B 0E 0B │ ▌..É≤ªuW&ïG.Öï..
A0 │ 00 03 C1 48 F7 F1 80 3E 71 01 60 75 02 B0 14 96 │ ..┴H÷±Ç>q.`u.░.û
B0 │ A1 11 00 B1 04 D3 E8 E8 3B 00 FF 36 1E 00 C4 1E │ í..▌.╙ΦΦ;. 6..─.
C0 │ 6F 01 E8 39 00 E8 64 00 2B F0 76 0D E8 26 00 52 │ o.Φ9.Φd.+≡v.Φ&.R
D0 │ F7 26 0B 00 03 D8 5A EB E9 CD 11 B9 02 00 D3 E0 │ ≈&...╪ZδΘ═.╣..╙α
E0 │ 80 E4 03 74 04 FE C4 8A CC 5B 58 FF 2E 6F 01 BE │ Çä.t.■─ì╠[X .o.╛
F0 │ 89 01 EB 55 90 01 06 1E 00 11 2E 20 00 C3 A1 18 │ ë.δU É...... .├í.
```

Figure 16-3. The Display with Closed Boxes.

```
A>
```

The former (incrementing) is exactly what we want to do. We want to go through the pattern, one byte at a time, starting at the beginning, and that is what our LODSB instruction does, because we used the other new instruction, CLD (*Clear Direction Flag*) to clear the direction flag. If we had set the direction flag, the LODSB instruction would decrement the SI register, instead. We'll use the LODSB instruction in a few other places in Dskpatch, always with the direction flag cleared, to increment.

Aside from LODSB and CLD, notice that we also used the PUSHF and POPF instructions to save and restore the flag register. We did this just in case we later decide to use the direction flag in a procedure that calls WRITE_PATTERN.

Adding Numbers to the Display

We're almost through with Part II of this book now. We'll create one more procedure, then we'll move on to Part III, and bigger and better things.

Right now, notice that our display lacks a row of numbers across the top. Such numbers—00 01 02 03 and so forth—would allow us to sight down the columns to find the address for any byte. So, let's write a procedure to print this row of numbers. Add this procedure, WRITE_TOP_HEX_NUMBERS, to DISP_SEC.ASM, just after INIT_SEC_DISP:

Listing 16-9. Add This Procedure to DISP_SEC.ASM

```
        EXTRN   WRITE_CHAR_N_TIMES:NEAR, WRITE_HEX:NEAR, WRITE_CHAR:NEAR
        EXTRN   WRITE_HEX_DIGIT:NEAR, SEND_CRLF:NEAR
;------------------------------------------------------------------;
; This procedure writes the index numbers (0 through F) at the top of ;
; the half-sector display.                                         ;
;                                                                  ;
; Uses:         WRITE_CHAR_N_TIMES, WRITE_HEX, WRITE_CHAR          ;
;               WRITE_HEX_DIGIT, SEND_CRLF                         ;
;------------------------------------------------------------------;
WRITE_TOP_HEX_NUMBERS   PROC    NEAR
        PUSH    CX
        PUSH    DX
        MOV     DL,' '                  ;Write 9 spaces for left side
        MOV     CX,9
        CALL    WRITE_CHAR_N_TIMES
        XOR     DH,DH                   ;Start with 0
HEX_NUMBER_LOOP:
        MOV     DL,DH
        CALL    WRITE_HEX
        MOV     DL,' '
        CALL    WRITE_CHAR
        INC     DH
        CMP     DH,10h                  ;Done yet?
        JB      HEX_NUMBER_LOOP

        MOV     DL,' '                  ;Write hex numbers over ASCII window
        MOV     CX,2
        CALL    WRITE_CHAR_N_TIMES
        XOR     DL,DL
HEX_DIGIT_LOOP:
        CALL    WRITE_HEX_DIGIT
        INC     DL
        CMP     DL,10h
        JB      HEX_DIGIT_LOOP
        CALL    SEND_CRLF
        POP     DX
        POP     CX
        RET
WRITE_TOP_HEX_NUMBERS   ENDP
```

Modify INIT_SEC_DISP (also in DISP_SEC.ASM) as follows, so it calls WRITE_TOP_HEX_NUMBERS before it writes the rest of the half-sector display:

Listing 16-10. Changes to INIT_SEC_DISP in DISP_SEC.ASM

```
;----------------------------------------------------------------;
; Uses:          WRITE_PATTERN, SEND_CRLF, DISP_HALF_SECTOR       ;
;                WRITE_TOP_HEX_NUMBERS                            ;
; Reads:         TOP_LINE_PATTERN, BOTTOM_LINE_PATTERN            ;
;----------------------------------------------------------------;
INIT_SEC_DISP   PROC    NEAR
        PUSH    DX
        CALL    WRITE_TOP_HEX_NUMBERS
        LEA     DX,TOP_LINE_PATTERN
        CALL    WRITE_PATTERN
        CALL    SEND_CRLF
        XOR     DX,DX                   ;Start at the beginning of the sector
        CALL    DISP_HALF_SECTOR
        LEA     DX,BOTTOM_LINE_PATTERN
        CALL    WRITE_PATTERN
        POP     DX
        RET
INIT_SEC_DISP   ENDP
```

Now we have a complete half-sector display, as you can see in Figure 16-4.
There are still some differences between this display and the final version.
We'll change WRITE_CHAR so it will print all 256 characters the IBM PC

Figure 16-4.   A Complete Half Sector Display.

can display, and then we'll clear the screen and center this display vertically, using the ROM BIOS routines inside the IBM Personal Computer. We'll do that next.

Summary

We've done a lot of building on our Dskpatch program, adding new procedures, changing old ones, and moving from one source file to another. From now on, if you find yourself losing track of what you're doing, refer to the complete listing of Dskpatch in Appendix B. The listing there is the final version, but you'll probably see enough resemblances to help you along.

Most of our changes in this chapter didn't rely on tricks, just hard work. But we did learn two new instructions: LODSB and CLD. LODSB is one of the string instructions that allow us to use one instruction to do the work of several. We used LODSB in WRITE_PATTERN to read consecutive bytes from the pattern table, always loading a new byte into the AL register. CLD clears the direction flag, which sets the direction for increment. Each following LODSB instruction loads the next byte from memory.

In the next part of this book we'll learn about the IBM PC's ROM BIOS routines. They will save us a lot of time.

PART III

The IBM PC's ROM BIOS

THE ROM BIOS ROUTINES

Inside your IBM Personal Computer are some computer chips, or ICs (*Integrated Circuits*), known as ROMs (*Read-Only Memory*). One of these ROMs contains a number of routines, very much like procedures, that provide all the basic routines for doing input and output to several different parts of your IBM PC. Because this ROM provides routines for performing input and output at a very low level, it is frequently referred to as the BIOS, for Basic Input Output System. DOS uses the ROM BIOS for such activities as sending characters to the screen and reading and writing to the disk, and we're free to use the ROM BIOS routines in our programs.

We'll concentrate on the BIOS routines we need for Dskpatch. Among them is a set for video display, which includes a number of functions we couldn't otherwise reach without working directly with the hardware—a very difficult job.

VIDEO_IO, the ROM BIOS Routines

We refer to the elements of the ROM BIOS as routines in order to distinguish them from procedures. We use procedures with a CALL instruction, whereas we call routines with INT instructions, not CALLs. We'll use an INT 10h instruction, for example, to call the video I/O routines, just as we used an INT 21h instruction to call routines in DOS.

Specifically, INT 10h calls the routine VIDEO_IO in the ROM BIOS. Other numbers call other routines, but we won't see any of them; VIDEO_IO provides all the functions we need outside of DOS. (Just for your information, however, DOS calls one of the other ROM BIOS routines when we ask for a sector from the disk.)

In this chapter, we'll use ROM BIOS routines to add two new procedures to Dskpatch: one to clear the screen, and the other to move the cursor to any screen location we choose. Both are very useful functions, but neither is available directly through DOS. Hence, we'll use the ROM BIOS routines to do the job. Later, we'll see even more interesting things we can do with these ROM routines, but let's begin by using INT 10h to clear the screen before we display our half sector.

The INT 10h instruction is our entry to a number of different functions. Recall that, when we used the DOS INT 21h instruction, we selected a particular function by placing its function number in the AH register. We select a VIDEO_IO function in just the same way: by placing the appropriate function number in the AH register (a full list of these functions is given in Table 17-1).

Table 17-1.   INT 10h Functions

(AH) = 0   **Set the display mode.** The AL register contains the mode number.

TEXT MODES

(AL) = 0   40 by 25, black and white mode
(AL) = 1   40 by 25, color
(AL) = 2   80 by 25, black and white
(AL) = 3   80 by 25, color
(AL) = 7   80 by 25, monochrome display adapter

GRAPHICS MODE

(AL) = 4   320 by 200, color
(AL) = 5   320 by 200, black and white
(AL) = 6   640 by 200, black and white

(AH) = 1   **Set the cursor size.**

(CH)   Starting scan line of the cursor. The top line is 0 on both the monochrome and color graphics displays, while the bottom line is 7 for the color graphics adapter and 13 for the monochrome adapter. Valid range: 0 to 31.

(CL)   Last scan line of the cursor.

The power-on setting for the color graphics adapter is CH = 6 and CL = 7. For the monochrome display: CH = 11 and CL = 12.

(AH) = 2   **Set the cursor position.**

(DH,DL)   Row, column of new cursor position; the upper left corner is (0,0).

Table 17-1. *continued*

(AH) = 2	(BH)	Page number. This is the number of the display page. The color-graphics adapter has room for several display pages, but most programs use page 0.

(AH) = 3   **Read the cursor position.**

(BH)   Page number
On exit   (DH,DL)   Row, column of cursor
                 (CH,CL)   Cursor size

(AH) = 4   **Read light pen position** (see Tech. Ref. Man.).

(AH) = 5   **Select active display page.**

(AL)   New page number (from 0 to 7 for modes 0
                 and 1; from 0 to 3 for modes 2 and 3)

(AH) = 6   **Scroll up.**

(AL)   Number of lines to blank at the bottom of
                 the window. Normal scrolling blanks one
                 line. Set to zero to blank entire window.
(CH,CL)   Row, column of upper, left corner of window
(DH,DL)   Row, column of lower, right corner of
                 window
(BH)   Display attribute to use for blank lines

(AH) = 7   **Scroll down.**

Same as scroll up (function 6), but lines are left blank at
the top of the window instead of the bottom

(AH) = 8   **Read attribute and character under the cursor.**

(BH)   Display page (text modes only)

Table 17-1. *continued*

(AH) = 8	(AL)	Character read
	(AH)	Attribute of character read (text modes only)

(AH) = 9		**Write attribute and character under the cursor.**
	(BH)	Display page (text modes only)
	(CX)	Number of times to write character and attribute of screen
	(AL)	Character to write
	(BL)	Attribute to write

(AH) = 10		**Write character under cursor** (with normal attribute).
	(BH)	Display page
	(CX)	Number of times to write character
	(AL)	Character to write

(AH) = 11 to 13		**Various graphics functions.** (See Tech. Ref. Man. for the details)

(AH) = 14		**Write teletype.** Write one character to the screen and move the cursor to the next position.
	(AL)	Character to write
	(BL)	Color of character (graphics mode only)
	(BH)	Display page (text mode)

(AH) = 15		**Return current video state.**
	(AL)	Display mode currently set
	(AH)	Number of characters per line
	(BH)	Active display pages

We'll use the INT 10h function number 6, SCROLL ACTIVE PAGE UP, to clear the screen. We don't actually want to scroll the screen, but this function also doubles as a clear-screen function. Here is the procedure; enter it into the file CURSOR.ASM:

Listing 17-1. Add This Procedure to CURSOR.ASM

```
        PUBLIC  CLEAR_SCREEN
;------------------------------------------------------------------;
; This procedure clears the entire screen.                         ;
;------------------------------------------------------------------;
CLEAR_SCREEN    PROC    NEAR
        PUSH    AX
        PUSH    BX
        PUSH    CX
        PUSH    DX
        XOR     AL,AL                   ;Blank entire window
        XOR     CX,CX                   ;Upper left corner is at (0,0)
        MOV     DH,24                   ;Bottom line of screen is line 24
        MOV     DL,79                   ;Right side is at column 79
        MOV     BH,7                    ;Use normal attribute for blanks
        MOV     AH,6                    ;Call for SCROLL-UP function
        INT     10h                     ;Clear the window
        POP     DX
        POP     CX
        POP     BX
        POP     AX
        RET
CLEAR_SCREEN    ENDP
```

It appears that INT 10h function number 6 needs quite a lot of information, even though all we want to do is clear the display. This function is rather powerful: It can actually clear any rectangular part of the screen—*window*—as it's called. We have to set the window to the entire screen by setting the first and last lines to 0 and 24, and setting the columns to 0 and 79. The routines we are using here can also clear the screen to all white (for use with black characters), or all black (for use with white characters). We want the latter, and that is what is specfied with the instruction MOV BH,7. Then, too, setting AL to 0, the number of lines to scroll, tells this routine to clear the window, rather than to scroll it.

Now we need to modify our test procedure, READ_SECTOR, to call CLEAR_SCREEN just before it starts to write the sector display. We didn't place this CALL in INIT_SEC_DISP, because we'll want to use INIT_SEC_DISP to re-write just the half-sector display, without affecting the rest of the screen.

To modify READ_SECTOR, add an EXTRN declaration for CLEAR_SCREEN and insert the CALL to CLEAR_SCREEN. Make the following changes in the file DISK_IO.ASM:

Listing 17-2. Changes to READ_SECTOR in DISK_IO.ASM

```
        EXTRN   INIT_SEC_DISP:NEAR, CLEAR_SCREEN:NEAR
;-------------------------------------------------------------------;
; This procedure reads the first sector on disk A and dumps the first ;
; half of this sector.                                              ;
;-------------------------------------------------------------------;
READ_SECTOR     PROC    NEAR
        MOV     AL,0                    ;Disk drive A (number 0)
        MOV     CX,1                    ;Read only 1 sector
        MOV     DX,0                    ;Read sector number 0
        LEA     BX,SECTOR               ;Where to store this sector
        INT     25h                     ;Read the sector
        POPF                            ;Discard flags put on stack by DOS
        XOR     DX,DX                   ;Set offset to 0 within SECTOR
        CALL    CLEAR_SCREEN
        CALL    INIT_SEC_DISP           ;Dump the first half
        INT     20h                     ;Return to DOS
READ_SECTOR     ENDP
```

Just before you run the new version of Disk_io, note where the cursor is located. Then, run Disk_io. The screen will clear, and Disk_io will start writing the half sector display wherever the cursor happened to be before you ran the program—probably at the bottom of the screen.

Even though we cleared the screen, we didn't mention anything about moving the cursor back to the top. In BASIC, the CLS command clears the screen in two steps: It clears the screen, then it moves the cursor to the top of the screen. Our procedure doesn't do that; we'll have to move the cursor ourselves.

Moving the Cursor

The INT 10h function number 2 sets the cursor position in much the same way BASIC's LOCATE statement does. We can use GOTO_XY to move the cursor anywhere on the screen (such as to the top after a clear), but we won't. Enter this procedure into the file CURSOR.ASM:

Listing 17-3. Add This Procedure to CURSOR.ASM

```
        PUBLIC  GOTO_XY
;-------------------------------------------------------------------;
; This procedure moves the cursor                                   ;
;                                                                   ;
;       DH      Row (Y)                                             ;
;       DL      Column (X)                                          ;
;-------------------------------------------------------------------;
```

Listing 17-3. *continued*

```
    GOTO_XY         PROC    NEAR
            PUSH    AX
            PUSH    BX
            MOV     BH,0                    ;Display page 0
            MOV     AH,2                    ;Call for SET CURSOR POSITION
            INT     10h
            POP     BX
            POP     AX
            RET
    GOTO_XY         ENDP
```

We'll use GOTO_XY in a revised version of INIT_SEC_DISP, to move the
cursor to the second line just before we write the half-sector display. Here are
the modifications to INIT_SEC_DISP in DISP_SEC.ASM:

Listing 17-4. Changes to INIT_SEC_DISP in DISP_SEC.ASM

```
        PUBLIC  INIT_SEC_DISP
        EXTRN   WRITE_PATTERN:NEAR, SEND_CRLF:NEAR
        EXTRN   GOTO_XY:NEAR
;-------------------------------------------------------------------;
;  This procedure initializes the half-sector display.              ;
;                                                                   ;
; Uses:      WRITE_PATTERN, SEND_CRLF, DISP_HALF_SECTOR             ;
;            WRITE_TOP_HEX_NUMBERS, GOTO_XY                         ;
; Reads:     TOP_LINE_PATTERN, BOTTOM_LINE_PATTERN                 ;
;-------------------------------------------------------------------;
INIT_SEC_DISP   PROC    NEAR
        PUSH    DX
        XOR     DL,DL               ;Move cursor into position at beginning
        MOV     DH,2                ;of 3rd line
        CALL    GOTO_XY
        CALL    WRITE_TOP_HEX_NUMBERS
        LEA     DX,TOP_LINE_PATTERN
                        .
                        .
                        .
```

If you try it now, you'll see that the half-sector display is nicely centered.

As you can see now, it's easy to work with the screen when we have the
ROM BIOS routines. In the next chapter, we'll use another routine in the
ROM BIOS to improve WRITE_CHAR, so that it will write any character to
the screen. But before we continue let's make some other changes to our program, then finish up with a procedure called WRITE_HEADER, which will
write a status line at the top of the screen, to show the current disk drive and
sector number.

Rewiring Variable Usage

We have much that we need to revamp before we create WRITE_HEADER. As they are now, many of our procedures have numbers hard-wired into them; READ_SECTOR, for example, reads sector 0 on drive A. We want to place the disk drive and sector numbers into memory variables, so more than one procedure can read them.

We'll need to change these procedures so they'll use memory variables, but let's begin by putting all memory variables into one file, DSKPATCH.ASM, to make our work simpler. Dskpatch.asm will be the first file in our program Dskpatch, so the memory variables will be easy to find there. Here is DSKPATCH.ASM, complete with a long list of memory variables:

Listing 17-5. The New File DSKPATCH.ASM

```
CGROUP  GROUP    CODE_SEG, DATA_SEG
        ASSUME   CS:CGROUP, DS:CGROUP


CODE_SEG        SEGMENT PUBLIC
        ORG      100h

        EXTRN    CLEAR_SCREEN:NEAR, READ_SECTOR:NEAR
        EXTRN    INIT_SEC_DISP:NEAR
DISK_PATCH      PROC    NEAR
        CALL     CLEAR_SCREEN
        CALL     READ_SECTOR
        CALL     INIT_SEC_DISP
        INT      20h
DISK_PATCH      ENDP

CODE_SEG        ENDS


DATA_SEG        SEGMENT PUBLIC

        PUBLIC  SECTOR_OFFSET
;------------------------------------------------;
; SECTOR_OFFSET is the offset of the half        ;
; sector display into the full sector.  It must  ;
; be a multiple of 16, and not greater than 256  ;
;------------------------------------------------;
SECTOR_OFFSET   DW       0

        PUBLIC  CURRENT_SECTOR_NO, DISK_DRIVE_NO
CURRENT_SECTOR_NO       DW       0          ;Initially sector 0
DISK_DRIVE_NO           DB       0          ;Initially Drive A:

        PUBLIC  LINES_BEFORE_SECTOR, HEADER_LINE_NO
```

Listing 17-5. *continued*

```
          PUBLIC  HEADER_PART_1, HEADER_PART_2
;----------------------------------------------;
; LINES_BEFORE_SECTOR is the number of lines    ;
; at the top of the screen before the half      ;
; sector display.                               ;
;----------------------------------------------;
LINES_BEFORE_SECTOR     DB      2
HEADER_LINE_NO          DB      0
HEADER_PART_1           DB      'Disk ',0
HEADER_PART_2           DB      '             Sector ',0

          PUBLIC  SECTOR
;----------------------------------------------;
; The entire sector (up to 8192 bytes) is       ;
; stored in this part of memory.                ;
;----------------------------------------------;
SECTOR  DB      8192 DUP (0)

DATA_SEG        ENDS

    END     DISK_PATCH
```

The main procedure, DISK_PATCH, calls three other procedures. We've seen them all before; soon we'll rewrite both READ_SECTOR and INIT_SEC_ DISP to use the variables just placed into the data segment.

Before we can use Dskpatch, we need to modify Disp_sec, to replace the definition of SECTOR with an EXTRN. We also need to alter Disk_io, to change READ_SECTOR into an ordinary procedure we can call from Dskpatch.

Let's take SECTOR first. Since we've placed it in DSKPATCH.ASM as a memory variable, we need to change the definition of SECTOR in Disp_sec to an EXTRN declaration. Make these changes in DISP_SEC.ASM:

Listing 17-6. Changes to DISP_SEC.ASM

```
DATA_SEG        SEGMENT PUBLIC
    EXTRN       SECTOR:BYTE
    PUBLIC      SECTOR
SECTOR  DB      512 DUP(0)

TOP_LINE_PATTERN        LABEL   BYTE
        DB      ' ',7
        DB      UPPER_LEFT,1
                    .
                    .
                    .
```

Let's rewrite the file DISK_IO.ASM so that it contains only procedures, and READ_SECTOR uses memory variables (not hard-wired numbers) for the sector and disk-drive numbers. Here is the new version of DISK_IO.ASM:

Listing 17-7. Changes to DISK_IO.ASM

```
CGROUP  GROUP   CODE_SEG, DATA_SEG
        ASSUME  CS:CGROUP, DS:CGROUP

CODE_SEG        SEGMENT PUBLIC
        ORG     100h
        PUBLIC  READ_SECTOR
DATA_SEG        SEGMENT PUBLIC
        EXTRN   SECTOR:BYTE
        EXTRN   DISK_DRIVE_NO:BYTE
        EXTRN   CURRENT_SECTOR_NO:WORD
DATA_SEG        ENDS
        EXTRN   INIT_SEC_DISP:NEAR, CLEAR_SCREEN:NEAR
;------------------------------------------------------------------;
; This procedure reads one sector (512 bytes) into SECTOR.         ;
;                                                                  ;
; Reads:        CURRENT_SECTOR_NO, DISK_DRIVE_NO                   ;
; Writes:       SECTOR                                             ;
;------------------------------------------------------------------;
READ_SECTOR     PROC    NEAR
        PUSH    AX
        PUSH    BX
        PUSH    CX
        PUSH    DX
        MOV     AL,DISK_DRIVE_NO        ;Drive number
        MOV     CX,1                    ;Read only 1 sector
        MOV     DX,CURRENT_SECTOR_NO    ;Logical sector number
        LEA     BX,SECTOR               ;Where to store this sector
        INT     25h                     ;Read the sector
        POPF                            ;Discard flags put on stack by DOS
        XOR     DX,DX                   ;Set offset to 0 within SECTOR
        CALL    CLEAR_SCREEN
        CALL    INIT_SEC_DISP           ;Dump the first half
        INT     20h
        POP     DX
        POP     CX
        POP     BX
        POP     AX
        RET
READ_SECTOR     ENDP

CODE_SEG        ENDS

DATA_SEG        SEGMENT PUBLIC
        EXTRN   SECTOR:BYTE
DATA_SEG        ENDS
        END
```

This new version of Disk_io uses the memory variables DISK_DRIVE_NO and CURRENT_SECTOR_NO as the disk drive and sector numbers for the sector to read. Since these variables are already defined in DSKPATCH.ASM, we won't have to change Disk_io when we start reading different sectors from other disk drives.

If you're using the Make program to rebuild DSKPATCH.COM, you'll need to make some additions to your Make file named Dskpatch:

Listing 17-8. The New Version of DSKPATCH

```
dskpatch.obj:    dskpatch.asm
      masm dskpatch;

disk_io.obj:     disk_io.asm
      masm disk_io;

disp_sec.obj:    disp_sec.asm
      masm disp_sec;

video_io.obj:    video_io.asm
      masm video_io;

cursor.obj:      cursor.asm
      masm cursor;

dskpatch.com:    dskpatch.obj disk_io.obj disp_sec.obj video_io.obj cursor.obj
      link dskpatch disk_io disp_sec video_io cursor;
      exe2bin dskpatch dskpatch.com
```

If you're not using Make, be sure to reassemble all three files changed (Dskpatch, Disk_io, and Disp_sec), and to link all five files, with Dskpatch listed first:

```
LINK DSKPATCH DISK_IO DISP_SEC VIDEO_IO CURSOR;
EXE2BIN DSKPATCH DSKPATCH.COM
```

We've made quite a few changes, so test Dskpatch and make sure it works correctly before you move on.

Writing the Header

Now that we've converted the hard-wired numbers into direct references to memory variables, we can write the procedure WRITE_HEADER to write a status line, or header, at the top of the screen. Our header will look like this:

```
Disk A              Sector 0
```

WRITE_HEADER will use WRITE_DECIMAL to write the current sector number in decimal. It will also write two strings of characters, *Disk* and *Sector* (each followed by a blank space), and a disk letter, such as A. We'll place the procedure in the file VIDEO_IO.ASM.

To begin, since we'll have a reference to the data segment (DATA_SEG), change the first line (the GROUP statement) in VIDEO_IO.ASM to read:

```
CGROUP  GROUP   CODE_SEG, DATA_SEG
```

Place the following procedure in VIDEO_IO.ASM:

Listing 17-9. Add This Procedure to VIDEO_IO.ASM

```
        PUBLIC  WRITE_HEADER
DATA_SEG        SEGMENT PUBLIC
        EXTRN   HEADER_LINE_NO:BYTE
        EXTRN   HEADER_PART_1:BYTE
        EXTRN   HEADER_PART_2:BYTE
        EXTRN   DISK_DRIVE_NO:BYTE
        EXTRN   CURRENT_SECTOR_NO:WORD
DATA_SEG        ENDS
        EXTRN   GOTO_XY:NEAR
;----------------------------------------------------------------;
; This procedure writes the header with disk-drive and sector number. ;
;                                                                ;
; Uses:      GOTO_XY, WRITE_STRING, WRITE_CHAR, WRITE_DECIMAL     ;
; Reads:     HEADER_LINE_NO, HEADER_PART_1, HEADER_PART_2         ;
;            DISK_DRIVE_NO, CURRENT_SECTOR_NO                     ;
;----------------------------------------------------------------;
WRITE_HEADER    PROC    NEAR
        PUSH    DX
        XOR     DL,DL                   ;Move cursor to header line number
        MOV     DH,HEADER_LINE_NO
        CALL    GOTO_XY
        LEA     DX,HEADER_PART_1
        CALL    WRITE_STRING
        MOV     DL,DISK_DRIVE_NO
        ADD     DL,'A'                  ;Print drives A, B, ...
        CALL    WRITE_CHAR
        LEA     DX,HEADER_PART_2
        CALL    WRITE_STRING
        MOV     DX,CURRENT_SECTOR_NO
```

Listing 17-9. *continued*

```
        CALL    WRITE_DECIMAL
        POP     DX
        RET
WRITE_HEADER    ENDP
```

The procedure WRITE_STRING doesn't exist yet. As you can see, we plan to use it to write a string of characters to the screen. The two strings, HEADER_PART_1 and HEADER_PART_2, are already defined in DSKPATCH.ASM. WRITE_STRING will use DS:DX as the address for the string.

We've chosen to supply our own string-output procedure so that our strings can contain any character, including the $, which we couldn't print with the DOS function 9. Where DOS uses a $ to mark the end of a string, we'll use a hex 0. Here is the procedure. Enter it into VIDEO_IO.ASM:

Listing 17-10. Add This Procedure to VIDEO_IO.ASM

```
        PUBLIC  WRITE_STRING
;-----------------------------------------------------------------;
; This procedure writes a string of characters to the screen.  The ;
; string must end with          DB      0                          ;
;                                                                  ;
;       DS:DX   Address of the string                              ;
;                                                                  ;
; Uses:         WRITE_CHAR                                         ;
;-----------------------------------------------------------------;
WRITE_STRING    PROC    NEAR
        PUSH    AX
        PUSH    DX
        PUSH    SI
        PUSHF                           ;Save direction flag
        CLD                             ;Set direction for increment (forward)
        MOV     SI,DX                   ;Place address into SI for LODSB
STRING_LOOP:
        LODSB                           ;Get a character into the AL register
        OR      AL,AL                   ;Have we found the 0 yet?
        JZ      END_OF_STRING           ;Yes, we are done with the string
        MOV     DL,AL                   ;No, write character
        CALL    WRITE_CHAR
        JMP     STRING_LOOP
END_OF_STRING:
        POPF                            ;Restore direction flag
        POP     SI
        POP     DX
        POP     AX
        RET
WRITE_STRING    ENDP
```

As it stands now, WRITE_STRING will write characters with ASCII codes below 32 (the space character) as a period (.), because we don't have a version of WRITE_CHAR that will write *any* character. We'll take care of that detail in the next chapter.

After all our work in this chapter, let's put the icing on the cake. Change DISK_PATCH in DSKPATCH.ASM to include the CALL to WRITE_HEADER:

Listing 17-11. Changes to DISK_PATCH in DSKPATCH.ASM

```
        EXTRN   CLEAR_SCREEN:NEAR, READ_SECTOR:NEAR
        EXTRN   INIT_SEC_DISP:NEAR, WRITE_HEADER:NEAR
DISK_PATCH      PROC    NEAR
        CALL    CLEAR_SCREEN
        CALL    WRITE_HEADER
        CALL    READ_SECTOR
        CALL    INIT_SEC_DISP
        INT     20h
DISK_PATCH      ENDP
```

Dskpatch should now produce a display like the one in Figure 17-1.

```
Disk A          Sector 0

      00 01 02 03 04 05 06 07 08 09 0A 0B 0C 0D 0E 0F    0123456789ABCDEF

  00  EB 21 90 49 42 4D 20 20 33 2E 31 00 02 02 01 00    δ!ÉIBM  3.1.....
  10  02 70 00 D0 02 FD 02 00 09 00 02 00 00 00 00 00    .p.╨.²..........
  20  00 00 00 C4 5C 08 33 ED B8 C0 07 8E D8 33 C9 0A    ...─\.3φ╕└.Ä╪3╔.
  30  D2 79 0E 89 1E 1E 00 8C 06 20 00 88 16 22 00 B1    ╥y.ë...î. .ê.".▒
  40  02 8E C5 8E D5 BC 00 7C 51 FC 1E 36 C5 36 78 00    .Ä┼Ä╒╝.|Qⁿ.6┼6x.
  50  BF 23 7C B9 0B 00 F3 A4 1F 88 0E 2C 00 A0 18 00    ┐#|╣..≤ñ.ê.,.á..
  60  A2 27 00 BF 78 00 B8 23 7C AB 91 AB A1 16 00 D1    ó'.┐x.╕#|½æ½í..╤
  70  E0 40 E8 80 00 E8 86 00 BB 00 05 53 B0 01 E8 AB    α@ΦÇ.Φå.╗..S░.Φ½
  80  00 5F BE 73 01 B9 0B 00 90 F3 A6 75 62 83 C7 15    ._╛s.╣..É≤ªubâ╟.
  90  B1 0B 90 90 F3 A6 75 57 26 8B 47 1C 99 8B 0E 0B    ▒.ÉÉ≤ªuW&ïG.Öï..
  A0  00 03 C1 48 F7 F1 80 3E 71 01 60 75 02 B0 14 96    ..┴H≈±Ç>q.`u.░.û
  B0  A1 11 00 B1 04 D3 E8 E8 3B 00 FF 36 1E 00 C4 1E    í..▒.╙ΦΦ;. 6..─.
  C0  6F 01 E8 39 00 E8 64 00 2B F0 76 0D E8 26 00 52    o.Φ9.Φd.+≡v.Φ&.R
  D0  F7 26 0B 00 03 D8 5A EB E9 CD 11 B9 02 00 D3 E0    ≈&...╪ZδΘ═.╣..╙α
  E0  80 E4 03 74 04 FE C4 8A CC 5B 58 FF 2E 6F 01 BE    ÇΣ.t.■─è╠[X .o.╛
  F0  89 01 EB 55 90 01 06 1E 00 11 2E 20 00 C3 A1 18    ë.δUÉ...... .├í.

A>
```

Figure 17-1. Dskpatch with the Header at the Top.

Summary

At last, we've met the ROM BIOS routines inside our IBM PCs, and already used two of these routines to help us toward our goal of a full Dskpatch program.

First we learned about INT 10h, function number 6, which we used to clear the screen. We also saw (though very briefly) that this function has more uses than we'll take advantage of in this book. For example, you may eventually find it helpful for scrolling portions of the screen—in Dskpatch or in your own programs.

We then used function 2 of INT 10h to move the cursor to the third line on the screen (line number 2), where we started writing our sector dump.

To make our programs easier to work with, we also rewrote several procedures so they would use memory variables, rather than hard-wired numbers. Now, we'll be able to read other sectors and change the way our program works in other ways, just by changing a few central numbers in DSKPATCH.ASM.

Finally, we wrote the procedures WRITE_HEADER and WRITE_STRING, so we could write a header at the top of the screen. As mentioned, we'll write an improved version of WRITE_CHAR in the next chapter, replacing the dots in the ASCII window of our display with graphics characters. And thanks to modular design, we'll do this without changing any of the procedures that use WRITE_CHAR.

THE ULTIMATE
WRITE_CHAR

We made good use of the ROM BIOS routines in the last chapter to clear the screen and move the cursor. But there are many more uses for the ROM BIOS, and we'll see some of them in this chapter.

Using DOS alone, we haven't been able to display all 256 of the characters that the IBM PC is capable of displaying. So, in this chapter, we'll present a new version of WRITE_CHAR that displays any character, thanks to another VIDEO_IO function.

Then, we'll add another useful procedure, called CLEAR_TO_END_OF_ LINE, that clears the line from the cursor to the right edge of the screen. We'll put this to use in WRITE_HEADER, so that it will clear the rest of the line.

Suppose we go from sector number 10 (two digits) to sector number 9. A zero would be left over from the 10 after we call WRITE_HEADER with the sector set to 9. CLEAR_TO_END_OF_LINE will clear this zero, as well as anything else on the remainder of the line.

A New WRITE_CHAR

The ROM BIOS function 9 for INT 10h writes a character and its *attribute* at the current cursor position. The attribute controls such features as underlining, blinking, and color (see the description of the different color codes in your BASIC manual under COLOR). We'll use only two attributes for Dskpatch: attribute 7, which is the normal attribute, and attribute 70h, which is a foreground color of zero and background of 7 and produces inverse video (black characters on a white background). We can set the attributes individually for each character, and we'll do this later to create a block cursor in inverse video—known as a *phantom* cursor. For now, though, we'll just use the normal attribute when we write a character.

INT 10h, function 9 writes the character and attribute at the current cursor position. Unlike DOS, it doesn't advance the cursor to the next character position unless it writes more than one copy of the character. We'll use this fact later, in a different procedure, but now we only want one copy of each character, so we'll move the cursor ourselves.

Here is the new version of WRITE_CHAR, which writes a character and then moves the cursor right one character. Enter it into the file VIDEO_ IO.ASM:

Listing 18-1. Changes to WRITE_CHAR in VIDEO_IO.ASM

```
        PUBLIC  WRITE_CHAR
        EXTRN   CURSOR_RIGHT:NEAR
;-----------------------------------------------------------------------;
; This procedure outputs a character to the screen using the ROM BIOS   ;
; routines, so characters such as the backspace are treated as          ;
; any other character and are displayed.                                ;
;   This procedure must do a bit of work to update the cursor position. ;
;                                                                       ;
;       DL      Byte to print on screen                                 ;
;                                                                       ;
; Uses:         CURSOR_RIGHT                                            ;
;-----------------------------------------------------------------------;
WRITE_CHAR      PROC    NEAR
        PUSH    AX
        PUSH    BX
        PUSH    CX
        PUSH    DX
        MOV     AH,9            ;Call for output of character/attribute
        MOV     BH,0            ;Set to display page 0
        MOV     CX,1            ;Write only one character
        MOV     AL,DL           ;Character to write
        MOV     BL,7            ;Normal attribute
        INT     10h             ;Write character and attribute
        CALL    CURSOR_RIGHT    ;Now move to next cursor position
        POP     DX
        POP     CX
        POP     BX
        POP     AX
        RET
WRITE_CHAR      ENDP
```

In reading through this procedure, you may have wondered why we included the instruction MOV BH,0. If you have a graphics display adapter, your adapter has four text pages in normal text mode. We'll only use the first page, page 0; hence, the instruction.

As for the cursor, WRITE_CHAR uses the procedure CURSOR_RIGHT to move the cursor right one character position or to the beginning of the next line if the movement would take the cursor past column 79. Place the following procedure into CURSOR.ASM:

Listing 18-2. Add This Procedure to CURSOR.ASM

```
        PUBLIC  CURSOR_RIGHT
;-----------------------------------------------------------------------;
; This procedure moves the cursor one position to the right or to the   ;
; next line if the cursor was at the end of a line.                     ;
;                                                                       ;
; Uses:         SEND_CRLF                                               ;
;-----------------------------------------------------------------------;
```

Listing 18-2. *continued*

```
CURSOR_RIGHT      PROC      NEAR
          PUSH    AX
          PUSH    BX
          PUSH    CX
          PUSH    DX
          MOV     AH,3                ;Read the current cursor position
          MOV     BH,0                ;On page 0
          INT     10h                 ;Read cursor position
          MOV     AH,2                ;Set new cursor position
          INC     DL                  ;Set column to next position
          CMP     DL,79               ;Make sure column <= 79
          JBE     OK
          CALL    SEND_CRLF           ;Go to next line
          JMP     DONE
OK:       INT     10h
DONE:     POP     DX
          POP     CX
          POP     BX
          POP     AX
          RET
CURSOR_RIGHT      ENDP
```

CURSOR_RIGHT uses two new INT 10h functions. Function 3 reads the position of the cursor, and function 2 changes the cursor position. The procedure first uses function 3 to find the cursor position, which is returned in two bytes, the column number in DL, and the line number in DH. Then, CURSOR_RIGHT increments the column number (in DL) and moves the cursor. If DL was at the last column (79), the procedure sends a carriage-return/linefeed pair to move the cursor to the next line. We don't need this column 79 check in Dskpatch, but including it makes CURSOR_RIGHT a general-purpose procedure you can use in any of your own programs.

With these changes, Dskpatch should now display all 256 characters as shown in Figure 18.1.

You can verify that it does by searching for a byte with a value less than 20h and seeing whether some strange character has replaced the period that value formerly produced in the ASCII window.

Now let's do something perhaps even more interesting: let's write a procedure to clear a line from the cursor position to the end.

Clearing to the End of a Line

In the last chapter, we used INT 10h, function 6, to clear the screen in the CLEAR_SCREEN procedure. At that time, we mentioned that function 6

```
Disk A          Sector 0

     00 01 02 03 04 05 06 07 08 09 0A 0B 0C 0D 0E 0F   0123456789ABCDEF

 00  EB 21 90 49 42 4D 20 20 33 2E 31 00 02 02 01 00   δ!ÉIBM  3.1 ☻☻☺ 
 10  02 70 00 D0 02 FD 02 00 09 00 02 00 00 00 00 00   ☻p ╨☻²☻ ○ ☻     
 20  00 00 00 C4 5C 08 33 ED B8 C0 07 8E D8 33 C9 0A      ─\◘3φ╕└•Ä╪3╔◙
 30  D2 79 0E 89 1E 1E 00 8C 06 20 00 88 16 22 00 B1   ╥y♫ë▲▲ î♠  ê▬" ▒
 40  02 8E C5 8E D5 BC 00 7C 51 FC 1E 36 C5 36 78 00   ☻Ä┼Ä╒╝ |Qⁿ▲6┼6x 
 50  BF 23 7C B9 0B 00 F3 A4 1F 88 0E 2C 00 A0 18 00   ┐#|╣♂ ≤ñ▼ê♫, á↑ 
 60  A2 27 00 BF 78 00 B8 23 7C AB 91 AB A1 16 00 D1   ó' ┐x ╕#|½æ½í▬ ╤
 70  E0 40 E8 80 00 E8 86 00 BB 00 05 53 B0 01 E8 AB   α@ΦÇ Φå ╗ ♣S░☺Φ½
 80  00 5F BE 73 01 B9 0B 00 90 F3 A6 75 62 83 C7 15    _╛s☺╣♂ É≤ªubâ╟§
 90  B1 0B 90 90 F3 A6 75 57 26 8B 47 1C 99 8B 0E 0B   ▒♂ÉÉ≤ªuW&ïG∟Öï♫♂
 A0  00 03 C1 48 F7 F1 80 3E 71 01 60 75 02 B0 14 96    ♥┴H≈±Ç>q☺`u☻░¶û
 B0  A1 11 00 B1 04 D3 E8 E8 3B 00 FF 36 1E 00 C4 1E   í◄ ▒♦╙ΦΦ;  6▲ ─▲
 C0  6F 01 E8 39 00 E8 64 00 2B F0 76 0D E8 26 00 52   o☺Φ9 Φd +≡v♪Φ& R
 D0  F7 26 0B 00 03 D8 5A EB E9 CD 11 B9 02 00 D3 E0   ≈&♂ ♥╪ZδΘ═◄╣☻ ╙α
 E0  80 E4 03 74 04 FE C4 8A CC 5B 58 FF 2E 6F 01 BE   ÇΣ♥t♦■─è╠[X .o☺╛
 F0  89 01 EB 55 90 01 06 1E 00 11 2E 20 00 C3 A1 18   ë☺δUÉ☺♠▲ ◄.  ├í↑

A>
```

Figure 18-1. Dskpatch with the New WRITE_CHAR.

could be used to clear any rectangular window. That capability applies even if a window is only one line high and less than one line long, so we can use function 6 to clear part of a line—to the end of the line.

The left side of the window, in this case, is the column number of the cursor, which we get with a function 3 call (also used by CURSOR_RIGHT). The right side of the window is always at column 79. You can see the details in CLEAR_TO_END_OF_LINE; place the procedure in CURSOR.ASM:

Listing 18-3. Add This Procedure to CURSOR.ASM

```
        PUBLIC  CLEAR_TO_END_OF_LINE
;----------------------------------------------------------------------;
; This procedure clears the line from the current cursor position to   ;
; the end of that line.                                                ;
;----------------------------------------------------------------------;
CLEAR_TO_END_OF_LINE    PROC    NEAR
        PUSH    AX
        PUSH    BX
        PUSH    CX
        PUSH    DX
        MOV     AH,3                    ;Read current cursor position
        XOR     BH,BH                   ; on page 0
        INT     10h                     ;Now have (X,Y) in DL, DH
```

Listing 18-3. *continued*

```
        MOV     AH,6                    ;Set up to clear to end of line
        XOR     AL,AL                   ;Clear window
        MOV     CH,DH                   ;All on same line
        MOV     CL,DL                   ;Start at the cursor position
        MOV     DL,79                   ;And stop at the end of the line
        MOV     BH,7                    ;Use normal attribute
        INT     10h
        POP     DX
        POP     CX
        POP     BX
        POP     AX
        RET
CLEAR_TO_END_OF_LINE    ENDP
```

We'll use this procedure in WRITE_HEADER, to clear the rest of the line when we start reading other sectors (we'll do that very soon). There isn't any way for you to see CLEAR_TO_END_OF_LINE work with WRITE_HEADER until we add the procedures that allow us to read a different sector and update the display, but let's revise WRITE_HEADER now, just to get it out of the way. Make the following changes to WRITE_HEADER in VIDEO_IO.ASM, to call CLEAR_TO_END_OF_LINE at the end of the procedure:

Listing 18-4. Changes to WRITE_HEADER in VIDEO_IO.ASM

```
        PUBLIC  WRITE_HEADER
DATA_SEG        SEGMENT PUBLIC
        EXTRN   HEADER_LINE_NO:BYTE
        EXTRN   HEADER_PART_1:BYTE
        EXTRN   HEADER_PART_2:BYTE
        EXTRN   DISK_DRIVE_NO:BYTE
        EXTRN   CURRENT_SECTOR_NO:WORD
DATA_SEG        ENDS
        EXTRN   GOTO_XY:NEAR, CLEAR_TO_END_OF_LINE:NEAR
;----------------------------------------------------------------;
;  This procedure writes the header with disk-drive and sector number.  ;
;                                                                ;
; Uses:          GOTO_XY, WRITE_STRING, WRITE_CHAR, WRITE_DECIMAL ;
;                CLEAR_TO_END_OF_LINE                            ;
; Reads:         HEADER_LINE_NO, HEADER_PART_1, HEADER_PART_2    ;
;                DISK_DRIVE_NO, CURRENT_SECTOR_NO                ;
;----------------------------------------------------------------;
WRITE_HEADER    PROC    NEAR
        PUSH    DX
        XOR     DL,DL                   ;Move cursor to header line number
        MOV     DH,HEADER_LINE_NO
        CALL    GOTO_XY
        LEA     DX,HEADER_PART_1
```

Listing 18-4. *continued*

```
        CALL    WRITE_STRING
        MOV     DL,DISK_DRIVE_NO
        ADD     DL,'A'                  ;Print drives A, B, ...
        CALL    WRITE_CHAR
        LEA     DX,HEADER_PART_2
        CALL    WRITE_STRING
        MOV     DX,CURRENT_SECTOR_NO
        CALL    WRITE_DECIMAL
        CALL    CLEAR_TO_END_OF_LINE    ;Clear rest of sector number
        POP     DX
        RET
WRITE_HEADER    ENDP
```

This revision marks both the final version of WRITE_HEADER and the completion of the file CURSOR.ASM. We are still missing several important parts of Dskpatch, though. In the next chapter, we'll continue on and add the central dispatcher for keyboard commands, we'll be able to press F1 and F2 to read other sectors on the disk.

Summary

This chapter has been relatively easy, without much in the way of new information or tricks. We did learn how to use INT 10h, function number 9, in the ROM BIOS to write any character to the screen.

In the process, we also saw how to read the cursor position with INT 10h function 3, so we could move the cursor right one position after we wrote a character. The reason: INT 10h function 9 doesn't move the cursor after it writes just one character, unless it writes more than one copy of the character. Finally, we put INT 10h function 6 to work clearing part of just one line.

In the next chapter, we'll get down to business again as we build the central dispatcher.

19

THE DISPATCHER

In any language it's nice to have a well-written program that does something, but to really bring a program to life we need to make it interactive. It's human nature to say, "If I do this, you do that," so we'll use this chapter to add some interactivity to Dskpatch. We'll write a simple keyboard-input procedure and a central dispatcher. The dispatcher's job will be to call the correct procedure for each key pushed. For example, when we press the F1 key to read and display the previous sector, the dispatcher will call a procedure called PREVIOUS_SECTOR. To do this, we'll be making many changes to Dskpatch. We'll start by creating DISPATCHER, the central dispatcher, and some other procedures for display formatting. Next, we'll add two new procedures, PREVIOUS_SECTOR and NEXT_SECTOR, which we'll call through DISPATCHER.

The Dispatcher

The Dispatcher will be the central control for Dskpatch, so all keyboard input and editing will be done through it. DISPATCHER's job will be to read characters and call other procedures to do the work. You'll soon see how the dispatcher does its work, but first let's see how it fits into Dskpatch.

DISPATCHER will have its own prompt line, just under the half-sector display where the cursor waits for keyboard input. You won't be able to enter hex numbers in our first version of the keyboard-input procedure, but later on you will. Here are our first modifications to DSKPATCH.ASM; these add the data for a prompt line:

Listing 19-1. Additions to DATA_SEG in DSKPATCH.ASM

```
HEADER_LINE_NO          DB      0
HEADER_PART_1           DB      'Disk ',0
HEADER_PART_2           DB      '        Sector ',0
        PUBLIC  PROMPT_LINE_NO, EDITOR_PROMPT
PROMPT_LINE_NO          DB      21
EDITOR_PROMPT           DB      'Press function key, or enter'
                        DB      ' character or hex byte: ',0
```

We'll add more prompts later to take care of such matters as inputting a new sector number, so we'll make our job simpler by using a common procedure, WRITE_PROMPT_LINE, to write each prompt line. Each procedure that uses WRITE_PROMPT_LINE will supply it with the address of the prompt (here, the address of EDITOR_PROMPT), and then write the prompt on line 21 (because PROMPT_LINE_NO is 21). For example, this new version of DISK_PATCH (in DSKPATCH.ASM) uses WRITE_PROMPT_LINE just before it calls DISPATCHER:

Listing 19-2. Additions to DISK_PATCH in DSKPATCH.ASM

```
            EXTRN   CLEAR_SCREEN:NEAR, READ_SECTOR:NEAR
            EXTRN   INIT_SEC_DISP:NEAR, WRITE_HEADER:NEAR
            EXTRN   WRITE_PROMPT_LINE:NEAR, DISPATCHER:NEAR
DISK_PATCH  PROC    NEAR
            CALL    CLEAR_SCREEN
            CALL    WRITE_HEADER
            CALL    READ_SECTOR
            CALL    INIT_SEC_DISP
            LEA     DX,EDITOR_PROMPT
            CALL    WRITE_PROMPT_LINE
            CALL    DISPATCHER
            INT     20h
DISK_PATCH  ENDP
```

The dispatcher itself is a fairly simple program, but we do use some new tricks in it. The following listing is our first version of the file DISPATCH.ASM:

Listing 19-3. The New File DISPATCH.ASM.

```
CGROUP  GROUP   CODE_SEG, DATA_SEG
        ASSUME  CS:CGROUP, DS:CGROUP


CODE_SEG        SEGMENT PUBLIC

        PUBLIC  DISPATCHER
        EXTRN   READ_BYTE:NEAR
;-------------------------------------------------------------------;
; This is the central dispatcher. During normal editing and viewing, ;
; this procedure reads characters from the keyboard and, if the char ;
; is a command key (such as a cursor key), DISPATCHER calls the       ;
; procedures that do the actual work.  This dispatching is done for   ;
; special keys listed in the table DISPATCH_TABLE, where the procedure ;
; addresses are stored just after the key names.                     ;
;   If the character is not a special key, then it should be placed   ;
; directly into the sector buffer--this is the editing mode.         ;
;                                                                     ;
; Uses:          READ_BYTE                                            ;
;-------------------------------------------------------------------;
```

Listing 19-3. *continued*

```
DISPATCHER      PROC    NEAR
        PUSH    AX
        PUSH    BX
DISPATCH_LOOP:
        CALL    READ_BYTE               ;Read character into AX
        OR      AH,AH                   ;AX = 0 if no character read, -1
                                        ; for an extended code.
        JZ      DISPATCH_LOOP           ;No character read, try again
        JS      SPECIAL_KEY             ;Read extended code
; do nothing with the character for now
        JMP     DISPATCH_LOOP           ;Read another character
SPECIAL_KEY:
        CMP     AL,68                   ;F10--exit?
        JE      END_DISPATCH            ;Yes, leave
                                        ;Use BX to look through table
        LEA     BX,DISPATCH_TABLE
SPECIAL_LOOP:
        CMP     BYTE PTR [BX],0         ;End of table?
        JE      NOT_IN_TABLE            ;Yes, key was not in the table
        CMP     AL,[BX]                 ;Is it this table entry?
        JE      DISPATCH                ;Yes, then dispatch
        ADD     BX,3                    ;No, try next entry
        JMP     SPECIAL_LOOP            ;Check next table entry

DISPATCH:
        INC     BX                      ;Point to address of procedure
        CALL    WORD PTR [BX]           ;Call procedure
        JMP     DISPATCH_LOOP           ;Wait for another key

NOT_IN_TABLE:                           ;Do nothing, just read next character
        JMP     DISPATCH_LOOP

END_DISPATCH:
        POP     BX
        POP     AX
        RET
DISPATCHER      ENDP

CODE_SEG        ENDS


DATA_SEG        SEGMENT PUBLIC


CODE_SEG        SEGMENT PUBLIC
        EXTRN   NEXT_SECTOR:NEAR        ;In DISK_IO.ASM
        EXTRN   PREVIOUS_SECTOR:NEAR    ;In DISK_IO.ASM
CODE_SEG        ENDS
```

Listing 19-3. *continued*

```
;----------------------------------------+----------------------------------;
; This table contains the legal extended ASCII keys and the addresses   ;
; of the procedures that should be called when each key is pressed.      ;
;       The format of the table is                                       ;
;               DB      72              ;Extended code for cursor up      ;
;               DW      OFFSET CGROUP:PHANTOM_UP                          ;
;-------------------------------------------------------------------------;
DISPATCH_TABLE  LABEL   BYTE
        DB      59                              ;F1
        DW      OFFSET CGROUP:PREVIOUS_SECTOR
        DB      60                              ;F2
        DW      OFFSET CGROUP:NEXT_SECTOR
        DB      0                       ;End of the table
DATA_SEG        ENDS

        END
```

DISPATCH_TABLE holds the extended ASCII codes for the F1 and F2 keys. Each code is followed by the address of the procedure DISPATCHER should call when it reads that particular extended code. For example, when READ_BYTE, which is called by DISPATCHER, reads an F1 key (extended code 59), DISPATCHER calls the procedure PREVIOUS_SECTOR.

The addresses of the procedures we want DISPATCHER to call are in the dispatch table, so we used a new pseudo-op, OFFSET, to obtain them. The line

```
DW      OFFSET CGROUP:PREVIOUS_SECTOR
```

for example, tells the assembler to use the *offset* of our PREVIOUS_SECTOR procedure. This offset is calculated relative to the start of our group CGROUP, and it is why we need the CGROUP: in front of the procedure name. Had we not put CGROUP there, the assembler would calculate the address of PREVI-OUS_SECTOR from the start of the code segment, and that might not be what we want. (As it turns out here, this CGROUP isn't absolutely necessary, because the code segment is loaded first in our program. Still, in the interest of clarity, we'll write OFFSET CGROUP: anyway.)

Notice that DISPATCH_TABLE contains both byte and word data. This raises a few considerations. In the past, we've always dealt with tables of one type or the other: either all words, or all bytes. But here, we have both, so we have to tell the assembler which type of data to expect when we use a CMP or CALL instruction. In the case of an instruction written like this:

```
CMP     [BX],0
```

the assembler doesn't know whether we want to compare words or bytes. But by writing the instruction like this:

```
CMP     BYTE PTR [BX],0
```

we tell the assembler that BX points to a byte, and that we want a byte compare. Similarly, the instruction CMP WORD PTR [BX],0 would compare words. On the other hand, an instruction like CMP AL,[BX] doesn't cause any problems, because AL is a byte register, and the assembler knows without being told that we want a byte compare.

Then, too, remember that a CALL instruction can be either a NEAR or a FAR CALL. A NEAR CALL needs one word for the address, while the FAR CALL needs two. Here, the instruction:

```
CALL    WORD PTR [BX]
```

tells the assembler, with WORD PTR, that [BX] points to one word, so it should generate a short CALL and use the word pointed to by [BX] as the address, that being the address we stored in DISPATCH_TABLE. (For a FAR CALL, which uses a two-word address, we would use the instruction CALL DWORD PTR [BX]. DWORD stands for *Double Word*, or two words.)

As you'll see in Chapter 22, we can easily add more key commands to Dskpatch simply by adding more procedures and placing new entries in DIS-PATCH_TABLE. Right now, however, we still need to add four procedures before we can test this new version of Dskpatch. We're missing READ_BYTE, WRITE_PROMPT_LINE, PREVIOUS_SECTOR, and NEXT_SECTOR.

READ_BYTE is a procedure to read characters and extended ASCII codes from the keyboard. The final version will be able to read special keys (such as the function and cursor keys), ASCII characters, and two-digit hex numbers. At this point, we'll write a simple version of READ_BYTE—to read either a character or a special key. Here is the first version of KBD_IO.ASM, which is the file in which we'll store all our procedures to read from the keyboard:

```
Listing 19-4. The New File KBD_IO.ASM

  CGROUP  GROUP   CODE_SEG
          ASSUME  CS:CGROUP, DS:CGROUP


  CODE_SEG        SEGMENT PUBLIC
          PUBLIC  READ_BYTE
```

Listing 19-4. *continued*

```
;-----------------------------------------------------------------;
; This procedure reads a single ASCII character.  This is just    ;
; a test version of READ_BYTE.                                    ;
;                                                                 ;
; Returns byte in      AL      Character code (unless AH = 0)     ;
;                       AH      1 if read ASCII char              ;
;                               -1 if read a special key          ;
;-----------------------------------------------------------------;
READ_BYTE       PROC    NEAR
        MOV     AH,7                    ;Read character without echo
        INT     21h                     ; and place into AL
        OR      AL,AL                   ;Is it an extended code?
        JZ      EXTENDED_CODE           ;Yes
NOT_EXTENDED:
        MOV     AH,1                    ;Signal normal ASCII character
DONE_READING:
        RET

EXTENDED_CODE:
        INT     21h                     ;Read the extended code
        MOV     AH,0FFh                 ;Signal extended code
        JMP     DONE_READING
READ_BYTE       ENDP

CODE_SEG        ENDS

        END
```

We'll add WRITE_PROMPT_LINE to VIDEO_IO.ASM as follows:

Listing 19-5. Add This Procedure to VIDEO_IO.ASM

```
        PUBLIC  WRITE_PROMPT_LINE
        EXTRN   CLEAR_TO_END_OF_LINE:NEAR
        EXTRN   GOTO_XY:NEAR
DATA_SEG        SEGMENT PUBLIC
        EXTRN   PROMPT_LINE_NO:BYTE
DATA_SEG        ENDS
;-----------------------------------------------------------------;
; This procedure writes the prompt line to the screen and clears the ;
; end of the line.                                                ;
;                                                                 ;
;       DS:DX   Address of the prompt-line message                ;
;                                                                 ;
; Uses:         WRITE_STRING, CLEAR_TO_END_OF_LINE, GOTO_XY        ;
; Reads:        PROMPT_LINE_NO                                    ;
;-----------------------------------------------------------------;
```

Listing 19-5. *continued*

```
WRITE_PROMPT_LINE        PROC    NEAR
        PUSH    DX
        XOR     DL,DL                   ;Write the prompt line and
        MOV     DH,PROMPT_LINE_NO       ; move the cursor there
        CALL    GOTO_XY
        POP     DX
        CALL    WRITE_STRING
        CALL    CLEAR_TO_END_OF_LINE
        RET
WRITE_PROMPT_LINE        ENDP
```

There really isn't much to this procedure. It moves the cursor to the beginning of the prompt line, which we set (in DSKPATCH.ASM) to line 21. Then, it writes the prompt line and clears the rest of the line. The cursor is at the end of the prompt when WRITE_PROMPT_LINE is done, and the rest of the line is cleared by CLEAR_TO_END_OF_LINE.

Reading Other Sectors

Finally, we need the two procedures PREVIOUS_SECTOR and NEXT_ SECTOR, to read and redisplay the previous and next disk sectors. Add these two procedures to DISK_IO.ASM:

Listing 19-6. Add These Procedures to DISK_IO.ASM

```
        PUBLIC  PREVIOUS_SECTOR
        EXTRN   INIT_SEC_DISP:NEAR, WRITE_HEADER:NEAR
        EXTRN   WRITE_PROMPT_LINE:NEAR
DATA_SEG        SEGMENT PUBLIC
        EXTRN   CURRENT_SECTOR_NO:WORD, EDITOR_PROMPT:BYTE
DATA_SEG        ENDS
;-----------------------------------------------------------------;
; This procedure reads the previous sector, if possible.          ;
;                                                                 ;
; Uses:          WRITE_HEADER, READ_SECTOR, INIT_SEC_DISP         ;
;                WRITE_PROMPT_LINE                                ;
; Reads:         CURRENT_SECTOR_NO, EDITOR_PROMPT                 ;
; Writes:        CURRENT_SECTOR_NO                                ;
;-----------------------------------------------------------------;
PREVIOUS_SECTOR          PROC    NEAR
        PUSH    AX
        PUSH    DX
        MOV     AX,CURRENT_SECTOR_NO    ;Get current sector number
        OR      AX,AX                   ;Don't decrement if already 0
```

Listing 19-6. *continued*

```
        JZ      DONT_DECREMENT_SECTOR
        DEC     AX
        MOV     CURRENT_SECTOR_NO,AX    ;Save new sector number
        CALL    WRITE_HEADER
        CALL    READ_SECTOR
        CALL    INIT_SEC_DISP           ;Display new sector
        LEA     DX,EDITOR_PROMPT
        CALL    WRITE_PROMPT_LINE
DONT_DECREMENT_SECTOR:
        POP     DX
        POP     AX
        RET
PREVIOUS_SECTOR         ENDP

        PUBLIC  NEXT_SECTOR
        EXTRN   INIT_SEC_DISP:NEAR, WRITE_HEADER:NEAR
        EXTRN   WRITE_PROMPT_LINE:NEAR
DATA_SEG        SEGMENT PUBLIC
        EXTRN   CURRENT_SECTOR_NO:WORD, EDITOR_PROMPT:BYTE
DATA_SEG        ENDS
;-----------------------------------------------------------------;
; Reads the next sector.                                          ;
;                                                                 ;
; Uses:          WRITE_HEADER, READ_SECTOR, INIT_SEC_DISP         ;
;                WRITE_PROMPT_LINE                                ;
; Reads:         CURRENT_SECTOR_NO, EDITOR_PROMPT                 ;
; Writes:        CURRENT_SECTOR_NO                                ;
;-----------------------------------------------------------------;
NEXT_SECTOR     PROC    NEAR
        PUSH    AX
        PUSH    DX
        MOV     AX,CURRENT_SECTOR_NO
        INC     AX                      ;Move to next sector
        MOV     CURRENT_SECTOR_NO,AX
        CALL    WRITE_HEADER
        CALL    READ_SECTOR
        CALL    INIT_SEC_DISP           ;Display new sector
        LEA     DX,EDITOR_PROMPT
        CALL    WRITE_PROMPT_LINE
        POP     DX
        POP     AX
        RET
NEXT_SECTOR     ENDP
```

Now, you're ready to assembly all the files we created or changed: Dskpatch, Video_io, Kbd_io, Dispatch, and Disk_io. When you link the Dskpatch files, remember there are now seven of them: Dskpatch, Disp_sec, Disk_io, Video_io, Kbd_io, Dispatch, and Cursor.

If you are using Make, here are the additions you need to make to the file

Dskpatch (the backslash at the end of the fourth line from the bottom tells Make we're continuing the list of files onto the next line):

Listing 19-7. Changes to the DSKPATCH Make File

```
cursor.obj:     cursor.asm
        masm cursor;

dispatch.obj:   dispatch.asm
        masm dispatch;

kbd_io.obj:     kbd_io.asm
        masm kbd_io;

dskpatch.com:   dskpatch.obj disk_io.obj disp_sec.obj video_io.obj cursor.obj \
        dispatch.obj kbd_io.obj
        link dskpatch disk_io disp_sec video_io cursor dispatch kbd_io;
        exe2bin dskpatch dskpatch.com
```

If you do not have Make, you may wish to write the following short batch file to link and create your .COM file:

```
LINK DSKPATCH DISK_IO DISP_SEC VIDEO_IO CURSOR DISPATCH KBD_IO;
EXE2BIN DSKPATCH DSKPATCH.COM
```

As we add more files, you'll only need to change this batch file, rather than type this long link list each time you rebuild the .COM program.

This version of Dskpatch has three active keys: F1 reads and displays the previous sector, stopping at sector 0; F2 reads the next sector; F10 exits from Dskpatch. Give these keys a try. Your display should now look something like Figure 19-1.

Philosophy of the Following Chapters

We covered far more ground than usual in this chapter, and in that respect you've had a taste of the philosophy we'll be following in Chapters 20 through 27. From now on, we'll move along at a fairly rapid pace, so that we can get through more examples of how to write large programs. You'll also find more procedures that you can use in your own programs.

These chapters are here for you to learn from, hence the rather high density of new procedures. But in the final two chapters of the book, we'll come back to learning new subjects, so hang on, or (if you wish) skip the remaining chap-

```
Disk A        Sector 0

          00 01 02 03 04 05 06 07 08 09 0A 0B 0C 0D 0E 0F   0123456789ABCDEF

   00 ║ EB 21 90 49 42 4D 20 20 33 2E 31 00 02 02 01 00    δ!ÉIBM  3.1 ☺☺◙
   10 ║ 02 70 00 D0 02 FD 02 00 09 00 02 00 00 00 00 00    ☺p ▲☺²◙ ○ ◙
   20 ║ 00 00 00 C4 5C 08 33 ED B8 C0 07 8E D8 33 C9 0A    -\☐3φ┐ L·Ä┼3┌◙
   30 ║ D2 79 0E 89 1E 1E 00 8C 06 20 00 88 16 22 00 B1    πулë▲▲ î◆ ê."┃
   40 ║ 02 8E C5 8E D5 BC 00 7C 51 FC 1E 36 C5 36 78 00    êÄ┼Ä┌⌐ │Q▀▲6┼6x
   50 ║ BF 23 7C B9 0B 00 F3 A4 1F 88 0E 2C 00 A0 18 00    ┐#│╕♂ ∫ñ▼ê♫,  ↑
   60 ║ A2 27 00 BF 78 00 B8 23 7C AB 91 AB A1 16 00 D1    ó' ┐x ┐#│½z½í ▬ ╤
   70 ║ E8 40 E8 80 00 E8 86 00 BB 00 05 53 B0 01 E8 AB    ╢@Ç┤ Φ ╚ ♦S▌☺Φ½
   80 ║ 00 5F BE 73 01 B9 0B 00 90 F3 A6 75 62 83 C7 15    ┃δÉÉ┌ºuWàïG┘Ö¡ß
   90 ║ B1 0B 90 90 F3 A6 75 57 26 8B 47 1C 99 8B 0E 0B    ♦┴H≡±Ç)q⊖˙u⊖╖û
   A0 ║ 00 03 C1 48 F7 F1 80 3E 71 01 60 75 02 B0 14 96    í◄ ┌♦└▌§; 6▲ -▲
   B0 ║ A1 11 00 B1 04 D3 E8 E8 3B 00 FF 36 1E 00 C4 1E    o⊙%9 ♂å ┼≡√┌à R
   C0 ║ 6F 01 E8 39 00 E8 64 00 2B F0 76 0D E8 26 00 52    ≈åδ ♥↓Z╢⊖=◄┤◙ L╓
   D0 ║ F7 26 0B 00 03 D8 5A EB E9 CD 11 B9 02 00 D3 E8    Ç∑♥♦■-è╢IX .o⌐
   E0 ║ 80 E4 03 74 04 FE C4 8A CC 5B 58 FF 2E 6F 01 BE    ë⊖δÜÉ⊖◆▲ ◄. ├├í
   F0 ║ 89 01 EB 55 90 01 06 1E 00 11 2E 20 00 C3 A1 18
```

Press function key, or enter character or hex byte:

Figure 19-1.   Dskpatch with the Prompt Line.

ters on Dskpatch until you're ready to write your own programs. When you're ready to come back again, you'll find many useful tidbits for programming.

Of course, if you're champing at the bit and eager to write your own procedures, read the next chapter. There, you'll find a number of hints, and we'll give you a chance to write the procedures in following chapters by giving you enough details to forge ahead.

From Chapter 21 on, we'll present many different procedures and let you discover how they work. Why? There are two reasons, both related to setting you on your feet and on your way to assembly language programming. First, we want you to have a library of procedures you can use in your own programs; to use them comfortably, you need to exercise your own skills. Second, by presenting this large programming example, we want to show you not only how to write a large program, but to give you a feel for it as well.

So take the rest of this book in the way that suits you best. Chapter 20 is for those of you eager to write your own programs. In Chapter 21, we'll return to Dskpatch and build the procedures to write and move what we call a phantom cursor: a reverse-video cursor for the hex and ASCII displays.

20

A PROGRAMMING CHALLENGE

This book contains six more chapters of procedures. If you want to try navigating on your own, read this chapter. We'll chart a course for you here, and plot your way through Chapters 21 and 22. Then you can try to write the procedures in each chapter before you read it. If you don't wish to try writing pieces of Dskpatch just yet, skip this chapter for now. It's very brief and leaves many details to your imagination.

If you decide to read through this chapter, here's a suggestion on how to proceed: Read one section and then try to make your own corresponding changes to Dskpatch. When you feel you've made enough progress, read the chapter with the same name as the section title. After you've read the corresponding chapter, then you can go on to read the next section.

Note: You may want to make a copy of all your files before you start making changes. Then when you get to Chapter 21, you'll have the choice of following along with the changes, or using your own version.

The Phantom Cursors

In Chapter 21 we'll place two phantom cursors on the screen: one in the hex window, and one in the ASCII window. A phantom cursor is similar to a normal cursor, but it doesn't blink and the background turns white, with the characters black, as you can see in Figure 20-1.

The phantom cursor in the hex window is four characters wide, the one in the ASCII window is only one character wide.

How do we create a phantom cursor? Each character on the screen has an *attribute* byte. This byte tells your IBM PC how to display each character. An attribute code of 7h displays a normal character, while 70h displays a character in inverse video. The latter is exactly what we want for the phantom cursor, so the question is: How can we change the attribute of our characters to 70h?

INT 10h function 9 writes both a character and an attribute to the screen, and INT 10h function 8 reads the character code at the current cursor posi-

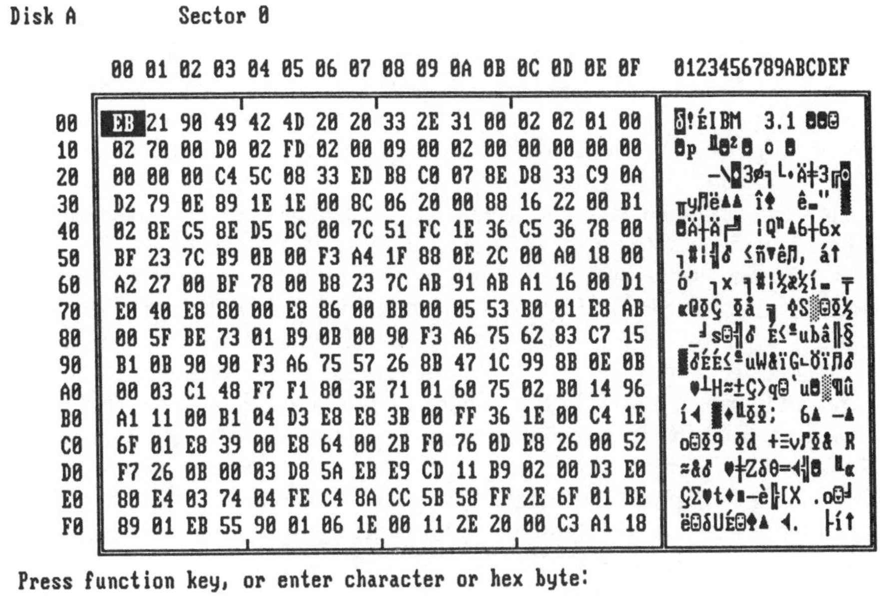

```
Disk A          Sector 0

          00 01 02 03 04 05 06 07 08 09 0A 0B 0C 0D 0E 0F   0123456789ABCDEF

    00   EB 21 90 49 42 4D 20 20 33 2E 31 00 02 02 01 00   §!ÉIBM  3.1 ███
    10   02 70 00 D0 02 FD 02 00 09 00 02 00 00 00 00 00   ®p ▐®²θ o █
    20   00 00 00 C4 5C 08 33 ED B8 C0 07 8E D8 33 C9 0A    ─\0▓3φ┐ Ļ·Ä‡3╓0
    30   D2 79 0E 89 1E 1E 00 8C 06 20 00 88 16 22 00 B1   ┬yΠë▲▲ îê ê_"
    40   02 8E C5 8E D5 BC 00 7C 51 FC 1E 36 C5 36 78 00   öÄ‡Ä╠┘ |Q"▲6†6x
    50   BF 23 7C B9 0B 00 F3 A4 1F 88 0E 2C 00 A0 18 00   ┐#!┤δ ◊ñvê∏, át
    60   A2 27 00 BF 78 00 B8 23 7C AB 91 AB A1 16 00 D1   ó' ┐x ┐ #!½æ¼í_ ┬
    70   E0 40 E8 80 00 E8 86 00 BB 00 05 53 B0 01 E8 AB   «@δÇ ₿å ┐ ÷S▓0δ½
    80   00 5F BE 73 01 B9 0B 00 90 F3 A6 75 62 83 C7 15   █ sθ┤δ E‡²ubâ║§
    90   B1 0B 90 90 F3 A6 75 57 26 8B 47 1C 99 8B 0E 0B   ♥⊥H≈±Ç⟩qθ`u█╗¶û
    A0   00 03 C1 48 F7 F1 80 3E 71 01 60 75 02 B0 14 96   í◀ █◆╙�ঽ; 6▲ _▲
    B0   A1 11 00 B1 04 D3 E8 E8 3B 00 FF 36 1E 00 C4 1E   o@§9 ðd +≡√Γ§ð R
    C0   6F 01 E8 39 00 E8 64 00 2B F0 76 0D E8 26 00 52   ≠åð ╫‡Zδθ=◀▐θ ▙к
    D0   F7 26 0B 00 03 D8 5A EB E9 CD 11 B9 02 00 D3 E0   Ç∑▼t◆■-è║[X .oθ┘
    E0   80 E4 03 74 04 FE C4 8A CC 5B 58 FF 2E 6F 01 BE   ëθ∂UÉθ▲▲ ◀. ├ít
    F0   89 01 EB 55 90 01 06 1E 00 11 2E 20 00 C3 A1 18
```

Press function key, or enter character or hex byte:

Figure 20-1.   A Display with Phantom Cursors.

tion. We can create a phantom cursor in the hex window with the following steps:

- Save the position of the real cursor (use INT 10h function 3 to read the cursor position and save this in variables).
- Move the real cursor to the start of the phantom cursor in the hex window.
- For the next four characters, read the character code (function 8) and write both the character and its attribute (setting the attribute to 70h).
- Finally, restore the old cursor position.

We write a phantom cursor in the ASCII window in much the same way. Once you have a working phantom cursor in the hex window, you can add the extra code for the ASCII window.

Keep in mind that your first try is only temporary. Once you have a working program with phantom cursors, you can go back and rewrite your changes, so you have a number of small procedures to do the work. Look at the procedures in Chapter 21 when you're done, to see one way of doing this.

Simple Editing

Once we have our phantom cursors, we'll want to move them around on the screen. We have to pay attention here to boundary conditions, in order to keep the phantom cursors inside each of the two windows. We also want our two phantom cursors to move together, since they represent the hex and ASCII representations of the same thing.

How can we move each phantom cursor? Each of the four cursor keys on the keypad sends out a special function number: 72 for cursor up, 80 for cursor down, 75 for cursor left, and 77 for cursor right. These are the numbers we need to add to DISPATCH_TABLE, along with the addresses of the four procedures to move the phantom cursors in each of these four directions.

To actually move each phantom cursor, erase it, then change its two coordinates and write it again. If you've been careful about how you wrote the phantom cursors, the four procedures to move them should be fairly simple.

Whenever you type a character on the keyboard, Dskpatch should read this character and replace the byte under the phantom cursor with the character just read. Here are the steps for simple editing:

- Read a character from the keyboard.
- Change the hex number in the hex window and the character in the ASCII window to match the character just read.
- Change the byte in the sector buffer, SECTOR.

Here's a simple hint: You don't have to make many changes to add editing. Dispatch requires little more than calling a new procedure (we've called it EDIT_BYTE) that does most of the work. EDIT_BYTE is responsible for changing both the screen and SECTOR.

Other Additions and Changes to Dskpatch

From Chapter 23 through Chapter 27, the changes start to become somewhat trickier and more involved. If you're still interested in writing your own version, consider this: What more would you like to see Dskpatch do than it does right now? We've used the following ideas in the remaining chapters.

We want a new version of READ_BYTE that will read either one character or a two-digit hex number and wait for us to press the Enter key before it returns a character to Dispatch. This part of our "wish list" isn't as simple as it sounds, and we'll spend two chapters (Chapters 23 and 24) working on this problem.

In Chapter 25, we'll go bug hunting, then in Chapter 26 we'll learn how to write modified sectors back to the disk using the DOS INT 26h function, which is analogous to the INT 25h that we used to read a sector from the disk. (In Chapter 26, we won't check for read errors, but you'll find such checks in the disk version of Dskpatch that is available with this book.)

Finally, in Chapter 27, we'll make some changes to Dskpatch so we can see the other half of our sector display. These changes won't allow us to scroll through the sector display as freely as we'd like but, again, those changes are on the disk version of Dskpatch.

21

THE PHANTOM CURSORS

In this chapter we'll build the procedures to write and erase a phantom cursor in the hex window, and another in the ASCII window. A phantom cursor is so called because it's not the PC's hardware cursor; it's a shadow ... albeit a rather unusual shadow, since it inverts the character, turning the background to white and the character to black. In the hex window, we have the room to make this cursor four characters wide so it will be easy to read. In the ASCII window, our phantom cursor will be just one character wide, because there is no room between characters.

We have a lot of procedures and code to cover here, so we'll describe these procedures only briefly.

The Phantom Cursors

INIT_SEC_DISP is the only procedure we have that changes the sector display. A new display appears when we start Dskpatch, and each time we read a new sector. Since our phantom cursors will be in the sector display, we'll begin our work here by placing a call to WRITE_PHANTOM in INIT_SEC_DISP. That way, we'll write the phantom cursors every time we write a new sector display.

Here is the revised—and final—version of INIT_SEC_DISP in DISP_SEC.ASM:

Listing 21-1. Changes to INIT_SEC_DISP in DISP_SEC.ASM

```
        PUBLIC  INIT_SEC_DISP
        EXTRN   WRITE_PATTERN:NEAR, SEND_CRLF:NEAR
        EXTRN   GOTO_XY:NEAR, WRITE_PHANTOM:NEAR
DATA_SEG        SEGMENT PUBLIC
        EXTRN   LINES_BEFORE_SECTOR:BYTE
        EXTRN   SECTOR_OFFSET:WORD
DATA_SEG        ENDS
;---------------------------------------------------------------;
;  This procedure initializes the half-sector display.          ;
;                                                               ;
; Uses:          WRITE_PATTERN, SEND_CRLF, DISP_HALF_SECTOR     ;
;                WRITE_TOP_HEX_NUMBERS, GOTO_XY, WRITE_PHANTOM  ;
; Reads:         TOP_LINE_PATTERN, BOTTOM_LINE_PATTERN          ;
;                LINES_BEFORE_SECTOR                            ;
; Writes:        SECTOR_OFFSET                                  ;
;---------------------------------------------------------------;
```

Listing 21-1. *continued*

```
INIT_SEC_DISP   PROC    NEAR
        PUSH    DX
        XOR     DL,DL                   ;Move cursor into position
        MOV     DH,LINES_BEFORE_SECTOR
        CALL    GOTO_XY
        CALL    WRITE_TOP_HEX_NUMBERS
        LEA     DX,TOP_LINE_PATTERN
        CALL    WRITE_PATTERN
        CALL    SEND_CRLF
        XOR     DX,DX                   ;Start at the beginning of the sector
        MOV     SECTOR_OFFSET,DX        ;Set sector offset to 0
        CALL    DISP_HALF_SECTOR
        LEA     DX,BOTTOM_LINE_PATTERN
        CALL    WRITE_PATTERN
        CALL    WRITE_PHANTOM           ;Write the phantom cursor
        POP     DX
        RET
INIT_SEC_DISP   ENDP
```

Notice that we've also updated INIT_SEC_DISP to use and initialize variables. It now sets SECTOR_OFFSET to zero to display the first half of a sector.

Let's move on to WRITE_PHANTOM itself. This will take quite a bit of work. Altogether, we have to write six procedures, including WRITE_PHANTOM. The idea is fairly simple, though. First, we move the real cursor to the position of the phantom cursor in the hex window and change the attribute of the next four characters to inverse video (attribute 70h). This creates a block of white, four characters wide, with the hex number in black. Then we do the same in the ASCII window, but for a single character. Finally, we move the real cursor back to where it was when we started. All the procedures for the phantom cursors will be in PHANTOM.ASM, with the exception of WRITE_ATTRIBUTE_N_TIMES, the procedure that will set the attribute of characters.

Enter the following procedures into the file PHANTOM.ASM:

Listing 21-2. The New File PHANTOM.ASM

```
CGROUP  GROUP   CODE_SEG, DATA_SEG
        ASSUME  CS:CGROUP, DS:CGROUP


CODE_SEG        SEGMENT PUBLIC

        PUBLIC  MOV_TO_HEX_POSITION
        EXTRN   GOTO_XY:NEAR
```

Listing 21-2. *continued*

```
DATA_SEG          SEGMENT PUBLIC
        EXTRN     LINES_BEFORE_SECTOR:BYTE
DATA_SEG          ENDS
;-------------------------------------------------------------------;
; This procedure moves the real cursor to the position of the phantom  ;
; cursor in the hex window.                                            ;
;                                                                      ;
; Uses:           GOTO_XY                                              ;
; Reads:          LINES_BEFORE_SECTOR, PHANTOM_CURSOR_X, PHANTOM_CURSOR_Y ;
;-------------------------------------------------------------------;
MOV_TO_HEX_POSITION     PROC    NEAR
        PUSH      AX
        PUSH      CX
        PUSH      DX
        MOV       DH,LINES_BEFORE_SECTOR  ;Find row of phantom (0,0)
        ADD       DH,2                    ;Plus row of hex and horizontal bar
        ADD       DH,PHANTOM_CURSOR_Y     ;DH = row of phantom cursor
        MOV       DL,8                    ;Indent on left side
        MOV       CL,3                    ;Each column uses 3 characters,so
        MOV       AL,PHANTOM_CURSOR_X     ; we must multiply CURSOR_X by 3
        MUL       CL
        ADD       DL,AL                   ;And add to the indent, to get column
        CALL      GOTO_XY                 ; for phantom cursor
        POP       DX
        POP       CX
        POP       AX
        RET
MOV_TO_HEX_POSITION     ENDP

        PUBLIC  MOV_TO_ASCII_POSITION
        EXTRN   GOTO_XY:NEAR
DATA_SEG          SEGMENT PUBLIC
        EXTRN     LINES_BEFORE_SECTOR:BYTE
DATA_SEG          ENDS
;-------------------------------------------------------------------;
; This procedure moves the real cursor to the beginning of the phantom ;
; cursor in the ASCII window.                                          ;
;                                                                      ;
; Uses:           GOTO_XY                                              ;
; Reads:          LINES_BEFORE_SECTOR, PHANTOM_CURSOR_X, PHANTOM_CURSOR_Y ;
;-------------------------------------------------------------------;
MOV_TO_ASCII_POSITION   PROC    NEAR
        PUSH      AX
        PUSH      DX
        MOV       DH,LINES_BEFORE_SECTOR  ;Find row of phantom (0,0)
        ADD       DH,2                    ;Plus row of hex and horizontal bar
        ADD       DH,PHANTOM_CURSOR_Y     ;DH = row of phantom cursor
        MOV       DL,59                   ;Indent on left side
        ADD       DL,PHANTOM_CURSOR_X     ;Add CURSOR_X to get X position
        CALL      GOTO_XY                 ; for phantom cursor
        POP       DX
```

Listing 21-2. *continued*

```
        POP     AX
        RET
MOV_TO_ASCII_POSITION   ENDP

        PUBLIC  SAVE_REAL_CURSOR
;----------------------------------------------------------------------;
; This procedure saves the position of the real cursor in the two      ;
; variables REAL_CURSOR_X and REAL_CURSOR_Y.                           ;
;                                                                      ;
; Writes:       REAL_CURSOR_X, REAL_CURSOR_Y                           ;
;----------------------------------------------------------------------;
SAVE_REAL_CURSOR        PROC    NEAR
        PUSH    AX
        PUSH    BX
        PUSH    CX
        PUSH    DX
        MOV     AH,3                    ;Read cursor position
        XOR     BH,BH                   ; on page 0
        INT     10h                     ;And return in DL,DH
        MOV     REAL_CURSOR_Y,DL        ;Save position
        MOV     REAL_CURSOR_X,DH
        POP     DX
        POP     CX
        POP     BX
        POP     AX
        RET
SAVE_REAL_CURSOR        ENDP

        PUBLIC  RESTORE_REAL_CURSOR
        EXTRN   GOTO_XY:NEAR
;----------------------------------------------------------------------;
; This procedure restores the real cursor to its old position, saved in ;
; REAL_CURSOR_X and REAL_CURSOR_Y.                                     ;
;                                                                      ;
; Uses:         GOTO_XY                                                 ;
; Reads:        REAL_CURSOR_X, REAL_CURSOR_Y                           ;
;----------------------------------------------------------------------;
RESTORE_REAL_CURSOR     PROC    NEAR
        PUSH    DX
        MOV     DL,REAL_CURSOR_Y
        MOV     DH,REAL_CURSOR_X
        CALL    GOTO_XY
        POP     DX
        RET
RESTORE_REAL_CURSOR     ENDP

        PUBLIC  WRITE_PHANTOM
        EXTRN   WRITE_ATTRIBUTE_N_TIMES:NEAR
```

Listing 21-2. *continued*

```
;-----------------------------------------------------------------------;
; This procedure uses CURSOR_X and CURSOR_Y, through MOV_TO_..., as the ;
; coordinates for the phantom cursor.  WRITE_PHANTOM writes this        ;
; phantom cursor.                                                       ;
;                                                                       ;
; Uses:         WRITE_ATTRIBUTE_N_TIMES, SAVE_REAL_CURSOR              ;
;               RESTORE_REAL_CURSOR, MOV_TO_HEX_POSITION                ;
;               MOV_TO_ASCII_POSITION                                   ;
;-----------------------------------------------------------------------;
WRITE_PHANTOM   PROC    NEAR
        PUSH    CX
        PUSH    DX
        CALL    SAVE_REAL_CURSOR
        CALL    MOV_TO_HEX_POSITION     ;Coord. of cursor in hex window
        MOV     CX,4                    ;Make phantom cursor four chars wide
        MOV     DL,70h
        CALL    WRITE_ATTRIBUTE_N_TIMES
        CALL    MOV_TO_ASCII_POSITION   ;Coord. of cursor in ASCII window
        MOV     CX,1                    ;Cursor is one character wide here
        CALL    WRITE_ATTRIBUTE_N_TIMES
        CALL    RESTORE_REAL_CURSOR
        POP     DX
        POP     CX
        RET
WRITE_PHANTOM   ENDP

        PUBLIC  ERASE_PHANTOM
        EXTRN   WRITE_ATTRIBUTE_N_TIMES:NEAR
;-----------------------------------------------------------------------;
; This procedure erases the phantom cursor, just the opposite of        ;
; WRITE_PHANTOM.                                                        ;
;                                                                       ;
; Uses:         WRITE_ATTRIBUTE_N_TIMES, SAVE_REAL_CURSOR              ;
;               RESTORE_REAL_CURSOR, MOV_TO_HEX_POSITION                ;
;               MOV_TO_ASCII_POSITION                                   ;
;-----------------------------------------------------------------------;
ERASE_PHANTOM   PROC    NEAR
        PUSH    CX
        PUSH    DX
        CALL    SAVE_REAL_CURSOR
        CALL    MOV_TO_HEX_POSITION     ;Coord. of cursor in hex window
        MOV     CX,4                    ;Change back to white on black
        MOV     DL,7
        CALL    WRITE_ATTRIBUTE_N_TIMES
        CALL    MOV_TO_ASCII_POSITION
        MOV     CX,1
        CALL    WRITE_ATTRIBUTE_N_TIMES
        CALL    RESTORE_REAL_CURSOR
        POP     DX
        POP     CX
        RET
```

```
Listing 21-2. continued

ERASE_PHANTOM    ENDP

CODE_SEG         ENDS


DATA_SEG         SEGMENT PUBLIC
REAL_CURSOR_X             DB      0
REAL_CURSOR_Y             DB      0
      PUBLIC   PHANTOM_CURSOR_X, PHANTOM_CURSOR_Y
PHANTOM_CURSOR_X          DB      0
PHANTOM_CURSOR_Y          DB      0
DATA_SEG         ENDS


      END
```

WRITE_PHANTOM and ERASE_PHANTOM are much the same. In fact, the only difference is in the attribute used: WRITE_PHANTOM sets the attribute to 70h for inverse video, while ERASE_PHANTOM sets to attribute back to the normal attribute (7).

Both of these procedures save the old position of the real cursor with SAVE_REAL_CURSOR, which uses the INT 10h function number 3 to read the position of the cursor and then saves this position in the two bytes REAL_CURSOR_X and REAL_CURSOR_Y.

After saving the real cursor position, both WRITE_PHANTOM and ERASE_PHANTOM then call MOV_TO_HEX_POSITION, which moves the cursor to the start of the phantom cursor in the hex window. Next, WRITE_ATTRIBUTE_N_TIMES writes the inverse-video attribute for four characters, starting at the cursor and moving to the right. This writes the phantom cursor in the hex window. In much the same way, WRITE_PHAN-TOM then writes a phantom cursor one character wide in the ASCII window. Finally, RESTORE_REAL_CURSOR restores the position of the real cursor to the position it was in before the call to WRITE_PHANTOM.

The only procedure we have left unwritten is WRITE_ATTRIBUTE_N_TIMES, so let's take care of it now.

Changing Character Attributes

We're going to use WRITE_ATTRIBUTE_N_TIMES to do three things. First, it will read the character under the cursor position. We'll do this because the INT 10h function we use to set a character's attribute, function number 9, writes both the character *and* the attribute under the cursor. Thus, WRITE_ATTRIBUTE_N_TIMES will change the attribute by writing the new attribute along with the character just read. Finally, the procedure will move the cursor right to the next character position, so we can repeat the whole process N times. You can see the details in the procedure itself; place WRITE_ATTRIBUTE_N_TIMES in the file VIDEO_IO.ASM:

Listing 21-3. Add This Procedure to VIDEO_IO.ASM

```
        PUBLIC  WRITE_ATTRIBUTE_N_TIMES
        EXTRN   CURSOR_RIGHT:NEAR
;----------------------------------------------------------------------;
; This procedure sets the attribute for N characters, starting at the  ;
; current cursor position.                                             ;
;                                                                      ;
;       CX      Number of characters to set attribute for              ;
;       DL      New attribute for characters                           ;
;                                                                      ;
; Uses:         CURSOR_RIGHT                                           ;
;----------------------------------------------------------------------;
WRITE_ATTRIBUTE_N_TIMES          PROC    NEAR
        PUSH    AX
        PUSH    BX
        PUSH    CX
        PUSH    DX
        MOV     BL,DL                   ;Set attribute to new attribute
        XOR     BH,BH                   ;Set display page to 0
        MOV     DX,CX                   ;CX is used by the BIOS routines
        MOV     CX,1                    ;Set attribute for one character
ATTR_LOOP:
        MOV     AH,8                    ;Read character under cursor
        INT     10h
        MOV     AH,9                    ;Write attribute/character
        INT     10h
        CALL    CURSOR_RIGHT
        DEC     DX                      ;Set attribute for N characters?
        JNZ     ATTR_LOOP               ;No, continue
        POP     DX
        POP     CX
        POP     BX
        POP     AX
        RET
WRITE_ATTRIBUTE_N_TIMES          ENDP
```

This is both the first and final version of WRITE_ATTRIBUTE_N_TIMES. With it, we've also created the final version of VIDEO_IO.ASM, so you won't need to change or assemble it again.

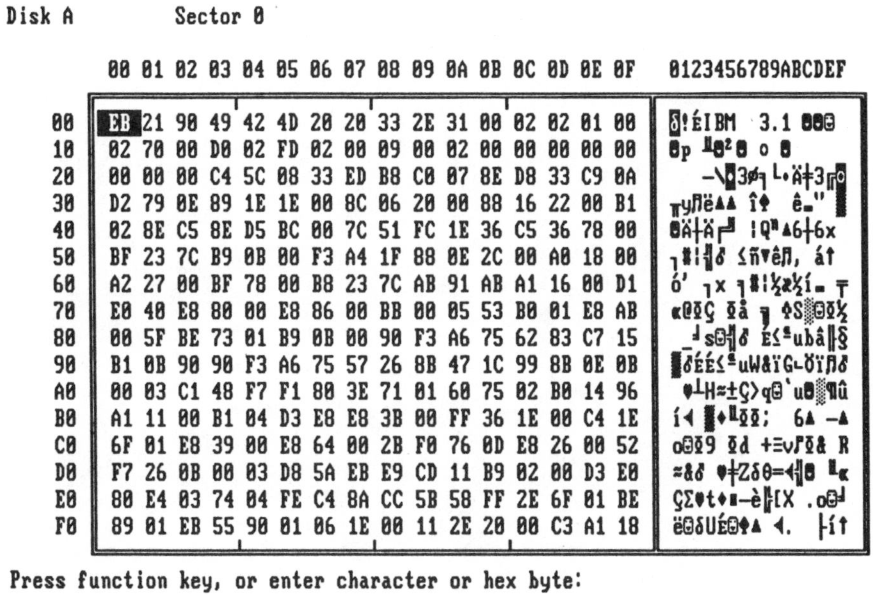

Disk A   Sector 0

```
         00 01 02 03 04 05 06 07 08 09 0A 0B 0C 0D 0E 0F   0123456789ABCDEF
    00   EB 21 90 49 42 4D 20 20 33 2E 31 00 02 02 01 00   ⌂!ÉIBM  3.1 ▓░▓
    10   02 70 00 D0 02 FD 02 00 09 00 02 00 00 00 00 00   ☻p ╨☻²☻ ○ ☻
    20   00 00 00 C4 5C 08 33 ED B8 C0 07 8E D8 33 C9 0A   ─\◘3φ┐ └·Ä‡3┌○
    30   D2 79 0E 89 1E 1E 00 8C 06 20 00 88 16 22 00 B1   ╥yⁿë▲▲ î▲ ê▬"  
    40   02 8E C5 8E D5 BC 00 7C 51 FC 1E 36 C5 36 78 00   ☻Ä┼Ä╒┘ !Q�ª▲6┼6x
    50   BF 23 7C B9 0B 00 F3 A4 1F 88 0E 2C 00 A0 18 00   ┐#!╣♂ ⌠ñvêⁿ, át
    60   A2 27 00 BF 78 00 B8 23 7C AB 91 AB A1 16 00 D1   ó' ┐x ╣#!½æ╜í ╥
    70   E0 40 E8 80 00 E8 86 00 BB 00 05 53 B0 01 E8 AB   α@Φ Φå ╗ ♣S░☺Φ½
    80   00 5F BE 73 01 B9 0B 00 90 F3 A6 75 62 83 C7 15   _┐s☺╣♂ É⌠ªubâ╟§
    90   B1 0B 90 90 F3 A6 75 57 26 8B 47 1C 99 8B 0E 0B   ♂ÉÉ⌠ªuW&ïG∟Öïⁿ♂
    A0   00 03 C1 48 F7 F1 80 3E 71 01 60 75 02 B0 14 96   ♥┴H≈±Ç>q☻`u░¶û
    B0   A1 11 00 B1 04 D3 E8 E8 3B 00 FF 36 1E 00 C4 1E   í◄ ♂♦╙ΦΦ; 6▲ ─▲
    C0   6F 01 E8 39 00 E8 64 00 2B F0 76 0D E8 26 00 52   o☺Φ9 Φd +≡v♪Φ& R
    D0   F7 26 0B 00 03 D8 5A EB E9 CD 11 B9 02 00 D3 E0   ≈& ♂ ♥╪ZΦΘ═◄╣☻ ╙α
    E0   80 E4 03 74 04 FE C4 8A CC 5B 58 FF 2E 6F 01 BE   ÇΣ♥t♦■─èⁿX .o☺┐
    F0   89 01 EB 55 90 01 06 1E 00 11 2E 20 00 C3 A1 18   ëⁿΦU É☺♠▲ ◄. ├ít
```

Press function key, or enter character or hex byte:

Figure 21-1. Screen Display with Phantom Cursors.

Summary

We now have eight files to link, with the main procedure still in Dskpatch. Of these, we've changed two files, Disp_sec and Video_io, and created one, Phantom. If you're using Make or the short batch file we suggested in Chapter 20, remember to add your new file, Phantom, to the list.

When you run Dskpatch now, you'll see it write the sector display, just as before, but Dskpatch will also write in the two phantom cursors. (See Figure 21-1.) Notice that the real cursor is back where it should be at the very end.

In the next chapter, we'll add procedures to move our newly formed phantom cursors, and we'll add a simple editing procedure to allow us to change the byte under the phantom cursor.

SIMPLE EDITING

We've almost reached the point at which we can begin to edit our sector display—change numbers in our half sector display. We'll soon add simple versions of the procedures for editing bytes in our display, but before we do, we need some way to move the phantom cursors to different bytes within the half sector display. This task turns out to be fairly simple, now that we have the two procedures ERASE_PHANTOM and WRITE_PHANTOM.

Moving the Phantom Cursors

Moving the phantom cursors in any direction depends on three basic steps: Erasing the phantom cursor at its current position; changing the cursor position by changing one of the variables, PHANTOM_CURSOR_X or PHANTOM_CURSOR_Y; and using WRITE_PHANTOM to write the phantom cursor at this new position. In the process, however, we must be careful not to let the cursor move outside the window, which is 16 bytes wide and 16 bytes high.

To move the phantom cursors, we'll need four new procedures, one for each of the arrow keys on the keyboard. DISPATCHER needs no changes, because all the information on procedures and extended codes is in the table DISPATCH_TABLE. We just need to add the extended ASCII codes and addresses of the procedures for each of the arrow keys. Here are the additions to DISPATCH.ASM that will bring the cursor keys to life:

Listing 22-1. Changes to DISPATCH.ASM

```
DATA_SEG        SEGMENT PUBLIC
CODE_SEG        SEGMENT PUBLIC
        EXTRN   NEXT_SECTOR:NEAR                        ;In DISK_IO.ASM
        EXTRN   PREVIOUS_SECTOR:NEAR                    ;In DISK_IO.ASM
        EXTRN   PHANTOM_UP:NEAR, PHANTOM_DOWN:NEAR      ;In PHANTOM.ASM
        EXTRN   PHANTOM_LEFT:NEAR, PHANTOM_RIGHT:NEAR
CODE_SEG        ENDS
;-------------------------------------------------------------------;
; This table contains the legal extended ASCII keys and the addresses   ;
; of the procedures that should be called when each key is pressed.      ;
;       The format of the table is                                  ;
;               DB      72              ;Extended code for cursor up   ;
;               DW      OFFSET CGROUP:PHANTOM_UP                    ;
;-------------------------------------------------------------------;
```

Listing 22-1. *continued*

```
DISPATCH_TABLE  LABEL   BYTE
         DB     59                              ;F1
         DW     OFFSET CGROUP:PREVIOUS_SECTOR
         DB     60                              ;F2
         DW     OFFSET CGROUP:NEXT_SECTOR
         DB     72                              ;Cursor up
         DW     OFFSET CGROUP:PHANTOM_UP
         DB     80                              ;Cursor down
         DW     OFFSET CGROUP:PHANTOM_DOWN
         DB     75                              ;Cursor left
         DW     OFFSET CGROUP:PHANTOM_LEFT
         DB     77                              ;Cursor right
         DW     OFFSET CGROUP:PHANTOM_RIGHT
         DB     0                               ;End of the table
DATA_SEG        ENDS
```

As you can see, it's simple to add commands to Dskpatch: We merely place the procedure names in DISPATCH_TABLE and write the procedures.

Speaking of writing procedures, the procedures PHANTOM_UP, PHANTOM_DOWN, and so on are fairly simple. They're also quite similar to one another, differing only in the boundary conditions used for each. We've already described how they work; see if you can write them yourself, in the file PHANTOM.ASM, before you read on.

Here are our versions of the procedures to move the phantom cursors:

Listing 22-2. Add These Procedures to PHANTOM.ASM

```
;----------------------------------------------------------------------;
; These four procedures move the phantom cursors.                      ;
;                                                                      ;
; Uses:         ERASE_PHANTOM, WRITE_PHANTOM                           ;
; Reads:        PHANTOM_CURSOR_X, PHANTOM_CURSOR_Y                     ;
; Writes:       PHANTOM_CURSOR_X, PHANTOM_CURSOR_Y                     ;
;----------------------------------------------------------------------;
        PUBLIC  PHANTOM_UP
PHANTOM_UP      PROC    NEAR
        CALL    ERASE_PHANTOM           ;Erase at current position
        DEC     PHANTOM_CURSOR_Y        ;Move cursor up one line
        JNS     WASNT_AT_TOP            ;Was not at the top, write cursor
        MOV     PHANTOM_CURSOR_Y,0      ;Was at the top, so put back there
WASNT_AT_TOP:
        CALL    WRITE_PHANTOM           ;Write the phantom at new position
        RET
PHANTOM_UP      ENDP

        PUBLIC  PHANTOM_DOWN
```

Listing 22-2. *continued*

```
PHANTOM_DOWN       PROC     NEAR
        CALL       ERASE_PHANTOM              ;Erase at current position
        INC        PHANTOM_CURSOR_Y           ;Move cursor down one line
        CMP        PHANTOM_CURSOR_Y,16        ;Was it at the bottom?
        JB         WASNT_AT_BOTTOM            ;No, so write phantom
        MOV        PHANTOM_CURSOR_Y,15        ;Was at bottom, so put back there
WASNT_AT_BOTTOM:
        CALL       WRITE_PHANTOM              ;Write the phantom cursor
        RET
PHANTOM_DOWN       ENDP


        PUBLIC     PHANTOM_LEFT
PHANTOM_LEFT       PROC     NEAR
        CALL       ERASE_PHANTOM              ;Erase at current position
        DEC        PHANTOM_CURSOR_X           ;Move cursor left one column
        JNS        WASNT_AT_LEFT             ;Was not at the left side, write cursor
        MOV        PHANTOM_CURSOR_X,0         ;Was at left, so put back there
WASNT_AT_LEFT:
        CALL       WRITE_PHANTOM              ;Write the phantom cursor
        RET
PHANTOM_LEFT       ENDP


        PUBLIC     PHANTOM_RIGHT
PHANTOM_RIGHT      PROC     NEAR
        CALL       ERASE_PHANTOM              ;Erase at current position
        INC        PHANTOM_CURSOR_X           ;Move cursor right one column
        CMP        PHANTOM_CURSOR_X,16        ;Was it already at the right side?
        JB         WASNT_AT_RIGHT
        MOV        PHANTOM_CURSOR_X,15        ;Was at right, so put back there
WASNT_AT_RIGHT:
        CALL       WRITE_PHANTOM              ;Write the phantom cursor
        RET
PHANTOM_RIGHT      ENDP
```

PHANTOM_LEFT and PHANTOM_RIGHT are the final versions, but we'll have to change PHANTOM_UP and PHANTOM_DOWN when we begin to scroll the display.

As Dskpatch stands now, we can see only the first half of a sector. In Chapter 27, we'll make some additions and changes to Dskpatch so we can scroll the display to see other parts of the sector. At that time, we'll change both PHANTOM_UP and PHANTOM_DOWN to scroll the screen when we try to move the cursor beyond the top or bottom of the screen. For example, when the cursor is at the bottom of the half-sector display, pushing the cursor-down key again should scroll the display up one line, adding another line at the bottom, so that we see the next 16 bytes. Scrolling is rather messy, however, so we'll keep these procedures until almost last. Through Chapter 26, we'll develop the editing and keyboard-input sections of Dskpatch by using only the first half sector.

Test Dskpatch now to see if you can move the phantom cursors around on the screen. They should move together, and they should stay within their own windows. Now, we'll go on to add editing, so we can change bytes on our display.

Simple Editing

We already have a simple keyboard-input procedure, READ_BYTE, which reads just one character from the keyboard without waiting for you to press the Enter key. We'll use this old, test version of READ_BYTE to develop editing. Then, in the next chapter, we'll write a more sophisticated version of the procedure that will wait until we press either the Enter key or a special key, such as a function or cursor key.

Our editing procedure will be called EDIT_BYTE, and it will change one byte both on the screen and in memory (SECTOR). EDIT_BYTE will take the character in the DL register, write it to the memory location within SECTOR that is currently pointed to by the phantom cursor, and then change the display.

DISPATCHER already has a nice niche where we can place a CALL to EDIT_BYTE. Here is the new version of DISPATCHER in DISPATCH.ASM, with the CALL to EDIT_BYTE and the changes to go along with it:

Listing 22-3. Changes to DISPATCHER in DISPATCH.ASM

```
        PUBLIC  DISPATCHER
        EXTRN   READ_BYTE:NEAR, EDIT_BYTE:NEAR
;---------------------------------------------------------------------;
; This is the central dispatcher.  During normal editing and viewing, ;
; this procedure reads characters from the keyboard and, if the character;
; is a command key (such as a cursor key), DISPATCHER calls the       ;
; procedures that do the actual work.  This dispatching is done for   ;
; special keys listed in the table DISPATCH_TABLE, where the procedure ;
; addresses are stored just after the key names.                      ;
;   If the character is not a special key, then it should be placed   ;
; directly into the sector buffer--this is the editing mode.          ;
;                                                                     ;
; Uses:         READ_BYTE, EDIT_BYTE                                  ;
;---------------------------------------------------------------------;
```

Listing 22-3. *continued*

```
DISPATCHER      PROC    NEAR
        PUSH    AX
        PUSH    BX
        PUSH    DX
DISPATCH_LOOP:
        CALL    READ_BYTE               ;Read character into AL
        OR      AH,AH                   ;AH = 0 if no character read, -1
                                        ; for an extended code.
        JZ      DISPATCH_LOOP           ;No character read, try again
        JS      SPECIAL_KEY             ;Read extended code
; do nothing with the character for now
        MOV     DL,AL
        CALL    EDIT_BYTE               ;Was normal character, edit byte
        JMP     DISPATCH_LOOP           ;Read another character

SPECIAL_KEY:
        CMP     AL,68                   ;F10--exit?
        JE      END_DISPATCH            ;Yes, leave
                                        ;Use BX to look through table
        LEA     BX,DISPATCH_TABLE
SPECIAL_LOOP:
        CMP     BYTE PTR [BX],0         ;End of table?
        JE      NOT_IN_TABLE            ;Yes, key was not in the table
        CMP     AL,[BX]                 ;Is it this table entry?
        JE      DISPATCH                ;Yes, then dispatch
        ADD     BX,3                    ;No, try next entry
        JMP     SPECIAL_LOOP            ;Check next table entry
DISPATCH:
        INC     BX                      ;Point to address of procedure
        CALL    WORD PTR [BX]           ;Call procedure
        JMP     DISPATCH_LOOP           ;Wait for another key
NOT_IN_TABLE:                           ;Do nothing, just read next character
        JMP     DISPATCH_LOOP

END_DISPATCH:
        POP     DX
        POP     BX
        POP     AX
        RET
DISPATCHER      ENDP
```

The EDIT_BYTE procedure itself does a lot of work, almost entirely by calling other procedures, and this is one feature of modular design. With modular design, we can often write rather complex procedures simply by giving a list of CALLs to other procedures that do the work. Many of the procedures in EDIT_BYTE work with a character in the DL register, but this is already set when we call EDIT_BYTE, so the only instruction other than a CALL (or PUSH, POP) is the LEA instruction to set the address of the prompt for

WRITE_PROMPT_LINE. Most of the procedure calls in EDIT_BYTE are for updating the display when we edit a byte. You'll see the other details of EDIT_BYTE when we come to the procedure listing in a moment.

Since EDIT_BYTE changes the byte on screen, we need another procedure, WRITE_TO_MEMORY, to change the byte in SECTOR. WRITE_TO_MEMORY uses the coordinates in PHANTOM_CURSOR_X and PHANTOM_CURSOR_Y to calculate the offset into SECTOR of the phantom cursor, then it writes the character (byte) in the DL register to the correct byte within SECTOR.

Here is the new file, EDITOR.ASM, which contains the final versions of both EDIT_BYTE and WRITE_TO_MEMORY:

```
Listing 22-4. The New File EDITOR.ASM


CGROUP  GROUP   CODE_SEG, DATA_SEG
        ASSUME  CS:CGROUP, DS:CGROUP

CODE_SEG        SEGMENT PUBLIC

DATA_SEG        SEGMENT PUBLIC
        EXTRN   SECTOR:BYTE
        EXTRN   SECTOR_OFFSET:WORD
        EXTRN   PHANTOM_CURSOR_X:BYTE
        EXTRN   PHANTOM_CURSOR_Y:BYTE
DATA_SEG        ENDS
;----------------------------------------------------------------;
; This procedure writes one byte to SECTOR, at the memory location ;
; pointed to by the phantom cursor.                                ;
;                                                                  ;
;       DL      Byte to write to SECTOR                            ;
;                                                                  ;
; The offset is calculated by                                      ;
;   OFFSET = SECTOR_OFFSET + (16 * PHANTOM_CURSOR_Y) + PHANTOM_CURSOR_X ;
;                                                                  ;
; Reads:        PHANTOM_CURSOR_X, PHANTOM_CURSOR_Y, SECTOR_OFFSET  ;
; Writes:       SECTOR                                             ;
;----------------------------------------------------------------;
WRITE_TO_MEMORY         PROC    NEAR
        PUSH    AX
        PUSH    BX
        PUSH    CX
        MOV     BX,SECTOR_OFFSET
        MOV     AL,PHANTOM_CURSOR_Y
        XOR     AH,AH
        MOV     CL,4                    ;Multiply PHANTOM_CURSOR_Y by 16
        SHL     AX,CL
        ADD     BX,AX                   ;BX = SECTOR_OFFSET + (16 * Y)
        MOV     AL,PHANTOM_CURSOR_X
```

Listing 22-4. *continued*

```
        XOR     AH,AH
        ADD     BX,AX                   ;That's the address!
        MOV     SECTOR[BX],DL           ;Now, store the byte
        POP     CX
        POP     BX
        POP     AX
        RET
WRITE_TO_MEMORY         ENDP

        PUBLIC  EDIT_BYTE
        EXTRN   SAVE_REAL_CURSOR:NEAR, RESTORE_REAL_CURSOR:NEAR
        EXTRN   MOV_TO_HEX_POSITION:NEAR, MOV_TO_ASCII_POSITION:NEAR
        EXTRN   WRITE_PHANTOM:NEAR, WRITE_PROMPT_LINE:NEAR
        EXTRN   CURSOR_RIGHT:NEAR, WRITE_HEX:NEAR, WRITE_CHAR:NEAR
DATA_SEG        SEGMENT PUBLIC
        EXTRN   EDITOR_PROMPT:BYTE
DATA_SEG        ENDS
;------------------------------------------------------------------;
; This procedure changes a byte in memory and on the screen.      ;
;                                                                  ;
;       DL      Byte to write into SECTOR, and change on screen    ;
;                                                                  ;
; Uses:         SAVE_REAL_CURSOR, RESTORE_REAL_CURSOR              ;
;               MOV_TO_HEX_POSITION, MOV_TO_ASCII_POSITION         ;
;               WRITE_PHANTOM, WRITE_PROMPT_LINE, CURSOR_RIGHT     ;
;               WRITE_HEX, WRITE_CHAR, WRITE_TO_MEMORY             ;
; Reads:        EDITOR_PROMPT                                      ;
;------------------------------------------------------------------;
EDIT_BYTE       PROC    NEAR
        PUSH    DX
        CALL    SAVE_REAL_CURSOR
        CALL    MOV_TO_HEX_POSITION     ;Move to the hex number in the
        CALL    CURSOR_RIGHT            ; hex window
        CALL    WRITE_HEX               ;Write the new number
        CALL    MOV_TO_ASCII_POSITION   ;Move to the char. in the ASCII window
        CALL    WRITE_CHAR              ;Write the new character
        CALL    RESTORE_REAL_CURSOR     ;Move cursor back where it belongs
        CALL    WRITE_PHANTOM           ;Rewrite the phantom cursor
        CALL    WRITE_TO_MEMORY         ;Save this new byte in SECTOR
        LEA     DX,EDITOR_PROMPT
        CALL    WRITE_PROMPT_LINE
        POP     DX
        RET
EDIT_BYTE       ENDP

CODE_SEG        ENDS

        END
```

Summary

Dskpatch now consists of nine files: Dskpatch, Dispatch, Disp_sec, Disk_io, Video_io, Kbd_io, Phantom, Cursor, and Editor. In this chapter, we changed Dispatch and added Editor. None of these files is very long, so none takes very long to assemble. Furthermore, we can make changes fairly quickly by editing just one of these files, reassembling it, and then linking all the files together again.

In terms of our current version of Dskpatch, push any key and you'll see a change in the number and character under the phantom cursor. Our editing works, but it's not very safe as yet, since we can change a byte by hitting any key. We need to build in some type of safeguard, such as pressing Enter to change a byte, so we don't make an accidental change by leaning on the keyboard unintentionally.

In addition, the current version of READ_BYTE doesn't allow us to enter a hex number to change a byte. In Chapter 24, we'll rewrite READ_BYTE, both so we'll have to push the Enter key before it will accept a new character, and to allow us to enter a two-digit hex number. First, we need to write a hex input procedure; in the next chapter, we'll write input procedures for both hex and decimal.

23

HEX AND DECIMAL INPUT

We'll encounter two new procedures for keyboard input in this chapter: one procedure for reading a byte by reading either a two-digit hex number or a single character, and another for reading a word by reading the characters of a decimal number. These will be our hex and decimal input procedures.

Both procedures are sufficiently tricky that we need to use a test program with them before we even consider linking them into Dskpatch. We'll be working with READ_BYTE, and a test procedure will be particularly important here, because this procedure will (temporarily) lose its ability to read special function keys. Since Dskpatch relies on the function keys, we won't be able to use our new READ_BYTE with Dskpatch. We'll also find out why we can't read special function keys with the READ_BYTE developed here, and in the next chapter we'll modify the file to make our function-key problems go away.

Hex Input

Let's begin by rewriting READ_BYTE. In the last chapter, READ_BYTE would read either an ordinary character or a special function key, and return one byte to Dispatch. Dispatch then called the Editor if READ_BYTE read an ordinary character, and EDIT_BYTE modified the byte pointed to by the phantom cursor. Otherwise, Dispatch looked for special function keys in DISPATCH_TABLE to see if the byte was there; if so, Dispatch called the procedure named in the table.

But, as mentioned in the last chapter, the old version of READ_BYTE makes it much too easy to change a byte by accident. If you unintentionally hit any key on the keyboard (other than special keys), EDIT_BYTE will change the byte under the phantom cursor. All of us are sometimes clumsy, and such an inadvertent change in a sector can lead to disaster.

We'll change READ_BYTE so that, henceforth, it won't return the character we type until we press the Enter key. We'll provide this feature by using the DOS INT 21h function 0Ah to read a string of characters. DOS only returns this string when we press Enter, so we get our anti-clumsy fix. But along the way, we lose special function keys, for reasons you'll see later.

To see exactly how our changes affect READ_BYTE, we need to write a test program to test READ_BYTE in isolation. That way, if anything strange happens, we'll know it's READ_BYTE and not some other part of Dskpatch. Our job of writing a test procedure will be simpler if we use a few procedures from

Kbd_io, Video_io, and Cursor to print information on the progress of READ_
BYTE. We'll use such procedures as WRITE_HEX and WRITE_DECIMAL to
print the character code returned and the number of characters read. The details are here, in TEST.ASM:

Listing 23-1. The Test Program TEST.ASM

```
CGROUP   GROUP    CODE_SEG, DATA_SEG
         ASSUME   CS:CGROUP, DS:CGROUP

CODE_SEG          SEGMENT PUBLIC
         ORG      100h

         EXTRN    WRITE_HEX:NEAR, WRITE_DECIMAL:NEAR
         EXTRN    WRITE_STRING:NEAR, SEND_CRLF:NEAR
         EXTRN    READ_BYTE:NEAR

TEST     PROC     NEAR
         LEA      DX,ENTER_PROMPT
         CALL     WRITE_STRING
         CALL     READ_BYTE
         CALL     SEND_CRLF
         LEA      DX,CHARACTER_PROMPT
         CALL     WRITE_STRING
         MOV      DL,AL
         CALL     WRITE_HEX
         CALL     SEND_CRLF
         LEA      DX,CHARACTERS_READ_PROMPT
         CALL     WRITE_STRING
         MOV      DL,AH
         XOR      DH,DH
         CALL     WRITE_DECIMAL
         CALL     SEND_CRLF
         INT      20h
TEST     ENDP

CODE_SEG          ENDS

DATA_SEG          SEGMENT PUBLIC
ENTER_PROMPT             DB      'Enter characters: ',0
CHARACTER_PROMPT        DB      'Character code: ',0
CHARACTERS_READ_PROMPT  DB      'Number of characters read: ',0
; and now dummy variables
         PUBLIC   HEADER_LINE_NO, DISK_DRIVE_NO, HEADER_PART_1, HEADER_PART_2
         PUBLIC   PROMPT_LINE_NO, CURRENT_SECTOR_NO
HEADER_LINE_NO          DB      0
DISK_DRIVE_NO           DB      0
HEADER_PART_1           DB      0
HEADER_PART_2           DB      0
```

Listing 23-1. *continued*

```
PROMPT_LINE_NO          DB      0
CURRENT_SECTOR_NO       DB      0
DATA_SEG        ENDS

        END     TEST
```

Try linking this with your current versions of Kbd_io, Video_io, and Cursor (place Test first in the LINK list). If you press any special function key, Test will tell you it read 255 characters. Why? We placed the −1 from AH into DL and set the upper byte of DX to zero, leaving DX set to 255 (FFh), not −1 (FFFFh).

We won't be so careless when we actually use READ_BYTE in Dskpatch. This is a test program, and as long as we know what to expect, we can test READ_BYTE and all its boundary conditions. Before we move on to rewrite READ_BYTE, however, we need to account for one feature of TEST.ASM that you may have noticed: its variable definitions.

The bulk of the instructions in TEST.ASM are for formatting—making the display look nice. The variable definitions at the end of Test are included only to satisfy the linker. When we link Test with Kbd_io, Video_io, and Cursor, the linker searches for a number of variables used by Kbd_io, Video_io, and Cursor. We defined the variables in Dskpatch, but since we aren't linking in Dskpatch, we need to redefine these variables in TEST.ASM. We won't actually use the variables, because we don't call any procedures in Video_io and Cursor that require them. But we need these variables anyway, to satisfy the linker there won't be any loose ends.

Let's move on to rewriting READ_BYTE to accept a string of characters. Not only will this save us from our clumsiness when we use Dskpatch, it will also allow us to use the Backspace key to delete characters if we change our mind about what we want to type in—another nice feature since it's easy to make mistakes. READ_BYTE will use the procedure READ_STRING to read a string of characters.

READ_STRING is very simple, almost trivial, but we've placed it in a separate procedure so we can rewrite it in the next chapter to read special function keys without having to press the Enter key. To save time, we'll also add three other procedures that READ_BYTE uses: STRING_TO_UPPER, CONVERT_HEX_DIGIT, and HEX_TO_BYTE.

STRING_TO_UPPER and HEX_TO_BYTE both work on strings. STRING_TO_UPPER converts all the lowercase letters in a string to uppercase. That means you can type either f3 or F3 for the hex number F3h. By

allowing hex numbers to be typed in either lower- or uppercase letters, we add
user-friendliness to Dskpatch.

HEX_TO_BYTE takes the string read by DOS, after we call STRING_
TO_UPPER, and converts the two-digit hex string to a single-byte number.
HEX_TO_BYTE makes use of CONVERT_HEX_DIGIT to convert each hex
digit to a four-bit number.

How do we ensure that DOS won't read more than two hex digits? The DOS
function 0Ah reads an entire string of characters into an area of memory defined like this:

```
CHAR_NUM_LIMIT  DB      0
NUM_CHARS_READ  DB      0
STRING          DB      80 DUP (0)
```

The first byte ensures we don't read too many characters. CHAR_NUM_
LIMIT tells DOS how many characters, at most, to read. If we set this to three,
DOS will read up to two characters, plus the carriage-return character (DOS
always counts the carriage return). Any characters we type after that will be
discarded—thrown away—and for each extra character, DOS will beep to let
us know we've passed the limit. When we press the Enter key, DOS sets the
second byte, NUM_CHARS_READ, to the number of characters it actually
read, not including the carriage return.

STRING_TO_UPPER, READ_BYTE, and STRING_TO_UPPER all use
NUM_CHARS_READ. For example, READ_BYTE checks NUM_CHARS_
READ to find out whether you typed a single character or a two-digit hex
number. If NUM_CHARS_READ was set to one, READ_BYTE returns a
single character in the AL register. If NUM_CHARS_READ was set to two,
READ_BYTE uses HEX_TO_BYTE to convert the two-digit hex string to a
byte.

Without further ado, here is the new file KBD_IO.ASM, with all four new
procedures:

Listing 23-2. The New Version of KBD_IO.ASM

```
CGROUP  GROUP   CODE_SEG, DATA_SEG
        ASSUME  CS:CGROUP, DS:CGROUP

CODE_SEG        SEGMENT PUBLIC

        PUBLIC  STRING_TO_UPPER
```

Listing 23-2. *continued*

```
;-----------------------------------------------------------------;
; This procedure converts the string, using the DOS format for strings, ;
; to all uppercase letters.                                       ;
;                                                                 ;
;       DS:DX    Address of string buffer                         ;
;-----------------------------------------------------------------;
STRING_TO_UPPER         PROC    NEAR
        PUSH    AX
        PUSH    BX
        PUSH    CX
        MOV     BX,DX
        INC     BX                      ;Point to character count
        MOV     CL,[BX]                 ;Character count in 2nd byte of buffer
        XOR     CH,CH                   ;Clear upper byte of count
UPPER_LOOP:
        INC     BX                      ;Point to next character in buffer
        MOV     AL,[BX]
        CMP     AL,'a'                  ;See if it is a lowercase letter
        JB      NOT_LOWER               ;Nope
        CMP     AL,'z'
        JA      NOT_LOWER
        ADD     AL,'A'-'a'              ;Convert to uppercase letter
        MOV     [BX],AL
NOT_LOWER:
        LOOP    UPPER_LOOP
        POP     CX
        POP     BX
        POP     AX
        RET
STRING_TO_UPPER         ENDP


;-----------------------------------------------------------------;
; This procedure converts a character from ASCII (hex) to a nibble (4  ;
; bits).                                                          ;
;                                                                 ;
;               AL      Character to convert                      ;
; Returns:      AL      Nibble                                    ;
;               CF      Set for error, cleared otherwise          ;
;-----------------------------------------------------------------;
CONVERT_HEX_DIGIT       PROC    NEAR
        CMP     AL,'0'                  ;Is it a legal digit?
        JB      BAD_DIGIT               ;Nope
        CMP     AL,'9'                  ;Not sure yet
        JA      TRY_HEX                 ;Might be hex digit
        SUB     AL,'0'                  ;Is decimal digit, convert to nibble
        CLC                             ;Clear the carry, no error
        RET
TRY_HEX:
        CMP     AL,'A'                  ;Not sure yet
        JB      BAD_DIGIT               ;Not hex
        CMP     AL,'F'                  ;Not sure yet
```

Listing 23-2. *continued*

```
        JA      BAD_DIGIT               ;Not hex
        SUB     AL,'A'-10               ;Is hex, convert to nibble
        CLC                             ;Clear the carry, no error
        RET
BAD_DIGIT:
        STC                             ;Set the carry, error
        RET
CONVERT_HEX_DIGIT       ENDP

        PUBLIC  HEX_TO_BYTE
;----------------------------------------------------------------------;
; This procedure converts the two characters at DS:DX from hex to one  ;
; byte.                                                                 ;
;                                                                      ;
;       DS:DX   Address of two characters for hex number               ;
; Returns:                                                             ;
;       AL      Byte                                                    ;
;       CF      Set for error, clear if no error                       ;
;                                                                      ;
; Uses:         CONVERT_HEX_DIGIT                                       ;
;----------------------------------------------------------------------;
HEX_TO_BYTE     PROC    NEAR
        PUSH    BX
        PUSH    CX
        MOV     BX,DX                   ;Put address in BX for indirect addr
        MOV     AL,[BX]                 ;Get first digit
        CALL    CONVERT_HEX_DIGIT
        JC      BAD_HEX                 ;Bad hex digit if carry set
        MOV     CX,4                    ;Now multiply by 16
        SHL     AL,CL
        MOV     AH,AL                   ;Retain a copy
        INC     BX                      ;Get second digit
        MOV     AL,[BX]
        CALL    CONVERT_HEX_DIGIT
        JC      BAD_HEX                 ;Bad hex digit if carry set
        OR      AL,AH                   ;Combine two nibbles
        CLC                             ;Clear carry for no error
DONE_HEX:
        POP     CX
        POP     BX
        RET
BAD_HEX:
        STC                             ;Set carry for error
        JMP     DONE_HEX
HEX_TO_BYTE     ENDP


;----------------------------------------------------------------------;
; This is a simple version of READ_STRING.                             ;
;                                                                      ;
;       DS:DX   Address of string area                                 ;
;----------------------------------------------------------------------;
```

Listing 23-2. *continued*

```
READ_STRING     PROC    NEAR
        PUSH    AX
        MOV     AH,0Ah              ;Call for buffered keyboard input
        INT     21h                 ;Call DOS function for buffered input
        POP     AX
        RET
READ_STRING     ENDP

        PUBLIC  READ_BYTE
;------------------------------------------------------------------------;
; This procedure reads either a single ASCII character or a two-digit    ;
; hex number.  This is just a test version of READ_BYTE.                 ;
;                                                                        ;
; Returns byte in        AL      Character code (unless AH = 0)          ;
;                        AH      1 if read ASCII char                    ;
;                                0 if no characters read                 ;
;                                -1 if read a special key                ;
;                                                                        ;
; Uses:          HEX_TO_BYTE, STRING_TO_UPPER, READ_STRING               ;
; Reads:         KEYBOARD_INPUT, etc.                                    ;
; Writes:        KEYBOARD_INPUT, etc.                                    ;
;------------------------------------------------------------------------;
READ_BYTE       PROC    NEAR
        PUSH    DX
        MOV     CHAR_NUM_LIMIT,3    ;Allow only two characters (plus Enter)
        LEA     DX,KEYBOARD_INPUT
        CALL    READ_STRING
        CMP     NUM_CHARS_READ,1    ;See how many characters
        JE      ASCII_INPUT         ;Just one, treat as ASCII character
        JB      NO_CHARACTERS       ;Only Enter key hit
        CALL    STRING_TO_UPPER     ;No, convert string to uppercase
        LEA     DX,CHARS            ;Address of string to convert
        CALL    HEX_TO_BYTE         ;Convert string from hex to byte
        JC      NO_CHARACTERS       ;Error, so return 'no characters read'
        MOV     AH,1                ;Signal read one character
DONE_READ:
        POP     DX
        RET
NO_CHARACTERS:
        XOR     AH,AH               ;Set to 'no characters read'
        JMP     DONE_READ
ASCII_INPUT:
        MOV     AL,CHARS            ;Load character read
        MOV     AH,1                ;Signal read one character
        JMP     DONE_READ
READ_BYTE       ENDP

CODE_SEG        ENDS

DATA_SEG        SEGMENT PUBLIC
KEYBOARD_INPUT  LABEL   BYTE
```

Listing 23-2. *continued*

```
CHAR_NUM_LIMIT  DB      0              ;Length of input buffer
NUM_CHARS_READ  DB      0              ;Number of characters read
CHARS           DB      80 DUP (0)     ;A buffer for keyboard input
DATA_SEG        ENDS

       END
```

Reassemble Kbd_io and link the four files Test, Kbd_io, Video_io, and Cursor to try this version of READ_BYTE.

At this point, we have two problems with READ_BYTE. Remember the special function keys? We can't read them with DOS function 0Ah. It just doesn't work. Try pressing a function key when you run Test. DOS doesn't return two bytes, with the first set to zero as you might expect.

We have no way to read extended codes with DOS' buffered input, using function 0Ah. We used this function so we could use the Backspace key to delete characters before we press the Enter key. But now, since we can't read special function keys, we have to write our own READ_STRING procedure. We'll have to replace function 0Ah to ensure we can press a special function key without pressing Enter.

The other problem with DOS' function 0Ah for keyboard input has to do with the line-feed character. Press Control-Enter (line feed) after you type one character, and then try the Backspace key. You'll find that you're on the next line, with no way to return to the one above. Our new version of Kbd_io in the next chapter will treat the line-feed character (Control-Enter) as an ordinary character; then, pressing line feed won't move the cursor to the next line.

But before we move on to fix the problems with READ_BYTE and READ_STRING, let's write a procedure to read an unsigned decimal number. We won't use the procedure in this book, but the version of Dskpatch on the companion disk does use it so that we can, for example, ask Dskpatch to display sector number 567.

Decimal Input

Recall that the largest unsigned decimal number we can put into a single word is 65536. When we use READ_STRING to read a string of decimal digits, we'll tell DOS to read no more than six characters (five digits and a carriage return at the end). Of course, that means READ_DECIMAL will still be able to read numbers from 65536 to 99999, even though these numbers don't fit into one word. We'll have to keep watch for such numbers and return an error code if READ_DECIMAL tries to read a number larger than 65535, or if it tries to read a character that is not between zero and nine.

To convert our string of up to five digits into a word, use multiplication as we did in Chapter 1: take the first (leftmost) digit, multiply it by ten, tack on the second digit, multiply it by ten, and so on. Using this method, we could, for example, write 49856 as:

$$4*10^4 + 9*10^3 + 8*10^2 + 5*10^1 + 6*10^0$$

or, as we'll do the calculation:

$$10*(10*(10*(10*4+9) +8) +5) +6$$

Of course, we must watch for errors as we do these multiplications and return with the carry flag set whenever an error occurs. How do we know when we try to read a number larger than 65535? With larger numbers, the last MUL will overflow into the DX register. The CF flag is set when DX is not zero after a word MUL, so we can use a JC (*Jump if Carry set*) instruction to handle an error. Here is READ_DECIMAL, which also checks each digit for an error (a digit that is not between 0 and 9). Place this procedure in the file KBD_IO.ASM:

Listing 23-3. Add This Procedure to KBD_IO.ASM

```
        PUBLIC  READ_DECIMAL
;----------------------------------------------------------------;
; This procedure takes the output buffer of READ_STRING and converts  ;
; the string of decimal digits to a word.                        ;
;                                                                ;
;       AX      Word converted from decimal                      ;
;       CF      Set if error, clear if no error                  ;
;                                                                ;
; Uses:         READ_STRING                                      ;
; Reads:        KEYBOARD_INPUT, etc.                             ;
; Writes:       KEYBOARD_INPUT, etc.                             ;
;----------------------------------------------------------------;
READ_DECIMAL    PROC    NEAR
        PUSH    BX
        PUSH    CX
        PUSH    DX
        MOV     CHAR_NUM_LIMIT,6        ;Max number is 5 digits (65535)
        LEA     DX,KEYBOARD_INPUT
        CALL    READ_STRING
        MOV     CL,NUM_CHARS_READ       ;Get number of characters read
```

Listing 23-3. *continued*

```
            XOR     CH,CH                   ;Set upper byte of count to 0
            CMP     CL,0                    ;Return error if no characters read
            JLE     BAD_DECIMAL_DIGIT       ;No chars read, signal error
            XOR     AX,AX                   ;Start with number set to 0
            XOR     BX,BX                   ;Start at beginning of string
CONVERT_DIGIT:
            MOV     DX,10                   ;Multiply number by 10
            MUL     DX                      ;Multiply AX by 10
            JC      BAD_DECIMAL_DIGIT       ;CF set if MUL overflowed one word
            MOV     DL,CHARS[BX]            ;Get the next digit
            SUB     DL,'0'                  ;And convert to a nibble (4 bits)
            JS      BAD_DECIMAL_DIGIT       ;Bad digit if < 0
            CMP     DL,9                    ;Is this a bad digit?
            JA      BAD_DECIMAL_DIGIT       ;Yes
            ADD     AX,DX                   ;No, so add it to number
            INC     BX                      ;Point to next character
            LOOP    CONVERT_DIGIT           ;Get the next digit
DONE_DECIMAL:
            POP     DX
            POP     CX
            POP     BX
            RET
BAD_DECIMAL_DIGIT:
            STC                             ;Set carry to signal error
            JMP     DONE_DECIMAL
READ_DECIMAL    ENDP
```

To make certain it works properly, we need to test this procedure with all
the boundary conditions. Here is a simple test program for READ_DECIMAL
that uses much the same approach we used to test READ_BYTE:

Listing 23-4. Changes to TEST.ASM

```
CGROUP  GROUP   CODE_SEG, DATA_SEG
        ASSUME  CS:CGROUP, DS:CGROUP

CODE_SEG        SEGMENT PUBLIC
        ORG     100H

        EXTRN   WRITE_HEX:NEAR, WRITE_DECIMAL:NEAR
        EXTRN   WRITE_STRING:NEAR, SEND_CRLF:NEAR
        EXTRN   READ_DECIMAL:NEAR

TEST    PROC    NEAR
        LEA     DX,ENTER_PROMPT
        CALL    WRITE_STRING
        CALL    READ_DECIMAL
        JC      ERROR
```

Listing 23-4. *continued*

```
        CALL    SEND_CRLF
        LEA     DX,NUMBER_READ_PROMPT
        CALL    WRITE_STRING
        MOV     DX,AX
        CALL    WRITE_DECIMAL
ERROR:  CALL    SEND_CRLF
        INT     20h
TEST    ENDP

CODE_SEG        ENDS

DATA_SEG        SEGMENT PUBLIC
ENTER_PROMPT            DB      'Enter decimal number: ',0
NUMBER_READ_PROMPT      DB      'Number read: ',0
; and now dummy variables
        PUBLIC  HEADER_LINE_NO, DISK_DRIVE_NO, HEADER_PART_1, HEADER_PART_2
        PUBLIC  PROMPT_LINE_NO, CURRENT_SECTOR_NO
HEADER_LINE_NO          DB      0
DISK_DRIVE_NO           DB      0
HEADER_PART_1           DB      0
HEADER_PART_2           DB      0
PROMPT_LINE_NO          DB      0
CURRENT_SECTOR_NO       DB      0
DATA_SEG        ENDS

        END     TEST
```

Again, we need to link four files: Test (the preceding file), Kbd_io, Video_io, and Cursor. Try the boundary conditions, using both valid digits and invalid ones (such as A, which is not a valid decimal digit), and with such numbers as 0, 65535, and 65536.

Summary

We'll return to the two simple test procedures later on, when we discuss ways you can write your own programs. Then, we'll see how you can use a slightly more advanced version of TEST.ASM to write a program that will convert numbers between hex and decimal.

But now, we're ready to move on to the next chapter, where we'll write improved versions of READ_BYTE and READ_STRING.

24

IMPROVED KEYBOARD INPUT

We mentioned we would present the development of Dskpatch just as we first wrote it—including bugs and clumsily designed procedures, some of which you've already seen. In this chapter, we'll write a new version of READ_BYTE, and it will place a subtle bug into Dskpatch. In the next chapter, we'll find a can of RAID to exorcise this small bug, but see if you can find it yourself first. (Hint: Carefully check all the boundary conditions for READ_BYTE when it's attached to Dskpatch.)

A New READ_STRING

Our modular-design philosophy calls for short procedures, therefore no single procedure is too difficult to understand. The new version of READ_ STRING will be an example of a clumsy procedure: much too long. It should be rewritten with more procedures, but we'll leave this rewrite to you. This book is quickly drawing to an end, and we still have a few more procedures left to write before Dskpatch is a useful program. Right now, we can still edit only the first half of any sector, and we can't write this sector back to the disk yet.

In this chapter, we'll give READ_STRING a new procedure, BACK_ SPACE, to emulate the function of the Backspace key found in the DOS function 0Ah. When we push the Backspace key, BACK_SPACE will erase the last character typed, from both the screen and the string in memory.

On screen, BACK_SPACE will erase the character by moving the cursor left one character, writing a space over it, and then moving right one character again. This sequence will perform the same backspace deletion provided by DOS.

In the buffer, BACK_SPACE will erase a character by changing the buffer pointer, DS:SI + BX, so it points to the next lower byte in memory. In other words, BACK_SPACE will simply decrement BX: (BX = BX − 1). The character will still be in the buffer, but our program won't see it. Why not? READ_ STRING tells us how many characters it's read. If we try to read more than this number from the buffer, we'll see characters we erased. Otherwise, we won't.

We have to be careful not to erase any characters when the buffer is empty. Remember that our string-data area looked something like this:

```
CHAR_NUM_LIMIT   DB        0
NUM_CHARS_READ   DB        0
STRING           DB        80 DUP (0)
```

The string buffer starts at the second byte of this data area, or at an *offset* of 2 from the start. So, BACK_SPACE won't erase a character if BX is set to 2, the start of the string buffer, because the buffer is empty when BX equals 2.

Here is BACK_SPACE; place it into KBD_IO.ASM:

Listing 24-1. Add This Procedure to KBD_IO.ASM

```
            PUBLIC   BACK_SPACE
            EXTRN    WRITE_CHAR:NEAR
;-------------------------------------------------------------------;
; This procedure deletes characters, one at a time, from the buffer and ;
; the screen when the buffer is not empty.  BACK_SPACE simply returns   ;
; when the buffer is empty.                                             ;
;                                                                       ;
;       DS:SI+BX        Most recent character still in buffer           ;
;                                                                       ;
; Uses:          WRITE_CHAR                                             ;
;-------------------------------------------------------------------;
BACK_SPACE      PROC     NEAR            ;Delete one character
        PUSH    AX
        PUSH    DX
        CMP     BX,2                    ;Is buffer empty?
        JE      END_BS                  ;Yes, read the next character
        DEC     BX                      ;Remove one character from buffer
        MOV     AH,2                    ;Remove character from screen
        MOV     DL,BS
        INT     21h
        MOV     DL,20h                  ;Write space there
        CALL    WRITE_CHAR
        MOV     DL,BS                   ;Back up again
        INT     21h
END_BS: POP     DX
        POP     AX
        RET
BACK_SPACE      ENDP
```

Let's move on to the new version of READ_STRING. It will be a large mouthful; the listing you'll see is for only one procedure. By far the longest procedure we've written, READ_STRING is, as we said, too large. That's because it's complicated by so many possible conditions.

Why does READ_STRING do so many things? We added a few more features. If you press the Escape key, READ_STRING will clear the string buffer and remove all the characters from the screen. DOS also erases all the characters in the string buffer when you press Escape, but it doesn't erase any characters from the screen. Instead, it simply writes a backslash (\) character at the end of the line and moves to the next line. Our version of READ_STRING will be more versatile than the DOS READ_STRING function.

READ_STRING uses three special keys: the Backspace, Escape, and Enter keys. We could write the ASCII codes for each of these keys in READ_STRING whenever we need them, but instead we'll add a few definitions to the beginning of KBD_IO.ASM to make READ_STRING more readable. Here are the definitions:

Listing 24-2. Additions to KBD_IO.ASM

```
CGROUP  GROUP   CODE_SEG, DATA_SEG
        ASSUME  CS:CGROUP, DS:CGROUP

BS      EQU     8                       ;Backspace character
CR      EQU     13                      ;Carriage-return character
ESC     EQU     27                      ;Escape character

CODE_SEG        SEGMENT PUBLIC
                  .
                  .
                  .
```

Here is READ_STRING. Although it's rather long, you can see from the listing that it's not very complicated—just long. Replace the old version of READ_STRING in KBD_IO.ASM with this new version:

Listing 24-3. The New READ_STRING in KBD_IO.ASM

```
        PUBLIC  READ_STRING
        EXTRN   WRITE_CHAR:NEAR
;----------------------------------------------------------------------;
; This procedure performs a function very similar to the DOS 0Ah       ;
; function.  But this function will return a special character if a    ;
; function or keypad key is pressed--no return for these keys.  And    ;
; ESC will erase the input and start over again.                       ;
;                                                                      ;
;       DS:DX   Address for keyboard buffer.  The first byte must      ;
;               contain the maximum number of characters to read (plus ;
;               one for the return).  And the second byte will be used ;
;               by this procedure to return the number of characters   ;
;               actually read.                                         ;
;                     0         No characters read                     ;
;                     -1        One special character read             ;
;                     otherwise number actually read (not including    ;
;                               Enter key)                             ;
;                                                                      ;
; Uses:         BACK_SPACE, WRITE_CHAR                                 ;
;----------------------------------------------------------------------;
```

Listing 24-3. *continued*

```
READ_STRING     PROC    NEAR
        PUSH    AX
        PUSH    BX
        PUSH    SI
        MOV     SI,DX                   ;Use SI for index register and
START_OVER:
        MOV     BX,2                    ;BX for offset to beginning of buffer
        MOV     AH,7                    ;Call for input with no checking
        INT     21h                     ; for CTRL-BREAK and no echo
        OR      AL,AL                   ;Is character extended ASCII?
        JZ      EXTENDED                ;Yes, read the extended character
NOT_EXTENDED:                           ;Extnd char is error unless buf empty
        CMP     AL,CR                   ;Is this a carriage return?
        JE      END_INPUT               ;Yes, we are done with input
        CMP     AL,BS                   ;Is it a backspace character?
        JNE     NOT_BS                  ;Nope
        CALL    BACK_SPACE              ;Yes, delete character
        CMP     BL,2                    ;Is buffer empty?
        JE      START_OVER              ;Yes, can now read extended ASCII again
        JMP     SHORT READ_NEXT_CHAR    ;No, continue reading normal characters
NOT_BS: CMP     AL,ESC                  ;Is it an ESC--purge buffer?
        JE      PURGE_BUFFER            ;Yes, then purge the buffer
        CMP     BL,[SI]                 ;Check to see if buffer is full
        JA      BUFFER_FULL             ;Buffer is full
        MOV     [SI+BX],AL              ;Else save char in buffer
        INC     BX                      ;Point to next free character in buffer
        PUSH    DX
        MOV     DL,AL                   ;Echo character to screen
        CALL    WRITE_CHAR
        POP     DX
READ_NEXT_CHAR:
        MOV     AH,7
        INT     21h
        OR      AL,AL                   ;An extended ASCII char is not valid
                                        ; when the buffer is not empty
        JNE     NOT_EXTENDED            ;Char is valid
        MOV     AH,7
        INT     21h                     ;Throw out the extended character

;-----------------------------------------------;
; Signal an error condition by sending a beep   ;
; character to the display: chr$(7).            ;
;-----------------------------------------------;
SIGNAL_ERROR:
        PUSH    DX
        MOV     DL,7                    ;Sound the bell by writing chr$(7)
        MOV     AH,2
        INT     21h
        POP     DX
        JMP     SHORT READ_NEXT_CHAR    ;Now read next character
```

Listing 24-3. *continued*

```
;------------------------------------------------;
; Empty the string buffer and erase all the      ;
; characters displayed on the screen.            ;
;------------------------------------------------;
PURGE_BUFFER:
        PUSH    CX
        MOV     CL,[SI]               ;Backspace over maximum number of
        XOR     CH,CH
PURGE_LOOP:                           ; characters in buffer.  BACK_SPACE
        CALL    BACK_SPACE            ; will keep the cursor from moving too
        LOOP    PURGE_LOOP            ; far back
        POP     CX
        JMP     START_OVER            ;Can now read extended ASCII characters
                                      ; since the buffer is empty

;------------------------------------------------;
; The buffer was full, so can't read another     ;
; character.  Send a beep to alert user of       ;
; buffer-full condition.                         ;
;------------------------------------------------;
BUFFER_FULL:
        JMP     SHORT SIGNAL_ERROR    ;If buffer full, just beep

;------------------------------------------------;
; Read the extended ASCII code and place this     ;
; in the buffer as the only character, then       ;
; return -1 as the number of characters read.     ;
;------------------------------------------------;
EXTENDED:                             ;Read an extended ASCII code
        MOV     AH,7
        INT     21h
        MOV     [SI+2],AL             ;Place just this char in buffer
        MOV     BL,0FFh               ;Num chars read = -1 for special
        JMP     SHORT END_STRING

;------------------------------------------------;
; Save the count of the number of characters      ;
; read and return.                                ;
;------------------------------------------------;
END_INPUT:                            ;Done with input
        SUB     BL,2                  ;Count of characters read
END_STRING:
        MOV     [SI+1],BL             ;Return number of chars read
        POP     SI
        POP     BX
        POP     AX
        RET
READ_STRING     ENDP
```

Stepping through the procedure, we can see that READ_STRING first checks to see if we pressed a special function key. It allows us to do so only when the string is empty. For example, if we press the F1 key after we press the *a* key, READ_STRING will ignore the F1 key and beep to tell us we pressed a special key at the wrong time. We can, however, press Escape, then F1, because the Escape key causes READ_STRING to clear the string buffer.

If READ_STRING reads a carriage-return character, it places the number of characters it read into the second byte of the string area and returns. Our new version of READ_BYTE looks at this byte to see how many characters READ_STRING actually read.

Next, READ_STRING checks to see if we typed a backspace character. If so, it CALLs BACK_SPACE to erase one character. If the string buffer becomes empty (BX becomes equal to 2, the start of the string buffer), then READ_STRING goes back to the start, where it can read a special key. Otherwise, it just reads the next character.

Finally, READ_STRING checks for the ESC character. BACK_SPACE erases characters only when there are characters in the buffer, so we can clear the string buffer by calling the BACK_SPACE procedure CHAR_NUM_LIMIT times, because READ_STRING can never read more than CHAR_NUM_LIMIT characters. Any other character is stored in the string buffer and echoed to the screen with WRITE_CHAR. Unless, that is, the buffer is full.

In the last chapter, we changed READ_BYTE in such a way that it couldn't read special function keys. We need only add a few lines here to allow READ_BYTE to work with our new version of READ_STRING, which can read special function keys. Here are the changes to make to READ_BYTE in KBD_IO.ASM:

Listing 24-4. Changes to READ_BYTE in KBD_IO.ASM

```
        PUBLIC  READ_BYTE
;-------------------------------------------------------------;
; This procedure reads a single ASCII character of a hex number. ;
;                                                             ;
; Returns byte in      AL      Character code (unless AH = 0)  ;
;                      AH      1 if read ASCII char or hex number ;
;                              0 if no characters read          ;
;                              -1 if read a special key         ;
;                                                             ;
; Uses:        HEX_TO_BYTE, STRING_TO_UPPER, READ_STRING       ;
; Reads:       KEYBOARD_INPUT, etc.                            ;
;-------------------------------------------------------------;
READ_BYTE       PROC    NEAR
        PUSH    DX
```

Listing 24-4. *continued*

```
            MOV     CHAR_NUM_LIMIT,3        ;Allow only two characters (plus Enter)
            LEA     DX,KEYBOARD_INPUT
            CALL    READ_STRING
            CMP     NUM_CHARS_READ,1        ;See how many characters
            JE      ASCII_INPUT            ;Just one, treat as ASCII character
            JB      NO_CHARACTERS          ;Only Enter key hit
            CMP     BYTE PTR NUM_CHARS_READ,OFFh    ;Special function key?
            JE      SPECIAL_KEY            ;Yes
            CALL    STRING_TO_UPPER        ;No, convert string to uppercase
            LEA     DX,CHARS               ;Address of string to convert
            CALL    HEX_TO_BYTE            ;Convert string from hex to byte
            JC      NO_CHARACTERS          ;Error, so return 'no characters read'
            MOV     AH,1                   ;Signal read one character
DONE_READ:
            POP     DX
            RET
NO_CHARACTERS:
            XOR     AH,AH                  ;Set to 'no characters read'
            JMP     DONE_READ
ASCII_INPUT:
            MOV     AL,CHARS               ;Load character read
            MOV     AH,1                   ;Signal read one character
            JMP     DONE_READ
SPECIAL_KEY:
            MOV     AL,CHARS[0]            ;Return the scan code
            MOV     AH,OFFh                ;Signal special key with -1
            JMP     DONE_READ
READ_BYTE   ENDP
```

Dskpatch, with the new versions of READ_BYTE and READ_STRING, should be much nicer to use. But there is a bug here, as we said. To try to find it, run Dskpatch and try all the boundary conditions for READ_BYTE and HEX_TO_BYTE.

IN SEARCH OF BUGS

If you try the new version of Dskpatch with *ag*, which isn't a hex number, you'll notice that Dskpatch doesn't do anything when you press the Enter key. Since the string *ag* isn't a hex number, there is nothing wrong with Dskpatch ignoring it, but the program should, at least, erase it from the screen.

This error is the sort we can find only by thoroughly checking the boundary conditions of a program. Not just the pieces, but the entire program. The bug here isn't the fault of READ_BYTE, even though it appeared when we re-wrote that procedure. Rather, the problem is in the way we wrote DIS-PATCHER and EDIT_BYTE.

EDIT_BYTE is designed so it calls WRITE_PROMPT_LINE to rewrite the editor prompt line and clear the rest of the line. This will remove any charac-ter we typed. But if we type a string like ag, READ_BYTE reports that it read a string of zero length, and DISPATCH doesn't call EDIT_BYTE. What's the solution?

Fixing DISPATCHER

There are actually two ways to solve this problem. The best solution would be to rewrite Dskpatch to be more modular, and to redesign DISPATCHER. We won't do that. Remember: Programs are never complete, but we have to stop somewhere. Instead, we'll add a fix to DISPATCHER so it will rewrite the prompt line whenever READ_BYTE reads a string of zero length.

Here are the modifications to DISPATCHER (in DISPATCH.ASM) to fix the bug:

Listing 25-1. Changes to DISPATCHER in DISPATCH.ASM

```
        PUBLIC  DISPATCHER
        EXTRN   READ_BYTE:NEAR, EDIT_BYTE:NEAR
        EXTRN   WRITE_PROMPT_LINE:NEAR
DATA_SEG        SEGMENT PUBLIC
        EXTRN   EDITOR_PROMPT:BYTE
DATA_SEG        ENDS
;-----------------------------------------------------------------;
; This is the central dispatcher.  During normal editing and viewing,   ;
; this procedure reads characters from the keyboard and, if the character;
; is a command key (such as a cursor key), DISPATCHER calls the          ;
; procedures that do the actual work.  This dispatching is done for      ;
; special keys listed in the table DISPATCH_TABLE, where the procedure   ;
; addresses are stored just after the key names.                         ;
```

Listing 25-1. *continued*

```
;   If the character is not a special key, then it should be placed   ;
; directly into the sector buffer--this is the editing mode.          ;
;                                                                     ;
; Uses:       READ_BYTE, EDIT_BYTE, WRITE_PROMPT_LINE                 ;
; Reads:      EDITOR_PROMPT                                           ;
;--------------------------------------------------------------------;
DISPATCHER      PROC    NEAR
        PUSH    AX
        PUSH    BX
        PUSH    DX
DISPATCH_LOOP:
        CALL    READ_BYTE               ;Read character into AX
        OR      AH,AH                   ;AX = 0 if no character read, -1
                                        ; for an extended code.
        JZ      NO_CHARS_READ           ;No character read, try again
        JS      SPECIAL_KEY             ;Read extended code
        MOV     DL,AL
        CALL    EDIT_BYTE               ;Was normal character, edit byte
        JMP     DISPATCH_LOOP           ;Read another character

SPECIAL_KEY:
        CMP     AL,68                   ;F10--exit?
        JE      END_DISPATCH            ;Yes, leave
                                        ;Use BX to look through table
        LEA     BX,DISPATCH_TABLE
SPECIAL_LOOP:
        CMP     BYTE PTR [BX],0         ;End of table?
        JE      NOT_IN_TABLE            ;Yes, key was not in the table
        CMP     AL,[BX]                 ;Is it this table entry?
        JE      DISPATCH                ;Yes, then dispatch
        ADD     BX,3                    ;No, try next entry
        JMP     SPECIAL_LOOP            ;Check next table entry

DISPATCH:
        INC     BX                      ;Point to address of procedure
        CALL    WORD PTR [BX]           ;Call procedure
        JMP     DISPATCH_LOOP           ;Wait for another key

NOT_IN_TABLE:                           ;Do nothing, just read next character
        JMP     DISPATCH_LOOP

NO_CHARS_READ:
        LEA     DX,EDITOR_PROMPT
        CALL    WRITE_PROMPT_LINE       ;Erase any invalid characters typed
        JMP     DISPATCH_LOOP           ;Try again

END_DISPATCH:
        POP     DX
        POP     BX
        POP     AX
        RET
    DISPATCHER  ENDP
```

This bug fix doesn't create any great problems, but it does make DIS-PATCHER slightly less elegant. Elegance is a virtue to strive for. Elegance and clarity often go hand in hand, and our rules of modular design are aimed at increasing elegance.

Summary

DISPATCHER is elegant because it's such a simple solution to a problem. Rather than using many comparisons for each special character we might type, we built a table we can search. Doing so made DISPATCHER simpler, and hence more reliable, than a program containing different instructions for each possible condition that might arise. By adding our small fix, we complicated DISPATCHER—not by much in this case, but some bugs might require us to really complicate a procedure.

If you find yourself adding fixes that make a procedure too complicated, rewrite whichever procedures you must to remove this complexity. And always check the boundary conditions both before and after you add a procedure to your main program. You'll save yourself a lot of debugging effort if you do.

We can't overemphasize the importance of testing procedures with boundary conditions and of following the rules of modular design. Both techniques lead to better and more reliable programs. In the next chapter, we'll look at another method for debugging programs.

26

WRITING MODIFIED SECTORS

We almost have a usable Dskpatch program. In this chapter, we'll build the procedure to write a modified sector back to disk, and in the next chapter, we'll write a procedure to show the second half of a sector. Dskpatch won't be finished then, as we said, programs never are; but the scope of our coverage in this book will be complete. You'll find many extras in the version of Dskpatch on the disk available to complement this book.

Writing to the Disk

Writing a modified sector back to the disk can be disastrous if it's not done intentionally. All of Dskpatch's functions thus far depend on the function keys F1, F2, and F10, and on the cursor keys. But any of these keys could be pressed quite by accident. Fortunately, the same doesn't hold true for the shifted function keys, so we'll use the shifted F5 key for writing a disk sector. This will prevent us from writing a sector back to disk unless we really want to.

Make the following changes to DISPATCH.ASM, to add WRITE_SECTOR to the table:

Listing 26-1. Changes to DISPATCH.ASM

```
DATA_SEG        SEGMENT PUBLIC
        EXTRN   NEXT_SECTOR:NEAR                        ;In DISK_IO.ASM
        EXTRN   PREVIOUS_SECTOR:NEAR                    ;In DISK_IO.ASM
        EXTRN   PHANTOM_UP:NEAR, PHANTOM_DOWN:NEAR      ;In PHANTOM.ASM
        EXTRN   PHANTOM_LEFT:NEAR, PHANTOM_RIGHT:NEAR
        EXTRN   WRITE_SECTOR:NEAR                       ;In DISK_IO.ASM
;-------------------------------------------------------------------------;
; This table contains the legal extended ASCII keys and the addresses     ;
; of the procedures that should be called when each key is pressed.       ;
;       The format of the table is                                        ;
;               DB      72              ;Extended code for cursor up       ;
;               DW      OFFSET CGROUP:PHANTOM_UP                          ;
;-------------------------------------------------------------------------;
DISPATCH_TABLE  LABEL   BYTE
        DB      59                              ;F1
        DW      OFFSET CGROUP:PREVIOUS_SECTOR
        DB      60                              ;F2
        DW      OFFSET CGROUP:NEXT_SECTOR
        DB      72                              ;Cursor up
        DW      OFFSET CGROUP:PHANTOM_UP
        DB      80                              ;Cursor down
```

Listing 2b-1. *continued*

```
        DW      OFFSET CGROUP:PHANTOM_DOWN
        DB      75                              ;Cursor left
        DW      OFFSET CGROUP:PHANTOM_LEFT
        DB      77                              ;Cursor right
        DW      OFFSET CGROUP:PHANTOM_RIGHT
        DB      88                              ;Shift F5
        DW      OFFSET CGROUP:WRITE_SECTOR
        DB      0                               ;End of the table
DATA_SEG        ENDS
```

WRITE_SECTOR itself is almost identical to READ_SECTOR. The only change is that we wish to write, rather than read, a sector. Whereas the INT 25h asks DOS to read one sector, its companion function, INT 26h, asks DOS to write a sector to the disk. Here is WRITE_SECTOR; place it into DISK_ IO.ASM:

Listing 2b-2. Add This Procedure to DISK_IO.ASM

```
        PUBLIC  WRITE_SECTOR
;------------------------------------------------------------------;
; This procedure writes the sector back to the disk.              ;
;                                                                 ;
; Reads:        DISK_DRIVE_NO, CURRENT_SECTOR_NO, SECTOR          ;
;------------------------------------------------------------------;
WRITE_SECTOR    PROC    NEAR
        PUSH    AX
        PUSH    BX
        PUSH    CX
        PUSH    DX
        MOV     AL,DISK_DRIVE_NO        ;Drive number
        MOV     CX,1                    ;Write 1 sector
        MOV     DX,CURRENT_SECTOR_NO    ;Logical sector
        LEA     BX,SECTOR
        INT     2bh                     ;Write the sector to disk
        POPF                            ;Discard the flag information
        POP     DX
        POP     CX
        POP     BX
        POP     AX
        RET
WRITE_SECTOR    ENDP
```

Now, reassemble both Dispatch and Disk_io, but don't try Dskpatch's write function just yet. Find an old disk you don't care much about and put it in drive A, with your program disk in some other drive, such as B. Run Dskpatch from drive B (or whatever drive you choose), so that Dskpatch reads the first sector from your scratch disk in drive A. Before you go on, make sure this is a scratch disk you have no qualms about if it's destroyed.

Change one byte in your sector display and make a note of the one you changed. Then, press the shifted F5 key. You'll see the red drive light come on: You've just written a modified sector back to drive A.

Next, press F2 to read the next sector (sector 1), then F1 to read the previous sector (your original sector, number 0). You should see the modified sector back again. Restore this sector and write it back to Drive A to restore the integrity of your scratch disk.

More Debugging Techniques

What would happen if we had made a small error in our program? Dskpatch is sufficiently large that we'd expect to have problems using Debug to find the bug. Besides, Dskpatch is composed of nine different files we must link to form DSKPATCH.COM. How do we find any one procedure in this large program without tracing slowly through much of the program? As you'll see in this chapter, there are two ways to find procedures: by using a road map we can get from LINK, or by using Microsoft's SYMDEB in place of DEBUG.

When we originally wrote Dskpatch, something went wrong when we added WRITE_SECTOR; pressing the Shift-F5 key caused our machine to hang. But we couldn't find anything wrong with WRITE_SECTOR and the only other changes were to DISPATCH_TABLE. Everything appeared to be correct.

Finally, we traced the bug to a faulty definition in the dispatcher. The bug turned out to be an error in the DISPATCH_TABLE entry for WRITE_SEC- TOR. Somehow, we had typed a DW rather than a DB in the table, so WRITE_SECTOR's address was stored one byte higher in memory than it should have been. You can see the bug shown in italics here:

```
DISPATCH_TABLE  LABEL    BYTE
                   .
                   .
                   .
        DB       77                          ;Cursor right
        DW       OFFSET CGROUP:PHANTOM_RIGHT
        DW       88                          ;Shift F5
        DW       OFFSET CGROUP:WRITE_SECTOR
        DB       0                           ;End of the table
DATA_SEG         ENDS
```

As an exercise in debugging, make this change to your file DIS-PATCH.ASM, then follow the directions in the next section.

Building a Road Map

Let's learn how to use LINK to build a map of Dskpatch. This map will help us find procedures and variables in memory.

The LINK command we've used so far has grown to be fairly long:

```
LINK DSKPATCH DISK_IO DISP_SEC VIDEO_IO CURSOR DISPATCH KBD_IO PHANTOM EDITOR;
```

and we'll want to add even more to it. Does that mean we'll have to keep typing file after file after file? No, there is a much easier way. LINK allows us to supply an *automatic response* file containing all the information. With such a file, which we'll call linkinfo, we can simply type:

```
LINK @LINKINFO
```

and LINK will read all of its information from this file.

With the file names that we've used so far, linkinfo looks like this:

```
DSKPATCH DISK_IO DISP_SEC VIDEO_IO CURSOR +
DISPATCH KBD_IO PHANTOM EDITOR
```

The plus (+) at the end of the first line tells LINK to continue reading file names from the next line.

We can also add some more information that tells LINK to create a map of the procedures and variables in our program to this simple linkinfo file. Here is the entire linkinfo file:

```
DSKPATCH DISK_IO DISP_SEC VIDEO_IO CURSOR +
DISPATCH KBD_IO PHANTOM EDITOR
DSKPATCH
DSKPATCH /MAP;
```

The last two lines are new parameters. The first, *dskpatch*, tells LINK we want the .EXE file to be named DSKPATCH.EXE; the second new line tells LINK to create a listing file called DSKPATCH.MAP—to create our road map. The */map* switch tells LINK to provide a list of all the procedures and variables we've declared to be public.

Create the map file by relinking Dskpatch with this linkinfo response file.

The map file produced by the linker is about 120 lines long. That's a bit too long for us to reproduce in its entirety, so we'll reproduce the parts that are of particular interest. Here is our partial listing of the map file, DSKPATCH.MAP:

```
Warning: no stack segment

Start   Stop    Length  Name                        Class
00000H  007E5H  007E6H  CODE_SEG
007F0H  0291FH  02130H  DATA_SEG

Origin    Group
0000:0    CGROUP

  Address           Publics by Name

  0000:0677         BACK_SPACE
  0000:048F         CLEAR_SCREEN
  0000:04D1         CLEAR_TO_END_OF_LINE
  0000:07F2         CURRENT_SECTOR_NO
  0000:04B1         CURSOR_RIGHT
  0000:07F4         DISK_DRIVE_NO
  0000:04F0         DISPATCHER
  0000:01F3         DISP_HALF_SECTOR
                 .
                 .
                 .
  0000:0370         WRITE_HEX_DIGIT
  0000:03DB         WRITE_PATTERN
  0000:06FE         WRITE_PHANTOM
  0000:0440         WRITE_PROMPT_LINE
  0000:013A         WRITE_SECTOR
  0000:0428         WRITE_STRING

  Address           Publics by Value

  0000:0120         READ_SECTOR
  0000:013A         WRITE_SECTOR
  0000:0154         PREVIOUS_SECTOR
  0000:0174         NEXT_SECTOR
  0000:0190         INIT_SEC_DISP
  0000:01F3         DISP_HALF_SECTOR
                 .
                 .
                 .
  0000:07F5         LINES_BEFORE_SECTOR
  0000:07F6         HEADER_LINE_NO
  0000:07F7         HEADER_PART_1
  0000:07FD         HEADER_PART_2
  0000:080E         PROMPT_LINE_NO
  0000:080F         EDITOR_PROMPT
```

```
0000:0844        SECTOR
0000:2912        PHANTOM_CURSOR_X
0000:2913        PHANTOM_CURSOR_Y
```

Program entry point at 0000:0100

There are three main parts to this *load map* (so called because it tells us where our procedures are loaded in memory). The first shows a list of segments in our program. Dskpatch has just two segments, CODE_SEG and DATA_SEG, which are grouped together, so you'll see these two segments in the list.

The next part of the load map shows our public procedures and variables, listed in alphabetic order. LINK lists only those procedures and variables you've declared to be PUBLIC—visible to the outside world. If you're debugging a long program, you may want to declare all procedures and variables to be public, just so you can find them in this map.

The final section of the map lists all the procedures and memory variables again, but this time in the order they appear in memory.

Both of these lists include the memory address for each PUBLIC procedure or variable. If you check this list, you'll find that our procedure DISPATCHER starts at address 4F0h. We'll use this address now, to track down the bug in Dskpatch.

Tracking Down Bugs

If you were to try running the version of Dskpatch with the bug in it, you'd find that everything works, with the exception of Shift-F5, which on our machine caused Dskpatch to hang. You probably don't want to try Shift-F5; there's no telling what it will do on your machine.

Since everything worked (and works now) except for Shift-F5, our first guess when we wrote the program was that we had introduced a bug into WRITE_ SECTOR. To find this bug, we could start debugging Dskpatch by tracing through WRITE_SECTOR. Instead, we'll take a somewhat different tack.

We know that DISPATCHER works correctly, because everything else (the cursor keys, F1, F2, and F10) all work correctly. That means DISPATCHER is a good starting point to search for the bug in Dskpatch.

If you look at the program listing for DISPATCHER (in Chapter 25), you'll see that the instruction

```
CALL    WORD PTR [BX]
```

is the heart of DISPATCHER, because it calls all the other routines. In particular, this CALL instruction will call WRITE_SECTOR when we press Shift-F5. Let's start our search here.

We'll use Debug to start Dskpatch with a breakpoint set on this instruction. Of course, that means we need the address of this instruction, and we can find that by unassembling DISPATCHER, which starts at 4F0h. After a U 4F0, followed by another U command, you should see the CALL command:

```
          .
          .
          .
2C14:0517 EBF2        JMP      050B
2C14:0519 43          INC      BX
2C14:051A FF17        CALL     [BX]
2C14:051C EBD5         JMP      04F3
          .
          .
          .
```

Now that we know the CALL instruction is at location 51Ah, we can set a breakpoint at this address, then single-step into and through WRITE_SECTOR.

First, use the command G 51A to execute Dskpatch up to this instruction. You'll see Dskpatch start up, then wait for you to type a command. Press Shift-F5, since this is the command that is causing problems. You'll see the following:

```
-G 51A


AX=FF58  BX=28A3  CX=2820  DX=080F  SP=FFF6  BP=419A  SI=03CC  DI=0001
DS=2C14  ES=2C14  SS=2C14  CS=2C14  IP=051A    NV UP DI PL NZ NA PE NC
2C14:051A FF17        CALL     [BX]                          DS:28A3=3A00
```

At this point the BX register is pointing to a word that should contain the address of WRITE_SECTOR. Let's see if it does:

```
-D 28A3 L 2
2C14:28A0           00 3A                                     .:
-
```

In other words, we're trying to CALL a procedure located at 3A00h (remember the lower byte is displayed first). But if we look at our memory map, we can see that WRITE_SECTOR should be at 13Ah. In fact, we can also tell from this load map that we don't have *any* procedures at 3A00h. The address is totally wrong!

In our original bug-hunting, once we discovered that this address was wrong, it didn't take us very long to find the error. We knew that DISPATCHER and the table were basically sound, because all the other keys worked, so we took a closer look at the data for Shift-F5 and found the DW where we should have had a DB. Having a road map makes debugging much simpler. Now let's take a look at Symdeb.

Symdeb

Symdeb (*Symbolic Debugging*) is a program that Microsoft includes with version 3.00 and above of its macro assembler package. As you'll see in this section, Symdeb is so useful that, if you don't have it, you may well want to consider upgrading your macro assembler.

Since both Debug and Symdeb were written by Microsoft, Symdeb shares most, if not all, of Debug's commands. It also includes a number of very useful commands you won't find in Debug, *and* it includes some other features that are worth their weight in gold. We'll use two of these new features in this chapter: symbolic debugging and screen swapping.

Symbolic Debugging

Symbolic debugging, which gives Symdeb its name, lets us see procedure and variable names, rather than addresses, in our Unassemble (U) listings. For example, if we use Debug to unassemble the first line in Dskpatch, we see:

```
2C14:0100 E88C03      CALL    048F
```

With Symdeb, on the other hand, we see the following:

```
3245:0100 E88C03      CALL    CLEAR_SCREEN
```

Which of these is easier to read? We rest our case.

Screen Swapping

The second new feature, screen swapping, is handy for debugging Dskpatch. Dskpatch jumps around the screen, writing in different places. In the last section, where we used Debug, Debug started writing to this screen and we eventually lost the Dskpatch screen.

Symdeb, however, maintains two separate screens: one for Dskpatch and one for itself. Whenever Dskpatch is active, we see its screen; whenever Symdeb is active, we see *its* screen. We'll get a clearer idea of screen swapping as we run through the following examples.

Before we can use Symdeb's symbolic debugging feature, we need to create a symbol file with a program called Mapsym. Mapsym takes the .MAP file we created earlier in this chapter and turns it into a symbol file:

```
A>MAPSYM DSKPATCH
Microsoft (R) Symbol File Generator  Version 4.00
Copyright (C) Microsoft Corp 1984, 1985.  All rights reserved.

        Program entry point at 0000:0100
```

In this case, Mapsym has created a symbol file called DSKPATCH.SYM. We then start Symdeb with both the symbol file and the .COM file:

```
A>SYMDEB /S DSKPATCH.SYM DSKPATCH.COM
Microsoft (R) Symbolic Debug Utility  Version 4.00
Copyright (C) Microsoft Corp 1984, 1985.  All rights reserved.

Processor is [8086]
-
```

The /S switch in our command tells Symdeb to use its screen-swapping feature. It doesn't use this feature by default, because screen swapping can make Symdeb noticeably slower.

Before we run through a repetition of our previous debugging session, let's take a quick look at the start of Dskpatch:

```
-U
330E:0100 E88C03        CALL    CLEAR_SCREEN
330E:0103 E8F402        CALL    WRITE_HEADER
330E:0106 E81700        CALL    READ_SECTOR
330E:0109 E88400        CALL    INIT_SEC_DISP
330E:010C 8D160F08      LEA     DX,[EDITOR_PROMPT]
```

```
330E:0110 E82D03        CALL    WRITE_PROMPT_LINE
330E:0113 E8DA03        CALL    DISPATCHER
330E:0116 CD20          INT     20
-
```

You can see how nicely Symdeb displays all the names, rather than the addresses.

When we last unassembled DISPATCHER to find the address of the CALL WORD PTR [BX] instruction, we first had to look in the map file to find the address of the procedure, then type U 4F0 to unassemble it. With Symdeb, life is much simpler: We can simply type U DISPATCHER to unassemble our procedure.

```
-U DISPATCHER
CGROUP:DISPATCHER:
330E:04F0 50            PUSH    AX
330E:04F1 53            PUSH    BX
330E:04F2 52            PUSH    DX
330E:04F3 E80401        CALL    READ_BYTE
330E:04F6 0AE4          OR      AH,AH
330E:04F8 7426          JZ      DISPATCHER+30 (0520)
330E:04FA 7807          JS      DISPATCHER+13 (0503)
-
```

After two more U commands, we find our CALL instruction:

```
330E:0514 83C303        ADD     BX,+03
330E:0517 EBF2          JMP     DISPATCHER+1B (050B)
330E:0519 43            INC     BX
330E:051A FF17          CALL    [BX]
330E:051C EBD5          JMP     DISPATCHER+03 (04F3)
-
```

Type G 51A, as before, and follow that with Shift-F5. If you have Symdeb, you'll see Dskpatch draw its screen. Then, you'll return to Symdeb after you push Shift-F5. This time, though, you won't see the Dskpatch screen, because Symdeb will swap screens. To flip back to the Dskpatch screen, press the back-slash (\) key and press Enter. Once the Dskpatch screen comes up, pressing any other key will return you to Symdeb's screen again.

There is one subtle point you may have noticed about Symdeb as we've used it here. If we look at the unassembly listings, we see instructions like this:

```
330E:051C EBD5          JMP     DISPATCHER+03 (04F3)
```

rather than this:

```
330E:051C EBD5          JMP     DISPATCH_LOOP
```

Why didn't Symdeb use the label DISPATCH_LOOP? We didn't define the labels in this procedure to be PUBLIC. If we went back and wrote PUBLIC declarations for all the labels in DISPATCHER, we'd see these labels in the unassembly listing. (If you do this, remember to rebuild the symbol file with Mapsym).

Summary

That ends our discussion of debugging techniques. We have only three chapters left in the book. In the next chapter, we'll add the procedures to scroll the screen between the two half sectors. Then, in the final two chapters, we'll learn more about the differences between .COM and .EXE files, and take a last look at the ASSUME statement and segment overrides.

By the way: Don't forget to fix the bug we placed in DISPATCH_TABLE.

27

THE OTHER HALF SECTOR

Ideally, Dskpatch should behave like a word processor when you try to move the cursor below the bottom of the half-sector display: The display should move up one line, with a new line appearing at the bottom. The version of Dskpatch on the disk available with this book does just that, but we won't get quite so sophisticated here. In this chapter, we'll add skeletal versions of the two procedures, SCROLL_UP and SCROLL_DOWN, that scroll the screen. In the disk version of Dskpatch, SCROLL_UP and SCROLL_DOWN can scroll by any number of lines from one to sixteen (there are sixteen lines in our half-sector display). The versions of SCROLL_UP and SCROLL_DOWN that we'll add to Dskpatch here scroll by full half sectors, so we'll see either the first or second half of the sector.

Scrolling by Half a Sector

Our old versions of PHANTOM_UP and PHANTOM_DOWN restore the cursor to the top or bottom of the half-sector display whenever we try to move the cursor off the top or bottom of the display. We'll change PHANTOM_UP and PHANTOM_DOWN so that we call either SCROLL_UP or SCROLL_DOWN when the cursor moves off the top or bottom of the display. These two new procedures will scroll the display and place the cursor at its new position.

Here are the modified versions of PHANTOM_UP and PHANTOM_DOWN (in PHANTOM.ASM):

Listing 27-1. Changes to PHANTOM.ASM

```
PHANTOM_UP      PROC    NEAR
        CALL    ERASE_PHANTOM           ;Erase at current position
        DEC     PHANTOM_CURSOR_Y        ;Move cursor up one line
        JNS     WASNT_AT_TOP            ;Was not at the top, write cursor
        MOV     PHANTOM_CURSOR_Y,0      ;Was at the top, so put back there
        CALL    SCROLL_DOWN             ;Was at the top, scroll
WASNT_AT_TOP:
        CALL    WRITE_PHANTOM           ;Write the phantom at new position
        RET
PHANTOM_UP      ENDP


PHANTOM_DOWN    PROC    NEAR
        CALL    ERASE_PHANTOM           ;Erase at current position
```

Listing 27-1. *continued*

```
        INC     PHANTOM_CURSOR_Y            ;Move cursor up one line
        CMP     PHANTOM_CURSOR_Y,16         ;Was it at the bottom?
        JB      WASNT_AT_BOTTOM             ;No, so write phantom
        MOV     PHANTOM_CURSOR_Y,15         ;Was at bottom, so put back there
        CALL    SCROLL_UP                   ;Was at bottom, scroll
WASNT_AT_BOTTOM:
        CALL    _WRITE_PHANTOM              ;Write the phantom cursor
        RET
PHANTOM_DOWN    ENDP
```

Don't forget to change the comment header for PHANTOM_UP and PHAN-TOM_DOWN, to mention that these procedures now use SCROLL_UP and SCROLL_DOWN:

Listing 27-2. Changes to PHANTOM.ASM

```
;--------------------------------------------------------------------;
; These four procedures move the phantom cursors.                    ;
;                                                                    ;
; Uses:         ERASE_PHANTOM, WRITE_PHANTOM                         ;
;               SCROLL_DOWN, SCROLL_UP                               ;
; Reads:        PHANTOM_CURSOR_X, PHANTOM_CURSOR_Y                   ;
; Writes:       PHANTOM_CURSOR_X, PHANTOM_CURSOR_Y                   ;
;--------------------------------------------------------------------;
```

SCROLL_UP and SCROLL_DOWN are both fairly simple procedures, since they switch the display to the other half sector. For example, if we're looking at the first half sector, and PHANTOM_DOWN calls SCROLL_UP, we'll see the second half sector. SCROLL_UP changes SECTOR_OFFSET to 256, the start of the second half sector, moves the cursor to the start of the sector display, writes the half sector display for the second half, and finally writes the phantom cursor at the top of this display.

You can see all the details for both SCROLL_UP and SCROLL_DOWN in the following listing. Add it to PHANTOM.ASM.

Listing 27-3. Add These Procedures to PHANTOM.ASM

```
        EXTRN   DISP_HALF_SECTOR:NEAR, GOTO_XY:NEAR
DATA_SEG        SEGMENT PUBLIC
        EXTRN   SECTOR_OFFSET:WORD
        EXTRN   LINES_BEFORE_SECTOR:BYTE
DATA_SEG        ENDS
```

Listing 27-3. *continued*

```
;-------------------------------------------------------------------;
; These two procedures move between the two half-sector displays.   ;
;                                                                   ;
; Uses:          WRITE_PHANTOM, DISP_HALF_SECTOR, ERASE_PHANTOM, GOTO_XY ;
;                SAVE_REAL_CURSOR, RESTORE_REAL_CURSOR              ;
; Reads:         LINES_BEFORE_SECTOR                                ;
; Writes:        SECTOR_OFFSET, PHANTOM_CURSOR_Y                    ;
;-------------------------------------------------------------------;
SCROLL_UP       PROC    NEAR
        PUSH    DX
        CALL    ERASE_PHANTOM           ;Remove the phantom cursor
        CALL    SAVE_REAL_CURSOR        ;Save the real cursor position
        XOR     DL,DL                   ;Set cursor for half-sector display
        MOV     DH,LINES_BEFORE_SECTOR
        ADD     DH,2
        CALL    GOTO_XY
        MOV     DX,256                  ;Display the second half sector
        MOV     SECTOR_OFFSET,DX
        CALL    DISP_HALF_SECTOR
        CALL    RESTORE_REAL_CURSOR     ;Restore the real cursor position
        MOV     PHANTOM_CURSOR_Y,0      ;Cursor at top of second half sector
        CALL    WRITE_PHANTOM           ;Restore the phantom cursor
        POP     DX
        RET
SCROLL_UP       ENDP

SCROLL_DOWN     PROC    NEAR
        PUSH    DX
        CALL    ERASE_PHANTOM           ;Remove the phantom cursor
        CALL    SAVE_REAL_CURSOR        ;Save the real cursor position
        XOR     DL,DL                   ;Set cursor for half-sector display
        MOV     DH,LINES_BEFORE_SECTOR
        ADD     DH,2
        CALL    GOTO_XY
        XOR     DX,DX                   ;Display the first half sector
        MOV     SECTOR_OFFSET,DX
        CALL    DISP_HALF_SECTOR
        CALL    RESTORE_REAL_CURSOR     ;Restore the real cursor position
        MOV     PHANTOM_CURSOR_Y,15     ;Cursor at bottom of first half sector
        CALL    WRITE_PHANTOM           ;Restore the phantom cursor
        POP     DX
        RET
SCROLL_DOWN     ENDP
```

SCROLL_UP and SCROLL_DOWN both work nicely, although there is one minor problem with them as Dskpatch stands now. Start Dskpatch and leave the cursor at the top of the screen. Press the cursor-up key, and you'll see Dskpatch rewrite the first half-sector display. Why? We didn't check for this boundary condition. Dskpatch rewrites the screen whenever you try to move the cursor off the top or bottom of the half-sector display.

Here's a challenge for you: Modify Dskpatch so that it checks for two boundary conditions. If the phantom cursor is at the top of the first half-sector display and you press the cursor-up key, Dskpatch should do nothing. If you're at the bottom of the second half-sector display and press the cursor-down key, again Dskpatch should do nothing.

Summary

This ends our work on Dskpatch in this book. Our intent was to use Dskpatch as a "live" example of the evolution of an assembly language program, at the same time providing you with a usable program, and a set of procedures you'll find helpful in your own programming. But the Dskpatch you've developed here isn't as finished as it could be. You'll find more features in the disk version of Dskpatch available with this book. And you may find yourself changing that disk version, for "a program is never done . . . but there comes a time when it has to be shipped to users."

We'll wrap up this book with a change of pace. In the next two chapters we'll move on to two advanced subjects: relocation and more about segments.

PART IV

Odds and Ends

RELOCATION

One subject that always seems to be shrouded in mystery is the difference between .EXE and .COM files and the meaning of relocatable programs. As part of our change of pace in these final two chapters, let's look at relocation and see how you can build programs larger than 64K—not that you'd necessarily want to, although many people do.

Multiple Segments

As soon as we start to build programs that use more than 64K of memory we find ourselves running into problems with .COM files. Why? That's what we're here to find out.

First of all, any program must be built from one or more segments, each no more than 64K long. But many programs extend their use of memory by using several different segments; for example, a code segment for the program, a data segment for the data, and a stack segment for the stack and temporary data. If each of these three segments were fully used, we'd fill 3 * 64K = 192K of memory. That's how we gain access to more memory, and that's where the difference between .COM and .EXE programs comes in: .EXE programs are designed specifically for this kind of job.

All our programs in this book have been .COM files, with either one segment or one group. Remember that the GROUP pseudo-op simply combines several different segments into a single unit that acts like one segment. If we wanted to use more than one segment to span more than 64K of memory, we'd have to do some more work. Let's look at an example.

Our program for printing a string of characters in Chapter 3 will serve nicely. That example, written with groups in assembly language, looks like this:

```
CGROUP  GROUP   CODE_SEG, DATA_SEG
        ASSUME  CS:CGROUP, DS:CGROUP


CODE_SEG        SEGMENT PUBLIC
        ORG     100h
WRITE_STRING    PROC    FAR
        MOV     AH,9                    ;Call for string output
        MOV     DX,OFFSET CGROUP:STRING ;Load address of string
        INT     21h                     ;Write string
        INT     20h                     ;Return to DOS
WRITE_STRING    ENDP
```

```
CODE_SEG        ENDS


DATA_SEG        SEGMENT PUBLIC
STRING  DB      "Hello, DOS here.$"
DATA_SEG        ENDS


        END     WRITE_STRING
```

The two segments CODE_SEG and DATA_SEG are placed into a single 64K group, CGROUP, so OFFSET CGROUP:STRING gives the offset of STRING from the beginning of the group CGROUP.

When DOS loads a .COM program into memory, it sets all four segment registers (CS, DS, ES, and SS) to the start of CGROUP, therefore DS:OFFSET CGROUP:STRING is the full address of STRING. What if we had two different segments and no group? We wouldn't have a limit of 64K for two segments: it would be 128K. How would we set the segment registers to point to their respective segments? By using an .EXE program, which allows us to use several segments, all starting at different addresses.

DOS allows us to set the segment registers for an .EXE program with the help of some assembler instructions. These assignments aren't as simple as they might seem, but we'll come back to that. First, let's rebuild WRITE_STRING as an .EXE program.

We must have at least two segments for any .EXE program: the code segment and the stack segment. These two segments are special cases for DOS. DOS sets the four registers—CS, SS, IP, and SP—when it loads an .EXE program into memory. DOS sets the CS:IP register to point to the first instruction whose address appears after the END pseudo-op. In an .EXE program, this first instruction can be anywhere, whereas in a .COM program, this instruction *must* be the first instruction in the code segment.

Similarly, SS:IP points to the end of stack region defined with the SEGMENT STACK pseudo-op. For example, the following version of WRITE_STRING contains a stack that is 80 bytes long, thus IP will be set to 80—the end of this stack region within the stack segment. Here is the program:

```
        ASSUME  CS:CODE_SEG, DS:DATA_SEG, SS:STACK_SEG


CODE_SEG        SEGMENT PUBLIC
WRITE_STRING    PROC    FAR
        MOV     AX,DATA_SEG             ;Segment address for DATA_SEG
        MOV     DS,AX                   ;Set up DS register for DATA_SEG
        MOV     AH,9                    ;Call for string output
        MOV     DX,OFFSET STRING        ;Load address of string
```

```
        INT     21h                     ;Write string

        PUSH    ES                      ;Save return address for long RET below
        XOR     AX,AX                   ;There is an INT 20h inst. at ES:0
        PUSH    AX


        RET                             ;Return to DOS
WRITE_STRING    ENDP

CODE_SEG        ENDS


DATA_SEG        SEGMENT PUBLIC
STRING  DB      "Hello, DOS here.$"
DATA_SEG        ENDS


STACK_SEG       SEGMENT STACK
        DB      10 DUP ('STACK    ')    ;'STACK' followed by three spaces
STACK_SEG       ENDS


        END     WRITE_STRING
```

This program will be ready to run after you link it, but first erase
WRITESTR.COM. If you have two versions of a file, one with the extension
.COM and one with the extension .EXE, DOS will execute the .COM file.

There are a number of differences between this .EXE file and our original
.COM file. In place of the INT 20h instruction to return to DOS, we now have
several cryptic instructions, beginning with PUSH ES. The two PUSH instructions push a long return address, ES:0, onto the stack. This is the address
of the first byte in the 256 byte data area DOS puts into memory before our
program, and the first instruction in this data area is an INT 20h instruction.

The CS register must point to the start of this data area when we execute
the INT 20h instruction. This was the case in our .COM program, right from
the start. But our .EXE program begins with the CS register set to the start of
the code segment, not the the data area. By doing a FAR RET to ES:0, we set
CS to the start of the data area and, as you can see, ES:0 holds the INT 20h
instruction:

```
A>DEBUG WRITESTR.EXE
-U ES:0
39AF:0000 CD20            INT     20
39AF:0002 006000          ADD     [BX+SI+00],AH
        .
        .
        .
```

The GROUP pseudo-op is missing, because we now have three different segments that are not confined to a total area of 64K or less. Each of these three segments is independent, and each of the segment registers (CS, DS, and SS) points to a different segment. Both CS and SS are set by DOS, as we can see with the help of Debug:

```
A>DEBUG WRITESTR.EXE
-R
AX=0000  BX=0000  CX=0100  DX=0000  SP=0050  BP=0000  SI=0000  DI=0000
DS=39AF  ES=39AF  SS=39C3  CS=39BF  IP=0000   NV UP DI PL NZ NA PO NC
39BF:0000 B8C139        MOV     AX,39C1
```

DS and ES point to a segment lower in memory than either CS or SS. As you saw in Chapter 11, both DS and ES point to the data area, 256 bytes long, placed by DOS before our program. In .COM program, we reserved this area with an ORG 100h statement. For .EXE files, we don't need to do the same, because the code and data segments are in different parts of memory. The data segment is elsewhere, but DS isn't pointing to DATA_SEG. This is the reason for the first instruction in WRITE_STRING. The MOV AX,DATA_SEG instruction moves the segment number of DATA_SEG into the AX register. If we look at our program in memory:

```
-U
39BF:0000 B8C139        MOV     AX,39C1
39BF:0003 8ED8          MOV     DS,AX
39BF:0005 B409          MOV     AH,09
39BF:0007 BA0000        MOV     DX,0000
39BF:000A CD21          INT     21
39BF:000C 06            PUSH    ES
39BF:000D 33C0          XOR     AX,AX
39BF:000F 50            PUSH    AX
39BF:0010 CB            RETF
39BF:0011 0000          ADD     [BX+SI],AL
                           .
                           .
                           .
```

we see that this MOV instruction has been translated into MOV AX,39C1, where 39C1 is the segment number of for DATA_SEG. We needed two MOV instructions to move this number into the DS register, because we can't move a number directly into any segment register. (See the chart of addressing modes in Appendix E.)

Where did the 39C1 come from? Surely, neither the assembler nor the linker knew ahead of time where DOS would load this program; only DOS can know that. In fact, it is DOS that sets this number to 39C1, and the process of calculating such numbers is known as *relocation*. DOS makes relocation calculations for .EXE programs, but not for .COM programs. It is for this reason that .COM programs load into memory more quickly. They are also more compact, because they don't contain the special information DOS uses to make relocation calculations.

Out of curiosity, let's see what happens if we try to convert our .EXE program into a .COM program using Exe2bin:

```
A>EXE2BIN WRITESTR WRITESTR.COM
File cannot be converted
A>
```

Exe2bin knows that it can't create a .COM program from our file, but it doesn't tell us why. It leaves us to figure that out for ourselves. Let's take a look at the problem

DOS loads a .COM program directly into memory after it creates the 256 byte header. If we want different segments, as in WRITE_STRING, and want to create a .COM file, we have to do any relocation ourselves, with instructions in our program. It's not very difficult, and we'll show you how it's done, so you can get a better insight into the way DOS relocates programs. If you ever need to write a large .COM program that needs to use more than 64K of memory, you'll find this technique useful.

Relocation

Our goal is to set the DS register to the beginning of DATA_SEG, and the SS register to the beginning of STACK_SEGMENT. We can do this with a bit of trickery. First, we need to ensure that our three segments are loaded into memory in the correct order:

    Code segment
    Data segment
    Stack segment

Fortunately, we've already taken care of this. The linker loads these three segments in the order in which they appear in our file. A word of warning though: When you use the following technique in a .COM file to set segment registers, make sure you know the order in which LINK will load your segments.

How do we calculate the value for DS? Let's begin by looking at three labels we've placed into various segments in the following listing. Those labels are END_OF_CODE_SEG, END_OF_DATA_SEG, and END_OF_STACK_ SEG. They aren't exactly where you might have expected them to be. Why not? Well, when we define a segment like:

```
CODE_SEG       SEGMENT       PUBLIC
```

we don't really tell the linker how to stitch together various segments. So, it starts each new segment on a paragraph boundary—at a hex address that ends with a zero, such as 32C40h. Because the Linker skips to the next paragraph boundary to start each segment, there will very often be a short, blank area between segments. By placing the label END_OF_CODE_SEG at the beginning of DATA_SEG, we include this blank area. If we had put END_ OF_CODE_SEG at the end of CODE_SEG, we wouldn't include the blank area between segments. (Look at the unassemble listing of our program on page 307. You'll see a blank area filled with zeros that is 15 bytes long.)

As for the value of the DS register, DATA_SEG starts at 39AF:0130, or 39C2:0000. The instruction OFFSET CODE_SEG:END_OF_CODE_SEG will return 130h, which is the number of bytes used by CODE_SEG. Divide this number by 16 to get the number we need to add to DS so that DS points to DATA_SEG. We use the same technique to set SS.

Here's the listing for our program, including the relocation instructions needed for a .COM file:

```
        ASSUME  CS:CODE_SEG, DS:DATA_SEG, SS:STACK_SEG


CODE_SEG        SEGMENT PUBLIC
        ORG     100h                    ;Reserve data area for .COM program
WRITE_STRING    PROC    FAR
        MOV     AX,OFFSET CODE_SEG:END_OF_CODE_SEG
        MOV     CL,4                    ;Calculate number of paragraphs
        SHR     AX,CL                   ; (16 bytes) used by the code segment
        MOV     BX,CS
        ADD     AX,BX                   ;Add CS to this
        MOV     DS,AX                   ;Set the DS register to DATA_SEG

        MOV     BX,OFFSET DATA_SEG:END_OF_DATA_SEG
        SHR     BX,CL                   ;Calculate paras used by data segment
        ADD     AX,BX                   ;Add to value used for data segment
        MOV     SS,AX                   ;Set the SS register for STACK_SEG
        MOV     AX,OFFSET STACK_SEG:END_OF_STACK_SEG
        MOV     SP,AX                   ;Set SP to end of stack area
```

```
        MOV     AH,9                    ;Call for string output
        MOV     DX,OFFSET STRING        ;Load address of string
        INT     21h                     ;Write string

        PUSH    ES                      ;Save return address for long RET below
        XOR     AX,AX                   ;There is an INT 20h inst. at ES:0
        PUSH    AX
        RET                             ;Return to DOS
WRITE_STRING    ENDP

CODE_SEG        ENDS


DATA_SEG        SEGMENT PUBLIC
END_OF_CODE_SEG         LABEL   BYTE
STRING  DB      "Hello, DOS here.$"
DATA_SEG        ENDS


STACK_SEG       SEGMENT         PUBLIC
END_OF_DATA_SEG         LABEL   BYTE
        DB      10 DUP ('STACK   ')     ;'STACK' followed by three spaces
END_OF_STACK_SEG        LABEL   BYTE
STACK_SEG       ENDS


        END     WRITE_STRING
```

You can see the results of all this work in the following Debug session:

```
A>DEBUG WRITESTR.COM
-U
39AF:0100 B83001        MOV     AX,0130
39AF:0103 B104          MOV     CL,04
39AF:0105 D3E8          SHR     AX,CL
39AF:0107 8CCB          MOV     BX,CS
39AF:0109 03C3          ADD     AX,BX
39AF:010B 8ED8          MOV     DS,AX
39AF:010D BB2000        MOV     BX,0020
39AF:0110 D3EB          SHR     BX,CL
39AF:0112 03C3          ADD     AX,BX
39AF:0114 8ED0          MOV     SS,AX
39AF:0116 B85000        MOV     AX,0050
39AF:0119 8BE0          MOV     SP,AX
39AF:011B B409          MOV     AH,09
39AF:011D BA0000        MOV     DX,0000
-U
39AF:0120 CD21          INT     21
39AF:0122 06            PUSH    ES
39AF:0123 33C0          XOR     AX,AX
39AF:0125 50            PUSH    AX
39AF:0126 CB            RETF
```

```
39AF:0127 0000          ADD     [BX+SI],AL
39AF:0129 0000          ADD     [BX+SI],AL
39AF:012B 0000          ADD     [BX+SI],AL
39AF:012D 0000          ADD     [BX+SI],AL
39AF:012F 004865        ADD     [BX+SI+65],CL
39AF:0132 6C            DB      6C
39AF:0133 6C            DB      6C
39AF:0134 6F            DB      6F
39AF:0135 2C20          SUB     AL,20
39AF:0137 44            INC     SP
39AF:0138 4F            DEC     DI
39AF:0139 53            PUSH    BX
39AF:013A 206865        AND     [BX+SI+65],CH
39AF:013D 7265          JB      01A4
39AF:013F 2E            CS:
39AF:0140 2400          AND     AL,00
-G 120

AX=0950  BX=0002  CX=0004  DX=0000  SP=0050  BP=0000  SI=0000  DI=0000
DS=39C2  ES=39AF  SS=39C4  CS=39AF  IP=0120   NV UP DI PL NZ NA PO NC
39AF:0120 CD21          INT     21
```

By doing the relocation for more than one segment ourselves, we've increased the amount of memory the .COM program can use. Most people never have need of such tricks, but knowing how relocation works helps us understand how DOS does the relocation with .EXE files.

.COM versus .EXE Programs

We'll finish this chapter by summarizing the difference between .COM and .EXE files.

A .COM program stored on disk is essentially a memory image of the program. Because of this, a .COM program is restricted to a single segment, unless it does its own relocation, as we did in this chapter.

An .EXE program, on the other hand, lets DOS take care of the relocation. This delegating makes it very easy for .EXE programs to use multiple segments. For this reason, most large programs are .EXE rather than .COM programs.

For our final look at .COM versus .EXE programs, let's take a closer look at how DOS loads and starts both of them. This should make the differences between these types of program clearer and more concrete. We'll begin with .COM programs.

When DOS loads a .COM program into memory, it follows these steps:

- First, DOS creates the program segment prefix (PSP), which is the 256 byte scratch area we saw in Chapter 11. Among other things, this PSP contains the command line typed.
- DOS next copies the entire .COM file from the disk into memory, immediately after the 256 byte PSP.
- DOS then sets all four segment registers (CS, DS, ES, and SS) to the start of the PSP.
- Finally, DOS sets the IP register to 100h (which is the start of the .COM program) and sets the SP register to the end of the segment—usually FFFE, which is the last word in the segment.

In contrast, the steps involved in loading an .EXE file are somewhat more involved, because DOS does the relocation. Where does DOS finds the information it needs to do the relocation?

As it turns out, every .EXE file has a header that's stored at the start of the file. This header, or *relocation table*, is always at least 512 bytes long, and contains all the information DOS needs to do the relocation. With recent releases of its macro assembler, Microsoft has included a program called EXEMOD we can use to look at some of the information in this header:

```
A>EXEMOD WRITESTR
Microsoft (R) EXE File Header Utility  Version 4.00
Copyright (C) Microsoft Corp 1985.  All rights reserved.

WRITESTR                        (hex)          (dec)


.EXE size (bytes)                290            656
Minimum load size (bytes)         90            144
Overlay number                     0              0
Initial CS:IP                0000:0000
Initial SS:SP                0004:0050             80
Minimum allocation (para)          0              0
Maximum allocation (para)       FFFF          65535
Header size (para)                20             32
Relocation table offset           1E             30
Relocation entries                 1              1


A>
```

At the bottom of this table, you can see that we have a single relocation entry for our program WRITESTR. Anytime we make a reference to a segment address, as we did with MOV AX,DATA_SEG, LINK will add a relocation entry to the table. The segment address isn't known until DOS loads our program into memory, so we must let DOS supply the segment number.

There are also some other interesting pieces of information in the table; for example, the initial CS:IP and SS:SP values. These pairs tell us the initial values for IP and SP. The table also tells DOS how much memory our program needs before it can run: the Minimum load size.

Because DOS uses this relocation table to supply absolute addresses for such locations as segment addresses, there are a few extra steps it takes when loading a program into memory. Here are the steps DOS follows in loading an .EXE program:

- DOS creates the program-segment prefix (PSP), just as it does for a .COM program.
- Second, DOS checks the .EXE header to find where the header ends and the program starts. It then loads the rest of the program into memory after the PSP.
- Next, using the header information, DOS finds and patches all the references in the program that need to be relocated, such as references to segment addresses.
- DOS then sets the ES and DS registers so they point to the start of the PSP. If your program has its own data segment, your program needs to change DS and/or ES so they point to your data segment.
- Finally, DOS sets the CS register to the start of the code segment, with IP set from the information in the .EXE header. Similarly, it sets SS:SP according to the information in the .EXE header. In the case illustrated, the header states that SS:SP will be placed at 0004:0050. That means DOS will set SP to 0050, and set SS so that it is four paragraphs higher in memory than the end of the PSP.

29

MORE ON SEGMENTS AND ASSUME

In this, our final chapter, we'll take another look at the ASSUME statement and see how it relates to our use of segments. Along the way, we'll learn about a feature called *segment overrides*, which we touched on very briefly. We'll see that segment overrides go hand in hand with the ASSUME statement.

Segment Override

So far we've always read and written data located in the data segment. We've been dealing with a single segment in this book (through the use of groups), so we've had no reason to read or write data in other segments.

But, as we've seen, .EXE programs contain multiple segments, and even .COM programs can contain or use multiple segments. A classic example is writing directly to the screen: Many commercial programs write to the screen by moving the data directly into screen memory and completely bypassing the ROM BIOS routines in the interest of speed. Screen memory on the IBM PC is located at segment B800h for a color/graphics adapter and at segment B000h for monochrome display adapters. To write directly to the screen means we'd want to write in different segments.

In this section, we'll write a short program showing how we can write to two different segments, using the DS and ES registers to point to the two segments. In fact, many programs that write directly to screen memory do use the ES register to point to screen memory.

Here is our program. It's very short, and you can see that it has two data segments, along with one variable in each data segment:

```
DATA_SEG        SEGMENT PUBLIC
DS_VAR          DW      1
DATA_SEG        ENDS


EXTRA_SEG       SEGMENT PUBLIC
ES_VAR          DW      2
EXTRA_SEG       ENDS


STACK_SEG       SEGMENT STACK
        DB      10 DUP ('STACK   ')      ;'STACK' followed by three spaces
STACK_SEG       ENDS


CODE_SEG        SEGMENT PUBLIC
```

```
            ASSUME  CS:CODE_SEG, DS:DATA_SEG, ES:EXTRA_SEG, SS:STACK_SEG

TEST                PROC    FAR
            PUSH    ES                      ;Save return address for long RET below
            XOR     AX,AX                   ;There is an INT 20h inst. at ES:0
            PUSH    AX

            MOV     AX,DATA_SEG             ;Segment address for DATA_SEG
            MOV     DS,AX                   ;Set up DS register for DATA_SEG
            MOV     AX,EXTRA_SEG            ;Segment address for EXTRA_SEG
            MOV     ES,AX                   ;Set up ES register for EXTRA_SEG

            MOV     AX,DS_VAR               ;Read a variable from data segment
            MOV     BX,ES:ES_VAR            ;Read a variable from extra segment

            RET                             ;Return to DOS
TEST                ENDP

CODE_SEG            ENDS


            END     TEST
```

We'll use this program to learn about both the ASSUME pseudo-op and segment overrides.

Notice we've put both data segments and the stack segment *before* our code segment, and that we've also put the ASSUME pseudo-op after all the segment declarations. As we'll see in this section, this arrangement is a direct result of using two data segments.

Let's take a look at the two MOV instructions in this program:

```
            MOV     AX,DS_VAR
            MOV     BX,ES:ES_VAR
```

The ES: in front of the second instruction tells the 8088 to use the ES, rather than the DS, register for this operation (to read the data from our extra segment). Every instruction has a default segment register it uses when it refers to data. But, as we've done with the ES register here, we can also tell the 8088 we want to use some other segment register for data.

Here's how it works: The 8088 has four special instructions, one for each of the four segment registers. These instructions are the segment-override instructions, and they tell the 8088 to use a specific segment register, rather than the default, when the following instruction tries to read or write memory.

For example, our instruction MOV AX,ES:ES_VAR is actually encoded as two instructions. You'll see the following if you unassemble our test program:

```
2CF4:0011 26           ES:
2CF4:0012 8B1E0000      MOV     BX,[0000]
```

This shows that the assembler translated our instruction into a segment-override instruction, followed by the MOV instruction. Now the MOV instruction will read its data from the ES, rather than the DS, segment.

If you trace through this program, you'll see that the first MOV instruction sets AX equal to 1 (DS_VAR) and the second MOV sets BX equal to 2 (ES_VAR). In other words: We've read data from two different segments.

Another Look at ASSUME

Let's take a look at what happens when we remove the ES: from our program. Change the line:

```
MOV     BX,ES:ES_VAR
```

so it reads:

```
MOV     BX,ES_VAR
```

We're no longer telling the assembler we want to use the ES register when we read from memory, so it should go back to using the default segment (DS), right? Wrong.

Use Debug to look at the result of this change. You'll see that we still have the ES: segment override in front of our MOV instruction. How could the assembler possibly have known that our variable is in the extra, rather than the data, segment? By using the information we gave it in the ASSUME pseudo-op.

Our ASSUME statement tells the assembler that the DS register points to the segment DATA_SEG, while ES points to EXTRA_SEG. Each time we write an instruction that uses a memory variable, the assembler searches for a declaration of this variable to see which segment it's declared in. Then, it searches through the ASSUME list to find out which segment register is pointing to this segment. The assembler uses this segment register when it generates the instruction.

In the case of our MOV BX,ES_VAR instruction, the assembler noticed ES_VAR was in the segment called EXTRA_SEG, and that the ES register was pointing to that segment, so it generated an ES: segment-override instruction on its own. If we were to move ES_VAR into STACK_SEG, the assembler would generate an SS: segment-override instruction. The assembler automatically generates any segment-override instructions we need, provided, of course, that our ASSUME pseudo-ops reflect the actual contents of the segment registers.

Phase Errors

Sometimes you'll find that the assembler displays a cryptic error message, such as *Phase error between passes*. This message can mean a number of things, but we'll look at one particular case to help you understand it.

Basically, the assembler makes a number of passes through a program as it generates the machine language version of it. Sometimes, as we'll see here, the program changes size between passes.

Using our sample program again, move the two data segments (DATA_ SEG and EXTRA_SEG) so they appear *after* your code SEGMENT. The assembler will now assemble the main program before it even looks at the data segments. As a result, it will generate a normal MOV instruction for MOV BX,ES_VAR, because it doesn't realize that this variable is in another segment.

Next, the assembler will assemble the two data segments. At this point, it will store the information that ES_VAR is in the segment EXTRA_SEG. On its next pass through this program, the assembler will notice it now needs room for a segment-override instruction. Since it didn't reserve room for this instruction the first time through, the assembler issues the error message: *Phase error between passes*.

This is why we placed all our data segments before the code segment: So the assembler would know which segments contained which variables. What isn't so obvious, though, is why we placed the ASSUME statement in CODE_SEG, rather than at the top of this file.

We also receive a phase-error message if we place our ASSUME first thing in the file. For some reason (not clear to us), we have to declare the segments *before* the ASSUME pseudo-op, *if* we're going to have any implicit segment overrides. The safest approach, then, is to declare all data before the code segment and to place the ASSUME pseudo-op in the code segment.

Closing Words

By now you've seen many examples of assembly-language programs. Throughout this book, we've constantly emphasized programming, rather than the details of the 8088 microprocessor inside your IBM Personal Computer. As a result, you haven't seen all the 8088 instructions, nor the assembler pseudo-ops. But most assembly language programs can be written with what you've learned here, and no more. Your best approach to learning more about writing assembly language programs is to take the programs in this book and modify them.

If you think of a better way to write any part of Dskpatch, by all means do so. This is how we first learned to write programs. Back then the programs were in BASIC, but the idea still holds. We found programs written in BASIC, and began to learn about the language itself by rewriting bits and pieces of those programs. You can do the same with Dskpatch.

After you've tried some of these examples, you'll be ready to write your own programs. Don't start from scratch here, either; that's rather difficult for your first time out. To begin with, use the programs in this book as a framework. Don't build a completely new structure or technique (your equivalent of modular design) until you feel comfortable with writing assembly language programs.

If you really become enthralled by assembly language, you'll also need a more complete book for use as a reference to the 8088 instruction set. Here is a list of good reference books available at the time we wrote this book. This list is by no means complete, and the books listed here are only the ones we've read.

The following two books are good programmers' references:

iAPX 88 Book, Intel, 1981. This is the definitive source book, and a very good reference.

Rector, Russel, and Alexy, George, *The 8086 Book*, Osborne/McGraw-Hill, 1980. This is another good reference, but rather thick and dense.

The next three books were all written for the IBM PC. Much of the information in each of these is generic; only the examples in the latter part of these books are specific to the IBM PC. We recommend that you look at all three books in a bookstore to see which one you find most interesting:

Scanlon, Leo J., *IBM PC & XT Assembly Language: A Guide for Programmers, Enhanced and Enlarged*, Brady Communication Co., 1985. This book is easy reading. It's a complete introduction to 8088 assembly language. If you're still feeling somewhat shaky about assembly language, this might be a good book for you. Otherwise, look at Morse's book.

Willen, David C., and Krantz, Jeffrey I., *8088 Assembler Language Programming: The IBM PC*, Howard W. Sams & Co., 1983. This is another good second book on the 8088 microprocessor, written for the IBM PC.

Bradley, David J., *Assembly Language Programming for the IBM Personal Computer,* Prentice-Hall, 1984. The author helped design the IBM PC, and he's included many examples for the IBM PC. These examples aren't complete, but they may give you ideas of programs to work on. He also talks about more advanced subjects, such as the 8087 numeric processor, than do the authors of the preceding two books.

The next recommendation is neither a reference book, nor an introduction for the IBM PC. It's an introduction to the 8088 microprocessor, written by a member of the design team at Intel:

Morse, Stephen P., *The 8086/8088 Primer*, Hayden, 1982. This is a delightful book. As one of the designers at Intel, Morse provides many insights into the design of the 8088 and also talks about some of the design flaws and bugs in the 8088. While not very good as a reference, this book is complete, and it's very readable and informative.

Finally, the last book is a reference that's useful to anyone programming the IBM PC. We like to think of it as a compendium of everything a programmer might need to know about the IBM PC and 8086 microprocessor family.

Norton, Peter, *Programmer's Guide to the IBM PC*, Microsoft Press, 1985. Includes a complete reference to all DOS and BIOS functions, descriptions of important memory locations, a summary of 8086 instructions, and a host of other useful (or at least interesting) information.

APPENDIX A

GUIDE TO THE DISK

The companion disk to this book contains most of the Dskpatch examples you've seen in the preceding chapters, as well as an advanced version of the program that includes a lot of improvements. The files are in two groups: the chapter examples and the advanced Dskpatch program. This appendix will explain what's on the disk, and why.

Chapter Examples

All the chapter examples are from Chapters 9 through 27. The examples in earlier chapters are short enough so you can type them in quickly. But starting in Chapter 9, we began to build Dskpatch, which, by the end of this book, had grown to nine different files.

In any one chapter, only a few of these nine files changed. Since they do evolve throughout each chapter, however, there wasn't enough room on the disk to store each version of each example. You will find the examples on the disk, as they stand after each chapter. Thus, if we modify a program several times in, say, Chapter 19, the disk contains the final version.

The table on page 324 shows when each file changes. It also shows the name of the disk file for that chapter. If you want to make sure you're still on course, or you don't feel like typing in the changes for some chapter, just look at this table to find the names of the new files. Then you can either check your work or copy the file(s) to your disk.

Here's the complete list of all the files on the companion disk (not including the advanced version of Dskpatch):

```
VIDEO_9.ASM    VIDEO_10.ASM   VIDEO_13.ASM   TEST13.ASM
DISP_S14.ASM   CURSOR14.ASM   VIDEO_14.ASM   DISP_S15.ASM
DISK_I15.ASM   DISP_S16.ASM   VIDEO_16.ASM   DISK_I16.ASM
DSKPAT17.ASM   DISP_S17.ASM   CURSOR17.ASM   VIDEO_17.ASM
DISK_I17.ASM   CURSOR18.ASM   VIDEO_18.ASM   DSKPAT19.ASM
DISPAT19.ASM   KBD_IO19.ASM   VIDEO_19.ASM   DISK_I19.ASM
DISP_S21.ASM   PHANTO21.ASM   VIDEO_21.ASM   DISPAT22.ASM
EDITOR22.ASM   PHANTO22.ASM   KBD_IO23.ASM   TEST23.ASM
KBD_IO24.ASM   DISPAT25.ASM   DISPAT26.ASM   DISK_I26.ASM
PHANTO27.ASM
```

Advanced Version of Dskpatch

The disk contains more than just the examples in this book. We didn't really finish Dskpatch by the end of Chapter 27, and there are many things we should have put into Dskpatch to make it a usable program. The disk contains an almost-finished version. Here's a quick overview of what you'll find there.

As it stands in this book, Dskpatch can only read the next or previous sector. Thus, if you wanted to read sector 576, you'd have to push the F2 key 575 times. That's too much work. What if you wanted to look at sectors within a file? Right now, you'd have to look at the directory sector and figure out where to look for the sectors of that file. Again, not much fun. The disk version of Dskpatch can read either absolute sectors, just as the book version can, or it can read sectors within a file. In its advanced form, Dskpatch is a very usable program.

The advanced version of Dskpatch has too many changes to describe in detail here, so let's look at the new functions we added to the disk version. You'll find many of the changes by exploring Dskpatch and making your own changes.

The advanced Dskpatch still has nine files, all of which you'll find on the disk:

```
DSKPATCH.ASM   DISPATCH.ASM   DISP_SEC.ASM   KBD_IO.ASM
CURSOR.ASM     EDITOR.ASM     PHANTOM.ASM    VIDEO_IO.ASM
DISK_IO.ASM    DSKPATCH.COM
```

You'll also find an assembled and linked .COM version ready to run, so you can try out the new version without assembling it.

When you do, you'll be able to tell that there are several improvements just by looking at the screen display. The advanced Dskpatch now uses eight function keys. That's more than you can remember, if you don't use Dskpatch very often, so the advanced Dskpatch has a "key line" at the bottom of the display. Here's a description of the function keys:

F1, F2   were used in this book. F1 reads the previous sector, and F2 reads the next sector.

F3   changes the disk-drive number or letter. Just press F3 and enter a letter, such as A (without a colon, :), or enter a drive number, such as 0. When you press the Enter key, Dskpatch will change drives and read a sector from the new disk drive. You may want to change Dskpatch so that it doesn't read a new sector when you change drives. We set it up so that it's very difficult to write a sector to the wrong disk.

F4   changes the sector number. Just press F4 and type a sector number, in decimal. Dskpatch will read that sector.

F5   is in this book. Press the Shift key and F5 to write a sector back to the disk.

F6   changes Dskpatch to file mode. Just enter the file name and Dskpatch will read a sector from that file. From then on, F1 (Previous Sector) and F2 (Next Sector) read sectors from within that file. F3 ends file mode and switches back to absolute-sector mode.

F7   asks for an offset within a file. This is just like F4 (Sector) except that it reads sectors within a file. If you enter an offset of 3, Dskpatch will read the fourth sector in your file.

F10   exits from Dskpatch. If you accidentally press this key, you'll find yourself back in DOS, and you'll lose any changes you've made to the last sector. You may want to change Dskpatch so that it asks if you really want to leave Dskpatch.

A number of other changes aren't as obvious as those just mentioned. For example, Dskpatch now scrolls the screen one line at a time. If you move the cursor to the bottom line of the display and press the Cursor-Down key, Dskpatch will scroll the display by one line, putting a new line at the bottom. In addition, some of the other keys on the keyboard also work now:

Home moves the phantom cursor to the top of the half-sector display and scrolls the display so you see the first half-sector.

End moves the phantom cursor to the bottom right of the half-sector display and scrolls the display so you see the second half-sector.

PgUp scrolls the half-sector display by four lines. This is a nice feature when you want to move partway through the sector display. If you press PgUp four times, you'll see the last half sector.

PgDn scrolls the half-sector display by four lines in the opposite direction from PgUp.

If you like, you can modify the advanced Dskpatch to better suit your own needs. That's why the disk has all the source files for the advanced Dskpatch: So you can modify Dskpatch any way you like and learn from a complete example. For instance, you might spruce up the error-checking capabilities. As it stands, if pressing F2 causes you to fall off the end of a disk or file, Dskpatch doesn't reset the sector to the last sector on the disk or file. If you feel ambitious, see if you can modify Dskpatch so it catches and corrects such errors.

Or, you may want to speed up screen updates. To do this you'd have to rewrite some of the procedures, such as WRITE_CHAR and WRITE_ATTRIBUTE_N_TIMES, to write directly to screen memory. Now, they use the very slow ROM BIOS routines. If you're really ambitious, try to write your own character-output routines that send characters to the screen very quickly.

Good luck.

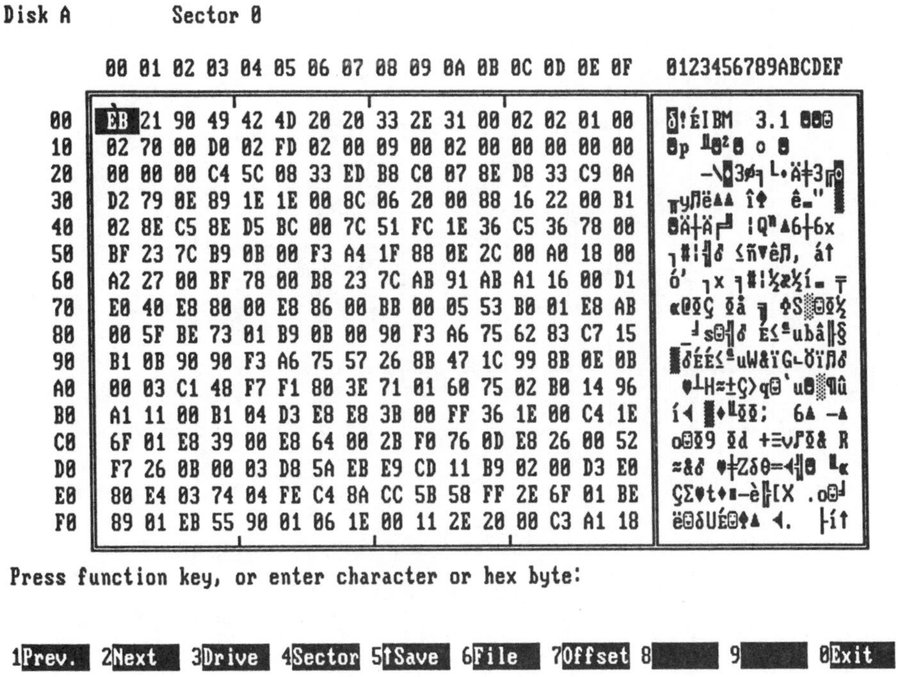

Figure A-1. The Advanced Version of Dskpatch

Chapter Number	DSKPATCH	DISPATCH	DISP_SEC	KBD_IO	CURSOR	EDITOR	PHANTOM	VIDEO_IO	DISK_IO	TEST
9								VIDEO_9.ASM		
10								VIDEO_10.ASM		
13								VIDEO_13.ASM		TEST13.ASM
14			DISP_S14.ASM		CURSOR14.ASM			VIDEO_14.ASM		
15			DISP_S15.ASM						DISK_I15.ASM	
16			DISP_S16.ASM					VIDEO_16.ASM	DISK_I16.ASM	
17	DSKPAT17.ASM		DISP_S17.ASM		CURSOR17.ASM			VIDEO_17.ASM	DISK_I17.ASM	
18					CURSOR18.ASM			VIDEO_18.ASM		
19	DSKPAT19.ASM	DISPAT19.ASM		KBD_IO19.ASM				VIDEO_19.ASM	DISK_I19.ASM	
21			DISP_S21.ASM				PHANT021.ASM	VIDEO_21.ASM		
22		DISPAT22.ASM				EDITOR22.ASM	PHANT022.ASM			
23				KBD_IO23.ASM						TEST23.ASM
24				KBD_IO24.ASM						
25		DISPAT25.ASM								
26		DISPAT26.ASM								
27							PHANT027.ASM		DISK_I26.ASM	

APPENDIX B
LISTING OF DSKPATCH

T his appendix contains the final version of Dskpatch. If you're writing your own programs, you'll find many general-purpose procedures in this appendix to help you on your way. We've included short descriptions of each procedure.

Descriptions of Procedures

CURSOR.ASM

CLEAR_SCREEN Like the BASIC CLS command; clears the text screen.

CLEAR_TO_END_OF_LINE Clears all the characters from the cursor position to the end of the current line.

CURSOR_RIGHT Moves the cursor one character position to the right, without writing a space over the old character.

GOTO_XY Very much like the BASIC LOCATE command; moves the cursor on the screen.

SEND_CRLF Sends a carriage-return/line-feed pair of characters to the screen. This procedure simply moves the cursor to the start of the next line.

DISK_IO.ASM

NEXT_SECTOR Adds one to the current sector number, then reads that sector into memory and rewrites the Dskpatch screen.

PREVIOUS_SECTOR Reads the previous sector. The procedure subtracts one from the old sector number (CURRENT_SECTOR_NO) and reads the new sector into the memory variable SECTOR. It also rewrites the screen display.

READ_SECTOR Reads one sector (512 bytes) from the disk into the memory buffer, SECTOR.

WRITE_SECTOR   Writes one sector (512 bytes) from the memory buffer, SECTOR, to the disk.

DISPATCH.ASM

DISPATCHER   The central dispatcher, reads characters from the keyboard and then calls on other procedures to do all the work of Dskpatch. Add any new commands to DISPATCH_TABLE in this file.

DISP_SEC.ASM

DISP_HALF_SECTOR   Does the work of displaying all the hex and ASCII characters that appear in the half-sector display by calling DISP_ LINE 16 times.

DISP_LINE   Displays one line of the half-sector display. DISP_HALF_ SECTOR calls this procedure 16 times to display all 16 lines of the half-sector display.

INIT_SEC_DISP   Initializes the half-sector display you see in Dskpatch. This procedure redraws the half-sector display, along with the boundaries and top hex numbers, but does not write the header or the editor prompt.

WRITE_TOP_HEX_NUMBERS   Writes the line of hex numbers across the top of the half-sector display. The procedure is not useful for much else.

DSKPATCH.ASM

DISK_PATCH   The (very short) main program of Dskpatch. DISK_ PATCH simply calls a number of other procedures, which do all the work. It also includes many of the definitions for the variables used throughout Dskpatch.

EDITOR.ASM

EDIT_BYTE *Edits* a byte in the half-sector display by changing one byte both in memory (SECTOR) and on the screen. Dskpatch uses this procedure to change bytes in a sector.

WRITE_TO_MEMORY Called upon by EDIT_BYTE to change a single byte in SECTOR. This procedure changes the byte pointed to by the phantom cursor.

KBD_IO.ASM

BACK_SPACE Used by the READ_STRING procedure to delete one character, both from the screen and from the keyboard buffer, whenever you press the Backspace key.

CONVERT_HEX_DIGIT Converts a single ASCII character into its hexadecimal equivalent. For example, the procedure converts the letter A into the hex number 0AH. **NOTE**: CONVERT_HEX_DIGIT works only with uppercase letters.

HEX_TO_BYTE Converts a two-character string of characters from a hexadecimal string, such as A5, into a single byte with that hex value. HEX_TO_BYTE expects the two characters to be digits or uppercase letters.

READ_BYTE Uses READ_STRING to read a string of characters. This procedure returns the special function key, a single character, or a hex byte if you typed a two-digit hex number.

READ_DECIMAL Reads an an unsigned decimal number from the keyboard, using READ_STRING to read the characters. READ_DECIMAL can read numbers from 0 to 65535.

READ_STRING Reads a DOS-style string of characters from the keyboard. This procedure also reads special function keys; the DOS READ_STRING function does not.

STRING_TO_UPPER   A general-purpose procedure, converts a DOS-style string to all uppercase letters.

PHANTOM.ASM

ERASE_PHANTOM   Removes the two phantom cursors from the screen by returning the character attribute to normal (7) for all characters under the phantom cursors.

MOV_TO_ASCII_POSITION   Moves the real cursor to the start of the phantom cursor in the ASCII window of the half-sector display.

MOV_TO_HEX_POSITION   Moves the real cursor to the start of the phantom cursor in the hex window of the half-sector display.

PHANTOM_DOWN   Moves the phantom cursor down and scrolls the screen if you try to move past the sixteenth line of the half-sector display.

PHANTOM_LEFT   Moves the phantom cursor left one entry, but not past the left side of the half-sector display.

PHANTOM_RIGHT   Moves the phantom cursor right one entry, but not past the right side of the half-sector display.

PHANTOM_UP   Moves the phantom cursor up one line in the half-sector display, or scrolls the display if you try to move the cursor off the top.

RESTORE_REAL_CURSOR   Moves the cursor back to the position recorded by SAVE_REAL_CURSOR.

SAVE_REAL_CURSOR   Saves the position of the real cursor in two variables. Call this procedure before you move the real cursor if you want to restore its position when you've finished making changes to the screen.

SCROLL_DOWN   Displays the first half of the sector. You'll find a more advanced version of SCROLL_DOWN on the disk available with this book. The advanced version scrolls the half-sector display by just one line.

SCROLL_UP Called by PHANTOM_DOWN when you try to move the phantom cursor off the bottom of the half-sector display. The version in this book doesn't actually scroll the screen: It writes the second half of the sector. On the disk, more advanced versions of SCROLL_UP and SCROLL_DOWN scroll the display by one line, instead of 16.

WRITE_PHANTOM Draws the phantom cursors in the half-sector display: one in the hex window, and one in the ASCII window. This procedure simply changes the character attributes to 70H, to use black characters on a white background.

VIDEO_IO.ASM

Contains most of the general-purpose procedures you'll want to use in your own programs.

WRITE_ATTRIBUTE_N_TIMES A handy procedure you can use to change the attributes for a group of N characters. WRITE_PHANTOM uses this procedure to draw the phantom cursors, and ERASE_PHANTOM uses it to remove the phantom cursors.

WRITE_CHAR Writes a character to the screen. Since it uses the ROM BIOS routines, this procedure doesn't attach special meaning to any characters. A carriage-return character will appear on the screen as a musical note (the character for 0DH). Call SEND_CRLF if you want to move the cursor to the start of the next line.

WRITE_CHAR_N_TIMES Writes N copies of one character to the screen. This procedure is useful for drawing lines of characters, such as the ones used in patterns.

WRITE_DECIMAL Writes a word to the screen as an unsigned decimal number in the range 0 to 65535.

WRITE_HEADER Writes the header at the top of the screen you see in Dskpatch. There, the procedure displays the disk-drive number and the number of the sector you see in the half-sector display.

WRITE_HEX   Takes a one-byte number and writes it on the screen as a two-digit hex number.

WRITE_HEX_DIGIT   Writes a single-digit hex number on the screen. This procedure converts a four-bit nibble into the ASCII character and writes it to the screen.

WRITE_PATTERN   Draws boxes around the half-sector display, as defined by a pattern. Use WRITE_PATTERN to draw arbitrary patterns of characters on the screen.

WRITE_STRING   A very useful, general-purpose procedure with which you can write a string of characters to the screen. The last character in your string must be a zero byte.

WRITE_PROMPT_LINE   Writes a string at the prompt line, then clears the rest of the line to remove any characters from the old prompt.

Program Listings for Dskpatch Procedures

DSKPATCH Make File

Here is the Make file that you can use with Microsoft's Make utility to build Dskpatch automatically.

```
DSKPATCH.OBJ:   DSKPATCH.ASM
        MASM DSKPATCH;

DISK_IO.OBJ:    DISK_IO.ASM
        MASM DISK_IO;

DISP_SEC.OBJ:   DISP_SEC.ASM
        MASM DISP_SEC;

VIDEO_IO.OBJ:   VIDEO_IO.ASM
        MASM VIDEO_IO;

CURSOR.OBJ:     CURSOR.ASM
        MASM CURSOR;

DISPATCH.OBJ:   DISPATCH.ASM
        MASM DISPATCH;

KBD_IO.OBJ:     KBD_IO.ASM
        MASM KBD_IO;

PHANTOM.OBJ:    PHANTOM.ASM
        MASM PHANTOM;

EDITOR.OBJ:     EDITOR.ASM
        MASM EDITOR;

DSKPATCH.COM:   DSKPATCH.OBJ DISK_IO.OBJ DISP_SEC.OBJ VIDEO_IO.OBJ CURSOR.OBJ \
                DISPATCH.OBJ KBD_IO.OBJ PHANTOM.OBJ EDITOR.OBJ
        LINK @LINKINFO
        EXE2BIN DSKPATCH DSKPATCH.COM
```

CURSOR.ASM

```
CR         EQU     13                        ;Carriage return
LF         EQU     10                        ;Line feed


CGROUP     GROUP    CODE_SEG
           ASSUME  CS:CGROUP, DS:CGROUP


CODE_SEG         SEGMENT PUBLIC


       PUBLIC  SEND_CRLF
;--------------------------------------------------------------------;
; This routine just sends a carriage-return/line-feed pair to the    ;
; display, using the DOS routines so that scrolling will be handled  ;
; correctly.                                                         ;
;--------------------------------------------------------------------;
SEND_CRLF        PROC    NEAR
       PUSH    AX
       PUSH    DX
       MOV     AH,2
       MOV     DL,CR
       INT     21h
       MOV     DL,LF
       INT     21h
       POP     DX
       POP     AX
       RET
SEND_CRLF        ENDP


       PUBLIC  CLEAR_SCREEN
;--------------------------------------------------------------------;
; This procedure clears the entire screen.                           ;
;--------------------------------------------------------------------;
CLEAR_SCREEN     PROC    NEAR
       PUSH    AX
       PUSH    BX
       PUSH    CX
       PUSH    DX
       XOR     AL,AL                     ;Blank entire window
       XOR     CX,CX                     ;Upper left corner is at (0,0)
```

CURSOR.ASM *continued*

```
        MOV     DH,24           ;Bottom line of screen is line 24
        MOV     DL,79           ;Right side is at column 79
        MOV     BH,7            ;Use normal attribute for blanks
        MOV     AH,6            ;Call for SCROLL_UP function
        INT     10h             ;Clear the window
        POP     DX
        POP     CX
        POP     BX
        POP     AX
        RET
CLEAR_SCREEN    ENDP


        PUBLIC  GOTO_XY
;-----------------------------------------------------------------;
; This procedure moves the cursor                                 ;
;                                                                 ;
;       DH      Row (Y)                                           ;
;       DL      Column (X)                                        ;
;                                                                 ;
;-----------------------------------------------------------------;
GOTO_XY         PROC    NEAR
        PUSH    AX
        PUSH    BX
        MOV     BH,0            ;Display page 0
        MOV     AH,2            ;Call for SET CURSOR POSITION
        INT     10h
        POP     BX
        POP     AX
        RET
GOTO_XY         ENDP


        PUBLIC  CURSOR_RIGHT
;-----------------------------------------------------------------;
; This procedure moves the cursor one position to the right or to the  ;
; next line if the cursor was at the end of a line.               ;
;                                                                 ;
; Uses:         SEND_CRLF                                         ;
;-----------------------------------------------------------------;
```

CURSOR.ASM *continued*

```
CURSOR_RIGHT      PROC      NEAR
        PUSH      AX
        PUSH      BX
        PUSH      CX
        PUSH      DX
        MOV       AH,3                  ;Read the current cursor position
        MOV       BH,0                  ;On page 0
        INT       10h                   ;Read cursor position
        MOV       AH,2                  ;Set new cursor position
        INC       DL                    ;Set column to next position
        CMP       DL,79                 ;Make sure column <= 79
        JBE       OK
        CALL      SEND_CRLF             ;Go to next line
        JMP       DONE
OK:     INT       10h
DONE:   POP       DX
        POP       CX
        POP       BX
        POP       AX
        RET
CURSOR_RIGHT      ENDP


        PUBLIC  CLEAR_TO_END_OF_LINE
;--------------------------------------------------------------------;
; This procedure clears the line from the current cursor position to  ;
; the end of that line.                                               ;
;--------------------------------------------------------------------;
CLEAR_TO_END_OF_LINE      PROC      NEAR
        PUSH      AX
        PUSH      BX
        PUSH      CX
        PUSH      DX
        MOV       AH,3                  ;Read current cursor position
        XOR       BH,BH                 ; on page 0
        INT       10h                   ;Now have (X,Y) in DL, DH
        MOV       AH,6                  ;Set up to clear to end of line
        XOR       AL,AL                 ;Clear window
        MOV       CH,DH                 ;All on same line
```

CURSOR.ASM *continued*

```
        MOV     CL,DL               ;Start at the cursor position
        MOV     DL,79               ;And stop at the end of the line
        MOV     BH,7                ;Use normal attribute
        INT     10h
        POP     DX
        POP     CX
        POP     BX
        POP     AX
        RET
CLEAR_TO_END_OF_LINE    ENDP

CODE_SEG        ENDS

        END
```

DISK_IO.ASM

```
CGROUP  GROUP    CODE_SEG, DATA_SEG
        ASSUME   CS:CGROUP, DS:CGROUP


CODE_SEG         SEGMENT PUBLIC


        PUBLIC   READ_SECTOR
DATA_SEG         SEGMENT PUBLIC
        EXTRN    SECTOR:BYTE
        EXTRN    DISK_DRIVE_NO:BYTE
        EXTRN    CURRENT_SECTOR_NO:WORD
DATA_SEG         ENDS
;----------------------------------------------------------------;
; This procedure reads one sector (512 bytes) into SECTOR.       ;
;                                                                ;
; Reads:        CURRENT_SECTOR_NO, DISK_DRIVE_NO                 ;
; Writes:       SECTOR                                           ;
;----------------------------------------------------------------;
READ_SECTOR     PROC     NEAR
        PUSH    AX
        PUSH    BX
        PUSH    CX
        PUSH    DX
        MOV     AL,DISK_DRIVE_NO        ;Drive number
        MOV     CX,1                    ;Read only 1 sector
        MOV     DX,CURRENT_SECTOR_NO    ;Logical sector number
        LEA     BX,SECTOR               ;Where to store this sector
        INT     25h                     ;Read the sector
        POPF                            ;Discard flags put on stack by DOS
        POP     DX
        POP     CX
        POP     BX
        POP     AX
        RET
READ_SECTOR     ENDP
```

DISK_IO.ASM *continued)*

```
        PUBLIC  WRITE_SECTOR
;--------------------------------------------------------------;
; This procedure writes the sector back to the disk.          ;
;                                                              ;
; Reads:        DISK_DRIVE_NO, CURRENT_SECTOR_NO, SECTOR       ;
;--------------------------------------------------------------;
WRITE_SECTOR    PROC    NEAR
        PUSH    AX
        PUSH    BX
        PUSH    CX
        PUSH    DX
        MOV     AL,DISK_DRIVE_NO        ;Drive number
        MOV     CX,1                    ;Write 1 sector
        MOV     DX,CURRENT_SECTOR_NO    ;Logical sector
        LEA     BX,SECTOR
        INT     26h                     ;Write the sector to disk
        POPF                            ;Discard the flag information
        POP     DX
        POP     CX
        POP     BX
        POP     AX
        RET
WRITE_SECTOR    ENDP


        PUBLIC  PREVIOUS_SECTOR
        EXTRN   INIT_SEC_DISP:NEAR, WRITE_HEADER:NEAR
        EXTRN   WRITE_PROMPT_LINE:NEAR
DATA_SEG        SEGMENT PUBLIC
        EXTRN   CURRENT_SECTOR_NO:WORD, EDITOR_PROMPT:BYTE
DATA_SEG        ENDS
;--------------------------------------------------------------;
; This procedure reads the previous sector, if possible.      ;
;                                                              ;
; Uses:         WRITE_HEADER, READ_SECTOR, INIT_SEC_DISP       ;
;               WRITE_PROMPT_LINE                              ;
; Reads:        CURRENT_SECTOR_NO, EDITOR_PROMPT               ;
; Writes:       CURRENT_SECTOR_NO                              ;
;--------------------------------------------------------------;
```

DISK_IO.ASM *continued)*

```
PREVIOUS_SECTOR         PROC    NEAR
        PUSH    AX
        PUSH    DX
        MOV     AX,CURRENT_SECTOR_NO    ;Get current sector number
        OR      AX,AX                   ;Don't decrement if already 0
        JZ      DONT_DECREMENT_SECTOR
        DEC     AX
        MOV     CURRENT_SECTOR_NO,AX    ;Save new sector number
        CALL    WRITE_HEADER
        CALL    READ_SECTOR
        CALL    INIT_SEC_DISP           ;Display new sector
        LEA     DX,EDITOR_PROMPT
        CALL    WRITE_PROMPT_LINE
DONT_DECREMENT_SECTOR:
        POP     DX
        POP     AX
        RET
PREVIOUS_SECTOR         ENDP

        PUBLIC  NEXT_SECTOR
        EXTRN   INIT_SEC_DISP:NEAR, WRITE_HEADER:NEAR
        EXTRN   WRITE_PROMPT_LINE:NEAR
DATA_SEG        SEGMENT PUBLIC
        EXTRN   CURRENT_SECTOR_NO:WORD, EDITOR_PROMPT:BYTE
DATA_SEG        ENDS

;-------------------------------------------------------------------;
; Reads the next sector.                                            ;
;                                                                   ;
; Uses:          WRITE_HEADER, READ_SECTOR, INIT_SEC_DISP           ;
;                WRITE_PROMPT_LINE                                  ;
; Reads:         CURRENT_SECTOR_NO, EDITOR_PROMPT                   ;
; Writes:        CURRENT_SECTOR_NO                                  ;
;-------------------------------------------------------------------;
NEXT_SECTOR     PROC    NEAR
        PUSH    AX
        PUSH    DX
        MOV     AX,CURRENT_SECTOR_NO
```

DISK_IO.ASM *continued)*

```
        INC     AX                          ;Move to next sector
        MOV     CURRENT_SECTOR_NO,AX
        CALL    WRITE_HEADER
        CALL    READ_SECTOR
        CALL    INIT_SEC_DISP               ;Display new sector
        LEA     DX,EDITOR_PROMPT
        CALL    WRITE_PROMPT_LINE
        POP     DX
        POP     AX
        RET
NEXT_SECTOR     ENDP


CODE_SEG        ENDS


        END
```

DISPATCH.ASM

```
CGROUP  GROUP   CODE_SEG, DATA_SEG
        ASSUME  CS:CGROUP, DS:CGROUP


CODE_SEG        SEGMENT PUBLIC


        PUBLIC  DISPATCHER
        EXTRN   READ_BYTE:NEAR, EDIT_BYTE:NEAR
        EXTRN   WRITE_PROMPT_LINE:NEAR
DATA_SEG        SEGMENT PUBLIC
        EXTRN   EDITOR_PROMPT:BYTE
DATA_SEG        ENDS
;--------------------------------------------------------------;
; This is the central dispatcher. During normal editing and viewing,  ;
; this procedure reads characters from the keyboard and if the char   ;
; is a command key (such as a cursor key), DISPATCHER calls the       ;
; procedures that do the actual work.  This dispatching is done for   ;
; special keys listed in the table DISPATCH_TABLE, where the procedure ;
; addresses are stored just after the key names.                      ;
;  If the character is not a special key, then it should be placed    ;
; directly into the sector buffer -- this is the editing mode.        ;
;                                                                     ;
; Uses:          READ_BYTE, EDIT_BYTE, WRITE_PROMPT_LINE              ;
; Reads:         EDITOR_PROMPT                                        ;
;--------------------------------------------------------------;
DISPATCHER      PROC    NEAR
        PUSH    AX
        PUSH    BX
        PUSH    DX
DISPATCH_LOOP:
        CALL    READ_BYTE               ;Read character into AX
        OR      AH,AH                   ;AH = 0 if no character read, -1
                                        ; for an extended code.
        JZ      NO_CHARS_READ           ;No character read, try again
        JS      SPECIAL_KEY             ;Read extended code
        MOV     DL,AL
        CALL    EDIT_BYTE               ;Was normal character, edit byte
        JMP     DISPATCH_LOOP           ;Read another character
```

DISPATCH.ASM *continued*

```
SPECIAL_KEY:
        CMP     AL,68                   ;F10--exit?
        JE      END_DISPATCH            ;Yes, leave
                                        ;Use BX to look through table
        LEA     BX,DISPATCH_TABLE
SPECIAL_LOOP:
        CMP     BYTE PTR [BX],0         ;End of table?
        JE      NOT_IN_TABLE            ;Yes, key was not in the table
        CMP     AL,[BX]                 ;Is it this table entry?
        JE      DISPATCH                ;Yes, then dispatch
        ADD     BX,3                    ;No, try next entry
        JMP     SPECIAL_LOOP            ;Check next table entry


DISPATCH:
        INC     BX                      ;Point to address of procedure
        CALL    WORD PTR [BX]           ;Call procedure
        JMP     DISPATCH_LOOP           ;Wait for another key


NOT_IN_TABLE:                           ;Do nothing, just read next character
        JMP     DISPATCH_LOOP


NO_CHARS_READ:
        LEA     DX,EDITOR_PROMPT
        CALL    WRITE_PROMPT_LINE       ;Erase any invalid characters typed
        JMP     DISPATCH_LOOP           ;Try again


END_DISPATCH:
        POP     DX
        POP     BX
        POP     AX
        RET
DISPATCHER      ENDP


CODE_SEG        ENDS



DATA_SEG        SEGMENT PUBLIC
```

DISPATCH.ASM *continued*

```
CODE_SEG        SEGMENT PUBLIC
    EXTRN       NEXT_SECTOR:NEAR                        ;In DISK_IO.ASM
    EXTRN       PREVIOUS_SECTOR:NEAR                    ;In DISK_IO.ASM
    EXTRN       PHANTOM_UP:NEAR, PHANTOM_DOWN:NEAR      ;In PHANTOM.ASM
    EXTRN       PHANTOM_LEFT:NEAR, PHANTOM_RIGHT:NEAR
    EXTRN       WRITE_SECTOR:NEAR                       ;In DISK_IO.ASM
CODE_SEG        ENDS
;---------------------------------------------------------------;
; This table contains the legal extended ASCII keys and the addresses  ;
; of the procedures that should be called when each key is pressed.    ;
;       The format of the table is                              ;
;               DB      72              ;Extended code for cursor up    ;
;               DW      OFFSET CGROUP:PHANTOM_UP                 ;
;---------------------------------------------------------------;
DISPATCH_TABLE LABEL    BYTE
    DB      59                      ;F1
    DW      OFFSET CGROUP:PREVIOUS_SECTOR
    DB      60                      ;F2
    DW      OFFSET CGROUP:NEXT_SECTOR
    DB      72                      ;Cursor up
    DW      OFFSET CGROUP:PHANTOM_UP
    DB      80                      ;Cursor down
    DW      OFFSET CGROUP:PHANTOM_DOWN
    DB      75                      ;Cursor left
    DW      OFFSET CGROUP:PHANTOM_LEFT
    DB      77                      ;Cursor right
    DW      OFFSET CGROUP:PHANTOM_RIGHT
    DB      88                      ;Shift F5
    DW      OFFSET CGROUP:WRITE_SECTOR
    DB      0                       ;End of the table
DATA_SEG        ENDS


        END
```

DISP_SEC.ASM

```
CGROUP  GROUP   CODE_SEG, DATA_SEG        ;Group two segments together
        ASSUME  CS:CGROUP, DS:CGROUP


;.................................................................;
; Graphics characters for border of sector.                      ;
;.................................................................;
VERTICAL_BAR      EQU     0BAh
HORIZONTAL_BAR    EQU     0CDh
UPPER_LEFT        EQU     0C9h
UPPER_RIGHT       EQU     0BBh
LOWER_LEFT        EQU     0C8h
LOWER_RIGHT       EQU     0BCh
TOP_T_BAR         EQU     0CBh
BOTTOM_T_BAR      EQU     0CAh
TOP_TICK          EQU     0D1h
BOTTOM_TICK       EQU     0CFh



CODE_SEG          SEGMENT PUBLIC

        PUBLIC  INIT_SEC_DISP
        EXTRN   WRITE_PATTERN:NEAR, SEND_CRLF:NEAR
        EXTRN   GOTO_XY:NEAR, WRITE_PHANTOM:NEAR
DATA_SEG          SEGMENT PUBLIC
        EXTRN   LINES_BEFORE_SECTOR:BYTE
        EXTRN   SECTOR_OFFSET:WORD
DATA_SEG          ENDS
;.................................................................;
; This procedure initializes the half-sector display.            ;
;                                                                 ;
; Uses:        WRITE_PATTERN, SEND_CRLF, DISP_HALF_SECTOR         ;
;              WRITE_TOP_HEX_NUMBERS, GOTO_XY, WRITE_PHANTOM      ;
; Reads:       TOP_LINE_PATTERN, BOTTOM_LINE_PATTERN              ;
;              LINES_BEFORE_SECTOR                                ;
; Writes:      SECTOR_OFFSET                                      ;
;.................................................................;
INIT_SEC_DISP   PROC    NEAR
        PUSH    DX
```

DISP_SEC.ASM *continued*

```
        XOR     DL,DL                       ;Move cursor into position
        MOV     DH,LINES_BEFORE_SECTOR
        CALL    GOTO_XY
        CALL    WRITE_TOP_HEX_NUMBERS
        LEA     DX,TOP_LINE_PATTERN
        CALL    WRITE_PATTERN
        CALL    SEND_CRLF
        XOR     DX,DX                       ;Start at the beginning of the sector
        MOV     SECTOR_OFFSET,DX            ;Set sector offset to 0
        CALL    DISP_HALF_SECTOR
        LEA     DX,BOTTOM_LINE_PATTERN
        CALL    WRITE_PATTERN
        CALL    WRITE_PHANTOM               ;Write the phantom cursor
        POP     DX
        RET
INIT_SEC_DISP   ENDP

        EXTRN   WRITE_CHAR_N_TIMES:NEAR, WRITE_HEX:NEAR, WRITE_CHAR:NEAR
        EXTRN   WRITE_HEX_DIGIT:NEAR, SEND_CRLF:NEAR
;--------------------------------------------------------------------;
; This procedure writes the index numbers (0 through F) at the top of ;
; the half-sector display.                                            ;
;                                                                     ;
; Uses:          WRITE_CHAR_N_TIMES, WRITE_HEX, WRITE_CHAR            ;
;                WRITE_HEX_DIGIT, SEND_CRLF                           ;
;--------------------------------------------------------------------;
WRITE_TOP_HEX_NUMBERS   PROC    NEAR
        PUSH    CX
        PUSH    DX
        MOV     DL,' '                      ;Write 9 spaces for left side
        MOV     CX,9
        CALL    WRITE_CHAR_N_TIMES
        XOR     DH,DH                       ;Start with 0
HEX_NUMBER_LOOP:
        MOV     DL,DH
        CALL    WRITE_HEX
        MOV     DL,' '
        CALL    WRITE_CHAR
```

DISP_SEC.ASM *continued*

```
        INC     DH
        CMP     DH,10h                  ;Done yet?
        JB      HEX_NUMBER_LOOP


        MOV     DL,' '                  ;Write hex numbers over ASCII window
        MOV     CX,2
        CALL    WRITE_CHAR_N_TIMES
        XOR     DL,DL
HEX_DIGIT_LOOP:
        CALL    WRITE_HEX_DIGIT
        INC     DL
        CMP     DL,10h
        JB      HEX_DIGIT_LOOP
        CALL    SEND_CRLF
        POP     DX
        POP     CX
        RET
WRITE_TOP_HEX_NUMBERS   ENDP


        PUBLIC  DISP_HALF_SECTOR
        EXTRN   SEND_CRLF:NEAR
;------------------------------------------------------------------------;
; This procedure displays half a sector (256 bytes)                      ;
;                                                                        ;
;       DS:DX   Offset into sector, in bytes--should be multiple of 16   ;
;                                                                        ;
; Uses:         DISP_LINE, SEND_CRLF                                     ;
;------------------------------------------------------------------------;
DISP_HALF_SECTOR        PROC    NEAR
        PUSH    CX
        PUSH    DX
        MOV     CX,16                   ;Display 16 lines
HALF_SECTOR:
        CALL    DISP_LINE
        CALL    SEND_CRLF
        ADD     DX,16
        LOOP    HALF_SECTOR
        POP     DX
```

DISP_SEC.ASM *continued*

```
        POP     CX
        RET
DISP_HALF_SECTOR        ENDP


        PUBLIC  DISP_LINE
        EXTRN   WRITE_HEX:NEAR
        EXTRN   WRITE_CHAR:NEAR
        EXTRN   WRITE_CHAR_N_TIMES:NEAR
;------------------------------------------------------------------;
; This procedure displays one line of data, or 16 bytes, first in hex,  ;
; then in ASCII.                                                   ;
;                                                                  ;
;       DS:DX   Offset into sector, in bytes                       ;
;                                                                  ;
; Uses:         WRITE_CHAR, WRITE_HEX, WRITE_CHAR_N_TIMES          ;
; Reads:        SECTOR                                             ;
;------------------------------------------------------------------;
DISP_LINE       PROC    NEAR
        PUSH    BX
        PUSH    CX
        PUSH    DX
        MOV     BX,DX                   ;Offset is more useful in BX
        MOV     DL,' '
        MOV     CX,3                    ;Write 3 spaces before line
        CALL    WRITE_CHAR_N_TIMES

                                        ;Write offset in hex
        CMP     BX,100h                 ;Is the first digit a 1?
        JB      WRITE_ONE               ;No, white space already in DL
        MOV     DL,'1'                  ;Yes, then place '1' into DL for output
WRITE_ONE:
        CALL    WRITE_CHAR
        MOV     DL,BL                   ;Copy lower byte into DL for hex output
        CALL    WRITE_HEX
                                        ;Write separator
        MOV     DL,' '
        CALL    WRITE_CHAR
        MOV     DL,VERTICAL_BAR         ;Draw left side of box
```

DISP_SEC.ASM *continued*

```
        CALL    WRITE_CHAR
        MOV     DL,' '
        CALL    WRITE_CHAR
                                        ;Now write out 16 bytes
        MOV     CX,16                   ;Dump 16 bytes
        PUSH    BX                      ;Save the offset for ASCII_LOOP
HEX_LOOP:
        MOV     DL,SECTOR[BX]           ;Get one byte
        CALL    WRITE_HEX               ;Dump this byte in hex
        MOV     DL,' '                  ;Write a space between numbers
        CALL    WRITE_CHAR
        INC     BX
        LOOP    HEX_LOOP

        MOV     DL,VERTICAL_BAR         ;Write separator
        CALL    WRITE_CHAR
        MOV     DL,' '                  ;Add another space before characters
        CALL    WRITE_CHAR
        MOV     CX,16
        POP     BX                      ;Get back offset into SECTOR
ASCII_LOOP:
        MOV     DL,SECTOR[BX]
        CALL    WRITE_CHAR
        INC     BX
        LOOP    ASCII_LOOP

        MOV     DL,' '                  ;Draw right side of box
        CALL    WRITE_CHAR
        MOV     DL,VERTICAL_BAR
        CALL    WRITE_CHAR

        POP     DX
        POP     CX
        POP     BX
        RET
DISP_LINE       ENDP

CODE_SEG        ENDS
```

DISP_SEC.ASM *continued*

```
DATA_SEG        SEGMENT PUBLIC
        EXTRN   SECTOR:BYTE


TOP_LINE_PATTERN        LABEL   BYTE
        DB      ' ',7
        DB      UPPER_LEFT,1
        DB      HORIZONTAL_BAR,12
        DB      TOP_TICK,1
        DB      HORIZONTAL_BAR,11
        DB      TOP_TICK,1
        DB      HORIZONTAL_BAR,11
        DB      TOP_TICK,1
        DB      HORIZONTAL_BAR,12
        DB      TOP_T_BAR,1
        DB      HORIZONTAL_BAR,18
        DB      UPPER_RIGHT,1
        DB      0
BOTTOM_LINE_PATTERN     LABEL   BYTE
        DB      ' ',7
        DB      LOWER_LEFT,1
        DB      HORIZONTAL_BAR,12
        DB      BOTTOM_TICK,1
        DB      HORIZONTAL_BAR,11
        DB      BOTTOM_TICK,1
        DB      HORIZONTAL_BAR,11
        DB      BOTTOM_TICK,1
        DB      HORIZONTAL_BAR,12
        DB      BOTTOM_T_BAR,1
        DB      HORIZONTAL_BAR,18
        DB      LOWER_RIGHT,1
        DB      0
DATA_SEG        ENDS



        END
```

DSKPATCH.ASM

```
CGROUP   GROUP    CODE_SEG, DATA_SEG
         ASSUME   CS:CGROUP, DS:CGROUP

CODE_SEG          SEGMENT PUBLIC
         ORG      100h

         EXTRN    CLEAR_SCREEN:NEAR, READ_SECTOR:NEAR
         EXTRN    INIT_SEC_DISP:NEAR, WRITE_HEADER:NEAR
         EXTRN    WRITE_PROMPT_LINE:NEAR, DISPATCHER:NEAR
DISK_PATCH        PROC    NEAR
         CALL     CLEAR_SCREEN
         CALL     WRITE_HEADER
         CALL     READ_SECTOR
         CALL     INIT_SEC_DISP
         LEA      DX,EDITOR_PROMPT
         CALL     WRITE_PROMPT_LINE
         CALL     DISPATCHER
         INT      20h
DISK_PATCH        ENDP

CODE_SEG          ENDS


DATA_SEG          SEGMENT PUBLIC

         PUBLIC   SECTOR_OFFSET
;----------------------------------------------;
; SECTOR_OFFSET is the offset of the half      ;
; sector display into the full sector.  It must ;
; be a multiple of 16, and not greater than 256 ;
;----------------------------------------------;
SECTOR_OFFSET    DW       0

         PUBLIC   CURRENT_SECTOR_NO, DISK_DRIVE_NO
CURRENT_SECTOR_NO        DW      0              ;Initially sector 0
DISK_DRIVE_NO            DB      0              ;Initially Drive A:

         PUBLIC   LINES_BEFORE_SECTOR, HEADER_LINE_NO
```

DSKPATCH.ASM *continued*

```
        PUBLIC  HEADER_PART_1, HEADER_PART_2
;----------------------------------------------;
; LINES_BEFORE_SECTOR is the number of lines    ;
; at the top of the screen before the half-     ;
; sector display.                               ;
;----------------------------------------------;
LINES_BEFORE_SECTOR    DB      2
HEADER_LINE_NO         DB      0
HEADER_PART_1          DB      'Disk ',0
HEADER_PART_2          DB      '        Sector ',0
        PUBLIC  PROMPT_LINE_NO, EDITOR_PROMPT
PROMPT_LINE_NO         DB      21
EDITOR_PROMPT          DB      'Press function key, or enter'
                       DB      ' character or hex byte: ',0


        PUBLIC  SECTOR
;----------------------------------------------;
; The entire sector (up to 8192 bytes) is       ;
; stored in this part of memory.                ;
;----------------------------------------------;
SECTOR  DB      8192 DUP (0)

DATA_SEG        ENDS

        END     DISK_PATCH
```

EDITOR.ASM

```
CGROUP  GROUP   CODE_SEG, DATA_SEG
        ASSUME  CS:CGROUP, DS:CGROUP


CODE_SEG        SEGMENT PUBLIC

DATA_SEG        SEGMENT PUBLIC
        EXTRN   SECTOR:BYTE
        EXTRN   SECTOR_OFFSET:WORD
        EXTRN   PHANTOM_CURSOR_X:BYTE
        EXTRN   PHANTOM_CURSOR_Y:BYTE
DATA_SEG        ENDS
;-----------------------------------------------------------;
; This procedure writes one byte to SECTOR, at the memory location    ;
; pointed to by the phantom cursor.                                   ;
;                                                                     ;
;       DL      Byte to write to SECTOR                               ;
;                                                                     ;
; The offset is calculated by                                         ;
;  OFFSET = SECTOR_OFFSET + (16 * PHANTOM_CURSOR_Y) + PHANTOM_CURSOR_X ;
;                                                                     ;
; Reads:        PHANTOM_CURSOR_X, PHANTOM_CURSOR_Y, SECTOR_OFFSET     ;
; Writes:       SECTOR                                                ;
;-----------------------------------------------------------;
WRITE_TO_MEMORY         PROC    NEAR
        PUSH    AX
        PUSH    BX
        PUSH    CX
        MOV     BX,SECTOR_OFFSET
        MOV     AL,PHANTOM_CURSOR_Y
        XOR     AH,AH
        MOV     CL,4                    ;Multiply PHANTOM_CURSOR_Y by 16
        SHL     AX,CL
        ADD     BX,AX                   ;BX = SECTOR_OFFSET + (16 * Y)
        MOV     AL,PHANTOM_CURSOR_X
        XOR     AH,AH
        ADD     BX,AX                   ;That's the address!
        MOV     SECTOR[BX],DL           ;Now, store the byte
```

EDITOR.ASM *continued*

```
        POP     CX
        POP     BX
        POP     AX
        RET
WRITE_TO_MEMORY         ENDP


        PUBLIC  EDIT_BYTE
        EXTRN   SAVE_REAL_CURSOR:NEAR, RESTORE_REAL_CURSOR:NEAR
        EXTRN   MOV_TO_HEX_POSITION:NEAR, MOV_TO_ASCII_POSITION:NEAR
        EXTRN   WRITE_PHANTOM:NEAR, WRITE_PROMPT_LINE:NEAR
        EXTRN   CURSOR_RIGHT:NEAR, WRITE_HEX:NEAR, WRITE_CHAR:NEAR
DATA_SEG        SEGMENT PUBLIC
        EXTRN   EDITOR_PROMPT:BYTE
DATA_SEG        ENDS
;------------------------------------------------------------------;
; This procedure changes a byte in memory and on the screen.      ;
;                                                                  ;
;       DL      Byte to write into SECTOR, and change on screen    ;
;                                                                  ;
; Uses:         SAVE_REAL_CURSOR, RESTORE_REAL_CURSOR              ;
;               MOV_TO_HEX_POSITION, MOV_TO_ASCII_POSITION         ;
;               WRITE_PHANTOM, WRITE_PROMPT_LINE, CURSOR_RIGHT     ;
;               WRITE_HEX, WRITE_CHAR, WRITE_TO_MEMORY             ;
; Reads:        EDITOR_PROMPT                                      ;
;------------------------------------------------------------------;
EDIT_BYTE       PROC    NEAR
        PUSH    DX
        CALL    SAVE_REAL_CURSOR
        CALL    MOV_TO_HEX_POSITION     ;Move to the hex number in the
        CALL    CURSOR_RIGHT            ; hex window
        CALL    WRITE_HEX               ;Write the new number
        CALL    MOV_TO_ASCII_POSITION   ;Move to the char. in the ASCII window
        CALL    WRITE_CHAR              ;Write the new character
        CALL    RESTORE_REAL_CURSOR     ;Move cursor back where it belongs
        CALL    WRITE_PHANTOM           ;Rewrite the phantom cursor
        CALL    WRITE_TO_MEMORY         ;Save this new byte in SECTOR
        LEA     DX,EDITOR_PROMPT
```

EDITOR.ASM *continued*

```
        CALL    WRITE_PROMPT_LINE
        POP     DX
        RET
EDIT_BYTE       ENDP

CODE_SEG        ENDS

        END
```

KBD_IO.ASM

```
CGROUP  GROUP    CODE_SEG, DATA_SEG
        ASSUME   CS:CGROUP, DS:CGROUP


BS      EQU      8                       ;Backspace character
CR      EQU      13                      ;Carriage-return character
ESC     EQU      27                      ;Escape character


CODE_SEG        SEGMENT PUBLIC

        PUBLIC   STRING_TO_UPPER
;-------------------------------------------------------------------;
; This procedure converts the string, using the DOS format for strings, ;
; to all uppercase letters.                                         ;
;                                                                   ;
;       DS:DX   Address of string buffer                            ;
;-------------------------------------------------------------------;
STRING_TO_UPPER         PROC    NEAR
        PUSH    AX
        PUSH    BX
        PUSH    CX
        MOV     BX,DX
        INC     BX                      ;Point to character count
        MOV     CL,[BX]                 ;Character count in 2nd byte of buffer
        XOR     CH,CH                   ;Clear upper byte of count
UPPER_LOOP:
        INC     BX                      ;Point to next character in buffer
        MOV     AL,[BX]
        CMP     AL,'a'                  ;See if it is a lowercase letter
        JB      NOT_LOWER               ;Nope
        CMP     AL,'z'
        JA      NOT_LOWER
        ADD     AL,'A'-'a'              ;Convert to uppercase letter
        MOV     [BX],AL
NOT_LOWER:
        LOOP    UPPER_LOOP
        POP     CX
```

KBD_IO.ASM *continued*

```
        POP     BX
        POP     AX
        RET
STRING_TO_UPPER         ENDP


;..................................................................;
; This procedure converts a character from ASCII (hex) to a nibble (4  ;
; bits).                                                           ;
;                                                                  ;
;               AL      Character to convert                      ;
; Returns:      AL      Nibble                                    ;
;               CF      Set for error, cleared otherwise          ;
;..................................................................;
CONVERT_HEX_DIGIT       PROC    NEAR
        CMP     AL,'0'                  ;Is it a legal digit?
        JB      BAD_DIGIT               ;Nope
        CMP     AL,'9'                  ;Not sure yet
        JA      TRY_HEX                 ;Might be hex digit
        SUB     AL,'0'                  ;Is decimal digit, convert to nibble
        CLC                             ;Clear the carry, no error
        RET
TRY_HEX:
        CMP     AL,'A'                  ;Not sure yet
        JB      BAD_DIGIT               ;Not hex
        CMP     AL,'F'                  ;Not sure yet
        JA      BAD_DIGIT               ;Not hex
        SUB     AL,'A'-10               ;Is hex, convert to nibble
        CLC                             ;Clear the carry, no error
        RET
BAD_DIGIT:
        STC                             ;Set the carry, error
        RET
CONVERT_HEX_DIGIT       ENDP
```

KBD_IO.ASM *continued*

```
        PUBLIC  HEX_TO_BYTE
;------------------------------------------------------------------;
; This procedure converts the two characters at DS:DX from hex to one ;
; byte.                                                            ;
;                                                                  ;
;       DS:DX   Address of two characters for hex number           ;
; Returns:                                                         ;
;       AL      Byte                                               ;
;       CF      Set for error, clear if no error                  ;
;                                                                  ;
; Uses:         CONVERT_HEX_DIGIT                                  ;
;------------------------------------------------------------------;
HEX_TO_BYTE     PROC    NEAR
        PUSH    BX
        PUSH    CX
        MOV     BX,DX               ;Put address in BX for indirect addr
        MOV     AL,[BX]             ;Get first digit
        CALL    CONVERT_HEX_DIGIT
        JC      BAD_HEX             ;Bad hex digit if carry set
        MOV     CX,4                ;Now multiply by 16
        SHL     AL,CL
        MOV     AH,AL               ;Retain a copy
        INC     BX                  ;Get second digit
        MOV     AL,[BX]
        CALL    CONVERT_HEX_DIGIT
        JC      BAD_HEX             ;Bad hex digit if carry set
        OR      AL,AH               ;Combine two nibbles
        CLC                         ;Clear carry for no error
DONE_HEX:
        POP     CX
        POP     BX
        RET
BAD_HEX:
        STC                         ;Set carry for error
        JMP     DONE_HEX
HEX_TO_BYTE     ENDP
```

KBD_IO.ASM *continued*

```
          PUBLIC  READ_STRING
          EXTRN   WRITE_CHAR:NEAR
;--------------------------------------------------------------;
; This procedure performs a function very similar to the DOS 0Ah ;
; function.  But this function will return a special character if a ;
; function or keypad key is pressed--no return for these keys.  And ;
; ESC will erase the input and start over again.               ;
;                                                              ;
;       DS:DX   Address for keyboard buffer.  The first byte must ;
;               contain the maximum number of characters to read (plus ;
;               one for the return).  And the second byte will be used ;
;               by this procedure to return the number of characters ;
;               actually read.                                 ;
;                       0       No characters read             ;
;                       -1      One special character read      ;
;                       otherwise number actually read (not including ;
;                               Enter key)                      ;
;                                                              ;
; Uses:         BACK_SPACE, WRITE_CHAR                         ;
;--------------------------------------------------------------;
READ_STRING     PROC    NEAR
          PUSH    AX
          PUSH    BX
          PUSH    SI
          MOV     SI,DX               ;Use SI for index register and
START_OVER:
          MOV     BX,2                ;BX for offset to beginning of buffer
          MOV     AH,7                ;Call for input with no checking
          INT     21h                 ; for CTRL-BREAK and no echo
          OR      AL,AL               ;Is character extended ASCII?
          JZ      EXTENDED            ;Yes, read the extended character
NOT_EXTENDED:                         ;Entnd char is error unless buf empty
          CMP     AL,CR               ;Is this a carriage return?
          JE      END_INPUT           ;Yes, we are done with input
          CMP     AL,BS               ;Is it a backspace character
          JNE     NOT_BS              ;Nope
          CALL    BACK_SPACE          ;Yes, delete character
          CMP     BL,2                ;Is buffer empty?
          JE      START_OVER          ;Yes, can now read extended ASCII again
```

KBD_IO.ASM *continued*

```
        JMP     SHORT READ_NEXT_CHAR    ;No, continue reading normal characters
NOT_BS: CMP     AL,ESC                  ;Is it an ESC--purge buffer?
        JE      PURGE_BUFFER            ;Yes, then purge the buffer
        CMP     BL,[SI]                 ;Check to see if buffer is full
        JA      BUFFER_FULL             ;Buffer is full
        MOV     [SI+BX],AL              ;Else save char in buffer
        INC     BX                      ;Point to next free character in buffer
        PUSH    DX
        MOV     DL,AL                   ;Echo character to screen
        CALL    WRITE_CHAR
        POP     DX
READ_NEXT_CHAR:
        MOV     AH,7
        INT     21h
        OR      AL,AL                   ;An extended ASCII char is not valid
                                        ; when the buffer is not empty
        JNE     NOT_EXTENDED            ;Char is valid
        MOV     AH,7
        INT     21h                     ;Throw out the extended character


;--------------------------------------------------;
; Signal an error condition by sending a beep      ;
; character to the display: chr$(7).               ;
;--------------------------------------------------;
SIGNAL_ERROR:
        PUSH    DX
        MOV     DL,7                    ;Sound the bell by writing chr$(7)
        MOV     AH,2
        INT     21h
        POP     DX
        JMP     SHORT READ_NEXT_CHAR    ;Now read next character


;--------------------------------------------------;
; Empty the string buffer and erase all the        ;
; characters displayed on the screen.              ;
;--------------------------------------------------;
PURGE_BUFFER:
        PUSH    CX
```

KBD_IO.ASM *continued*

```
        MOV     CL,[SI]                 ;Backspace over maximum number of
        XOR     CH,CH
PURGE_LOOP:                             ; characters in buffer.  BACK_SPACE
        CALL    BACK_SPACE              ; will keep the cursor from moving too
        LOOP    PURGE_LOOP              ; far back
        POP     CX
        JMP     START_OVER              ;Can now read extended ASCII characters
                                        ; since the buffer is empty
;------------------------------------------------;
; The buffer was full, so can't read another     ;
; character.  Send a beep to alert user of       ;
; buffer-full condition.                         ;
;------------------------------------------------;
BUFFER_FULL:
        JMP     SHORT SIGNAL_ERROR      ;If buffer full, just beep


;------------------------------------------------;
; Read the extended ASCII code and place this    ;
; in the buffer as the only character, then      ;
; return -1 as the number of characters read.    ;
;------------------------------------------------;
EXTENDED:                               ;Read an extended ASCII code
        MOV     AH,7
        INT     21h
        MOV     [SI+2],AL               ;Place just this char in buffer
        MOV     BL,0FFh                 ;Num chars read = -1 for special
        JMP     SHORT END_STRING


;------------------------------------------------;
; Save the count of the number of characters     ;
; read and return.                               ;
;------------------------------------------------;
END_INPUT:                              ;Done with input
        SUB     BL,2                    ;Count of characters read
END_STRING:
        MOV     [SI+1],BL               ;Return number of chars read
        POP     SI
        POP     BX
```

KBD_IO.ASM *continued*

```
        POP       AX
        RET
READ_STRING       ENDP


        PUBLIC  READ_BYTE
;------------------------------------------------------------------;
; This procedure reads either a single ASCII character or a two-digit   ;
; hex number.  This is just a test version of READ_BYTE.           ;
;                                                                  ;
; Returns byte in     AL      Character code (unless AH = 0)       ;
;                     AH      1 if read ASCII char                 ;
;                             0 if no characters read              ;
;                             -1 if read a special key             ;
;                                                                  ;
; Uses:       HEX_TO_BYTE, STRING_TO_UPPER, READ_STRING            ;
; Reads:      KEYBOARD_INPUT, etc.                                 ;
; Writes:     KEYBOARD_INPUT, etc.                                 ;
;------------------------------------------------------------------;
READ_BYTE       PROC    NEAR
        PUSH      DX
        MOV       CHAR_NUM_LIMIT,3        ;Allow only two characters (plus Enter)
        LEA       DX,KEYBOARD_INPUT
        CALL      READ_STRING
        CMP       NUM_CHARS_READ,1        ;See how many characters
        JE        ASCII_INPUT            ;Just one, treat as ASCII character
        JB        NO_CHARACTERS          ;Only Enter key hit
        CMP       BYTE PTR NUM_CHARS_READ,0FFh   ;Special function key?
        JE        SPECIAL_KEY            ;Yes
        CALL      STRING_TO_UPPER        ;No, convert string to uppercase
        LEA       DX,CHARS               ;Address of string to convert
        CALL      HEX_TO_BYTE            ;Convert string from hex to byte
        JC        NO_CHARACTERS          ;Error, so return 'no characters read'
        MOV       AH,1                   ;Signal read one character
DONE_READ:
        POP       DX
        RET
NO_CHARACTERS:
        XOR       AH,AH                  ;Set to 'no characters read'
```

KBD_IO.ASM *continued*

```
        JMP     DONE_READ
ASCII_INPUT:
        MOV     AL,CHARS            ;Load character read
        MOV     AH,1               ;Signal read one character
        JMP     DONE_READ
SPECIAL_KEY:
        MOV     AL,CHARS[0]         ;Return the scan code
        MOV     AH,0FFh            ;Signal special key with -1
        JMP     DONE_READ
READ_BYTE       ENDP


        PUBLIC  READ_DECIMAL
;-----------------------------------------------------------------;
; This procedure takes the output buffer of READ_STRING and converts ;
; the string of decimal digits to a word.                         ;
;                                                                 ;
;       AX      Word converted from decimal                      ;
;       CF      Set if error, clear if no error                  ;
;                                                                 ;
; Uses:         READ_STRING                                      ;
; Reads:        KEYBOARD_INPUT, etc.                             ;
; Writes:       KEYBOARD_INPUT, etc.                             ;
;-----------------------------------------------------------------;
READ_DECIMAL    PROC    NEAR
        PUSH    BX
        PUSH    CX
        PUSH    DX
        MOV     CHAR_NUM_LIMIT,6    ;Max number is 5 digits (65535)
        LEA     DX,KEYBOARD_INPUT
        CALL    READ_STRING
        MOV     CL,NUM_CHARS_READ   ;Get number of characters read
        XOR     CH,CH              ;Set upper byte of count to 0
        CMP     CL,0               ;Return error if no characters read
        JLE     BAD_DECIMAL_DIGIT   ;No chars read, signal error
        XOR     AX,AX              ;Start with number set to 0
        XOR     BX,BX              ;Start at beginning of string
CONVERT_DIGIT:
        MOV     DX,10              ;Multiply number by 10
```

KBD_IO.ASM *continued*

```
        MUL     DX                      ;Multiply AX by 10
        JC      BAD_DECIMAL_DIGIT       ;CF set if MUL overflowed one word
        MOV     DL,CHARS[BX]            ;Get the next digit
        SUB     DL,'0'                  ;And convert to a nibble (4 bits)
        JS      BAD_DECIMAL_DIGIT       ;Bad digit if < 0
        CMP     DL,9                    ;Is this a bad digit?
        JA      BAD_DECIMAL_DIGIT       ;Yes
        ADD     AX,DX                   ;No, so add it to number
        INC     BX                      ;Point to next character
        LOOP    CONVERT_DIGIT           ;Get the next digit
DONE_DECIMAL:
        POP     DX
        POP     CX
        POP     BX
        RET
BAD_DECIMAL_DIGIT:
        STC                             ;Set carry to signal error
        JMP     DONE_DECIMAL
READ_DECIMAL    ENDP


        PUBLIC  BACK_SPACE
        EXTRN   WRITE_CHAR:NEAR
;--------------------------------------------------------------------;
; This procedure deletes characters, one at a time, from the buffer and ;
; the screen when the buffer is not empty.  BACK_SPACE simply returns    ;
; when the buffer is empty.                                              ;
;                                                                        ;
;       DS:SI+BX        Most recent character still in buffer            ;
;                                                                        ;
; Uses:         WRITE_CHAR                                               ;
;--------------------------------------------------------------------;
BACK_SPACE      PROC    NEAR
        PUSH    AX
        PUSH    DX
        CMP     BX,2                    ;Is buffer empty?
        JE      END_BS                  ;Yes, read the next character
        DEC     BX                      ;Remove one character from buffer
        MOV     AH,2                    ;Remove character from screen
```

KBD_IO.ASM *continued*

```
        MOV     DL,BS
        INT     21h
        MOV     DL,20h              ;Write space there
        CALL    WRITE_CHAR
        MOV     DL,BS              ;Back up again
        INT     21h
END_BS: POP     DX
        POP     AX
        RET
BACK_SPACE      ENDP


CODE_SEG        ENDS



DATA_SEG        SEGMENT PUBLIC
KEYBOARD_INPUT  LABEL   BYTE
CHAR_NUM_LIMIT  DB      0          ;Length of input buffer
NUM_CHARS_READ  DB      0          ;Number of characters read
CHARS           DB      80 DUP (0) ;A buffer for keyboard input
DATA_SEG        ENDS


        END
```

PHANTOM.ASM

```
CGROUP   GROUP    CODE_SEG, DATA_SEG
         ASSUME   CS:CGROUP, DS:CGROUP


CODE_SEG         SEGMENT PUBLIC

         PUBLIC   MOV_TO_HEX_POSITION
         EXTRN    GOTO_XY:NEAR
DATA_SEG         SEGMENT PUBLIC
         EXTRN    LINES_BEFORE_SECTOR:BYTE
DATA_SEG         ENDS
;------------------------------------------------------------------;
; This procedure moves the real cursor to the position of the phantom ;
; cursor in the hex window.                                         ;
;                                                                   ;
; Uses:          GOTO_XY                                            ;
; Reads:         LINES_BEFORE_SECTOR, PHANTOM_CURSOR_X, PHANTOM_CURSOR_Y ;
;------------------------------------------------------------------;
MOV_TO_HEX_POSITION    PROC    NEAR
         PUSH    AX
         PUSH    CX
         PUSH    DX
         MOV     DH,LINES_BEFORE_SECTOR   ;Find row of phantom (0,0)
         ADD     DH,2                     ;Plus row of hex and horizontal bar
         ADD     DH,PHANTOM_CURSOR_Y      ;DH = row of phantom cursor
         MOV     DL,8                     ;Indent on left side
         MOV     CL,3                     ;Each column uses 3 characters, so
         MOV     AL,PHANTOM_CURSOR_X      ; we must multiply CURSOR_X by 3
         MUL     CL
         ADD     DL,AL                    ;And add to the indent, to get column
         CALL    GOTO_XY                  ; for phantom cursor
         POP     DX
         POP     CX
         POP     AX
         RET
MOV_TO_HEX_POSITION    ENDP

         PUBLIC   MOV_TO_ASCII_POSITION
         EXTRN    GOTO_XY:NEAR
DATA_SEG         SEGMENT PUBLIC
```

PHANTOM.ASM *continued*

```
        EXTRN   LINES_BEFORE_SECTOR:BYTE
DATA_SEG        ENDS
;------------------------------------------------------------;
; This procedure moves the real cursor to the beginning of the phantom ;
; cursor in the ASCII window.                                 ;
;                                                             ;
; Uses:          GOTO_XY                                      ;
; Reads:         LINES_BEFORE_SECTOR, PHANTOM_CURSOR_X, PHANTOM_CURSOR_Y ;
;------------------------------------------------------------;
MOV_TO_ASCII_POSITION   PROC    NEAR
        PUSH    AX
        PUSH    DX
        MOV     DH,LINES_BEFORE_SECTOR  ;Find row of phantom (0,0)
        ADD     DH,2                    ;Plus row of hex and horizontal bar
        ADD     DH,PHANTOM_CURSOR_Y     ;DH = row of phantom cursor
        MOV     DL,59                   ;Indent on left side
        ADD     DL,PHANTOM_CURSOR_X     ;Add CURSOR_X to get X position
        CALL    GOTO_XY                 ; for phantom cursor
        POP     DX
        POP     AX
        RET
MOV_TO_ASCII_POSITION   ENDP


        PUBLIC  SAVE_REAL_CURSOR
;------------------------------------------------------------;
; This procedure saves the position of the real cursor in the two ;
; variables REAL_CURSOR_X and REAL_CURSOR_Y.                  ;
;                                                             ;
; Writes:        REAL_CURSOR_X, REAL_CURSOR_Y                 ;
;------------------------------------------------------------;
SAVE_REAL_CURSOR        PROC    NEAR
        PUSH    AX
        PUSH    BX
        PUSH    CX
        PUSH    DX
        MOV     AH,3                    ;Read cursor position
        XOR     BH,BH                   ; on page 0
        INT     10h                     ;And return in DL,DH
        MOV     REAL_CURSOR_Y,DL        ;Save position
        MOV     REAL_CURSOR_X,DH
```

PHANTOM.ASM *continued*

```
        POP     DX
        POP     CX
        POP     BX
        POP     AX
        RET
SAVE_REAL_CURSOR        ENDP


        PUBLIC  RESTORE_REAL_CURSOR
        EXTRN   GOTO_XY:NEAR
;---------------------------------------------------------------;
; This procedure restores the real cursor to its old position, saved in ;
; REAL_CURSOR_X and REAL_CURSOR_Y.                               ;
;                                                                ;
; Uses:          GOTO_XY                                         ;
; Reads:         REAL_CURSOR_X, REAL_CURSOR_Y                    ;
;---------------------------------------------------------------;
RESTORE_REAL_CURSOR        PROC    NEAR
        PUSH    DX
        MOV     DL,REAL_CURSOR_Y
        MOV     DH,REAL_CURSOR_X
        CALL    GOTO_XY
        POP     DX
        RET
RESTORE_REAL_CURSOR        ENDP


        PUBLIC  WRITE_PHANTOM
        EXTRN   WRITE_ATTRIBUTE_N_TIMES:NEAR
;---------------------------------------------------------------;
; This procedure uses CURSOR_X and CURSOR_Y, through MOV_TO_..., as the ;
; coordinates for the phantom cursor.  WRITE_PHANTOM writes this ;
; phantom cursor.                                               ;
;                                                                ;
; Uses:          WRITE_ATTRIBUTE_N_TIMES, SAVE_REAL_CURSOR       ;
;               RESTORE_REAL_CURSOR, MOV_TO_HEX_POSITION         ;
;               MOV_TO_ASCII_POSITION                            ;
;---------------------------------------------------------------;
WRITE_PHANTOM   PROC    NEAR
        PUSH    CX
        PUSH    DX
```

PHANTOM.ASM *continued*

```
        CALL    SAVE_REAL_CURSOR
        CALL    MOV_TO_HEX_POSITION     ;Coord. of cursor in hex window
        MOV     CX,4                    ;Make phantom cursor four chars wide
        MOV     DL,70h
        CALL    WRITE_ATTRIBUTE_N_TIMES
        CALL    MOV_TO_ASCII_POSITION   ;Coord. of cursor in ASCII window
        MOV     CX,1                    ;Cursor is one character wide here
        CALL    WRITE_ATTRIBUTE_N_TIMES
        CALL    RESTORE_REAL_CURSOR
        POP     DX
        POP     CX
        RET
WRITE_PHANTOM   ENDP


        PUBLIC  ERASE_PHANTOM
        EXTRN   WRITE_ATTRIBUTE_N_TIMES:NEAR
;------------------------------------------------------------------;
; This procedure erases the phantom cursor, just the opposite of   ;
; WRITE_PHANTOM.                                                   ;
;                                                                  ;
; Uses:         WRITE_ATTRIBUTE_N_TIMES, SAVE_REAL_CURSOR          ;
;               RESTORE_REAL_CURSOR, MOV_TO_HEX_POSITION           ;
;               MOV_TO_ASCII_POSITION                              ;
;------------------------------------------------------------------;
ERASE_PHANTOM   PROC    NEAR
        PUSH    CX
        PUSH    DX
        CALL    SAVE_REAL_CURSOR
        CALL    MOV_TO_HEX_POSITION     ;Coord. of cursor in hex window
        MOV     CX,4                    ;Change back to white on black
        MOV     DL,7
        CALL    WRITE_ATTRIBUTE_N_TIMES
        CALL    MOV_TO_ASCII_POSITION
        MOV     CX,1
        CALL    WRITE_ATTRIBUTE_N_TIMES
        CALL    RESTORE_REAL_CURSOR
        POP     DX
        POP     CX
```

PHANTOM.ASM *continued*

```
        RET
ERASE_PHANTOM   ENDP

;-------------------------------------------------------------------;
; These four procedures move the phantom cursors.                   ;
;                                                                   ;
; Uses:          ERASE_PHANTOM, WRITE_PHANTOM                       ;
;                SCROLL_DOWN, SCROLL_UP                             ;
; Reads:         PHANTOM_CURSOR_X, PHANTOM_CURSOR_Y                 ;
; Writes:        PHANTOM_CURSOR_X, PHANTOM_CURSOR_Y                 ;
;-------------------------------------------------------------------;

        PUBLIC  PHANTOM_UP
PHANTOM_UP      PROC    NEAR
        CALL    ERASE_PHANTOM           ;Erase at current position
        DEC     PHANTOM_CURSOR_Y        ;Move cursor up one line
        JNS     WASNT_AT_TOP            ;Was not at the top, write cursor
        CALL    SCROLL_DOWN             ;Was at the top, scroll
WASNT_AT_TOP:
        CALL    WRITE_PHANTOM           ;Write the phantom at new position
        RET
PHANTOM_UP      ENDP


        PUBLIC  PHANTOM_DOWN
PHANTOM_DOWN    PROC    NEAR
        CALL    ERASE_PHANTOM           ;Erase at current position
        INC     PHANTOM_CURSOR_Y        ;Move cursor up one line
        CMP     PHANTOM_CURSOR_Y,16     ;Was; it at the bottom?
        JB      WASNT_AT_BOTTOM         ;No, so write phantom
        CALL    SCROLL_UP               ;Was at bottom, scroll
WASNT_AT_BOTTOM:
        CALL    WRITE_PHANTOM           ;Write the phantom cursor
        RET
PHANTOM_DOWN    ENDP


        PUBLIC  PHANTOM_LEFT
PHANTOM_LEFT    PROC    NEAR
        CALL    ERASE_PHANTOM           ;Erase at current position
        DEC     PHANTOM_CURSOR_X        ;Move cursor left one column
```

PHANTOM.ASM *continued*

```
        JNS     WASNT_AT_LEFT           ;Was not at the left side, write cursor
        MOV     PHANTOM_CURSOR_X,0      ;Was at left, so put back there
WASNT_AT_LEFT:
        CALL    WRITE_PHANTOM           ;Write the phantom cursor
        RET
PHANTOM_LEFT    ENDP


        PUBLIC  PHANTOM_RIGHT
PHANTOM_RIGHT   PROC    NEAR
        CALL    ERASE_PHANTOM           ;Erase at cursor position
        INC     PHANTOM_CURSOR_X        ;Move cursor right one column
        CMP     PHANTOM_CURSOR_X,16     ;Was it already at the right side?
        JB      WASNT_AT_RIGHT
        MOV     PHANTOM_CURSOR_X,15     ;Was at right, so put back there
WASNT_AT_RIGHT:
        CALL    WRITE_PHANTOM           ;Write the phantom cursor
        RET
PHANTOM_RIGHT   ENDP


        EXTRN   DISP_HALF_SECTOR:NEAR, GOTO_XY:NEAR
DATA_SEG        SEGMENT PUBLIC
        EXTRN   SECTOR_OFFSET:WORD
        EXTRN   LINES_BEFORE_SECTOR:BYTE
DATA_SEG        ENDS
;-------------------------------------------------------------------;
; These two procedures move between the two half-sector displays.   ;
;                                                                   ;
; Uses:         WRITE_PHANTOM, DISP_HALF_SECTOR, ERASE_PHANTOM, GOTO_XY ;
;               SAVE_REAL_CURSOR, RESTORE_REAL_CURSOR               ;
; Reads:        LINES_BEFORE_SECTOR                                 ;
; Writes:       SECTOR_OFFSET, PHANTOM_CURSOR_Y                     ;
;-------------------------------------------------------------------;
SCROLL_UP       PROC    NEAR
        PUSH    DX
        CALL    ERASE_PHANTOM           ;Remove the phantom cursor
        CALL    SAVE_REAL_CURSOR        ;Save the real cursor position
        XOR     DL,DL                   ;Set cursor for half-sector display
        MOV     DH,LINES_BEFORE_SECTOR
```

PHANTOM.ASM *continued*

```
            ADD       DH,2
            CALL      GOTO_XY
            MOV       DX,256                   ;Display the second half sector
            MOV       SECTOR_OFFSET,DX
            CALL      DISP_HALF_SECTOR
            CALL      RESTORE_REAL_CURSOR      ;Restore the real cursor position
            MOV       PHANTOM_CURSOR_Y,0       ;Cursor at top of second half sector
            CALL      WRITE_PHANTOM            ;Restore the phantom cursor
            POP       DX
            RET
SCROLL_UP       ENDP


SCROLL_DOWN     PROC      NEAR
            PUSH      DX
            CALL      ERASE_PHANTOM            ;Remove the phantom cursor
            CALL      SAVE_REAL_CURSOR         ;Save the real cursor position
            XOR       DL,DL                    ;Set cursor for half-sector display
            MOV       DH,LINES_BEFORE_SECTOR
            ADD       DH,2
            CALL      GOTO_XY
            XOR       DX,DX                    ;Display the first half sector
            MOV       SECTOR_OFFSET,DX
            CALL      DISP_HALF_SECTOR
            CALL      RESTORE_REAL_CURSOR      ;Restore the real cursor position
            MOV       PHANTOM_CURSOR_Y,15      ;Cursor at bottom of first half sector
            CALL      WRITE_PHANTOM            ;Restore the phantom cursor
            POP       DX
            RET
SCROLL_DOWN     ENDP


CODE_SEG        ENDS


DATA_SEG        SEGMENT PUBLIC
REAL_CURSOR_X             DB        0
REAL_CURSOR_Y             DB        0
        PUBLIC  PHANTOM_CURSOR_X, PHANTOM_CURSOR_Y
PHANTOM_CURSOR_X          DB        0
PHANTOM_CURSOR_Y          DB        0
DATA_SEG        ENDS


            END
```

VIDEO_IO.ASM

```
CGROUP  GROUP   CODE_SEG, DATA_SEG
        ASSUME  CS:CGROUP, DS:CGROUP

CODE_SEG        SEGMENT PUBLIC
        ORG     100h


        PUBLIC  WRITE_HEX
;-------------------------------------------------------------;
; This procedure converts the byte in the DL register to hex and writes ;
; the two hex digits at the current cursor position.          ;
;                                                             ;
;       DL      Byte to be converted to hex                  ;
;                                                             ;
; Uses:         WRITE_HEX_DIGIT                               ;
;-------------------------------------------------------------;
WRITE_HEX       PROC    NEAR            ;Entry point
        PUSH    CX                      ;Save registers used in this procedure
        PUSH    DX
        MOV     DH,DL                   ;Make a copy of byte
        MOV     CX,4                    ;Get the upper nibble in DL
        SHR     DL,CL
        CALL    WRITE_HEX_DIGIT         ;Display first hex digit
        MOV     DL,DH                   ;Get lower nibble into DL
        AND     DL,0Fh                  ;Remove the upper nibble
        CALL    WRITE_HEX_DIGIT         ;Display second hex digit
        POP     DX
        POP     CX
        RET
WRITE_HEX       ENDP


        PUBLIC  WRITE_HEX_DIGIT
;-------------------------------------------------------------;
; This procedure converts the lower 4 bits of DL to a hex digit and ;
; writes it to the screen.                                    ;
;                                                             ;
;       DL      Lower 4 bits contain number to be printed in hex ;
;                                                             ;
; Uses:         WRITE_CHAR                                    ;
;-  ----------------------------------------------------------;
```

VIDEO_IO.ASM *continued*

```
WRITE_HEX_DIGIT PROC     NEAR
        PUSH    DX              ;Save registers used
        CMP     DL,10           ;Is this nibble <10?
        JAE     HEX_LETTER      ;No, convert to a letter
        ADD     DL,"0"          ;Yes, convert to a digit
        JMP     Short WRITE_DIGIT ;Now write this character
HEX_LETTER:
        ADD     DL,"A"-10       ;Convert to hex letter
WRITE_DIGIT:
        CALL    WRITE_CHAR      ;Display the letter on the screen
        POP     DX              ;Restore old value of AX
        RET
WRITE_HEX_DIGIT ENDP


        PUBLIC  WRITE_CHAR
        EXTRN   CURSOR_RIGHT:NEAR
;-------------------------------------------------------------------;
; This procedure outputs a character to the screen using the ROM BIOS ;
; routines, so that characters such as the backspace are treated as  ;
; any other character and are displayed.                             ;
;    This procedure must do a bit of work to update the cursor position. ;
;                                                                    ;
;       DL      Byte to print on screen                              ;
;                                                                    ;
; Uses:         CURSOR_RIGHT                                         ;
;-------------------------------------------------------------------;
WRITE_CHAR      PROC     NEAR
        PUSH    AX
        PUSH    BX
        PUSH    CX
        PUSH    DX
        MOV     AH,9            ;Call for output of character/attribute
        MOV     BH,0            ;Set to display page 0
        MOV     CX,1            ;Write only one character
        MOV     AL,DL           ;Character to write
        MOV     BL,7            ;Normal attribute
        INT     10h             ;Write character and attribute
        CALL    CURSOR_RIGHT    ;Now move to next cursor position
```

VIDEO_IO.ASM *continued*

```
        POP     DX
        POP     CX
        POP     BX
        POP     AX
        RET
WRITE_CHAR      ENDP


        PUBLIC  WRITE_DECIMAL
;--------------------------------------------------------------------;
; This procedure writes a 16-bit, unsigned number in decimal notation.  ;
;                                                                    ;
;       DX      N : 16-bit, unsigned number                         ;
;                                                                    ;
; Uses:         WRITE_HEX_DIGIT                                      ;
;--------------------------------------------------------------------;
WRITE_DECIMAL   PROC    NEAR
        PUSH    AX                      ;Save registers used here
        PUSH    CX
        PUSH    DX
        PUSH    SI
        MOV     AX,DX
        MOV     SI,10                   ;Will divide by 10 using SI
        XOR     CX,CX                   ;Count of digits placed on stack
NON_ZERO:
        XOR     DX,DX                   ;Set upper word of N to 0
        DIV     SI                      ;Calculate N/10 and (N mod 10)
        PUSH    DX                      ;Push one digit onto the stack
        INC     CX                      ;One more digit added
        OR      AX,AX                   ;N = 0 yet?
        JNE     NON_ZERO                ;Nope, continue
WRITE_DIGIT_LOOP:
        POP     DX                      ;Get the digits in reverse order
        CALL    WRITE_HEX_DIGIT
        LOOP    WRITE_DIGIT_LOOP
END_DECIMAL:
        POP     SI
        POP     DX
        POP     CX
        POP     AX
```

VIDEO_IO.ASM *continued*

```
        RET
WRITE_DECIMAL    ENDP


        PUBLIC  WRITE_CHAR_N_TIMES
;------------------------------------------------------------------;
; This procedure writes more than one copy of a character         ;
;                                                                  ;
;       DL      Character code                                    ;
;       CX      Number of times to write the character            ;
;                                                                  ;
; Uses:         WRITE_CHAR                                         ;
;------------------------------------------------------------------;
WRITE_CHAR_N_TIMES      PROC    NEAR
        PUSH    CX
N_TIMES:
        CALL    WRITE_CHAR
        LOOP    N_TIMES
        POP     CX
        RET
WRITE_CHAR_N_TIMES      ENDP


        PUBLIC  WRITE_PATTERN
;------------------------------------------------------------------;
; This procedure writes a line to the screen, based on data in the ;
; form                                                             ;
;                                                                  ;
;       DB      {character, number of times to write character}, 0 ;
; Where {x} means that x can be repeated any number of times       ;
;       DS:DX   Address of above data statement                    ;
;                                                                  ;
; Uses:         WRITE_CHAR_N_TIMES                                 ;
;------------------------------------------------------------------;
WRITE_PATTERN   PROC    NEAR
        PUSH    AX
        PUSH    CX
        PUSH    DX
```

VIDEO_IO.ASM *continued*

```
        PUSH    SI
        PUSHF                           ;Save the direction flag
        CLD                             ;Set direction flag for increment
        MOV     SI,DX                   ;Move offset into SI register for LODSB
PATTERN_LOOP:
        LODSB                           ;Get character data into AL
        OR      AL,AL                   ;Is it the end of data (0h)?
        JZ      END_PATTERN             ;Yes, return
        MOV     DL,AL                   ;No, set up to write character N times
        LODSB                           ;Get the repeat count into AL
        MOV     CL,AL                   ;And put in CX for WRITE_CHAR_N_TIMES
        XOR     CH,CH                   ;Zero upper byte of CX
        CALL    WRITE_CHAR_N_TIMES
        JMP     PATTERN_LOOP
END_PATTERN:
        POPF                            ;Restore direction flag
        POP     SI
        POP     DX
        POP     CX
        POP     AX
        RET
WRITE_PATTERN   ENDP


        PUBLIC  WRITE_HEADER
DATA_SEG        SEGMENT PUBLIC
        EXTRN   HEADER_LINE_NO:BYTE
        EXTRN   HEADER_PART_1:BYTE
        EXTRN   HEADER_PART_2:BYTE
        EXTRN   DISK_DRIVE_NO:BYTE
        EXTRN   CURRENT_SECTOR_NO:WORD
DATA_SEG        ENDS
        EXTRN   GOTO_XY:NEAR, CLEAR_TO_END_OF_LINE:NEAR
;--------------------------------------------------------------------;
; This procedure writes the header with disk-drive and sector number. ;
;                                                                     ;
; Uses:         GOTO_XY, WRITE_STRING, WRITE_CHAR, WRITE_DECIMAL      ;
;               CLEAR_TO_END_OF_LINE                                  ;
; Reads:        HEADER_LINE_NO, HEADER_PART_1, HEADER_PART_2          ;
;               DISK_DRIVE_NO, CURRENT_SECTOR_NO                      ;
;--------------------------------------------------------------------;
```

VIDEO_IO.ASM *continued*

```
WRITE_HEADER    PROC    NEAR
        PUSH    DX
        XOR     DL,DL                   ;Move cursor to header line number
        MOV     DH,HEADER_LINE_NO
        CALL    GOTO_XY
        LEA     DX,HEADER_PART_1
        CALL    WRITE_STRING
        MOV     DL,DISK_DRIVE_NO
        ADD     DL,'A'                  ;Print drives A, B, ...
        CALL    WRITE_CHAR
        LEA     DX,HEADER_PART_2
        CALL    WRITE_STRING
        MOV     DX,CURRENT_SECTOR_NO
        CALL    WRITE_DECIMAL
        CALL    CLEAR_TO_END_OF_LINE    ;Clear rest of sector number
        POP     DX
        RET
WRITE_HEADER    ENDP


        PUBLIC  WRITE_STRING
;--------------------------------------------------------------------;
; This procedure writes a string of characters to the screen.  The   ;
; string must end with          DB      0                            ;
;                                                                    ;
;       DS:DX    Address of the string                               ;
;                                                                    ;
; Uses:          WRITE_CHAR                                          ;
;--------------------------------------------------------------------;
WRITE_STRING    PROC    NEAR
        PUSH    AX
        PUSH    DX
        PUSH    SI
        PUSHF                           ;Save direction flag
        CLD                             ;Set direction for increment (forward)
        MOV     SI,DX                   ;Place address into SI for LODSB
STRING_LOOP:
        LODSB                           ;Get a character into the AL register
        OR      AL,AL                   ;Have we found the 0 yet?
```

VIDEO_IO.ASM *continued*

```
            JZ      END_OF_STRING           ;Yes, we are done with the string
            MOV     DL,AL                   ;No, write character
            CALL    WRITE_CHAR
            JMP     STRING_LOOP
END_OF_STRING:
            POPF                            ;Restore direction flag
            POP     SI
            POP     DX
            POP     AX
            RET
WRITE_STRING    ENDP


            PUBLIC  WRITE_PROMPT_LINE
            EXTRN   CLEAR_TO_END_OF_LINE:NEAR
            EXTRN   GOTO_XY:NEAR
DATA_SEG        SEGMENT PUBLIC
            EXTRN   PROMPT_LINE_NO:BYTE
DATA_SEG        ENDS
;-------------------------------------------------------------------;
; This procedure writes the prompt line to the screen and clears the ;
; end of the line.                                                   ;
;                                                                    ;
;       DS:DX   Address of the prompt-line message                  ;
;                                                                    ;
; Uses:         WRITE_STRING, CLEAR_TO_END_OF_LINE, GOTO_XY          ;
; Reads:        PROMPT_LINE_NO                                       ;
; -------------------------------------------------------------------;
WRITE_PROMPT_LINE       PROC    NEAR
            PUSH    DX
            XOR     DL,DL                   ;Write the prompt line and
            MOV     DH,PROMPT_LINE_NO       ; move the cursor there
            CALL    GOTO_XY
            POP     DX
            CALL    WRITE_STRING
            CALL    CLEAR_TO_END_OF_LINE
            RET
WRITE_PROMPT_LINE       ENDP

            PUBLIC  WRITE_ATTRIBUTE_N_TIMES
            EXTRN   CURSOR_RIGHT:NEAR
```

VIDEO_IO.ASM *continued*

```
;------------------------------------------------------------;
; This procedure sets the attribute for N characters, starting at the  ;
; current cursor position.                                   ;
;                                                            ;
;       CX      Number of characters to set attribute for   ;
;       DL      New attribute for characters                ;
;                                                            ;
; Uses:         CURSOR_RIGHT                                 ;
;------------------------------------------------------------;
WRITE_ATTRIBUTE_N_TIMES        PROC    NEAR
        PUSH    AX
        PUSH    BX
        PUSH    CX
        PUSH    DX
        MOV     BL,DL                   ;Set attribute to new attribute
        XOR     BH,BH                   ;Set display page to 0
        MOV     DX,CX                   ;CX is used by the BIOS routines
        MOV     CX,1                    ;Set attribute for one character
ATTR_LOOP:
        MOV     AH,8                    ;Read character under cursor
        INT     10h
        MOV     AH,9                    ;Write attribute/character
        INT     10h
        CALL    CURSOR_RIGHT
        DEC     DX                      ;Set attribute for N characters?
        JNZ     ATTR_LOOP               ;No, continue
        POP     DX
        POP     CX
        POP     BX
        POP     AX
        RET
WRITE_ATTRIBUTE_N_TIMES ENDP

CODE_SEG        ENDS

        END
```

APPENDIX C

SEGMENT LOAD ORDER

The IBM Macro Assembler (version 1.0 and 2.0) loads segments in an order different from that used by all the more recent versions of the Microsoft Macro Assembler. In this appendix, we'll look at the question of segment load order, and see how knowledge of this order can be useful when EXE2BIN gives you the error message *File cannot be converted.*

Segment Load Order

All of the examples after Chapter 13 use two segments, CODE_SEG and DATA_SEG. The IBM versions of the assembler tell LINK to load these segments into memory in alphabetic order. So, when we wrote:

```
CGROUP  GROUP   CODE_SEG, DATA_SEG
        ASSUME_CS:CGROUP, DS:CGROUP

DATA_SEG        SEGMENT PUBLIC
DATA_SEG        ENDS

CODE_SEG        SEGMENT PUBLIC
CODE_SEG        ENDS

        END
```

The IBM versions of the Macro Assembler tell LINK to load DATA_SEG into memory after loading CODE_SEG. Let's turn this code fragment into a real program, so that we can look at the load map.

Here's our new version. It doesn't do much, but it's enough for us to see how LINK loads the segments into memory.

```
CGROUP  GROUP   CODE_SEG, DATA_SEG
        ASSUME  CS:CGROUP, DS:CGROUP

DATA_SEG        SEGMENT PUBLIC
        DB      0
DATA_SEG        ENDS

CODE_SEG        SEGMENT PUBLIC
        ORG     100h
MAIN:   INT     20h
CODE_SEG        ENDS

        END     MAIN
```

Type in this file, name it SEGTEST.ASM, and then assemble and link it to create a load map:

```
A>LINK SEGTEST,SEGTEST,SEGTEST/MAP;
```

If you've got an IBM version of the assembler, you'll see this load map:

```
Warning: no stack segment

Start  Stop   Length Name                  Class
00000H 00101H 00102H CODE_SEG
00110H 00110H 00001H DATA_SEG


Origin  Group
0000:0  CGROUP


Address          Publics by Name

Address          Publics by Value

Program entry point at 0000:0100
```

LINK loaded CODE_SEG into memory before DATA_SEG. This is exactly the order we want. In fact, CODE_SEG *must* be the first segment in memory, so our program will begin at 100h from the start of the group.

On the other hand, your map may have had these two segments in reverse order. That's a sign that you have a Microsoft version of the assembler. If you do, you'll see the following load map, instead:

```
Warning: no stack segment


Start  Stop   Length Name                  Class
00000H 00000H 00001H DATA_SEG
00010H 00111H 00102H CODE_SEG


Origin  Group
0000:0  CGROUP


Address          Publics by Name

Address          Publics by Value

Program entry point at 0000:0110
```

Nothing's right in this load map. DATA_SEG appears in memory before CODE_SEG, and that means the ORG 100h statement gives us an offset from the end of DATA_SEG, rather than from the start of the group.

The last line in this map shows that the starting address of our program is now 110h. But it has to be at 100H for a .COM file. So, what will happen if we try to create a .COM file from this?

Run EXE2BIN and you'll see the following:

```
A>EXE2BIN SEGTEST SEGTEST.COM
File cannot be converted
A>
```

That's not a very useful error message—it doesn't give us a clue about why it can't convert our program. But that's where the load map comes in handy. By looking at the load map, we can see that LINK loaded our segments into memory in the wrong order. Then we just have to figure out how to fix the problem.

We've been careful in this book to make sure that all the programs will run with both the Microsoft and IBM versions of the assembler. This is the reason we've placed the data segment *after* the code segment in all of our source files.

If, in your work with assembly language programs, you either create or encounter programs in which the data segments appear at the top of the file, use the /A switch available with the Microsoft versions of MASM. The /A option tells MASM you want segments loaded in alphabetical order. To try out this option, reassemble our sample test program, SEGTEST.ASM, with the following command:

```
A>MASM SEGTEST/A;
```

Link this file again and create a new load map. You should now see the two segments in alphabetic order, with CODE_SEG first in the file.

Phase Errors

We've been very careful that the examples run with all versions of the Macro Assembler—IBM and Microsoft—by placing the data segment at the end of our files. But this is not a good idea in many cases. In this section we'll look at the problems, and at better ways to organize your segments.

Let's look at a concrete example:

```
CODE_SEG        SEGMENT PUBLIC
        ASSUME  CS:CODE_SEG, ES:DATA_SEG

BEGIN   PROC    NEAR
        MOV     AX,DATA_SEG          ;Get the segment number
        MOV     ES,AX                ;Set ES so it points to our data
        MOV     AL,VARIABLE          ;Read ""variable'' into AL
        MOV     AH,4Ch               ;Exit to DOS
        INT     21h
BEGIN   ENDP


CODE_SEG        ENDS


DATA_SEG        SEGMENT PUBLIC
VARIABLE        DB      0
DATA_SEG        ENDS

        END     BEGIN
```

We've placed the data segment at the end of this program to ensure that DATA_SEG will be loaded into memory after CODE_SEG. But the assembler generates a *phase error* message when we try to assemble it:

```
A>MASM TEST;
Microsoft (R) Macro Assembler  Version 4.00
Copyright (C) Microsoft Corp 1981, 1983, 1984, 1985.  All rights reserved.

TEST.ASM(10) : error 6: Phase error between passes

  51036 Bytes symbol space free

      0 Warning Errors
      1 Severe  Errors
```

What does phase error mean?

It turns out that the Macro Assembler makes several passes through a file as it assembles it. On the first pass, it collects information it needs, such as the type and segments of variables. In the interest of efficiency, the assembler also starts to assemble the program on the first past; here is where we run into problems.

MASM assembles the instruction MOV AL,VARIABLE *before* it knows what segment contains VARIABLE, so it assembles the MOV instruction as if we don't need a segment override (which is ES: in this case). On the second pass, however, MASM notices that it needs to add a segment override since VARIABLE is in the segment pointed to by the ES register. Unfortunately,

MASM didn't reserve room for this override instruction during the first pass (or phase), so it generates a *phase error* message.

We need to declare all variables *before* we use them in a file. If we do this, and we're using the Microsoft Macro Assembler, the data segment will be first in memory, which usually isn't a problem with .EXE files where we're most likely to use multiple segments.

If, on the other hand, you want the code segment to be loaded into memory first, there is a simple solution: Simply place a *dummy* segment before your data segment. You can see the details in the following example.

```
CODE_SEG        SEGMENT PUBLIC          ;Load CODE_SEG first
CODE_SEG        ENDS


DATA_SEG        SEGMENT PUBLIC
VARIABLE        DB      0
DATA_SEG        ENDS


CODE_SEG        SEGMENT PUBLIC
        ASSUME  CS:CODE_SEG, ES:DATA_SEG

BEGIN   PROC    NEAR
        MOV     AX,DATA_SEG             ;Get the segment number
        MOV     ES,AX                   ;Set ES so it points to our data
        MOV     AL,VARIABLE             ;Read "variable" into AL
        MOV     AH,4Ch                  ;Exit to DOS
        INT     21h
BEGIN   ENDP

CODE_SEG        ENDS


        END     BEGIN
```

EXE2BIN File Cannot be Converted

If you have problems with EXE2BIN, first check the load map to make sure that CODE_SEG is the first segment. Also, make certain you only have two segments listed. It's possible to have several different versions of the same segment listed. For example:

```
00000H 00103H 00104H CODE_SEG
00110H 00105H 00006H DATA_SEG
00120H 00101H 00102H CODE_SEG
```

In this case, CODE_SEG is fragmented. If you see more than one piece of a single segment in the load map, it means you've got problems, and they could stem from several possible sources.

- You may not have a PUBLIC pseudo-op after all of your segment definitions.
- You may have slightly different SEGMENT definitions in your source files. Check all your source files and verify that all the SEGMENT definitions are identical.
- One of your source files may be missing a GROUP statement or the GROUP statement may not be correct. Check all of the group statements carefully to make sure they're the same.
- If the GROUP statements are in order, check the ASSUME statements to make sure they read:

```
ASSUME  CS:CGROUP, DS:CGROUP
```

- You've defined a STACK segment. .COM programs don't need a STACK segment, and, in fact, you *must not* define one.
- The entry point is not at 100h. This may be because you didn't place the starting procedure's name after the END pseudo-op in the main source file, or that you've linked the files in the wrong order. The main procedure *must* be in the first file named in the LINK list.

You'll also find more information on error messages and what they may mean in Appendix D.

APPENDIX D

COMMON ERROR MESSAGES

This appendix lists many of the more common error messages you may encounter as you use MASM, LINK, and EXE2BIN. If you don't find an error message listed here, check either your macro assembler or your DOS manual.

The error messages are in three groups: one for MASM, one for LINK, and one for EXE2BIN. Within each section, you'll find the error messages listed alphabetically.

MASM

Block nesting error   You'll probably see this error message along with either an *Open procedures* or an *Open segments* message. See the following descriptions for these two error messages.

End of file, no END directive   You're either missing the END statement at the end of your file, or you need to add a blank line after the existing END statement. The Microsoft versions of the macro assembler expect to find a blank line at the very end of the file. If you don't have at least one blank line after END, MASM won't read the END statement.

Must be declared in pass 1   This error message usually appears in connection with a GROUP statement. It means you haven't defined one of the segments you listed in the GROUP statement. For example, if you have the line *CGROUP GROUP CODE_SEG, DATA_SEG*, but you never defined a segment called DATA_SEG, you'll probably see this message. Verify that you've declared all the segments listed in the GROUP statement.

No or unreachable CS   MASM needs to see an ASSUME statement in order to know how to assemble some instructions, such as branch or CALL instructions. This error message means MASM either couldn't find an ASSUME statement or the ASSUME it found had an error in it. Check your source file to make sure you have an ASSUME statement in it, and that the statement is correct.

Open procedures   This means that either you're missing a PROC or an ENDP statement, or that the names aren't the same on one PROC/ENDP pair. Make sure every PROC has a matching ENDP statement, and check the procedure name in both the PROC and the ENDP statements to make sure they match.

Open segments You're missing a SEGMENT or an ENDS statement, or the names aren't the same on one SEGMENT/ENDS pair. Make sure every SEGMENT has a matching ENDS statement, and check the procedure name in both the SEGMENT and ENDS statements to make sure they match.

Symbol not defined There are three things you should look for if you see this error message:

1. You may have misspelled a name. Check the line you see in the error display to make certain you've typed the name correctly.
2. You may have misspelled the name when you first declared a PROC or a variable. Check the spelling of the names you see in the faulty line against the names in the PROC or variable declarations.
3. You may be missing an EXTRN declaration, or the name in the EXTRN may be misspelled.

LINK

Fixup offset exceeds field width This is a tricky one, and it's often the hardest bug to swat. This message usually means you've declared some procedure as a FAR procedure, but later declared that same procedure as a NEAR procedure in an EXTRN declaration.

It can also mean that a group has grown larger than the the 64K limit for groups. You can check for such errors by looking at the size field in the map file.

This message can also appear when your segment has become fragmented. In such cases, the two fragments may be more than 64K apart, which means that CALLs must be FAR CALLs to work. You'll find more information on fragmented segments in Appendix C.

If that doesn't seem to be the problem, you'll have to search deeper. Read Appendix C carefully, then create a load map of your program. You may find a hint in this load map. For example, check the order of the segments. You may find they are out of order.

Symbol defined more than once This means you've probably defined the same procedure or variable in two source files. Make sure you've defined each name in only one source file, then use EXTRNs in other places where you need to use the same procedure or variable.

Unresolved externals   When you see this message, either a PUBLIC is missing from the file in which you declared the procedure or variable, or you misspelled the name in an EXTRN declaration in some other source file.

Warning: no stack segment   This isn't really an error message, it's simply a warning. You'll see this warning message for the examples in this book, because we're creating .COM files, and .COM files don't use a separate segment for the stack. See Chapter 28 for a sample program that doesn't cause LINK to display this warning.

EXE2BIN

File cannot be converted   This is probably the only error message you'll see from EXE2BIN, and it's not a very helpful one. Most of the time it can mean one of three things:

1.   Your segments are in the wrong order, thus you have a segment in memory before CODE_SEG. Check the load map to see if this is your problem. For more information, read Appendix C.
2.   Your main program is not the first file you listed in your LINK list. It must be, so try relinking to make sure this isn't the problem. Again, you can often spot this type of problem by looking at the load map.
3.   Your main program does not have an ORG 100h as the first statement after the *CODE_SEG SEGMENT PUBLIC* declaration. Also, make sure the END statement in your main source file includes the label of the instruction at which you want to start—for example, *END DSKPATCH*.

If these suggestions don't help, check Appendix C for more information.

APPENDIX E

MISCELLANEOUS TABLES

Table E-1. ASCII Character Codes

Dec	Hex	Char	Dec	Hex	Char	Dec	Hex	Char	Dec	Hex	Char
0	0		43	2B	+	86	56	V	129	81	ü
1	1	☺	44	2C	,	87	57	W	130	82	é
2	2	☻	45	2D	–	88	58	X	131	83	â
3	3	♥	46	2E	.	89	59	Y	132	84	ä
4	4	♦	47	2F	/	90	5A	Z	133	85	à
5	5	♣	48	30	0	91	5B	[	134	86	å
6	6	♠	49	31	1	92	5C	\	135	87	ç
7	7	•	50	32	2	93	5D	]	136	88	ê
8	8	◘	51	33	3	94	5E	^	137	89	ë
9	9	○	52	34	4	95	5F	_	138	8A	è
10	A	◙	53	35	5	96	60	`	139	8B	ï
11	B	♂	54	36	6	97	61	a	140	8C	î
12	C	♀	55	37	7	98	62	b	141	8D	ì
13	D	♪	56	38	8	99	63	c	142	8E	Ä
14	E	♫	57	39	9	100	64	d	143	8F	Å
15	F	☼	58	3A	:	101	65	e	144	90	É
16	10	►	59	3B	;	102	66	f	145	91	æ
17	11	◄	60	3C	<	103	67	g	146	92	Æ
18	12	↕	61	3D	=	104	68	h	147	93	ô
19	13	‼	62	3E	>	105	69	i	148	94	ö
20	14	¶	63	3F	?	106	6A	j	149	95	ò
21	15	§	64	40	@	107	6B	k	150	96	û
22	16	▬	65	41	A	108	6C	l	151	97	ù
23	17	↨	66	42	B	109	6D	m	152	98	ÿ
24	18	↑	67	43	C	110	6E	n	153	99	Ö
25	19	↓	68	44	D	111	6F	o	154	9A	Ü
26	1A	→	69	45	E	112	70	p	155	9B	¢
27	1B	←	70	46	F	113	71	q	156	9C	£
28	1C	∟	71	47	G	114	72	r	157	9D	¥
29	1D	↔	72	48	H	115	73	s	158	9E	₧
30	1E	▲	73	49	I	116	74	t	159	9F	ƒ
31	1F	▼	74	4A	J	117	75	u	160	A0	á
32	20		75	4B	K	118	76	v	161	A1	í
33	21	!	76	4C	L	119	77	w	162	A2	ó
34	22	"	77	4D	M	120	78	x	163	A3	ú
35	23	#	78	4E	N	121	79	y	164	A4	ñ
36	24	$	79	4F	O	122	7A	z	165	A5	Ñ
37	25	%	80	50	P	123	7B	{	166	A6	ª
38	26	&	81	51	Q	124	7C	¦	167	A7	º
39	27	'	82	52	R	125	7D	}	168	A8	¿
40	28	(	83	53	S	126	7E	~	169	A9	⌐
41	29	)	84	54	T	127	7F	⌂	170	AA	¬
42	2A	*	85	55	U	128	80	Ç	171	AB	½

Table E-1. *continued*

Dec	Hex	Char	Dec	Hex	Char	Dec	Hex	Char	Dec	Hex	Char
172	AC	¼	193	C1	⊥	214	D6		235	EB	δ
173	AD	¡	194	C2	⊤	215	D7		236	EC	∞
174	AE	«	195	C3	├	216	D8		237	ED	ø
175	AF	»	196	C4	─	217	D9		238	EE	∈
176	B0		197	C5	┼	218	DA		239	EF	∩
177	B1		198	C6		219	DB		240	F0	≡
178	B2		199	C7		220	DC		241	F1	±
179	B3		200	C8		221	DD		242	F2	≥
180	B4		201	C9		222	DE		243	F3	≤
181	B5		202	CA		223	DF		244	F4	⌠
182	B6		203	CB		224	E0	α	245	F5	⌡
183	B7		204	CC		225	E1	β	246	F6	÷
184	B8		205	CD	=	226	E2	Γ	247	F7	≈
185	B9		206	CE		227	E3	π	248	F8	°
186	BA		207	CF		228	E4	Σ	249	F9	∙
187	BB		208	D0		229	E5	σ	250	FA	·
188	BC		209	D1	⊤	230	E6	μ	251	FB	√
189	BD		210	D2		231	E7	τ	252	FC	ⁿ
190	BE		211	D3		232	E8	Φ	253	FD	²
191	BF		212	D4		233	E9	θ	254	FE	■
192	C0		213	D5		234	EA	Ω	255	FF	

Many of the keys on the keyboard (such as the function keys) return a two-character code when you read the keys through DOS: A decimal 0 followed by a scan code. The following table shows the scan codes for all the keys that have no equivalent ASCII code.

Table E-2.   Extended Keyboard Codes

15	Shift Tab
16–25	Alt keys for Q, W, E, R, T, Y, U, I, O, P
30–38	Alt keys for A, S, D, F, G, H, J, K, L
44–50	Alt keys for Z, X, C, V, B, N, M
59–68	F1 through F10
71	Home
72	Cursor Up
73	PgUp
75	Cursor Left
77	Cursor Right
79	End
80	Cursor Down
81	PgDn
82	Ins
83	Del
84–93	Shift F1 through F10
94–103	Control F1 through F10
104–113	Alt F1 through F10
114	Control PrtSc
115	Control Left Cursor
116	Control Right Cursor
117	Control End
118	Control PgDn
119	Control Home
120–131	Control Alt for 1, 2, 3, 4, 5, 6, 7, 8, 9, 0, -, =
132	Control PgUp

Table E-3. The Addressing Modes

Addressing Mode	Format of Address	Segment Register Used
Register	register (such as AX)	None
Immediate	data (such as 12345)	None
	Memory Addressing Modes	
Register Indirect	[BX]	DS
	[BP]	SS
	[DI]	DS
	[SI]	DS
Base Relative*	label[BX]	DS
	label[BP]	SS
Direct Indexed*	label[DI]	DS
	label[SI]	DS
Base Indexed*	label[BX + SI]	DS
	label[BX + DI]	DS
	label [BP + SI]	SS
	label[BP + DI]	SS
String Commands: (MOVSW, LODSB, *and so on*)		Read from DS:SI Write to ES:DI

* Label[...] can be replaced by [disp + ...], where disp is a displacement. Thus, we could write [10 + BX] and the address would be 10 + BX.

Table E-4.   INT 10h Functions

(AH) = 0

Set the display mode. The AL registers contain the mode number.

TEXT MODES

(AL) = 0   40 by 25, black and white mode
(AL) = 1   40 by 25, color
(AL) = 2   80 by 25, black and white
(AL) = 3   80 by 25, color
(AL) = 7   80 by 25, monochrome display adapter

GRAPHICS MODE

(AL) = 4   320 by 200, color
(AL) = 5   320 by 200, black and white
(AL) = 6   640 by 200, black and white

(AH) = 1

Set the cursor size.

(CH)   Starting scan line of the cursor. The top line is 0 on both the monochrome and color graphics displays, while the bottom line is 7 for the color graphics adapter and 13 for the monochrome adapter. Valid range: 0 to 31.

(CL)   Last scan line of the cursor.

The power-on setting for the color graphics adapter is CH = 6 and CL = 7. For the monochrome display: CH = 11 and CL = 12.

(AH) = 2

Set the cursor position.

(DH,DL)   Row, column of new cursor position; the upper, left corner is (0,0).

(BH)   Page number. This is the number of the display page. The color-graphics adapter has room for several display pages, but most programs use page 0.

(AH) = 3

Read the cursor position.

(BH)   Page number
On exit   (DH,DL)   Row, column of cursor
(CH,CL)   Cursor size

Table E-4. *(continued)*

(AH) = 4   **Read light pen position** (See Tech. Ref. Man.)

(AH) = 5   **Select active display page**.

(AL)	New page number (from 0 to 7 for modes 0 and 1; from 0 to 3 for modes 2 and 3)

(AH) = 6   **Scroll up.**

(AL)	Number of lines to blank at the bottom of the window. Normal scrolling blanks one line. Set to zero to blank entire window.
(CH,CL)	Row, column of upper, left corner of window
(DH,DL)	Row, column of lower, right corner of window
(BH)	Display attribute to use for blank lines

(AH) = 7   **Scroll down.**

Same as scroll up (function 6), but lines are left blank at the top of the window instead of the bottom

(AH) = 8   **Read attribute and character under the cursor.**

(BH)	Display page (text modes only)
(AL)	Character read
(AH)	Attribute of character read (text modes only)

(AH) = 9   **Write attribute and character under the cursor.**

(BH)	Display page (text modes only)
(CX)	Number of times to write character and attribute on screen
(AL)	Character to write
(BL)	Attribute to write

(AH) = 10   **Write character under cursor** (with normal attribute).

(BH)	Display page
(CX)	Number of times to write character
(AL)	Character to write

(AH) = 11 to 13   **Various graphics functions**. (See Tech. Ref. Man. for the details.)

Table E-4. *(continued)*

(AH) = 14   **Write teletype.** Write one character to the screen and move the cursor to the next position.

(AL)	Character to write
(BL)	Color of character (graphics mode only)
(BH)	Display page (text mode)

(AH) = 15   **Return current video state.**

(AL)	Display mode currently set
(AH)	Number of characters per line
(BH)	Active display pages

This table contains the INT 21h functions used in this book. For a more complete list, you should buy the IBM *DOS Technical Reference* manual.

Table E-5.   INT 21h Functions

(AH) = 1

Keyboard input.   This function waits for you to type a character on the keyboard. It echoes the character to the screen, and returns the ASCII code in the AL register. For extended keyboard codes, this function returns two characters: an ASCII 0 followed by the scan code (see Table E-2).

(AL)   Character read from the keyboard.

(AH) = 2

Display output.   Displays one character on the screen. Several characters have special meaning to this function:

7	Beep: Send a one-second tone to the speaker.
8	Backspace: move the cursor left one character position.
9	Tab: Move to the next tab stop. Tab stops are set to every 8 characters.
0Ah	Line feed: Move to the next line.
0Dh	Carriage return: Move to the start of the current line.

(DL)   Character to display on the screen.

(AH) = 8

Keyboard input without echo.   Reads a character from the keyboard, but doesn't display the character on the screen.

(AL)   Character read from keyboard.

(AH) = 9

Display string.   Displays the string pointed to by the DS:DX pair of registers. You must mark the end of the string with the $ character. ·

DS:DX   Points to the string to display.

(AH) = 0Ah

Read string.   Reads a string from the keyboard. See Chapter 23 for more details.

Table E-5. *(continued)*

(AH) = 4Ch   **Exit to DOS.**   Returns to DOS, like INT 20h, but it works for *both* .COM and .EXE programs. The INT 20h function used in this book only works for .COM programs.

         (AL)   Return code. Normally set to 0, but you can set it to any other number and use the DOS batch commands IF and ERRORLEVEL to detect errors.

INDEX

D

E

F

G

H

I

J

K

L

About the Authors

Peter Norton is well-known in the personal computing arena for both his writing and programming. Starting in the earliest days of the IBM Personal Computer, he began writing about the IBM/PC, helping other people understand how these wonderful machines work. He has written a half a dozen books on the PC family, including the best-selling *Inside the IBM/PC*; his columns appear in each issue of *PC* and *PC Week* magazines. His set of programs called The Norton Utilities has helped many PC users rescue lost data and explore the inner workings of their computers. Peter grew up in Seattle, Washington, attended Reed College in Portland, Oregon; he now lives in Santa Monica, California with his wife.

John Socha is better known for his public-domain utilities than by his name. In the early days of the IBM PC, he wrote a column for the now defunct magazine *Softalk*, where he published such programs as ScreenSave (the first screen blanker), KbdBuffer (extends the keyboard buffer), and Whereis (finds files on a hard disk). After the demise of *Softalk*, John concentrated on finishing his PhD in Physics and writing a commercial program called The Norton Commander. John grew up in the woods of Wisconsin, earned a BS degree in Electrical Engineering from the University of Wisconsin, and a PhD in Applied Physics from Cornell University; he now lives in southern California.

Norton's here and BRADY'S got him.

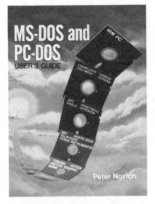

1. An inside look at how Disk Operation Systems work as only Peter Norton can give. A how-to-book for beginners and experienced users alike. Practical and simply written, this book has all you'll need to understand the operating system of your microcomputer as well as practical advice about what to buy and what to use. $17.95 (0-89303-645-5)

2. Peter Norton has updated and expanded his bestseller to include *every* model of the IBM microcomputer family. Beginning with a review of the fundamentals, the book then moves on to discover new ways to master the important facets of using your microcomputer to its fullest potential. $21.95 (0-89303-583-1)

3. The most comprehensive guide available from America's most respected authority, Peter Norton, *PC-DOS* tells you everything you need to know to use your operating system to customize your PC. $18.95 (0-89303-752-4)

Now at your book or computer store.
Or order today: **201-767-5937**

BRADY Knows Programming

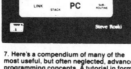